PROUD CO-OWNER OF IELTS

4技能対策＋模試2回

IDP Education
IELTS
公認問題集

IDP Education / イングリッシュイノベーションズ 共著

桐原書店

はじめに　～IELTSエキスパートがスコアUPをサポート！～

皆さん、こんにちは。

　本書は、IELTSの共同所有機関である**IDP Education**による初の公認問題集で、**アカデミック・モジュールの対策に特化**し、豊富な練習・実践問題に加えて、Practice Test（模試）2回分を収録しています。

　IELTSの受験者数は、今や世界で年間数百万人にのぼります。日本でも海外留学や移住を目指す目的で受験する方が増え、特に近年は、国内の大学入試で活用するために受験する高校生も増加しています。

 憧れの海外留学への一歩を踏み出したい！

目標の大学に入るためにスコアを取りたい！

　きっと本書を手にしてくださった皆さんは、このような目標をお持ちのはずです。しかし、IELTSの試験は問題のタイプが特殊で、難易度が高めです。実際に「目標スコアを取るにはどうしたらいいのか」と、悩んでいる方が多いのではないでしょうか。

初めての受験で、何をすればいいかわからない
何回受けてもスコアが目標に届かない…
本番通りの難易度の問題や模試を解きたい！
IELTSを熟知している先生に習いたい！

　本書では、こういったお悩みを解決すべく、特に以下のポイントにこだわりました。
- 練習問題、実践問題、模試（2回）は、すべて**本番さながらの難易度と質を再現**
- IELTSエキスパートチームによる**IELTS初心者にもわかりやすい解説**
- 英語圏のさまざまなアクセントに慣れるように**イギリス、アメリカ、オーストラリア、カナダのナレーターによる音声を収録**

　本書は、読者が日本人の受験生であること、また幅広いレベルの受験者がいることを想定して制作しています。例えば、ライティングのサンプル回答では、中級者と上級者の二通りのエッセイを掲載しているので、自分の目標、レベルに合ったエッセイを参考にできます。

IELTSエキスパートチームのメンバー

「IDP公認のIELTSエキスパートたち」が「日米で通算8,500人以上に英語試験対策を提供してきた実績のある専門学校English Innovations」とタッグを組み、本企画を立ち上げました。主なメンバーを紹介します。

ドン・オリヴァー先生（IDP公認IELTSエキスパート）

　　オーストラリア出身。30年以上もIELTSに関わってきたIDP公認IELTSエキスパート。英語教師としても30年以上のキャリアを持つ。

　　IELTS専門校でカリキュラム・アドバイザーを担当する一方、定期的にセミナーを開催して学習者に直接関わり、彼らが苦手とする点を把握したうえで指導している。

キャロライン・ヤング先生（IDP公認IELTSエキスパート）

　　アイルランド出身。10年以上IELTSに関わってきたIDP公認IELTSエキスパート。ネパールや西アフリカでIELTSに関わった後、現在は日本でIELTS対策を教えているほか、高校生にも英語を指導している。

　　IELTS教授法の指導経験が豊富で、IELTSの深いところまで知り尽くしている。特に、スピーキングとライティングのわかりやすく、スコアUPに直結する指導に定評がある。

キアラ・ニコール・ウォルドバーグ先生（English Innovations 講師）

　　アメリカ出身。講師として生徒のライティングの添削を重ねるなど、IELTS教育の最前線で受験者をサポートしている。

　　日本滞在歴は7年にのぼり、日本人に対する指導経験が豊富で、生徒からの信頼が厚い。IELTSのほか、TOEFL®やTOEIC®など資格試験対策も熟知している。

　　ほか、IELTSを毎年受けており、IELTSを熟知している日本人スタッフも制作に関わることで、「日本人の苦手な部分を改善するにはどうすればいいのか」を踏まえた内容になっています。

　　初受験で右も左もわからない方でも、何回も受験しているけどスコアが伸び悩んでいる方でも大丈夫です。本書の問題を何回も解き、復習し、模試で本番形式に慣れることで、スコアUPが狙えます。一緒に頑張りましょう！

We are here to support your IELTS journey!
2022年2月　IDP Education / English Innovations

Table of Contents

About IELTS

Reading

▶ About Reading

▶ 問題タイプ別　練習問題

Listening

▶ About Listening

▶ Part 1 対策

▶ Part 2 対策

▶ Part 3 対策

▶ Part 4 対策

Writing

練習・実践問題について

本書に掲載している問題の一部は、IELTS公式の練習問題を使用しています。

Reading　　　練習2、練習3、練習4、練習5

Listening　　Part 1対策（練習2）、Part 2対策（練習1,2）、実践問題（Part 2）

Writing　　　Task 1（実践1）

ほかの公式練習問題を解きたい方はIDPのサイトにQRコードからアクセスしてください。

Speaking

▶ About Speaking

▶ Part 1 対策

▶ Part 2 対策

▶ Part 3 対策

▶ Part 1-3 実践問題

Practice Test（模試）

本書の特徴

攻略ルール（Reading, Listening, Writing, Speaking の各章）

スコア UP に役立つルールをまとめて解説

図やイラストつきでわかりやすい

Reading / Listening

問題タイプを丁寧に解説

[Reading]
練習問題：7問
実践問題：2パッセージ

[Listening]
練習問題：10問
実践問題：パート1－4の通し問題

Writing

中級者の
エッセイ

二通りのエッセ
イを比較しなが
ら学ぼう！

上級者の
エッセイ

Speaking

試験官との
会話をリア
ルに再現

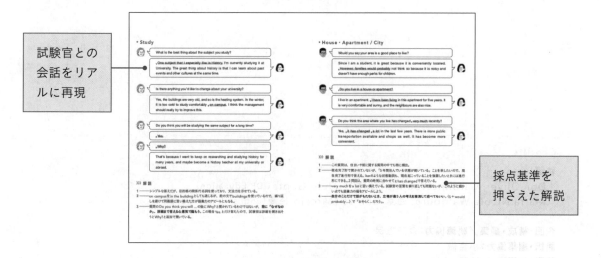

採点基準を
押さえた解説

Practice Test（模試）2回分を収録

・問題の難易度は、本番を再現

・本番と同じサイズの解答用紙がついているので、予行練習として最適

ダウンロード音声について

　リスニングとスピーキングの練習問題、実践問題、Practice Test（模試）の音声は、すべて無料でダウンロードできます。音声トラック番号は⓪で示されています。

ナレーターの国籍
リスニング：🇬🇧 イギリス、🇺🇸 アメリカ、🇦🇺 オーストラリア、🇨🇦 カナダ
スピーキング：試験官は🇬🇧 イギリス、🇺🇸 アメリカ、受験者は🇯🇵 日本

音声ファイル（MP3形式）の入手方法
パソコンからインターネットで専用サイトにアクセスする

　下記のURLにアクセスし、『IDP Education IELTS公認問題集』の商品紹介ページ内にあるリンクから音声をダウンロードしてください。

　https://www.kirihara.co.jp/product/detail/002199/

Credits
執筆：
Don Oliver, Caroline Young, 市川智子, Juhi Gupta（IDP Education）,
Kiarra Nicole Waldburg, 通堂 Gomes Marcalo 裕輝（English Innovations）

企画・構成・編集／執筆協力：余田志保
翻訳・編集協力：小宮徹
校正：仲慶次, 島村栄一
装丁：小口翔平＋三沢綾（tobufune）
本文デザイン：喜來詩織（エントツ）
本文イラスト：田島ミノリ
DTP：有限会社マーリンクレイン
録音：一般財団法人英語教育協議会（ELEC）
ナレーション：
Guy Perryman, Emma Howard, Nadia McKechnie, Stuart O, Sarah Greaves,
Howard Colefield, Jennifer Okano, Jon Mudryj, Andree Dufleit

About IELTS

About IELTS

Q IELTS（アイエルツ）は、どんな試験？

A IELTS（International English Language Testing System）は、アメリカ、オーストラリア、ニュージーランド、カナダ、およびイギリスを含む英語圏の国々に留学、就労または移住を希望する人々の英語力を測定する、英語4技能試験です。
世界140か国で実施されており、1万1000以上の大学と移民局を含む世界中の機関が、英語力の証明として広く認めています。日本でも全国で受験希望者が増えるなか、受験機会が拡大しています。

Q IELTSはどこが運営しているの？

A IELTSは、英語教育・言語研究機関であるIDP: IELTS Australia（オーストラリア）、Cambridge Assessment English（イギリス）、British Council（イギリス）の3団体が共同所有者として、1989年より運営しています。

Q アカデミック・モジュールとジェネラル・トレーニング・モジュールの違いは？

A アカデミック・モジュールは、英語圏の大学や大学院に留学する目的の方、またはプロフェッショナルな機関への登録申請を目的とする方向けのテストです。

一方、ジェネラル・トレーニング・モジュールは、英語圏での就職や移住を希望している人が、ビザを申請する際に英語力を証明するためのテストです。実践的な、日常生活での英語力を測ります。

リスニングとスピーキングの問題は共通で、ライティングとリーディングの問題はモジュールによって異なります。

どのモジュールを受験すればよいか迷った場合は、受験前にスコアの提出先に確認しましょう。

Q 受験方式は？

A 試験会場で受験する場合、コンピューター方式またはペーパー方式から選択できます（両者の違いはp.18を参照）。今後はご自宅などでご自身のパソコンを使用して受験するオンライン方式（IELTS Online）も、世界各国で開始されます。日本での受験日、受験料などの詳細はIDPの公式サイトをご確認ください。

Q IELTS for UKVI とは？

A 英国ビザ申請に必要な英語能力証明テスト Secure English Language Test（SELT）の1つとして、英国政府から認可された試験で、試験内容、難易度、採点方法などはすべて従来の IELTS と同じです。

違いは、不正防止のため、従来の IELTS 受験時よりもセキュリティーが厳しい点です。

また、国内での受験は British Council が運営する東京と大阪会場に限られています（2021年12月現在）。IELTS for UKVI の受験が必要かは、留学先や移民局に確認しましょう。

Q 結果の有効期限は？

A IELTSを認めている多くの機関は、**2年以内に取得したスコア**を求めています。

Q どのように評価されるの？ バンドスコアとは？

A IELTSに合格や不合格という評価はありません。また、級分けされている試験でもありません。
IELTSは英語初級者からネイティブレベルまでの幅広い英語力を測れるように設計されています。結果は4つのスキル（ライティング、リーディング、リスニング、スピーキング）ごとに1（最低）から9（最高）の段階評価で示されます。各スキルの「バンドスコア」と総合評価としての「オーバーオール・バンドスコア」が、0.5刻みで示されます。

9	エキスパート ユーザー	英語を自由自在に使いこなす能力を有する。 適切、正確、流暢、完全な理解力もある。
8	非常に優秀な ユーザー	不正確さや不適切さがみられるが、英語を自由自在に使いこなす能力を有している。慣れない状況下では誤解が生ずる可能性もある。込み入った議論にも対応できる。
7	優秀なユーザー	不正確さや不適切さがみられ、また状況によっては誤解が生ずる可能性もあるが、英語を使いこなす能力を有する。複雑な言葉遣いにも概ね対応でき、詳細な論理を理解できる。
6	有能なユーザー	不正確さ、不適切さ、誤解もみられるが、概ね効果的に英語を使いこなす能力を有する。特に、慣れた状況下では、かなり複雑な言葉遣いの使用と理解ができる。
5	中程度のユーザー	不完全だが英語を使う能力を有しており、ほとんどの状況でおおまかな意味を把握することができる。ただし、間違いを犯すことも多い。自身の専門分野では、基本的なコミュニケーションをとることが可能。
4	限定的なユーザー	慣れた状況においてのみ、基本的能力を発揮できる。理解力、表現力の問題が頻繁にみられる。複雑な言葉遣いはできない。
3	非常に限定的な ユーザー	慣れた状況において、一般的な意味のみを伝え、理解することができる。コミュニケーションの断絶が頻発する。
2	散発的ユーザー	慣れた状況下で、その場の必要性に対処するため、極めて基本的な情報を片言で伝える以外、現実的なコミュニケーションをとることは不可能。英語の会話や文章を理解することは困難である。
1	非ユーザー	単語の羅列のみで、基本的に単語を使用する能力を有していない。
0	試験放棄	必要情報が提供されていない。

日本人の平均バンドスコア　※2019年 アカデミック・モジュール

Reading	Listening	Writing	Speaking	Overall
6.1	5.9	5.5	5.5	5.8

 Q テスト内容は？

 A IELTSのテストは、ライティング、リーディング、リスニング、スピーキングに分かれています。
テストの概要は以下の通りですが、詳しいことは各章で解説しているので、そちらを参考にしてください。

✍️ **Writing**（アカデミック・モジュール）　→詳しくはP.89以降をチェック！

時間　：60分 問題数：2問 (Task 1、Task 2) 形式　：エッセイ	**Task 1:** 与えられたグラフ、表、図を分析し、数値の変化や特徴を客観的に伝える **Task 2:** 問題文の指示に従って、自分の意見を論理的に展開する

📖 **Reading**（アカデミック・モジュール）　→詳しくはP.21以降をチェック！

時間　：60分 問題数：40問 (3 Passages) 形式　：記述・選択問題	・Passageはすべて書籍、雑誌、新聞からの抜粋 ・内容は専門家向けではなく、専門知識を有しない一般向け

🔊 **Listening**　→詳しくはP.57以降をチェック！

時間　：30分 問題数：40問 (4 Parts) 形式　：記述・選択問題	・イギリス、アメリカ、カナダ、オーストラリア、ニュージーランドなどの国のアクセントによる登場人物の会話やモノローグを聞き、問題に答える ・音声は一度だけ流される **Part 1:** 日常生活における2人の会話（宿泊施設の予約など） **Part 2:** 日常生活におけるモノローグ（地域の施設に関する説明など） **Part 3:** キャンパスなど教育現場での最大4人の会話（課題を議論し合う大学教授と学生など） **Part 4:** 学術的なテーマに関するモノローグ（大学の講義など）

🗣️ **Speaking**　→詳しくはP.145以降をチェック！

時間　：11～14分 問題数：3 Parts 形式　：試験官と1対1の対面形式	**Part 1:** 会話形式のやり取り（4～5分） 　　　身近なトピック（家族、仕事、興味など）に関する質問に答える **Part 2:** ロングターン（3～4分） 　　　身近なトピックについて1～2分間話す。事前に1分間の準備時間がある **Part 3:** ディスカッション（4～5分） 　　　**Part 2**に関連した、社会的なトピックについてディスカッションする

Q 受験日は？

A ペーパー試験の場合は年間最大48日、コンピューター試験の場合は週に複数回、受験機会があります。
試験会場や受験方式によって受験日が異なるので、公式サイトで確認しましょう。

Q 受験会場は？

A 試験会場は全国に拡大中です。会場は公式テストセンターをはじめ大学や貸し会議室です。試験会場は試験日によって異なるので、公式サイトの最新情報を確認してください。

Q 申し込み方法は？

A 申し込みは公式サイトから試験日と試験会場を選択のうえ、オンラインで行います。**申し込みを完了するには、パスポートが必要**です。IDP公式テストセンターでは、試験日の3日前まで申し込みができますが、定員がいっぱいになると、その時点で締め切られてしまうので、早めに手続きを済ませましょう。

IDP運営の試験会場の受験日・会場・申し込み公式サイト

www.ieltsjp.com

Q 試験結果はいつ届く？

A ペーパーで受験するIELTSは試験後13日後に、コンピューターで受験するIELTSは、試験後3～5営業日で成績が開示され、オンラインで確認できます。
同時に成績証明書が郵送され、通常オンラインでの公開から5日以内にご自宅に届きます。試験会場によっては証明書を直接受け取ることも可能です。なお、メールやFAXでは送信していません。

IDP公式テストセンターでの申し込みから結果受け取りまでの流れ

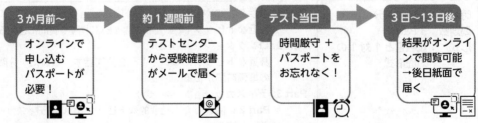

3か月前～	約1週間前	テスト当日	3日～13日後
オンラインで申し込む パスポートが必要！	テストセンターから受験確認書がメールで届く	時間厳守 ＋ パスポートをお忘れなく！	結果がオンラインで閲覧可能→後日紙面で届く

Q 当日の持ち物は？

A 必ず必要な持ち物は「**パスポート**」のみです。必ず有効期限が切れていない原本をご持参ください。当日パスポートを忘れてしまうと、いかなる理由でも受験ができませんのでご注意ください。

その他の持ち物
- 透明なボトルに入った水（ラベルがついていないもの）※必要な場合のみ
- 18歳未満の受験者は、**IELTS未成年者承認と同意書**

> IDP運営のテストセンターで受験する場合は、会場で鉛筆と消しゴムをご用意いたします。IDP以外の試験実施団体で受験される場合は、別途持ち物がある場合があるので、受験案内を確認しましょう。

 Q 試験中、トイレ休憩の時間はあるの？

A IELTSはライティング、リーディング、リスニングの3技能の受験中に休憩時間を設けていません。試験中にトイレに行きたい場合は、以下の時間を除き、離席できます。貴重な試験時間をロスしないように、試験前に済ませておきましょう。
- リスニングテスト中
- 各テストの間
- 各テストの終了前10分間

※スピーキングテスト中は離席できません

Q 最新情報はどこで得られるの？

A IELTSの試験対策、受験情報、お申し込みはIDPの公式サイトをご確認ください。

日本ではIDPのほか、British CouncilがIELTSを実施しています。両者は、まったく同じ公式の試験ですが、受験日、受験料、会場、予約サイトが異なるためご注意ください。

コンピューター試験とペーパー試験の違い

　IELTSは、コンピューター試験とペーパー試験の2つの方式から選んで受験ができます。試験内容、問題タイプ、採点基準はまったく同じです。また、コンピューターで受験できるのはライティング、リーディング、リスニングの3技能のみで、スピーキングテストは両方式ともに試験官との1対1の対面形式で行われます。

　主な違いを以下の表でまとめています。違いを理解して自分に合う方式を選びましょう。

	コンピューター	ペーパー
受験日	平日・土日祝日 （週複数回）	月3〜4回 （土曜日または木曜日）
試験結果	試験日から3〜5日後	試験日から13日後
試験時間・順番	午前または午後 **Listening**（30分） ↓ **Reading**（60分） ↓ **Writing**（60分） 午前または午後 **Speaking**（11〜14分） ※申し込み時に午前・午後の部、またスピーキングの時間を選択できます	午前 **Writing**（60分） ↓ **Reading**（60分） ↓ **Listening**（30分＋転記時間10分） 午後 **Speaking**（11〜14分）
試験会場※1	**東京・大阪** （2021年12月現在）	全国各地
受験料※2	26,400円	25,380円

※1　会場の場所は運営団体や時期によって異なる
※2　2021年12月現在、IDPが運営する試験会場の受験料（税込み）

コンピューター試験のメリット

1 ▸ [ライティング] 入力や修正が簡単。語数のカウントが不要

コンピューター試験で一番メリットがあるのがライティングだと言われています。

- タイピングに慣れている場合は、手書きよりも時間の短縮になる
- 書き間違いなどの修正や編集が、素早くできる
- 語数カウント機能がついている

2 ▸ [リスニング] ヘッドフォンで集中できる

ペーパー試験では（一部の会場を除き）※、スピーカーを通して音声が流れるので、ほかの受験者が立てる雑音が気になることがあるかもしれません。しかし、コンピューター試験であれば、ヘッドフォンが用意されているため、雑音が入らず集中して取り組めます。なお、ヘッドフォンはリスニング試験以外でも使用可能です。

　※IDPの運営する一部のペーパー試験会場では、リスニング時にヘッドフォンが使用できる会場もあります

3 ▸ [リーディング] パッセージと問題文を並列できる

　ペーパー試験では、パッセージと問題文が書かれているページを行ったり来たり、めくりながら、解いていきます。一方で、コンピューター試験の場合は、左右で分割画面になっており、左側にパッセージ、右側に問題文が表示されます。両者を見比べながら効率的に解ける点は大きなメリットでしょう。

4 ▸ 画面上に残り時間が表示されるため、時間管理がしやすい

　コンピューター試験では、パソコンの画面上に残り時間が表示されるので、時計にちらちら目をやるよりも無駄なく時間を確認できます。

5 ▸ 結果の開示が早い

コンピューター試験は、試験当日から早ければ3営業日後に結果が通知されます（ペーパー試験は13日後）。

ペーパー試験のメリット

1 ▶ なじみがあって受けやすい

　紙と筆記用具を用いたテスト形式は、私たちが小学生の頃から慣れ親しんでいるものです。コンピューターの操作に慣れていない方にとっては、紙ベースならテストの内容以外で余計な心配をしなくていいのでペーパー試験が適しているでしょう。

　また、コンピューター試験では、長時間画面を見続けなければいけないため、目が疲れてしまうという方もいます。特に、リーディングでは、1,000 words 近くのパッセージを素早く読む必要があり、集中力を要します。**普段から紙媒体で文章を読むことに慣れている方には、ペーパー試験が適している**でしょう。

2 ▶ 問題用紙への書き込みができる

　問題用紙に好きなようにメモを取ることができ、さらに**リーディングやリスニングの問題文のキーワードに、素早く線や印をつけられます。**コンピューター試験でもハイライト機能があり、メモの書き込みはできますが、慣れていないと時間がかかるでしょう。

> コンピューター試験かペーパー試験、どちらが自分に向いているかを判断するために、まずはデモ画面でサンプル問題を解いてみましょう。

Reading

About Reading

リーディングテストは3つのパッセージに分かれています。

- 制限時間　　　　　　　60分（時間配分の目安：1パッセージ20分）
- 1パッセージの語数　　約800〜900 words
- 内容　　　　　　　　　リーディングテストの文章はすべて書籍や雑誌、新聞からの抜粋。テーマは自然科学、文学、歴史など多岐にわたるが、専門知識は必要ない。

Passage	問題数の例
1	13問（Questions 1–13）
2	13問（Questions 14–26）
3	14問（Questions 27–40）

評価基準　　　40点満点（1問1点×40問）

配点は各1点で、合計得点は換算表に基づき、1〜9の0.5刻みのバンドスコアに換算されます。

バンドスコアの換算例

バンドスコア	40問中の正答数
5	15
6	23
7	30
8	35

減点対象となるもの

スペルミス

文法ミス

語数指定を守らない（part-timerなどハイフンでつなげている語は1単語と数える）

読み取れない文字（ペーパー受験のみ）

減点対象とならないもの

大文字・小文字（DOG, dog, Dog どれも可）

句読点等の表記（9.30 am / 9:30 a.m. どちらも可。ex-husband / exhusband どちらも可）

英米スペル（centre / center どちらも可）

Reading 攻略ルール

1 ▶ 問題文は正確に読み解く

問題文は注意深く読みましょう。問題部分に表や図がある場合は、そのタイトルや大まかな内容も確認します。

さらに、「要約やフローチャートを完成させる問題」や「文を完成させる問題」では、空欄の前後を読み込むことで、品詞は何が入るかなどを予想することができます。事前に目星がついていると解答を見つけやすくなります。

2 ▶ 制限時間内に1つでも多くの正答を

1パッセージに20分費やせると考えると、**1問にかけられるのは1分〜1分半**です。

もちろん1→3の順で解く必要はありません。各パッセージのテーマは自然科学、文学、歴史などさまざま。**最初に各タイトルを確認して、ご自身が解きやすいパッセージから挑んで**ください。

試験の目的は、「制限時間内に1問でも多く正答すること」です。パッセージのすべての内容を時間をかけて理解する必要はありません。解答できない問題は、時に諦める潔さも必要です。ただし、その場合でも解答欄を埋めるのを忘れずに！

3 ▶ パラフレーズを見抜こう

問題を解くときは、選択肢や問題文を読んで、その内容が合っているか確かめるためにパッセージ中に答えの根拠を探します。そのとき、問題にある表現と同じ言い回しをパッセージ中から探そうとしても、残念ながら見つかる確率は低いです。なぜなら大半の場合、「パッセージの文」と「問題文や選択肢」は違う表現で言い換えられているから。このように**「文意は保ったまま違う単語や構文で言い換えること」をパラフレーズ**と言います。

特にリーディングテストでは、ほとんどの問題でパラフレーズが起こっています。**パラフレーズを見抜く力が問われている**と言ってもいいでしょう。以下に、パラフレーズの代表的な例を挙げます。

品詞を変更

[名] novel about Russian history ⇄ [形] historical novel about Russia
[動] improve one's business performance ⇄ [名] improvement in one's business performance
[形] increasing volume of traffic ⇄ [名] an increase in the volume of traffic

同義語

consumer ⇄ customer   emphasise ⇄ focus on 〜
bread and butter ⇄ livelihood

構文の言い換え

> Staff **are less likely to** change jobs if cooperation is encouraged.
>
> ⇅
>
> Staff **are more likely to** stay with the company if cooperation is encouraged.
>
> （協力的な体制が奨励されたら、スタッフが転職する可能性は低い。⇄ 協力的な体制が奨励されたら、スタッフが会社に居続ける可能性は高い）

be less likely to change jobs（転職する可能性が低い）⇄ be more likely to stay with the company（会社に居続ける可能性が高い）の部分は反義語を使っていますが、結果的には同じ意味を表しています。

次は〈A＋be＋better than B〉⇄〈B＋be＋not as well ... as A〉の言い換えです。

> Previous generations' education standards **are** much **better than** those of today's young high-school graduates.
>
> ⇅
>
> Nowadays, young workers **are not as well** educated **as** older workers.
>
> （前の世代の教育基準は今日の若い高卒者よりはるかによい。⇄ 最近は、若い労働者は年配の労働者ほどよい教育を受けていない）

today's ⇄ Nowadays / high-school graduates ⇄ young workersなど、語句単位でもパラフレーズさせています。

4 ▶ 指示文をよく確認してから解こう

IELTSでは、問題タイプによって解答形式がさまざまであるうえ、解答方法に対しても、細かな指示がされることがあります。この指示文を理解して見落とさないことがケアレスミス削減につながるので、IELTSらしい代表的な3つの指示文を確認してください。

語数制限

空欄補充問題には、解答に対する語数制限が設けられて、リスニングでも同様の指示が頻繁に登場します。

解答が合っていても、指定の文字数で書かれていなければ間違いになります。数字も単語として書かれているので、指示文の読み間違いに注意しましょう。

指示文例	解答パターン
ONE WORD ONLY	1語
ONE WORD AND/OR A NUMBER	1語と1数字・1語・1数字
ONE OR TWO WORDS	1語・2語
NO MORE THAN TWO WORDS	1語・2語
NO MORE THAN TWO WORDS AND/OR A NUMBER	1語・2語・1数字・1語と1数字・2語と1数字

正答を複数選ぶ

　「複数の選択肢から選ぶ問題」では、以下の例のように正答を複数選ぶように指示されることがあります。この場合、指示通りの数を選び、該当する解答欄に答えを記入してください。なお、複数ある解答の順番は問いません。

　Choose **TWO** letters, **A-E**. / Choose **THREE** letters, **A-G**.

同じ選択肢を複数使用可

　選択問題では、時々以下のような追加指示があります。あまり見慣れないNBはNota Beneの略で「よく注意せよ」という意味です。NB以降は必ず、選択肢を複数回使用してよいという指示が続きます。「特徴を組み合わせる問題」と「情報を組み合わせる問題」で出てくるので、見落とさないように！

　NB *You may use any letter more than once.*

10の問題タイプを知ろう

リーディングテストには10の問題タイプがあります。各パッセージで1種類もしくは2種類以上の問題形式が出題されます。なお、制限内の語数で答える問題(Short answer questions)は、主にジェネラル・トレーニング・モジュールだけで出題されるので、本書では扱いません。

> **task type-1** 〉 **図を完成させる問題** Diagram label completion 　　　　〉〉〉 練習1

パッセージの内容を表す図を完成させる問題です。頻出なのは機械や建物の構造などで、手順や工程を説明しているものです。多くの場合、解答が特定の段落に集中しています。答え方には、引用型(パッセージからそのまま単語を引用。語数制限有り)と選択肢型(選択肢は空欄の数よりも多い)があります。

　　例：*Label the diagram below.*
　　*Choose **NO MORE THAN TWO WORDS** from the passage for each answer.*
　　→パッセージから2語以内を選び、図を完成させる。

> **task type-2** 〉 **メモ・表・フローチャートを完成させる問題** 　　〉〉〉 練習2
　　　　　　　　　　Note, table, flow-chart completion

メモや表、フローチャートなど、フォームの空欄を埋める問題です。普通、各フォームはパッセージの全体ではなく一部をまとめたものです。答え方には引用型と選択肢型があります。

　　例：*Complete the table below.*
　　*Choose **NO MORE THAN TWO WORDS** from the passage for each answer.*
　　→パッセージから2語以内を選び、表を完成させる。

> **task type-3** 〉 **要約を完成させる問題** Summary completion 　　　　〉〉〉 練習3
　　　　　　　　　　　　　　　　　　　　　　　　　　　　　　　　　 実践1

要約の空欄を埋める問題です。要約のうち大半はパッセージ全体ではなく一部をまとめたものです。答え方には引用型と選択肢型があります。

　　例：*Complete the summary below.*
　　*Choose **ONE OR TWO WORDS** from the passage for each answer.*
　　→パッセージから1語または2語を選び、要約を完成させる。
　　例：*Complete the summary using the list of words, **A-H**, below.*
　　→下記の単語A〜Hを使って要約を完成させる。

⟩ task type-4 ⟩ 文 を 完 成 さ せ る 問 題 Sentence completion   ⟫⟫ 練習7

パッセージに関する文の空欄を埋めて、文を完成させます。空欄に埋める単語はパッセージから引用します（語数制限有り）。

例：*Complete the sentences below.*
*Choose **ONE OR TWO WORDS** from the passage for each answer.*
→パッセージから1語または2語を選び、文を完成させる。

⟩ task type-5 ⟩ 複 数 の 選 択 肢 か ら 選 ぶ 問 題 Multiple choice   ⟫⟫ 練習4, 5 実践2

複数の選択肢から正答を選ぶ問題で、ほかの試験でも見られるようなオーソドックスなタイプです。ただし、**正答を1つ選ぶパターンだけではなく複数選ぶこともあり**、これはIELTSらしい形式です。
指示の内容は2つのパターンがあります。
・質問文があり、その答えとなる選択肢を選ぶ
・文の前半が与えられ、後半として適切なものを選ぶ

例：*Choose **TWO** letters, A–E.*
→A〜Eの選択肢から正しい答えを2つ選択する。

⟩ task type-6 ⟩ 特 定 す る 問 題
Identifying information / Identifying a writer's views [claims]

特定する問題には、以下の2種類があります。
・情報を特定する（TRUE, FALSE, NOT GIVENの3択）
・筆者の見解・主張を特定する（YES, NO, NOT GIVENの3択）
難所はFALSEとNOT GIVEN、NOとNOT GIVENの識別です。**パッセージ中に明確な根拠があれば FALSE / NO**となり、**根拠を特定できないものはNOT GIVEN**となります。

① 情 報 の 特 定 (TRUE, FALSE, NOT GIVEN)   ⟫⟫ 実践2

例：Do the following statements agree with the information given in the passage?
In boxes 1–4 on your answer sheet, write

TRUE　　　　　*if the statement agrees with the information*
FALSE　　　　*if the statement contradicts the information*
NOT GIVEN　*if there is no information on this*
→記述が情報と合致するならTRUE、矛盾するならFALSE、これに関する情報がないならNOT
　GIVENを解答欄に記入する。

② 筆者の見解・主張の特定 (YES, NO, NOT GIVEN)　　　　　>>> 練習6

例：Do the following statements agree with the claims of the writer in the passage?

In boxes 1–5 on your answer sheet, write

YES　　　　　*if the statement agrees with the claims of the writer*

NO　　　　　*if the statement contradicts the claims of the writer*

NOT GIVEN　*if it is impossible to say what the writer thinks about this*

→記述が筆者の見解と合致するならYES、相違するならNO、筆者がどう考えているか判断できなければNOT GIVENを解答欄に記入する。

> **task type-7** 〉 特 徴 を 組 み 合 わ せ る 問 題　Matching features　　　>>> 練習7

いくつか問題文があり、それと選択肢（A, B, C ...）を組み合わせる問題です。選択肢の数が多く、一度も選ばないこともあるので注意しましょう。一方で**同じ選択肢を複数回選ぶことも。**その場合、指示文でその旨が明記されます。選択肢は同じカテゴリーでまとめられています（例は「作者」）。

例：*Match each statement with the correct author, **A–C**.*

*Write the correct letter, **A–C**, in boxes 1-5 on your answer sheet.*

***NB** You may use any letter more than once.*

List of Authors

A Enid Blyton

B Roald Dahl

C Eric Carle

→問題文の記述が、A〜Cのどれに該当するか選ぶ。

　同じ選択肢を複数使用可

> **task type-8** 〉 文 の 前 半 と 後 半 を 組 み 合 わ せ る 問 題　　　>>> 実践1
> Matching sentence endings

問題文で与えられる「文の前半」に合う「文の後半」を選択肢から選ぶ問題です。どの選択肢も文法的にはつながるので、**文法をヒントに解くことはできません。**選択肢にはダミー（いずれの正解ともならないもの）もあります。

例：*Complete each sentences with the correct ending, **A–H**, below.*

　　*Write the correct letter, **A–H**, in boxes 1–6 on your answer sheet.*

→正しい文の後半を選択肢のA〜Hから選ぶ。

task type-9 〉 段落に合う見出しを選ぶ問題 Matching headings 〉〉〉 実践2

List of Headings（各段落の内容を表した「見出し」）の選択肢が与えられ、見出し（i, ii …）と段落（A, B …）を組み合わせます。選択肢はダミー（いずれの正解ともならないもの）を含みます。各段落の主旨を把握させる問題です。

> 例：The passage has seven paragraphs, **A–G**.
>
> *Choose the correct heading for each paragraph **A–G** from the list of headings below.*
>
> *Choose the correct number, **i–x**. in boxes 1–7 on your answer sheet.*
>
> →パッセージには7つの段落A〜Gがある。リストから、各段落の見出しとして正しいものを選ぶ。

task type-10 〉 情報を組み合わせる問題 Matching information 〉〉〉 実践1

問題文でいくつか情報（語句）が与えられ、それらがどの段落で言及されているかを選ぶ問題です。**同じものが複数回正答になることもあり、その場合はその旨が明記されます。**task type 9は、各段落の主旨を把握させる問題ですが、こちらは主旨に限らず具体的な情報を探します。

情報は「結果」「原因」など、以下のように機能的な働きをする語句であることが多いです。

- A result of 〜（結果）
- A cause of 〜（原因）
- An example of 〜（例）
- A definition of 〜（定義）
- A comparison of 〜（比較）

> 例：The passage has ten paragraphs, **A–J**.
>
> Which paragraph mentions the following information?
>
> *Write the correct letter, **A–J**, in boxes 1–7 on your answer sheet.*
>
> **NB** *You may use any letter more than once.*
>
> →パッセージにはA〜Jの10段落がある。どの段落で次の情報について述べているかを選ぶ。
>   同じ選択肢を複数使用可。

Readingの解法 2つのアプローチ

　リーディングは何と言っても時間との勝負。当然ながら、全パッセージの一字一句を精読している暇はなく、速読する必要があります。その代表的な方法としてスキャニングとスキミングを活用した解法を紹介しましょう。

スキャニング＝キーワードを求めて目を動かし特定する
　冒頭から文を読み進めるのではなく、とにかく情報を探すことに集中します。テレビの番組表から好きな番組の情報を見つけたいときなど、皆さんも無意識的にスキャニングをしているはずです。
スキミング＝パッセージの大意を把握するためにざっと読む
　日本語でいう「**斜め読み**」。例えば、ネットの記事を読むときに1文1文すべてを丁寧に読まずに、**見出しや大事そうな部分のみを追っていく**ことがあるはずです。

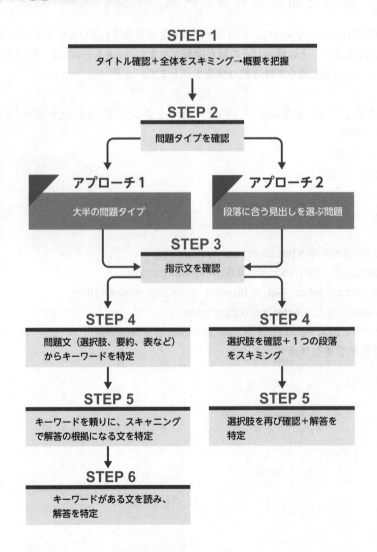

前提として、**リーディングの解法に絶対的なものは存在しません**。p. 30にある図のアプローチはあくまでも1つの方法なので、本書を参考にしながら、あなたにとって効率的なアプローチを是非見つけてください。図を見ていただくとわかる通り、アプローチ1と2に分かれる前に共通するSTEPである1〜3があります。まずは1と2を解説していきましょう。

STEP-1 タイトル確認＋全体をスキミング→概要を把握

最初にスキミングを行います。**パッセージの概要を理解せずに問題を解くのは不可能**です。問題文を見る前に、まずは数分かけて全体のスキミングをしてください。

概要を把握するためのスキミング方法
①パッセージのタイトル・サブタイトルを読む

②最初の段落と最終段落の全文を読む
1段落目にはパッセージの論点、筆者の主張に関する重要な情報が含まれています。一方で、最終段落には全体のまとめが書かれていることが多いので、パッセージの大意をつかむうえで外せません。

③各段落のトピックセンテンスを読む
アカデミックな文章は、**論理的に「1段落、1アイデア（主旨）」の原則**で書かれていることがほとんどです。大半の場合、段落の1文目に、各段落で展開するアイデアの要点を簡潔に表したトピックセンテンスがきます。ただし、これは段落の最後に来ることもあるので、各段落の最初と最後の文を注意して読みましょう。

STEP-2 問題タイプを確認

今から解く問題が、どの問題タイプに該当するのか見極めます（問題タイプの詳細はpp. 26〜29を参照）。問題タイプがわかったら、「段落に合う見出しを選ぶ問題」の場合は、図のアプローチ2に、それ以外の場合はアプローチ1に進んでください。アプローチ1ではスキャニングを、アプローチ2ではスキミングを活用します。では実際に、例題を解きながら各アプローチで解く過程を見ていきましょう。

スキャニングとスキミングの練習は、IELTS用の練習問題だけでなく、英語のネットニュースや雑誌の記事でも行えます。
初中級者の皆さんにオススメするのは、自分に合ったレベルや、「少し難しい」と感じるくらいの記事を見つけて、**一字一句を読まずに、その文章が伝えたいポイントを読み取る練習を毎日少しずつ続ける**ことです。

アプローチ1（スキャニングを活用）

この例題は「表を完成させる問題」の一部です。

World's Most Populated Cities

It shouldn't come as a surprise that China and India have some of the most populous cities in the world with Delhi in second place and Shanghai in third. However, the famous cosmopolitan Japanese city, Tokyo, happens to be at the top of the pile with approximately 37 million people living in the Greater Tokyo region. Incidentally, the top three most populated cities are in Asia but there are several non-Asian cities that also feature in the list of cities with the highest population in the world. Brazil's São Paulo and Mexico's Mexico City have not only been growing economically but also in terms of the number of people that call these cities home with populations of 21.65 million and 21.58 million respectively.

Complete the table below.

*Choose **ONE WORD AND/OR A NUMBER** from the passage for each answer.*

Top 5 Most Populated Cities in the World (UN 2018 estimates)			
City	Population (in millions)	Country	Continent
1 …………	37.47	Japan	Asia
Delhi	28.51	India	Asia
2 …………	25.58	China	Asia
São Paulo	3 …………	Brazil	South America
Mexico City	21.58	Mexico	North America

解答　1 ▸ Tokyo　　2 ▸ Shanghai　　3 ▸ 21.65

▶ パッセージの大意

世界で最も人口が多い都市

　中国とインドには世界で最も人口の多い都市があり、デリーが2位、上海が3位であることは驚かないが、有名な日本の国際都市、東京は、首都圏に約3,700万人がいて、最多である。上位3都市はアジアにあるが、世界ランキングではアジア以外も上位を占める。ブラジルのサンパウロとメキシコのメキシコシティーは、

経済だけでなく、そこを出身地と呼ぶ人々の数でも成長を続けており、それぞれ2,165万人と2,158万人を抱える。

STEP-3　指示文を確認

Complete the table below.
*Choose **ONE WORD AND/OR A NUMBER** from the passage for each answer.*

　パッセージから1語・1数字を選び、表を完成させる問題です。ここでは例として、空欄1を解答するプロセスを紹介します。

STEP-4　問題文（選択肢、要約、表など）からキーワードを特定

　キーワードとは、問題文の選択肢や表の中にあり、答えを導くうえでヒントになる語句のことです。**キーワードの代表格は名詞**で、ほかに動詞や形容詞などの内容語の場合もあります。

　特に、**人名・都市名などの固有名詞**、**日付や時間などの数詞**があったら必ず印をつけましょう。そして、パッセージを読むときも、それらを見つけたら印をつけてください。これらはパラフレーズするのが難しいので、パッセージ中にそのまま現れる可能性が高いのです。本例題のキーワードは人口の37.47と国名のJapanです。

STEP-5　キーワードを頼りに、スキャニングで解答の根拠になる文を特定

　ここからがスキャニングです。パッセージ中からキーワード、またはキーワードをパラフレーズしたものを探し、解答の根拠になりそうな文を特定しましょう。

However, the famous cosmopolitan **Japanese** city, Tokyo, happens to be at the top of the pile with approximately **37 million** people living in the Greater Tokyo region.

STEP-6　キーワードがある文を読み、解答を特定

　根拠になりそうな文を特定できたら、その文を詳しく読んで解答を特定しましょう。その文だけで特定できない場合は、その前後の文も読み込みます。本例題のケースでは、文の前後を読むと、Shanghai, São Paulo, Mexico Cityなど日本以外の都市しか出てこないため、解答はTokyoだと確信できます。

However, the famous cosmopolitan Japanese city, **Tokyo**, happens to be at the top of the pile with approximately 37 million people living in the Greater **Tokyo** region.

Source: United Nations, Department of Economic and Social Affairs, Population Division (2019). World Urbanization Prospects 2018 Highlights. Available at https://population.un.org/wup/Publications/Files/WUP2018-Highlights.pdf

アプローチ２（スキミングを活用）

この例題は「段落に合う見出しを選ぶ問題」の一部です。

Eco-friendly plastics for the future

A———For some time now, scientists have been promoting biodegradable alternatives to traditional plastics as the latter have an adverse effect on our environment. Even though there are many so-called eco-friendly products on the market, they still take as much time as conventional plastic to break down in home composts.

B———Recently, researchers at UC, Berkeley discovered a new variety of biodegradable plastic that dissolves completely in home composts. The new plastic contains enzymes that consume the plastic and turn it into nutrition for plants. Currently, the research is in its infancy and more experiments need to be conducted.

The passage has two sections, **A-B**.
Choose the correct heading for each section from the list of headings below.
Write the correct number, i-iii, in boxes 1-2 on your answer sheet.

List of Headings

i   Ecological plastics' slow degradation
ii   Scientists invent compostable plastic
iii   How to recycle plastic at home

---

1   Section **A** ....
2   Section **B** ....

解答	**1** ▸ i **2** ▸ ii

 パッセージの大意

未来のための環境に優しいプラスチック

A———科学者は生分解性の代替物で従来のプラスチックを置き換えることを提唱してきた。後者は環境に有害だからだ。「環境に優しい」製品が出回っているが、それらは家庭用コンポストで分解されるまでに、従来のプラスチックと同等の時間を要する。
B———カリフォルニア大学バークレー校の研究者は、新しい生分解性プラスチックを発見したが、それは家庭用コンポストで完全に分解でき、プラスチックを分解する酵素を含み、植物の栄養となる。研究は初期

段階で、まだ実験を行う必要がある。

STEP-3　指示文を確認

The passage has two sections, **A–B**.
Choose the correct heading for each section from the list of headings below.
*Write the correct number, **i-iii**, in boxes 1-2 on your answer sheet.*

　2つの段落A–Bに合う見出しをリストから選ぶ問題です。ここでは段落Bの見出しを特定するプロセスを解説します。

STEP-4　選択肢を確認＋1つの段落をスキミング

　選択肢リストでi-iiiの見出しを読んだ後に、段落ごとにスキミングをしていきます。
　スキミングでは、各段落の主旨を表すトピックセンテンスを読んで把握するのがポイントです。
　多くの場合、トピックセンテンスは段落の1文目にあります。一方で、段落の最終文は、その段落のまとめです。したがって「1文目＋最終文」の意味をとらえて判断すると、段落の主旨をより明確に把握できます。
　段落Bのトピックセンテンスは最初の文です。

STEP-5　選択肢を再び確認＋解答を特定

　段落Bのトピックセンテンス Recently, researchers at UC, Berkeley discovered ... を読むと、a new variety of biodegradable plastic that dissolves completely in home composts ⇄ compostable plastic がパラフレーズされており、iiの内容と一致します。

Source: Conroy, G. (2021). New type of plastic decomposes within days just by adding heat and water. Retrieved 24 June 2021, from https://www.abc.net.au/news/science/2021-04-22/biodegradable-plastic-compost-enzymes-environment-soil-green/100082958

問題タイプ別 練習問題

練習 **1** 図を完成させる問題 **3** min.

A Remarkable Beetle

Introducing dung[1] beetles into a pasture is a simple process: approximately 1,500 beetles are released, a handful at a time, into fresh cow pats[2] in the cow pasture. The beetles immediately disappear beneath the pats digging and tunnelling and, if they successfully adapt to their new environment, soon become a permanent, self-sustaining part of the local ecology. In time they multiply and within three or four years the benefits to the pasture are obvious.

Dung beetles work from the inside of the pat so they are sheltered from predators such as birds and foxes. Most species burrow into the soil and bury dung in tunnels directly underneath the pats, which are hollowed out from within. Some large species originating from France excavate tunnels to a depth of approximately 30 cm below the dung pat. These beetles make sausage-shaped brood chambers along the tunnels. The shallowest tunnels belong to a much smaller Spanish species that buries dung in chambers that hang like fruit from the branches of a pear tree. South African beetles dig narrow tunnels of approximately 20 cm below the surface of the pat. Some surface-dwelling beetles, including a South African species, cut perfectly-shaped balls from the pat, which are rolled away and attached to the bases of plants.

[Glossary]   1. dung: the droppings or excreta of animals   2. cow pats: droppings of cows

Questions 1–3

Label the tunnels on the diagram below using words from the box.
Write your answers in boxes 1–3 on your answer sheet.

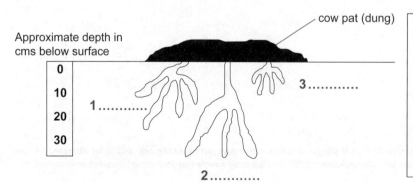

cow pat (dung)

Approximate depth in cms below surface

0
10
20
30

1 ....

2 ....

3 ....

Dung Beetle Types

French
Mediterranean
Australian native
Spanish
South African
South African ball-roller

The Serious Search for an Anti-Aging Pill

No treatment on the market today has been proved to slow human aging. But one intervention, consumption of a low-calorie* yet nutritionally balanced diet, works incredibly well in a broad range of animals, increasing longevity and prolonging good health. Those findings suggest that caloric restriction could delay aging and increase longevity in humans, too. But what if someone could create a pill that mimicked the physiological effects of eating less without actually forcing people to eat less, a 'caloric-restriction mimetic'?

The best-studied candidate for a caloric-restriction mimetic, 2DG (2-deoxy-D-glucose), works by interfering with the way cells process glucose. It has proved toxic at some doses in animals and so cannot be used in humans. But it has demonstrated that chemicals can replicate the effects of caloric restriction; the trick is finding the right one.

Cells use the glucose from food to generate ATP (adenosine triphosphate), the molecule that powers many activities in the body. By limiting food intake, caloric restriction minimises the amount of glucose entering cells and decreases ATP generation. When 2DG is administered to animals that eat normally, glucose reaches cells in abundance but the drug prevents most of it from being processed and thus reduces ATP synthesis. Researchers have proposed several explanations for why interruption of glucose processing and ATP production might retard aging. One possibility relates to the ATP-making machinery's emission of free radicals, which are thought to contribute to aging and to such age-related diseases as cancer by damaging cells. Reduced operation of the machinery should limit their production and thereby constrain the damage. Another hypothesis suggests that decreased processing of glucose could indicate to cells that food is scarce (even if it isn't) and induce them to shift into an anti-aging mode that emphasises preservation of the organism over such 'luxuries' as growth and reproduction.

*calorie: a measure of the energy value of food

Questions 1–3

Complete the flow-chart below.

*Choose **NO MORE THAN TWO WORDS** from the passage for each answer.*

Write your answers in boxes 1–3 on your answer sheet.

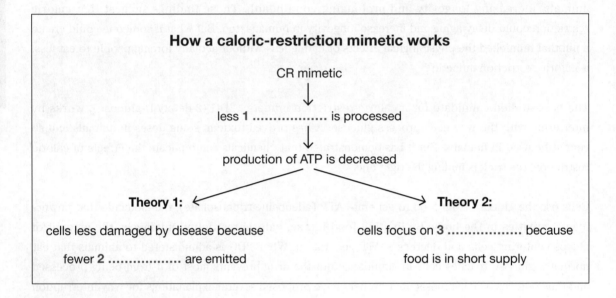

How a caloric-restriction mimetic works

CR mimetic

↓

less **1** .... is processed

↓

production of ATP is decreased

Theory 1:

cells less damaged by disease because

fewer **2** .... are emitted

Theory 2:

cells focus on **3** .... because

food is in short supply

This Marvellous Invention

Of all mankind's manifold creations, language must take pride of place. Other inventions—the wheel, agriculture, sliced bread—may have transformed our material existence, but the advent of language is what made us human. Compared to language, all other inventions pale in significance, since everything we have ever achieved depends on language and originates from it. Without language, we could never have embarked on our ascent to unparalleled power over all other animals, and even over nature itself.

But language is foremost not just because it came first. In its own right it is a tool of extraordinary sophistication, yet based on an idea of ingenious simplicity: 'this marvellous invention of composing out of twenty-five or thirty sounds that infinite variety of expressions which, whilst having in themselves no likeness to what is in our mind, allow us to disclose to others its whole secret, and to make known to those who cannot penetrate it all that we imagine, and all the various stirrings of our soul'. This was how, in 1660, the renowned French grammarians of the Port-Royal abbey near Versailles distilled the essence of language, and no one since has celebrated more eloquently the magnitude of its achievement. Even so, there is just one flaw in all these hymns of praise, for the homage to language's unique accomplishment conceals a simple yet critical incongruity. Language is mankind's greatest invention—except, of course, that it was never invented. This apparent paradox is at the core of our fascination with language, and it holds many of its secrets.

Questions 1–4

*Complete the summary using the list of words, **A–G**, below.*

*Write the correct letter, **A–G**, in boxes 1–4 on your answer sheet.*

The importance of language

The wheel is one invention that has had a major impact on **1** .... aspects of life, but no impact has been as **2** .... as that of language. Language is very **3** ...., yet composed of just a small number of sounds. Language appears to be **4** .... to use. However, its sophistication is often overlooked.

A difficult	**B** complex	**C** original	**D** admired
E material	**F** easy	**G** fundamental	

Grey Workers ①

Clearly, when older people do heavy physical work, their age may affect their productivity. But other skills may increase with age, including many that are crucial for good management, such as an ability to handle people diplomatically, to run a meeting or to spot a problem before it blows up. Peter Hicks, who coordinates OECD* work on the policy implications of aging, says that plenty of research suggests older people are paid more because they are worth more.

And the virtues of the young may be exaggerated. 'The few companies that have kept on older workers find they have good judgement and their productivity is good', says Peter Peterson, author of a recent book on the impact of ageing. 'Besides, their education standards are much better than those of today's young high-school graduates'. Companies may say that older workers are not worth training because they are reaching the end of their working lives; in fact, young people tend to switch jobs so frequently that they offer the worst returns on training. The median age for employer-driven training is the late 40s and early 50s, and this training goes mainly to managers.

* OECD: Organisation for Economic Co-operation and Development

Questions 1-2

Choose **TWO** letters, **A–G**.

Write the correct letter in boxes 1–2 on your answer sheet.

Which **TWO** advantages are mentioned by the writer about employing older workers?

1 ....   2 ....

A They are less likely to be involved in careless accidents.
B They can predict areas that may cause trouble in the future.
C They are able to train younger workers.
D They can deal with unexpected problems.
E They are more conscientious.
F They are prepared to work for lower salaries.
G They are more skilled in personal relationships.

Questions 3-4

*Choose **TWO** letters, **A–F**.*

Write the correct letter in boxes 3–4 on your answer sheet.

Which **TWO** disadvantages are mentioned by the writer about employing younger workers?

3 ....   4 ....

A They are too confident of their own skills.

B They may injure themselves.

C They do not stay with the same company for very long.

D Their training has been too theoretical.

E They are not as well educated as older workers.

F They demand higher salaries.

Tips ▶ 速読のために、英語を「英語で」理解しよう

　英語を読むときに頭で日本語に変換せずに、英語を「英語で」理解すれば、速く読めるようになります。とはいっても、IELTSで出題されるパッセージの内容を、いきなり日本語を介さずに理解するのは難しいはずです。まずは単語レベルでトレーニングを積みましょう。

　例えば、「violet＝すみれ＝紫色の花」ではなくviolet＝a purple flowerと、ダイレクトに英語で解釈します。
日頃から英英辞典を使って「英語と英語の変換」に慣れていくことをオススメします。

min.

Grey Workers ②

The general assumption is that older workers are paid more in spite of, rather than because of, their productivity. That might partly explain why, when employers are under pressure to cut costs, they persuade a 55-year-old to take early retirement. Take away seniority-based pay scales, and older workers may become a much more attractive employment proposition. But most employers and many workers are uncomfortable with the idea of reducing someone's pay in later life—although manual workers on piece-rates often earn less as they get older. So retaining the services of older workers may mean employing them in different ways.

One innovation was devised by IBM Belgium. Faced with the need to cut staff costs, and having decided to concentrate cuts on 55- to 60-year olds, IBM set up a separate company called Skill Team, which re-employed any of the early-retired who wanted to go on working up to the age of 60. An employee who joined Skill Team at the age of 55 on a five-year contract would work for 58% of his time, over the full period, for 88% of his last IBM salary. The company offered services to IBM, thus allowing it to retain access to some of the intellectual capital it would otherwise have lost.

The best way to tempt the old to go on working may be to build on such 'bridge' jobs: part-time or temporary employment that creates a more gradual transition from full-time work to retirement. Studies have found that, in the United States, nearly half of all men and women who had been in full-time jobs in middle age moved into such 'bridge' jobs at the end of their working lives. In general, it is the best-paid and worst-paid who carry on working. There seem to be two very different types of bridge job-holder—those who continue working because they have to and those who continue working because they want to, even though they could afford to retire.

If the job market grows more flexible, the old may find more jobs that suit them. Often, they will be self-employed. Sometimes, they may start their own businesses: a study by David Storey of Warwick University found that in Britain 70% of businesses started by people over 55 survived, compared with an overall national average of only 19%. But whatever pattern of employment they choose, in the coming years the skills of these 'grey workers' will have to be increasingly acknowledged and rewarded.

42

Questions 1–4

*Choose the correct letter, **A**, **B**, **C** or **D**.*

Write the correct letter in boxes 1–4 on your answer sheet.

1 In paragraph 1, the writer suggests that companies could consider ....

   A abolishing pay schemes that are based on age.

   B avoiding pay that is based on piece-rates.

   C increasing pay for older workers.

   D equipping older workers with new skills.

2 Skill Team is an example of a company which ....

   A offers older workers increases in salary.

   B allows people to continue working for as long as they want.

   C allows the expertise of older workers to be put to use.

   D treats older and younger workers equally.

3 According to the writer, 'bridge' jobs ....

   A tend to attract people in middle-salary ranges.

   B are better paid than some full-time jobs.

   C originated in the United States.

   D appeal to distinct groups of older workers.

4 David Storey's study found that ....

   A people demand more from their work as they get older.

   B older people are good at running their own businesses.

   C an increasing number of old people are self-employed.

   D few young people have their own businesses.

Environmental Psychology—Why Our Physical Environment Is Important to Us ①

I first became interested in the psychological impact of buildings when I was reading about the reconstruction of the House of Commons in the British Parliament after World War II. At the time, some people wanted a new semicircular horseshoe pattern currently in favour in many European parliaments, and the chamber to be enlarged. But thankfully, Prime Minister Winston Churchill persuaded the members to keep the traditional, rectangular layout, saying that this better suited the two-party system, with the parties sitting opposite each other. Churchill also opposed enlargement of the chamber, seeming to think that a restricted space added urgency to the atmosphere of the chamber. Insightfully, he said, "We shape our buildings, and later they shape us".

The study of the relationship between us, human beings, and the physical world around us is called *environmental psychology*. It is based on the belief that the spaces we occupy can also influence our behaviour, mood and mental health. It became a recognized field in 1970 when Harold Proshansky published *Environmental Psychology: Man and His Physical Setting.* Proshansky's contention was that our psychology is affected not only by our upbringing, as traditional psychology had taught, but also by the design of the buildings we live and move within.

At that time, there was some effort to apply environmental psychology to the serious housing problems in the United States. The most notorious case was the Pruitt-Igoe project in St. Louis. Constructed in 1954 to house thousands of the city's poor, the Pruitt-Igoe complex consisted of 33 high-rise apartment buildings. At the time of its construction it had been praised by new tenants as 'an oasis in the desert', and favourably compared to the extremely poor standard of housing they had occupied previously. However, within sixteen years the entire Pruitt-Igoe complex had rapidly decayed through neglect, and it needed to be demolished.

Now, it is clear that there were several causes of these problems. At Pruitt-Igoe, the existence of shared spaces and the lack of private spaces led to chronic neglect. The designers had anticipated that shared spaces would encourage everyone to look after the environment, but in fact nobody felt any sense of responsibility or personal pride. The deterioration of the site led to people living there feeling distressed, and displaying high rates of criminal behaviour and psychological problems.

Questions 1–5

Do the following statements agree with the claim of the writer in the passage?

In boxes 1–5 on your answer sheet, write

YES   *if the statement agrees with the claim of the writer*

NO   *if the statement contradicts the claim of the writer*

NOT GIVEN   *if it is impossible to say what the writer thinks about this*

1   The House of Commons was better in a semicircular layout.   ....

2   Churchill believed that a small debating chamber would make debates more relaxed.   ....

3   Environment affected people's mood more than it affected their behaviour.   ....

4   The Pruitt-Igoe complex failed because it was not cared for properly.   ....

5   There was a connection between environment and mental health in Pruitt-Igoe.   ....

Environmental Psychology—Why Our Physical Environment Is Important to Us ②

Environmental psychology was first applied to another context in 1973, when Philip Kotler coined the term 'atmospherics' in an article in the *Journal of Retailing.* He defined atmospherics as, 'the effort to design buying environments to produce specific emotional effects in the buyer that enhance the purchase probability'. In some cases, Kotler maintained, the atmosphere of a store was more important than the products it sold, and consumers might be drawn to a shop simply by the pleasure of being in that space.

He laid down four principles. The first was unity. Basically this meant that elements such as colour, shape and sound worked well together. The second, legibility, specified that the building was easy for people to navigate. The third, complexity, stipulated that the interior should also be just complex enough to keep people interested in moving within it. Related to this was the fourth precept, mystery. You never knew what was around the next corner. This satisfied the consumers' continual need to be attracted. All of these principles are reflected in the design of many of today's shopping malls.

No type of business demonstrates quite how far designers will go in modern times to influence their consumers more than the modern casino. The typical Las Vegas casino interior has a peculiar ambience. There are no windows, nor are there clocks on the walls. There is no sense of time of day. Casinos deliberately remove all these clues to the normal passing of time so that customers forget that they are 'wasting time' in a casino. Sound is also manipulated by the casino owners. The constant background noise maintains the timelessness of the ambience, while the regular sound of a cascade of coins whenever someone wins the jackpot keeps people hoping for success. In a sense, casino floors are not 'legible' because the casino designers want you to get figuratively lost, to forget the real world. However, they don't want you to really *feel* lost, because that makes you anxious. Thus, lighting and patterns in carpets subliminally lead you where the casino owners want you to go.

The application of environmental psychology has today become much more detailed and complex. Research continues to be done into, for example, hospital buildings, with a view to increasing a sense of well-being, and in turn, aiding patients' recovery. Research from many countries demonstrates that simply introducing 'green' spaces into hospitals not only makes patients feel better, it actually reduces recovery times from surgery and produces significantly more positive outcomes in cases of chronic illness. Background music, high ceilings, and giving patients control of lighting also have a positive effect.

All aspects of our lives are being enhanced by further refinement of environmental psychology, and we can look forward to many more improvements to our living environment in the future.

Questions 1–4

Complete the sentences below.

*Choose **ONE OR TWO WORDS** from the passage for each answer.*

Write your answers in boxes 1–4 on your answer sheet.

1 The emotional impact produced by the design of the store can increase a consumer's

....

2 Interiors should to some extent be complex so that people do not become bored, and there should also be an element of ....

3 The principles of atmospherics are shown in the design of many modern ....

4 If casinos had windows or clocks, people might think they were ....

Questions 5–7

*According to the passage, which of the following statements applies to these places, **A–C**.*

*Write the correct letter, **A–C**, in boxes 5–7 on your answer sheet.*

***NB** You may use any letter more than once.*

List of Places
A casinos only
B hospitals only
C both casinos and hospitals

5 Lighting plays a role in people's mental state.   ....

6 Sounds are important in influencing people's mental state.   ....

7 The height of indoor spaces has some effect.   ....

情報を組み合わせる問題
文の前半と後半を組み合わせる問題
要約を完成させる問題

実践問題では、本番と同程度の長さ、問題数のパッセージを2本掲載します。なお、実際のテストではパッセージは3本出題されます。

Tambora Volcano

A————The explosion was heard at a distance of 2,600 kilometres. Ash fell to earth at least 1,300 kilometres away. When, in 1815, the Tambora volcano on the Indonesian island of Sumbawa blew its top in the largest observed eruption in recorded history, the immediate impact was devastating. On Sumbawa itself and on the neighbouring islands of Lombok and Bali, many thousands of people lost their lives. Longer term effects were felt all over the world, as far away as Europe and the United States. Even today, among climatologists involved in the modern battle with climate change, the meteorological implications of the Tambora eruption continue to provoke debate.

B————Mount Tambora became active on 5 April 1815. The next morning, volcanic ash began to fall in East Java, with faint explosions heard on the breeze lasting until 10 April. On that day, the eruption intensified, the whole mountainside transformed into a flowing mass of liquid fire, and pyroclastic flows slid down the slopes to the sea, totally obliterating the small community of Tambora. The ash shroud spread as far as Batavia (modern Jakarta), where a nitrous stench hung in the air and heavy acid rain fell for days.

C————All vegetation on Sumbawa was wiped out. Fallen trees, mixed with pumice ash, were swept into the sea, where they formed floating islands up to five kilometres wide. A medium-sized tsunami hit the coastal areas of several islands in the Indonesian archipelago, causing death and destruction at a great distance. In East Java and in the Moluccan Islands it reached two to three metres in height. The estimated death toll varies depending on which authority you refer to. Taking all the principal sources into consideration, the number of direct fatalities caused by the pyroclastic flows can be put at 10,000. On Sumbawa, subsequently, 18,000 starved to death, while about 10,000 on Lombok died from hunger and related disease. In all, it is thought that 100,000 people in the Indonesian island chain died from the effects, direct and indirect, of the eruption.

D————The Tambora explosion thrust a column of ash into the stratosphere to an altitude of more than 43 kilometres. Ice-core evidence shows that this high-level cloud stayed in the earth's atmosphere from a few months to a few years at altitudes of 10–30 kilometres. Winds spread the fine particles around the globe, creating incredible optical phenomena. Brilliantly-coloured sunsets were seen frequently in London, where it is theorized that they inspired the vibrant painted landscapes of the celebrated JMW Turner. Darkened skies were also said to have inspired the novel *Frankenstein*.

E ———So much sulfur dioxide (SO_2) was emitted into the stratosphere that it significantly affected the climate. We now know that the year 1816 was the second-coldest year in the northern hemisphere since around 1400, and the 1810s are the coldest decade on record. 1816 became known as 'the year without summer'. Historians estimate that, in Europe, the significant cooling caused 90,000 deaths. Parts of Europe also experienced a stormier than usual winter, with cool temperatures and heavy rains resulting in failed crops across Britain and Ireland. The crops were so poor in Germany that food prices rose sharply, and demonstrations in front of grain markets and bakeries, followed by riots, arson, and looting were common in many cities. For that country, it was the worst famine of the 19th century. The change in climate has also been blamed for the severity of typhus epidemics in southeast Europe and along the coast of the eastern Mediterranean Sea between 1816 and 1819. In India it disrupted the monsoon, caused three failed harvests, and contributed to the spread of a new strain of cholera, all of these leading to the death of tens of millions of people there.

F ———In recent years some scientists have begun to ask whether cooling effects like those of Tambora could be produced artificially in order to tackle the problem of global warming. It has been proposed that injecting sulfur dioxide into the stratosphere using artillery or aircraft could be done at a reasonable cost, and could well be effective in reducing global temperatures. But this kind of geoengineering is controversial. Those who are opposed point to several risks. First, there is the threat to health. If any sulfate particles fell to ground level in quantities, they would harm asthma sufferers and others with respiratory ailments. Reduction in the ozone level is another probable side effect. Some people also point out that, should the geoengineering be stopped all at once, there would be very rapid increases in temperature and rainfall at five to ten times the rates of global warming.

G ———Instead of trying to recreate a Tambora effect, the critics add, we should be more concerned about a repetition of a real eruption on that scale. Historical meteorological data indicates that this kind of mega-eruption has happened somewhere in the world, on average, about once every two centuries. It is now more than two hundred years since Tambora blew. One can only shudder at the economic, social and environmental impacts such a disaster would have on today's interconnected world.

Questions 1–5

The passage has seven paragraphs, **A–G**.

Which paragraph contains the following information?

*Write the correct letter, **A–G**, in boxes 1–5 on your answer sheet.*

1   A warning about the future   ....

2   A reference to the destruction of a village   ....

3   A suggestion for addressing climate change   ....

4   A theory about an influence on the world of art   ....

5   A reference to social unrest   ....

Questions 6–10

*Complete each sentence with the correct ending, **A–H** below.*

*Write the correct letter, **A–H**, in boxes 6–10 on your answer sheet.*

6   The immediate ash cloud caused   ....

7   Wood and ash in the sea together caused   ....

8   A tsunami caused   ....

9   Fine ash in the stratosphere caused   ....

10   Bad harvests caused   ....

A	disturbances and protests.
B	a bad stink in the air in Batavia.
C	pyroclastic flows.
D	epidemics in German cities.
E	dramatic visual effects.
F	deaths in the Moluccan Islands.
G	intense debate among climatologists.
H	the formation of huge rafts.

Questions 11–14

Complete the summary below.

*Choose **ONE WORD** from the passage for each answer.*

Write your answers in boxes 11–14 on your answer sheet.

Concerns about geoengineering

Geoengineering has been suggested as a way to overcome climate change. Introducing sulfur dioxide into the stratosphere could be effective, and the **11** .... would be acceptable. However, such a policy might have downsides, too. Particles could cause harm to people with respiratory disease, and there might be loss of **12** .... in the atmosphere. Also, if the geoengineering came to a halt suddenly, **13** .... and temperature levels would rise sharply. Pessimists point out that we are due for another **14** .... soon, if we take history as a guide.

> **Tips** コンピューター試験では、コピー＆ペーストを活用しよう
>
> パッセージから単語を抜き出して解答する「引用型」の問題では、手書きで写すとスペルミスをするリスクがあります。したがって、コンピューター試験で受ける場合には、**コピー＆ペースト機能を使いましょう。これは入力時間の短縮にもなります**。ただし、マウスの右クリックは使えないので、必ずショートカットキーを使ってください。
> ・Ctrl + C：コピー
> ・Ctrl + V：ペースト
> なお、コピー＆ペーストはライティングテストでエッセイを書くときにも役に立ちます！

段落に合う見出しを選ぶ問題
特定する問題
複数の選択肢から選ぶ問題

Why Do We Have Time Zones?

A————What time is it right now where you are? Let us imagine you are reading this in Singapore, and it is 19:24 on a Monday evening. The sun has just set. In half an hour or so, you may sit down to dinner with your family. Elsewhere in the world, it is earlier, or later. In London it is mid-morning. In New York it is 6:24 and early risers are enjoying their morning coffee. In Auckland, New Zealand, it is already Tuesday. Nowadays, we take for granted that the world is divided into time zones. We are so familiar with this concept we may not realize that the very idea of time zones is relatively modern in human history.

B————Two hundred years ago, time zones did not exist. Before the invention of the telegraph in the mid-nineteenth century, in an age when people did not travel any faster than a horse could carry them, official time zones were simply not needed. In those days, nobody cared what hour of the day it was in a town just 100 km away, much less what time it was on the other side of the world, and city governments simply established their own time. When the sun reached its highest point in the sky, everyone set their clock to 12 o'clock noon and calculated the hours of the day from that. In effect, every town had its own private time zone.

C————This all changed with the invention of rail travel and telegraph communication. Once people started moving around more, it did start to matter what time it was in a distant city. You might have a connecting train leaving from that city, and you might miss that train. How could national train systems work when everyone's watches told different times? In Europe, by the mid-nineteenth century, an international rail network had begun to develop, closely followed by the transcontinental railroad in the US. Without a standard time, how could these systems run?

D————One day in 1876, a Scottish-Canadian engineer named Sandford Fleming missed a train and experienced frustration. He came up with the plan of dividing the world into 24 time zones. Since 1855 Great Britain had been using a standard time, called Railway Time, founded on the old maritime reference time known as Greenwich Mean Time (GMT). Fleming took that as his starting point and proposed that the entire world should be divided into 24 zones, all relating to GMT. Zones lying to the east of Greenwich would be earlier; those lying to the west would be later. For example, Istanbul would be GMT plus 3, and Buenos Aires would be GMT minus 3. Fleming's plan is now 150 years old and is a fundamental component of global communication and business. In reality, the picture today is not 24 time zones. Since certain countries have elected to distinguish themselves by 30 minutes, there are actually 39 time zones in all. In the USA there are four time zones, Eastern, Central, Mountain and Pacific. China, however, only has one time zone, even though its geographic spread should really span about five.

E ———But this may not be the end of the story. As air travel has compressed travel time even more, and the internet has brought the world even closer together, some people have started to ask why we need time zones at all. Why do we not just all have the same time everywhere in the world? Two American professors, Richard Conn Henry and Steve Hanke, have proposed Universal Time, according to which we should all just set our clocks to London time, which used to be called GMT. This is already happening in some fields. Financial traders, wherever they are, tend to set their clocks to GMT, as do the military in some countries.

F ———Henry and Hanke point out that clock time is an artificial human construct, so there is no scientific reason why we should not all march to exactly the same drum. Would it not be simpler if nine o'clock in New York were also nine o'clock in Tokyo and in Karachi and Auckland? The benefits, they emphasize, would be immediate and profound. Life would be simpler. We would never have to calculate what time it was elsewhere in the world, and planning long-distance travel would be far easier. Businesses and governments would save money. The problems due to current artificially-imposed time zones—said to include lack of sleep and higher rates of heart disease—could disappear as local areas set their own timetables. Above all, the long-term, positive psychological impact of all humanity keeping exactly the same time would be immense.

G ———Critics, however, point out that, mentally, it might not be that easy to get used to. If you live in Japan, for instance, every new date would start half way through the morning. In Los Angeles the new date would start in late afternoon. On some islands in the Pacific, the date would change with the sun high in the sky. People would wake up on Friday and go to bed on Saturday. So Universal Time would take a long time to grow used to, and there would be other drawbacks, too. Cultural phrases like, 'We are going to party till two in the morning', and, 'I have a nine to five job', would become meaningless. And anyway, whenever we took a long-haul flight, we would still get jet lag.

Questions 1–6

The passage has seven paragraphs, **A–G**.

Choose the correct heading for each paragraph from the list of headings below.

Paragraph A has been done for you.

Write the correct number, *i–x*, in boxes 1–6 on your answer sheet.

List of Headings

i   Advantages of a future change

ii   A long-lasting system

iii   One country, five time zones

iv   Time for another change?

v   Thousands of time zones

vi   A long adjustment period?

vii   Financial benefits

viii   A familiar part of modern life

ix   The impact of the internet

x   Time zones become needed

     Paragraph **A**   ....viii............

1   Paragraph **B**   ....

2   Paragraph **C**   ....

3   Paragraph **D**   ....

4   Paragraph **E**   ....

5   Paragraph **F**   ....

6   Paragraph **G**   ....

Questions 7–12

Do the following statements agree with the information given in the passage?

In boxes 7–12 on your answer sheet, write

> **TRUE**   *if the statement agrees with the information*
> **FALSE**   *if the statement contradicts the information*
> **NOT GIVEN** *if there is no information on this*

7   19th century horse-riders could only travel 100 km per day.   ....

8   Train travel contributed to a need for official time zones.   ....

9   Fleming based his system on an existing convention.   ....

10   All time zones are at least one hour apart.   ....

11   Air travel has made time zones even more necessary.   ....

12   Universal Time would not have any health benefits.   ....

Question 13

Choose the correct letter, *A*, *B*, *C* or *D*.

Write the correct letter in box 13 on your answer sheet.

Universal Time …   ....

A   would not be economically beneficial.

B   would mostly affect Pacific islands.

C   would mean people feel better psychologically.

D   could be changed by local areas.

高得点ホルダーの勉強法を公開！①

C.F さん 女性 24 歳／オーバーオール 7.0
（リスニング：8.0、リーディング：7.5、ライティング：6.0、スピーキング：6.0）

リスニング

- さまざまな問題集のほか、ウェブサイトに掲載されている問題も解いた
  - →古い問題集でもIELTSの対策には変わりはないと考え、数をこなした。一方で、「解いて終わり」ではなく、見直しは丁寧に行い、**最低3回はスクリプトを聞いた。**
- YouTubeで、BBC Learning Englishをほぼ毎日見るようにした

English Innovationsが実施したアンケートでは、**3割以上の生徒さんがリスニング対策としてBBCを活用**していました。「リスニングが苦手」と漠然と訴える生徒さんに、まずはBBCの音声を毎日聞いてもらうと、スコアがUPすることがあります。本書はさまざまなアクセントの音声を収録しているので、自分が苦手とする国のアクセントはどれかを分析して、その国のニュースを聞きましょう。

リーディング

- 問題タイプごとに練習問題を解いた
- 制限時間内にすべて解き切ることを目標に、3つのパッセージを50分以内で解けるように練習を積んだ
  - →本番でも時間に余裕ができ、「スペルミスをしていないか」などの見直しもできるようになった。

ライティング

- 「同じ単語を3回以上使わない」「同じ接続詞を2回以上使わない」などルールを作って書く練習をした
  - →特に、対比を表す語句（on the one handとon the other handやwhileなど）は、タスク1、2共通で使えるので、必ずと言っていいほど使ってエッセイを構成した。
- 自分のレベルに合った単語や文法を使ってミスを少なくした

確かに関係代名詞や分詞構文を使った文を使いこなせると、スコアに直結しますが、**ご自身のレベルを超えて難しい文法を使うと、ミスが起こり逆効果**です。最初は基本的な接続詞を使えるようにする、次に、少し複雑な文にチャレンジする…というふうに、段階的にレベルUPしましょう。

スピーキング

- パート1：大体のトピックは予測できるので、そのトピックに関する語彙力をつけた
- パート2：求められているポイントに答えつつ、2分間話し続けられるように練習した
  - →具体的にはネイティブ講師の助言を聞き、ストーリーを作って、順を追って話すようにした。そうすると「流れ」ができ、スムーズに回答できるようになった。
- パート3：難しい問題に備えて、時間を稼ぐ回答（I've never thought about it, but ...など）をインプットしておいた。
  - →実際に**日本語でも回答できないようなことも多々聞かれたが、回答内容の出来にこだわるのではなく、自分が思ったことを伝える**ようにした。

Listening

About Listening

リスニングテストは4つのパートから成ります。
- 問題数： 40問（各パート10問）
- 試験時間： 30分（各パート6〜8分）
  ペーパー試験のみ、最後に10分の転記時間がある
- 音声のアクセント：イギリス、アメリカ、カナダ、オーストラリア、ニュージーランドなど
- 質問の順番： 音声が流れる順番で出題される

Part	シチュエーションの例	話者の数	内容
1	・予約手続き ・問い合わせ	2人	日常的 社会的
2	・ツアーや施設の案内	1人	
3	・学生同士、または学生と教授の会話やディスカッション （課題や科目選択など）	2〜4人	学術的 教育的
4	・講義や講演	1人	
転記	解答を解答用紙に書き写す時間（10分）		

※コンピューター試験の場合、転記時間はないので、すぐに解答を打ち込む必要があります

評価基準 40点満点（1問1点×40問）
配点は各1点で、合計得点は換算表に基づき、1〜9の0.5刻みのバンドスコアに換算されます。

バンドスコアの換算例

バンドスコア	40問中の正答数
5	16
6	23
7	30
8	35

なお、減点対象になるもの／ならないものの基準はリーディングと同じです（p.22参照）。

Listening 攻略ルール

1 ▶ プレヴュータイムは、ゴールデンタイム

パート1〜3では問題の開始前と途中に、それぞれ30秒ほどのプレヴュータイムがあります。パート4だけは全10問分の音声が途中の切れ目なく流れるので、最初のプレヴュータイムで一気に問題を追っていきましょう。

プレヴュータイム中にぼーっとしてしまうのは論外で、前のパートのことを考え続けるのもいけません！ **必ずこれから解く問題に目を通して**ください。

プレヴュータイムにすべきこと
- 空欄を埋める問題では、語数制限を確認する
- 空欄に入れる語の見当をつけておく
- キーワードになりそうな語句には印をつける
  （特に、数字や固有名詞は必ずチェック）
- 問題文のキーワードから内容を予測する
  （room, name, reservationなどの単語があったら「ホテルを予約するときの会話？」と**放送内容を推測**できる）

> **Part 1–3の音声タイムライン例**
> プレヴュー（約30秒）
> ↓
> 音声（前半5問）
> ↓
> プレヴュー（約30秒）
> ↓
> 音声（後半5問）
> ↓
> 解答の確認（30秒〜1分）

プレヴュータイム
＝集中！

2 ▶ 空欄に入れる語の見当をつけておく

1の「プレヴュータイムにすべきこと」の「空欄に入れる語の見当をつけておく」を詳しく説明していきます。「フォームを完成させる問題」や「要約を完成させる問題」などの空欄補充系では、空欄のある文全体の構造や、空欄前後の語句を確認して、文法的にはどんな単語が入るか判断しましょう。「品詞は何か」「複数名詞か単数名詞か」「可算名詞か不可算名詞か」など見当がついていれば、音声を聞きながら解答を拾いやすくなります。

Walk or take a .... to the bus station.
→ aの後なので単数名詞が入る。文脈から「乗り物」表す名詞が解答になると判断できる。

Maryland Guest House location: .... Street
→ Streetから通りの名前が入ると判断できる。

3 ▸ ディストラクターに要注意！

ディストラクターは、あなたを混乱させる引っ掛けの選択肢のことです。**答えになりそうな単語が聞こえたからといって、すぐに飛びつくのは危険！** 答えになりそうな単語の前後の文脈を聞き取り、正答できるようにしましょう。

ディストラクターはすべてのパートを通じて度々出てくるので、パートごとの傾向を知っておく必要があります。詳しくは「Part別にディストラクターを攻略しよう」を参考にしてください（p.63参照）。

4 ▸ 放送中に解答用紙を埋めない

ペーパー受験の場合は、パート4の音声が終了した後、10分間転記する時間があります。これは**リスニングの問題用紙から解答用紙に解答を転記する**ための時間です。

逆に言えば、各パートの合間には解答を解答用紙に記入しない方がいいのです。合間の時間は先に述べたとおりゴールデンタイム。次のパートの準備に専念すべきです。ただし、コンピューター試験の場合、転記時間はなく、放送中に解答していく必要があるので注意しましょう。

5 ▸ わからない問題は、一度捨てる勇気を持つ

答えられない問題にあたったら、潔くその問題のことはいったん忘れてしまいましょう。次の問題に移っても前のことを考え続けていると集中力がなくなり、最悪パニック状態になることも考えられます。

実際、同じパート内でも**難易度にばらつき**があります。難問にあたったら一度そこから離れ、**最後に時間があったら戻る**方が賢明です。

もし「答えはわかるけどスペルを思い出せない」ときは、ペーパー試験の場合なら、とりあえずカタカナでもよいので解答を書いておきましょう。その上で、最後の転記時間になったときに正しいスペルを検討して最終解答とするのがオススメです。

6 ▸ パラフレーズを見抜こう

問題文の表現（文や語句）が、音声では違う表現に言い換えられていることがあり、これをパラフレーズと言います。語彙を増やすときは、1つの単語だけではなく、パラフレーズ対策として同義語や反義語もあわせて覚えるとよいでしょう。これはリーディングの章で詳しく解説しているので、是非参考にしてください（pp.23-24参照）。

6つの問題タイプを知ろう

リスニングテストには6つの問題タイプがあります。各パートで1種類もしくは2種類以上の問題形式が出題されます。

⟩ task type-1 フォーム・メモ・表・フローチャート・要約を完成させる問題 Form, notes, table, flowchart, summary completion ⟫⟫⟫ Part 1, 4 の練習1、2／実践

申し込み用紙、料金表、フローチャートや、要約にある空欄を埋めます。解答は、音声に出てくる語を使用して記入します。指示文で語数制限が指定されています。**人名や住所、数字の聞き取りは頻出**です。

例：*Complete the notes below. Write **ONE WORD ONLY** for each answer.*
→1単語のみで空欄を埋めてメモを完成させる。

⟩ task type-2 文を完成させる問題 Sentence completion ⟫⟫⟫ Part 3の練習1／実践

音声に出てくる語を使用して、文中の空欄を埋める問題です。指示文に語数制限の指定があります。

例：*Complete the sentences below. Write **ONE WORD AND/OR A NUMBER** for each answer.*
→1つの単語か1つの数字、またはその両方を使って文を完成させる。

⟩ task type-3 制限内の語数で答える問題 Short-answer questions ⟫⟫⟫ Part 2の練習1

音声に出てくる語を使用して、解答します。質問文の疑問詞（what, who, where, whichなど）を確認して何が問われているのか把握し、答えを聞き逃さないようにしてください。指示文では語数制限の指定があります。

例：*Write **NO MORE THAN TWO WORDS AND/OR A NUMBER** for each answer.*
→質問に、2つ以下の単語か1つの数字、またはその両方を使って答える。

⟩ task type-4 マッチングする問題 Matching information ⟫⟫⟫ Part 3の練習3

音声を聞き、それぞれの問題に最も適切な解答を囲みの中の選択肢から選ぶ問題です。選択肢が問題数より多いこともあります。

例：*Choose **THREE** answers from the box and write the correct letter, **A-E**, next to Questions 1–3.*
→囲みの中から3つの答えを選び、解答欄の1〜3にA-Eの正しい文字を記入する。

Part 3の
練習2
／実践

task type-5 〉 複数の選択肢から選ぶ問題　Multiple choice

音声を聞き、選択肢から解答を選ぶ問題で、複数の解答を選ぶこともあります。また、選択肢から解答を選ぶシンプルな問題のほか、文の前半が与えられ、後半を選択する問題もあります。

　　　　例：*Choose **TWO** letters, **A–E**.*
　　　　→ A〜Eから2つ選ぶ。

Part 2の
練習2、3

task type-6 〉 プラン・地図・図を完成させる問題
Plan, map, diagram labelling

音声を聞き、与えられた図などを完成させる問題です。以下のバリエーションがあります。
- プラン（例：建物の中のフロアプラン）
- 地図（例：町）
- 図（例：機器の仕組みや工程）

音声をもとに選択肢から選ぶほか、単語を記入するパターンもあります。
このタイプでは、**空間的な関係を表す語、道順を伝える語など、頻出の語句を押さえる**のが重要。実際に音声が始まったら、最初に現在地を必ず把握してください。その後は聞きながら手を動かしてルートをたどり、途中で聞き逃しても、だいたいの見当がつくようにしていきましょう。

　　　　例：*Label the map below. Write the correct letter, **A–H**, next to Questions 1–5.*
　　　　→次の地図を完成させる。正しい文字を1〜5の解答欄に書く。

Tips 〈 Partごとに、出題されやすい問題タイプがある

ここで紹介した問題タイプは、すべてのパートで出題される可能性があります。しかし、パートごとに出題されやすい問題タイプがあり、その傾向を把握していると対策を立てやすいでしょう。以下に出題傾向をまとめたので参考にしてください。

パート1
task type 1 が頻出で、ほかにも穴埋め系の問題が多い。

パート2
task type 5, 6のように選択肢から選ぶ問題が多い。

パート3
task type 4の出題が多い。

パート4
task type 1の中でも、特に「メモを完成させる問題」は定番。

Part別にディストラクターを攻略しよう

全パートで度々登場し、受験者を惑わせるディストラクターを攻略すべく、ここではパートごとに典型的な例を紹介していきます。まずは大前提として「ディストラクターになりやすいもの」を理解したうえで、例題を読みましょう。

ディストラクターになりやすいもの
- 誰かからの提案（日時の提案で実際には採用されないものなど）
- 間違った情報（誰かが間違えた情報を言い、その後に訂正されるものなど）
- 音声の語句が選択肢でパラフレーズされているが、実際には正答ではないもの

Part-1 　日にちや時刻は、ディストラクターの大定番！

　エイミーが面接のためにサンフランシスコに行く日程について、マットと話しています。「エイミーの面接日はいつか」と問われたら、正答はCの7日です。複数の日にちが会話に出てきており、それらがすべてディストラクターです。

M=Matt　A=Amy

M　I heard that you were looking for a new job. How's it going?

A　Quite well, actually. I'm flying to San Francisco on the 3rd for an interview with a big IT company.

M　That's wonderful. You must be pretty excited. So, I guess your interview is on the 5th, right?

A　Not exactly. It's on the 7th, but I want to get over the jet lag before my interview day. Also, even if the flight is delayed, I'm sure I'll still be able to reach San Francisco by the 6th at the latest.

M　That's a good plan. Best of luck for your interview.

Question: When is Amy's interview?

A on the 5th　　**B** on the 3rd　　**C** on the 7th　　**D** on the 6th

Part-2 　質問文で聞かれていることを明確にしておこう

　入居者にごみの収集日について説明をしています。ごみの種類によって収集日が異なり、複数の曜日が出てきます。「リサイクル不可のごみ収集日はいつか」と問われたら、正答はDのTuesdayです。

We have prepared this welcome guide to help new residents settle in and learn more about our beautiful town. First, in order to keep our surroundings clean, we request all residents to follow the community rules for garbage collection. All recyclable garbage bins are collected on

Mondays and non-recyclable garbage bins on Tuesdays. If you have any oversized garbage, please let the council office know and it will be collected on a Friday. Finally, please note that food and garden waste doesn't go in the non-recyclable bins as we have separate collection for such waste every Thursday.

Question: When is non-recyclable garbage collected?

    A Friday   **B** Thursday   **C** Monday   **D** Tuesday

Part-3　賛成・反対など、会話の流れをつかもう

　2人の学生がプレゼンテーションのトピックについて話し合っています。「学生たちが決めたプレゼンテーションのトピックは何か」と聞かれたら、正答はBの primary schools（小学校）です。ミサが提案したが採用されなかった schools や、全体のテーマである education が先に聞こえてくるので、飛びつかないように。最後まで文脈を理解しながら聞く必要があります。また、他のグループのテーマである vocational colleges（専門学校）も、presenting on に続いており、問題文と同じ表現で話しているので要注意のディストラクターです。

G=George　M=Misa

G　By the way, before I forget, shouldn't we decide on a topic for our presentation next month?

M　Oh yes. Thanks for reminding me. Since the overall theme is education, I was wondering if we could prepare a presentation on schools.

G　Sounds good, but that's still a pretty broad topic. I guess it's a good idea to focus on a specific sector. What about looking at primary schools?

M　That's a great idea. I heard the other group is presenting on vocational colleges, so there is going to be no overlap.

Question: Which topic did the students decide to present on?

    A schools   **B** primary schools

    C vocational colleges   **D** education

Part-4　選択肢と音声のパラフレーズにも注意！

　大学教授がプロジェクトの進捗について話しています。「プロジェクトの遅れの原因は何か」と問われたら、正答はBの mistake in the questions（質問の間違い）です。

　ディストラクターは、summer holidays（夏季休暇）、lack of volunteers（ボランティアの不足）、number of respondents（アンケートへの回答数）です。これらは話の中で懸念点として言及されていますが、最終的にはプロジェクトの遅れに影響しなかったことです。

There were a number of challenges that we encountered throughout the surveying phase of this project. Firstly, the timing couldn't have been worse. As it was the middle of the summer break, finding volunteers was quite difficult. Luckily, thanks to social media, we were able to find enough students who were happy to participate in the survey. Unfortunately, despite having enough respondents, midway through, we realised there was a critical flaw in the survey questions, so we had to redo the entire survey. As a result, this phase took three weeks longer than expected.

Question: What caused the delay with the project?

A summer holidays   **B** mistake in the questions

C lack of volunteers   **D** number of respondents

Tips 生きた英語を毎日聞く習慣を作ろう！

リスニングテストでは、アカデミック・モジュールとジェネラル・トレーニング・モジュールで共通の問題が出題されます。つまり、流れてくる音声のシチュエーションは、英語圏の日常生活で遭遇するようなシーンが想定されています。

英語特有の会話の流れや、さまざまな表現を身につけるには、生きた英語を聞くことを習慣化するのがオススメです。平日は、通勤、通学中に、YouTubeやPodcastで興味があるものを見たり聞いたりするといいでしょう。週末は、TED Talksや海外ドラマを楽しみながら視聴するのはどうでしょうか。毎日の積み重ねが、必ずスコアUPにつながります！

Part 1 対策

　パート1では、2人の話者による日常的な会話が出題されます。本パートは、最も得点しやすいパートと言われているので、ハイスコアを目指す方は、パート1でしっかり正答を重ねていくようにしましょう。よく出るのは次のようなシーンです。
- ホテル予約の電話
- ジムやスクールの申し込み
- ツアーの問い合わせ
- 空港でのチェックイン時の会話

細かい情報の聞き取り問題は頻出
　パート1における最大の特徴は、細かい情報を正確に聞き取らせる問題が多く出題される点です。固有名詞（人名・場所名・会社名）、数字・番号（申し込み番号・電話番号・パスポートナンバー）、日付、時刻、単位、メールアドレス、値段などの聞き取りは頻出です。

固有名詞
　多くの場合、一度音声で流れた後に、1文字ずつアルファベットが流れます。ただし、JoeやMaryなど一般的なものはスペルアウトされないこともあります。
　　　例：Arthur→A-R-T-H-U-R

数字・番号
　数字には特殊な読み方のルールがあります。
　　329-0887　読み上げ方 →THREE, TWO, NINE, ZERO, EIGHT, EIGHT, SEVEN
　088の部分は、以下の読み上げ方もあるので注意しましょう。
　　　0 → OH （「オゥ」に近い音）
　　　88 → double eight （同じ数字が2回続く場合にdoubleを使う）
　なお、888と3つ続く場合は、triple eightと読まれることもあります。

日付
　表記はアメリカ／イギリス式のどちらでも問題ありません。年号は2桁ずつ読み上げます。
　　　October 10(th) （アメリカ式）
　　　10(th) October （イギリス式）　　※OctoberはOct. またはOctでも可

in 2021　読み上げ方→ in twenty twenty one

時刻

〈分＋past＋時〉（〜時…分過ぎ）と、〈分＋to＋時〉（〜時…分前）の言い方に慣れましょう。

時刻	読み上げ方
9:00	nine o'clock
9:15	nine fifteen / fifteen（minutes）**past** nine / quarter **past** nine
9:20	nine twenty / twenty（minutes）**past** nine
9:30	nine thirty / half **past** nine / half nine
9:40	nine forty / twenty **to** ten
9:45	nine forty five / quarter **to** ten

単位

　通貨や長さなどの単位は日本人にとってなじみのないものが多く、時にアメリカやイギリスで使われている単位が音声で流れてくることもあるので注意が必要です。単位の記号を書くことが求められる場合もあり、スペルミスで不正解とならないように**単位の記号も覚えておいた方がいいでしょう**。通貨単位の中では、特に＄と£が頻出です。

英語（日本語）	記号
dollar（ドル）	$
pound（ポンド）	£
euro（ユーロ）	€
cent（セント）	¢
kilogramme（キログラム）	kg
metre（メーター）	m
mile（マイル）	m

また、金額を答えさせる問題もあるので、お金の読み上げ方にも慣れておく必要があります。
　　$5.40 → five dollars (and) forty cents / five forty
　　£10.50 → ten pounds fifty

練習 **1** 表を完成させる問題

本問は、本番の試験よりも音声の長さは短くなっています。

Questions 1–5

Complete the table below.

*Write **NO MORE THAN TWO WORDS AND/OR A NUMBER** for each answer.*

Village Wellness Club	Membership Contracts
Minimum age requirement for membership:	
Gym access: 1 .... years old	For a membership Contract: 18 years old
Type 1: Full Service Membership	
Access: all equipment and 2	
Personalised programmes: exercise & weight loss professionals	
Fee: 3 .... / day	
Type 2: 4 .... Membership	
No personalised programmes	
Access: machines for strength and 5 ...., and free weights	
Fee: $1 / day	

練習 **2** フォームを完成させる問題

本問は、練習1よりは音声が長い問題ですが、本番の試験よりも音声の長さは短くなっています。

Questions 1–8

Complete the form below.

Write **NO MORE THAN THREE WORDS AND/OR A NUMBER** *for each answer.*

PACKHAM'S SHIPPING AGENCY — customer quotation from

> *Example*
> **Country of destination:** Kenya

Name: Jacob 1 ………

Address to be collected from: 2 ……… College, Downlands Rd

Town: Bristol

Postcode: 3 ………

Length: 1.5m

Width: 4 ………

Height: 5 ………

Contents: clothes

6 …………

7 …………

Total estimated value: 8 £…………

Part 2 対策

パート2では、日常的なシーンで1人の話者が説明や紹介をしている音声が流れます。
よく出題されるのは次のような説明です。

- 旅行ガイドによる説明
- 娯楽施設や公共施設での案内
- イベントの告知
- 会議室の手配方法

位置関係や道順を表す重要表現

パート2では「プラン・地図・図を完成させる問題」が頻出です。この問題タイプでは、位置関係や道順を表す語句を理解しておく必要があります。ここで力試しに例題を解いてみましょう。この地図を見ながら音声を聞いて、1〜9の施設や店がA–Iのどこにあるか、アルファベットを記入してください。

TRACK **3**

例題

1 library .... 　2 bookshop .... 　3 shoe store .... 　4 bus terminal ....
5 statue .... 　6 school .... 　7 bank .... 　8 hotel .... 　9 station ....

<table>
<tr><td rowspan="2">解答</td><td>1 ▸ D</td><td>2 ▸ F</td><td>3 ▸ E</td><td>4 ▸ C</td><td>5 ▸ B</td></tr>
<tr><td>6 ▸ G</td><td>7 ▸ A</td><td>8 ▸ I</td><td>9 ▸ H</td><td></td></tr>
</table>

▶ スクリプトと訳

1 The **library** is right next to the post office. （図書館は、郵便局のちょうど隣にある）

2 The **bookshop** is located at a crossroads of Homer Street and Yale Street.
（本屋は、ホーマー通りとイエール通りの十字路に位置している）

3 The **shoe store** is right opposite the pharmacy. （靴屋は、薬局のちょうど向かい側にある）

4 The **bus terminal** is located on the corner of Homer Street and Robson Street.
（バスターミナルは、ホーマー通りとロブソン通りの角に位置している）

5 The **statue** is behind a café, off the road. （像は、カフェの後ろ、道から外れたところにある）

6 Turn left on the first corner. Go right round a bend and you will see the **school** just after the bend. （最初の角を左にまがり、曲がり道を右に進んだところに学校がある）

7 Go down the road as far as the park, and there is the **bank** across the road on your right.
（公園まで進んで、道の向かい側、右手に銀行がある）

8 Take the second left, keep going to the end of the road, and the **hotel** is across the road.
（二番目の角を左に曲がり、そのまま突き当たりまで進むと、ホテルは道路の向こう側にある）

9 Go down Homer Street and take the third left. Then, walk down Water Street and go straight over the roundabout. The **station** is on your left.
（ホーマー通りを進み、三番目の角を左に曲がり、ウォーター通りを歩きラウンドアバウトを越えると、駅は左にある）

┤ Vocabulary ├

- **next to 〜** 〜の隣に
- **opposite** [前] 〜の向かい側に
- **behind** [前] 〜の後ろに
- **turn left** 左に曲がる
- **go down the road** 道を進む
- **take the second left** 二番目の角を左に行く
- **roundabout** [名] ラウンドアバウト、環状交差点
- **crossroad** [名] 十字路
- **on the corner of 〜** 〜の角に
- **off the road** 道から外れて
- **bend** [名] 曲がり、カーブ
- **as far as 〜** 〜まで
- **across the road** 道路の向こう側に

以下に、スクリプトに登場していない重要語句も紹介します。
- **head** [動] 〜に向かう
- **go past** 通り過ぎる
- **crosswalk** [名] 横断歩道
- **in front of 〜** 〜の前に
- **intersection** [名] 交差点
- **traffic light** 信号

本問の音声の長さは、本番のパート2と比較して半分ほどで、問題の数も半分です。
まずはパート2の形式に慣れるために解いてみましょう。

Questions 1–5

Answer the questions below.

Write **NO MORE THAN TWO WORDS AND/OR A NUMBER** *for each answer.*

1 How long is the whole A Taste of Niagara-on-the-Lake event? ....
2 What are you doing on Saturday morning? ....
3 When is the feature activity? ....
4 Which activity is more suitable for kids? ....
5 How should you buy the tickets after the 1st of March? ....

Tips さまざまな国のアクセントに慣れよう

先に説明した通り、IELTSのリスニングテストでは、イギリス、アメリカ、カナダ、オーストラリア、ニュージーランドなど、さまざまな国籍のナレーターによる音声が流れます。
本書では、皆さんが幅広いアクセントに慣れるように、**イギリス、アメリカ、オーストラリア、カナダ国籍のナレーターによる音声を収録**しています。ナレーターの国籍は、別冊の解答ページにある「国旗マーク」でわかるようになっています。
例えば「イギリス国籍のナレーターによる問題になると、正答率がいつも下がる」なら、「BBCのニュースを毎日聞く」など、対策ができるはず。苦手を得意に変えるために、是非「国旗マーク」に注目してみてください！

練習 **2** 地図を完成させる問題

本問の音声の長さは、本番のパート2と比較して半分ほどで、問題の数も少なくなっています。

「地図を完成させる問題」はIELTSらしい試験で、パート2で頻出です。

Questions 1–3

Label the map below.

Write the correct letter, **A**–**G**, next to Questions 1–3.

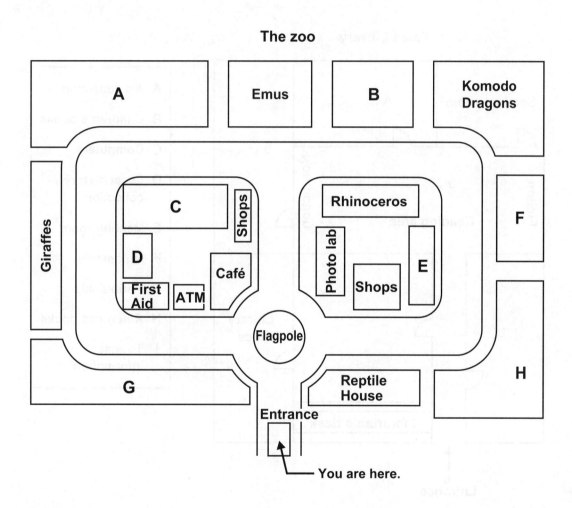

The zoo

1 Koalas ....

2 Tigers ....

3 African elephants ....

Listening

練習 3 ▶ プランを完成させる問題

本問も本番よりは音声が短い問題です。位置関係や道順を表す語句を理解していないと解きづらいので、語句をしっかりと頭に入れたうえで臨みましょう。

Questions 1–5

Label the plan below.

Choose **FIVE** answers from the box and write the correct letter, **A–I**, next to Questions 1–5.

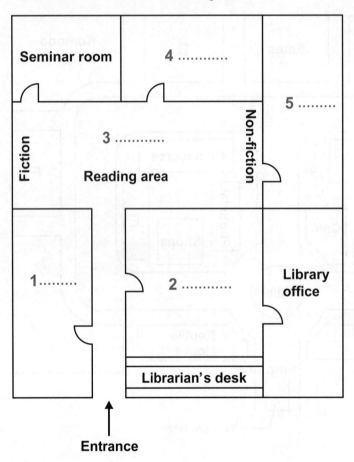

Part 3 対策

パート3では、2〜4人によるキャンパスを場面とした会話が出題されます。
会話の例は以下の通りです。
- チューターが学生に個別指導
- 課題について、教授と学生の議論
- 課題について、学生たちの話し合い

賛成・反対...話者の意見を理解しよう

パート3は、**話者の感情や態度を理解することが求められる唯一のパート**です。

上に挙げたような指導や議論の中で、さまざまな意見が飛び交い、話者がそれぞれ意思を表明していきます。話者が、賛成（ポジティブ）または反対（ネガティブ）意見を表明するとき、**agree / disagree や Yes / No といった明確な表現だけが使われるわけではありません**。いろいろな表現があるからこそ、話者の感情や態度を把握するのが難しくなります。次に紹介する語句をしっかり押さえておきましょう。

賛成する

Definitely. / Certainly. / Absolutely. / Exactly.　（［いずれも強い肯定で］絶対に、もちろんです）
That's true.　（その通りです）
You can say that again.　（おっしゃる通りです）
I suppose you're right.　（その通りだと思います）
You have a point.　（もっともです）

反対する

I don't see how you can ...　（...が可能とは思えません）
I'm not sure about that.　（それについて確信が持てません）
Actually, I'd rather ...　（実際のところ、むしろ...した方がいいと思います）
Personally, I don't think (that) S＋V　（個人的には、SVだと思いません）
I'm not convinced of 〜.　（〜には納得できません）

反対を不安として表現する

I'm not exactly confident about 〜. （〜について必ずしも自信がありません）

My worry [concern] is ... （私が不安に感じているのは ... です）

I struggled with 〜. （〜で苦労しました）

I'm not clear [sure] about 〜. （〜について確信が持てません）

賛成か反対なのか決めかねている、態度がはっきりしない

It shouldn't matter. （関係ないと思います）

It's worth considering. （考える余地があります）

I'll think about that. （考えてみます）

That might be interesting. （それは興味深いかもしれません）

建設的批判（constructive criticism）に注意！

　反対や別の意見を表現するとき、**相手の意見を尊重したうえで自分の意見を述べるのが、大学や職場で使用する「丁寧な(polite / respectful)」英語の鉄則**です。

　特に、教える立場である教授やチューターは真っ向から学生の意見に反対するような表現は使いません。まずは学生の意見を評価・尊重してから、反対意見を伝える建設的批判の表現を使います。この表現では、話し始めに「賛成」を表明した後、butやthoughでつなぎ、あとに「反対」や別の意見を続けていきます。

You have a point, but in this first section of the essay, **you need to** provide an overview of the graph.
（的を射ていますが、エッセイの最初の段落で、グラフの要約を述べる必要があります）

That would be a good idea, though in this particular case, **I am not sure** if that method would work.
（それはよい考えでしょうが、この特殊な場合では、その方法がうまくいくか確信が持てません）

練習 **1** 文を完成させる問題

本問は、本番のパート3と比べて音声の長さが3分の1程度です。話者は2人と少ないため、難易度は下がります。
まずはパート3の形式に慣れるつもりで解いてみましょう。

Questions 1–4

Complete the sentences below.

*Write **NO MORE THAN TWO WORDS** for each answer.*

1 Studying with the Open University demanded a great deal of ....
2 Studying and working at the same time improved Rachel's .... skills.
3 It was helpful that the course was structured in ....
4 She enjoyed meeting other students at ....

練習 **2** 複数の選択肢から選ぶ問題

音声の長さは、本番のパート3の半分ほどです。
話者は3人で難易度が上がるので、それぞれの立場と意見をしっかり追いましょう。

Questions 1–5

*Choose the correct letter, **A, B** or **C**.*

1 Creativity ...   .
   A is totally learned.
   B is mostly innate.
   C can be improved no matter how old you are.

2 Creativity can be improved if ...   .
   A you have a lot of innate talent.
   B your environment is encouraging.
   C you have already invented something.

3 Creativity will be reduced if ...   .
   A your family culture is overly supportive.
   B you re-design old projects.
   C you are discouraged from thinking differently.

4 Comparing yourself with well-known creative people ... .
   A can inhibit your creativity.
   B can encourage you to be more creative.
   C can lead you to do more graphic designs.

5 One of the ways to improve your creativity is ...   .
   A collect logos, business cards, etc.
   B learn from the experts.
   C collaborate with other designers.

いよいよ話者が4人の問題です。「会話の中心者」が「会話の参加者」に話を振っていくので、その展開についていくようにしましょう。音声の長さは本番の半分ほどですが、話者が多いので難易度は上がります。

Questions 1–5

What are the five ideas that the students suggest about studying online?

Choose **FIVE** *answers from the box and write the correct letter,* **A–F,** *next to Questions 1–5.*

Ideas

A   develop a strict daily routine

B   study online with a team

C   create an inviting environment

D   take regular breaks

E   move to an alternative indoor location

F   study in the open air

Suggestions about studying online

1   Idea 1   ....
2   Idea 2   ....
3   Idea 3   ....
4   Idea 4   ....
5   Idea 5   ....

Part 4 対策

パート4では、大学の講義などを聞いて問題に答えます。**パート4には途中のプレヴュータイムがなく、約10問分の音声が一気に流れる**のが特徴です。

内容はテクノロジー、環境問題、生物学、教育など学術的で、ほかのパートに比べて少し専門性が上がります。

サインポスト・ランゲージで話の展開を追おう

パート2と4ではモノローグ形式で音声が流れるので、集中して聞いていないと「今、話者は何の話をしているのか」把握できず、話の展開についていけなくなる危険性があります。「迷子」にならないために欠かせないのが、サインポスト・ランゲージです。**サインポストとは「道しるべ」**という意味で、サインポスト・ランゲージは**「これからどういうことを話すか」を明確に示すサイン**の役割を果たします。ここでは、特にパート4で役立つものを厳選して紹介します。

順序立てて説明する

First of all / Firstly　（第一に）
Secondly　（次に）
Another point　（もうひとつのポイントは）
Finally　（最後に）
To summarise　（要約すると）
To conclude my presentation　（私のプレゼンテーションの結論としては）

話を始める

Let's take a look at the map.　（地図を見てみましょう）
Let's talk about the 'festival zones'.　（フェスティバルゾーンについて話しましょう）
Today, we're going to look at what makes Danish people so happy.
（今日は、なぜデンマーク人はそんなに幸せなのか見ていきます）
I will be talking about the Ainu people of Japan.　（日本のアイヌ民族について話します）
Let's start, first of all, with their way of life.　（最初に彼らの生活様式から始めましょう）

話題を転換する

OK, let's move on to looking at the history of this museum.
（では当ミュージアムの歴史を見ていきましょう）

Now, let's turn our attention to how the data was collected.
（さあ、次にデータ収集の方法に目を向けましょう）

情報を追加する

Two important factors in the climate of an area are temperature and precipitation.
There are also other factors, and you should, of course, consider them all.
（その地域の気候において2つの重要な要因は、気温と降水量です。ほかの要因もあり、もちろんそれらすべてを考慮する必要があります）

In addition, the yearly average temperature of the area needs to be considered.
（加えて、その地域の年間平均気温も考慮する必要があります）

例を挙げる

Let me give you an example. （例を挙げさせてください）
For instance, carbohydrates are one of the key macronutrients that your body requires daily. There are different types of carbohydrates such as starches, fiber, and sugars.
（例えば、炭水化物は体が毎日必要とする主要栄養素です。でんぷん、食物繊維、砂糖などさまざまな種類があります）

重要な情報を伝える

There is one thing you need to know about where the money goes.
（お金がどこに行くのかに関して、1つ知っておくべきことがあります）

重 要 語 句

以下に、パート4で頻出の分野の語句を紹介します。

エネルギー

nuclear （核）	coal （石炭）
generate （発電する）	hydro electrical power （水力発電）
solar power （太陽光発電）	wind turbine （風力原動機）
windmill （風車）	natural gas （天然ガス）
aluminum （アルミニウム）	source （元になるもの）
renewable （再生可能な）	non-renewable （再生不可能な）

環境問題

global warming （地球温暖化）	disaster （災害）
earthquake （地震）	tornado （竜巻）
blizzard （猛吹雪）	hurricane （大西洋および北東太平洋で発生した台風）
cyclone （南太平洋およびインド洋で発生した台風）	typhoon （北西太平洋で発生した台風）
pollution （汚染）	drought （干ばつ）
flood （洪水）	volcanic eruption （火山噴火）

deforestation （森林伐採）　　desertification （砂漠化）

健康

vegetarian （菜食主義者）　　vegan （完全菜食主義者）

leisure （余暇）　　disease （病気）

vitamin （ビタミン）　　protein （タンパク質）

carbohydrate （炭水化物）　　exercise （運動）

treatment （治療）　　obese （肥満）

overweight （太り過ぎ）　　check up （健康診断）

medicine （薬）　　pandemic （病気の世界的大流行）

virus （ウイルス）　　cure （治療、治す、癒す）

vaccination （予防接種）

動物と自然

mammals （哺乳類）　　reptile （爬虫類）

primate （霊長類）　　predators （捕食者）

prey （獲物）　　pond （沼）

stream （小川）　　endangered species （絶滅危惧種）

species （種類）　　bush fire （山火事）

Antarctica （南極大陸）　　Oceania （オセアニア）

政治

government （政府）　　politician （政治家）

senate （上院）　　senator （上院議員）

mayor （市長）　　regulation （規制）

president （大統領）　　society （社会）

individual （個人）　　council （目的を持って集まった人の会議）

そのほかの頻出単語

appointment （予約、任命）　　cooperation （協力）

employment （雇用）　　exhibition （展示）

occupation （職業）　　decade （10年）

century （100年、世紀）　　millennium （1000年）

creativity （創造性）　　guarantee （保証）

satellite （衛星）　　opportunity （機会）

licence （免許）

練習 **1** フローチャートを完成させる問題

TRACK
10

　本問は、本番のパート4と比べると音声は半分ほどの長さしかありません。まずはパート4の形式に慣れるつもりで解いてみましょう。

Questions 1–6

Complete the flowchart below.

Write **NO MORE THAN TWO WORDS** *for each answer.*

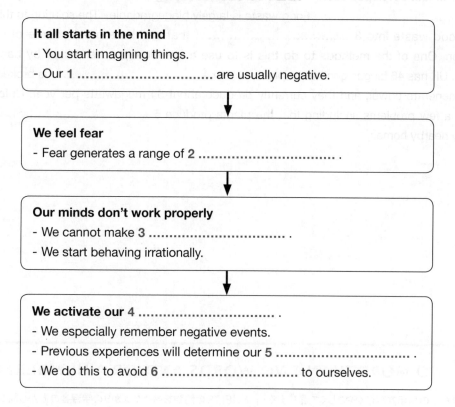

FOUR STAGES OF FEAR

It all starts in the mind
- You start imagining things.
- Our **1** .... are usually negative.

↓

We feel fear
- Fear generates a range of **2** ....

↓

Our minds don't work properly
- We cannot make **3** ....
- We start behaving irrationally.

↓

We activate our 4 ....
- We especially remember negative events.
- Previous experiences will determine our **5** ....
- We do this to avoid **6** .... to ourselves.

Listening

練習 **2** 要約を完成させる問題

本番よりも音声が短めですが、練習1よりは長くなります。少しずつ音声に慣れて、レベルUPしていきましょう。

Questions 1–5

Complete the summary below.

*Write **NO MORE THAN TWO WORDS AND/OR A NUMBER** for each answer.*

In the UK, each year restaurants and the food industry effectively waste over **1** .... of food. Not just developed countries waste food—developing countries do too, mostly because of bad **2** .... Food waste is largely biodegradable. The solution to this issue is turning food waste into **3** .... that can be a great source of electricity generation. One of the methods to do this is to use a chemical process aided by bacteria and microbes. UK has 46 biogas generation plants where **4** .... is broken down in order to generate power, and they currently produce about 54 megawatts per year. Unfortunately there are a few problems, including that the plants produce **5** .... that can affect any nearby homes.

Tips **NO MORE THAN TWO WORDS AND/OR A NUMBERとは!?**

「語数指定の指示内容がややこしくて混乱する!」と、IELTSの勉強を始めたばかりの学習者の方から聞くことがあります。語数でミスをするのはもったいないので、ここで整理しておきましょう。*Write **NO MORE THAN TWO WORDS AND/OR A NUMBER** for each answer.* を訳すと、「それぞれの解答として2つ以下の単語か1つの数字、もしくはその両方を記入しなさい」です。

解答例
- natural resources ←2つ以下の単語なのでOK
- 53 ←1つの数字なのでOK
- 217-3340355 ←電話番号は1つの数字とみなされるのでOK
- 7 million species←「1つの数字+2つの単語」=3単語でもOK

一番ややこしいのは最後の例です。指示文のNO MORE THAN TWO WORDSに惑わされて「単語と数字で2語以下」と解釈しないように気をつけましょう。なお、リーディングの章では、ほかの語数制限のパターンも紹介しています (p.24参照)。

84

実践問題 Part 1-4

ここからは実践としてパート1から4を一気に解いてみましょう。難易度や音声の長さは、本番どおりです。

Part 1

TRACK
12

Questions 1–5

Complete the reservation form below.

Write **ONE WORD AND/OR A NUMBER** for each answer.

RESERVATION FORM

First Name: Charlotte

Surname: **1** ....

Passport Number: **2** ....

Nationality: **3** ....

Check in: 6th July

Check out: **4** .... July

Special request: a **5** .... room

Questions 6–10

Complete the notes below.
Write **NO MORE THAN TWO WORDS AND/OR A NUMBER** for each answer.

- Maryland Guest House location: **6** .... Street.
- Walk or take a **7** .... to the bus station.
- The bus to the beach will have the words **8** .... written on the front.
- Printing in the business centre is **9** .... per page.
- The shop sells **10** .... things like phone cards and sweets.

Part 2

Questions 11–16

Complete the notes below.

Write **NO MORE THAN THREE WORDS AND/OR A NUMBER** for each answer.

THE NATIONAL ARTS CENTRE	
Well known for:	**11** ....
Complex consists of:	concert rooms theatres cinemas art galleries public library restaurants **12** ....
Historical background:	1940 – area destroyed by bombs 1960s – Centre was **13** .... in **14** ....–opened to public
Managed by:	**15** ....
Open:	**16** .... days per year

Questions 17–20

Complete the table below.

Write **NO MORE THAN THREE WORDS AND/OR A NUMBER** for each answer.

Day	Time	Event	Venue	Ticket price
Monday and Tuesday	7:30 pm	*The Magic Flute* (opera by Mozart)	**17**	from £8.00
Wednesday	8:00 pm	**18** .... (Canadian film)	Cinema 2	**19** ....
Saturday and Sunday	11 am to 10 pm	**20** .... (art exhibition)	Gallery 1	free

Part 3

Questions 21–25

*Choose the correct letter, **A**, **B** or **C**.*

21 Vicky wants a new career in …   ....
   A banking.
   B music.
   C finance.

22 The move into a new career should be done …   ....
   A all at once.
   B gradually.
   C strictly following your business plan.

23 When they talk about *keeping the process simple*, they mean: …   ....
   A The language in your website should be easy to read.
   B Have a simple name for your company.
   C Only do one thing initially, not more.

24 When people are developing their business, they should also …   ....
   A run special training for other people.
   B get even more skills for themselves.
   C work with a large group.

25 To get a reward from the new career …   ....
   A you must always wait a few years.
   B you must be patient.
   C you should try to make money immediately.

Questions 26–30

Complete the sentences below.
*Write **ONE WORD AND/OR A NUMBER** for each answer.*

26 When turning your hobby into your new job, you cannot use your hobby to ....
27 You have to be ready to work .... days per week.
28 Your new job can be hard work and be an emotional ....
29 Your new business should mirror your own unique ....
30 If you have to go back to your old career, you should not feel any ....

Listening

Part 4

Questions 31–40

Complete the notes below.

*Write **ONE WORD OR A NUMBER** for each answer.*

Deforestation is leading to more infectious diseases in humans

How Nipah virus initially spread

· Deforestation is clearing of forests by humans to make the land available for other uses.

· **31** .... worsened the forest fires in Indonesia in 1997.

· The fires made **32** .... migrate to fruit farms in Malaysia in search of food. Then pigs ate the fruit and got sick. After that, the deadly disease infected pig farmers too.

· Within two years, the disease had caused **33** .... in the brain of 265 people and killed 105.

· The more forests are cleared, the more often epidemics of infectious diseases will occur.

Malaria

· Globally, malaria is transmitted by mosquitoes and every year roughly **34** .... people die. It is also believed to be related to deforestation.

· Cases have increased gradually due to agricultural **35** ....

· How malaria spread in the Peruvian Amazon: the mosquitoes bred in a habitat along forest edges and larvae were found in warm and slightly **36** .... pools.

· Ten percent increase in forest removal brought about the increase of malaria cases by 3% between 2003–2015.

· Mosquito ecology depends on species and area. A direct link between malaria and deforestation in **37** .... is weak, while it's quite strong in Sabah.

How new diseases emerge

· As well as mosquitoes, a range of forest **38** .... also transmit deadly diseases to people.

· Transmission can happen when people move into untouched forest **39** ....

· Clearing of forests for plantations sends animals for **40** .... to nearby human habitats, making contact with people.

· Humans contracted the Lasso virus, which killed 36% of infected people, when they came into contact with the urine or faeces of rodents.

お疲れさまでした！ 通しで解くと、かなり集中力を使うのがわかったと思います。本書では、巻末に**模試を2回も用意しているので、まだまだ実践的なトレーニングが積めます**よ！ 日頃から海外ニュースを聞くなどしてリスニング力をUPさせたうえで、是非模試に臨んでください！

Writing

About Writing

ライティングテストは2つのタスクで構成されています。タスク1と2で、語数指定や書くべき内容が違い、個別の対策が必要となります。まずは、両者の違いを把握しましょう。

	語数指定 (words)	内容	時間配分の目安 (試験時間60分)	スコア配分 (対比)
Task 1	150以上	与えられたグラフや図を分析し、数値の変化や特徴を客観的に描写する。	20分	1
Task 2	250以上	問題文の指示に書かれている内容に従って論理的に自身の意見を展開する。トピックは、教育、環境、ビジネス、テクノロジーなど多岐にわたる。	40分	2 (Task 1の 2倍の比重)

評価基準

タスク1〈課題の達成度〉
- タスクの指示に従い、グラフや図などの情報を読み取り、**要約**を提示し、的確に説明できているか
- **具体的な数値**を挙げたり、**項目を比較**したりしながら、グラフや図の内容を客観的に描写できているか

タスク2〈課題への回答〉
- タスクの課題に対して、**自分の意見を明確に表現**し、論理的な議論ができているか
- タスクが課題として**要求していること**(本書でいう[要求ポイント])に、漏れなく言及しているか
- タスクの課題に沿った**主旨**を示しているか
- 主旨をサポートする**具体的な理由や詳細**が述べられているか

Task 1, Task 2 共通の基準

基準	内容
一貫性 まとまり	・段落構成が適切で、エッセイ全体がまとまっているか ・接続表現(cohesive devices)を適切に使い、論理的で一貫性のあるエッセイになっているか
語彙力	・幅広い語彙(単語やコロケーション)を適切な文脈で使えているか ・スペルミスがないか
文法知識 正確さ	・さまざまな構文を使えているか ・文脈に合う文法を正しく使えているか

タスク1、2ともに、4つの評価基準は1〜9まで0.5点刻みで採点され、その平均がスコアとなります。4つの基準間で採点比重に偏りはありません。

Writing 攻略ルール

1 ▶ 語数指定を守ろう

タスク1（150 words 以上）、タスク2（250 words 以上）の語数指定を大幅に下回ると減点になりかねません。さらに、**語数が足りないと、必然的に語彙力や構文の構成力を示せないので、タスクの指示や課題に応えられず、これも減点の原因になります。** 7以上を狙う上級者の方は、タスク1では200 words 以上、タスク2では300 words 以上を目指しましょう。ただし、長さに固執して不要な文を入れないように！ 同じ表現を何度も繰り返すのも不適切です。

なお、ライティングテストは時間との闘いなので、ペーパー試験の場合は、1行に書くだいたいの語数を決めておき、効率的に語数を数えてください。

2 ▶ 配点を意識した時間配分を

タスク1とタスク2の配点は「1：2」です。これは、**タスク2が2倍重要である**ことを意味します。

例えば、どんなにタスク1を完璧に仕上げても、タスク2のConclusionが書けずに時間切れになってしまうと、スコアに響きます。高得点を狙いたければ、タスク2に時間をかけ、完成度の高いエッセイに仕上げましょう。時間配分のイメージは「タスク1は20分と決め、時間がきたら潔く切り上げ、タスク2に進み、40分かけてしっかり書き上げる」です。ご自身のやりやすいように、もちろんタスク2から先に取り組んでも構いません。

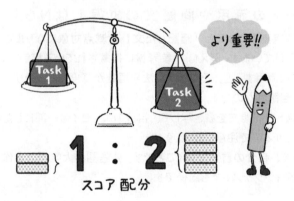

より重要!!

スコア配分

3 ▶ 高得点を目指すなら〈課題の達成度〉〈課題への回答〉を意識しよう

実のところ、IELTSのライティングテストは、ネイティブでも高得点を取るのが難しいと言われています。なぜかというと、評価基準のうちの〈一貫性とまとまり〉〈語彙力〉〈文法知識と正確さ〉を満たしていても、**タスク1の〈課題の達成度〉、タスク2の〈課題への回答〉をクリアしていなければ、7以上のスコアは見込めない**からです。評価基準をしっかり読んで、各タスクが求めているものは何か、把握しておきましょう（p.90参照）。

4 ▶ 読み手（試験官）のために、体裁の整ったエッセイに

　皆さんが書くエッセイの読み手は、紛れもなく試験官です。彼らにとって読みやすく、採点しやすいエッセイを目指しましょう。特に次に挙げる点に注意してください。

段落の間は1行空ける

　段落の区切りを明確にするために、IntroductionとBodyなどの段落と段落の間は1行空けてください。段落の最初の文字を字下げする方法もありますが、わかりやすさを重視して前者をオススメします。なお、**メモ形式や箇条書きはアカデミック・ライティングには適さない**のでやめましょう。1つの段落は1文のみで終わらせず、2文以上で構成する点も忘れずに。

1つの段落＝1つの主旨

　アカデミック・ライティングでは「1つの段落には1つの主旨のみを書く」のが原則です。特にタスク2では、1つのBodyに多くのことを詰め込み過ぎるミスを犯しがちです。例えば、ある議論に関して、肯定的、否定的な側面を書く場合、両者を1つのBodyに書くのではなく、Body 1と2に分けるのが正解です。

誰にでも判読可能なアルファベットを書く

　ペーパー試験の場合、試験官が読み取れるアルファベットを書きましょう。走り書きや、**癖字で読めない場合は、スコアに影響する**可能性があります。自分が書くアルファベットの中で読みにくいものはないか、第三者に判断してもらうのもいいでしょう。

5 ▶ テンプレートの流用や問題文の丸写しはNG！

　ライティングテストの採点基準によると**「暗記した文」は減点対象**になります。実際、試験官は「暗記した文」を見抜く訓練を受けています。例えば、参考書に掲載されている模範的なエッセイを丸暗記して、その一部を自分のエッセイに流用すると、そこだけ文法や語彙が高度になったり、内容がちぐはぐになったりするので、流用したのが一目瞭然なのです。

　また、ライティングテストの問題文を書き写して、自分のエッセイの一部にした場合、その部分は語数にカウントされず、減点につながるので注意しましょう。

　大切なことはシンプルで、**自分の言葉で書く**ことです。英語圏の大学では盗作（plagiarism）に対して厳しく罰しますが、それはライティングテストでも同様です。

6 ▶ 書き出す前のプランニングが重要！

60分間で、150 wordsと250 wordsものエッセイを書き上げることにプレッシャーを感じ、「テストが始まったら、すぐに書き出さなくては！」と思う方がいるかもしれません。

しかし、構成が決まっていないまま漫然と書き始めると、入れるべき情報が漏れたり、話が脱線したりして、締まりのないエッセイになりかねません。それに、途中で大幅な修正を加えることになったときのタイムロスは痛いものです。

特に、タスク2で犯しがちなのが、Introductionで書いた意見が、エッセイを書いているうちにブレてしまう、極端な場合は途中で意見が180度変わってしまうといったミスです。これは、評価基準の〈課題への回答〉のスコアに影響します。タスク2では、**エッセイを書き出す前に、自分の意見を明確にし、メモに書き出しましょう。**その上で、Bodyで、その意見の具体的な理由や詳細をどのように挙げて論じていくかを、必ずプランニングしてください。

本書では、4つのSTEPを踏んでエッセイを完成させていきます。タスク1、2ともに**実際に書き出す前の3〜4分(STEP 1, 2)が、スコアを左右する重要な時間**なのです。

エッセイ 完成までの4つの STEP

STEP 1	問題を分析する
↓	
STEP 2	構成を組み立てる
↓	
STEP 3	エッセイを書く
↓	
STEP 4	見直しをする

なお、構成を組み立てる際、ペーパー試験では問題用紙の余白を活用しましょう。コンピューター試験の場合は、画面上にタイプできるのはもちろん、ログインシートの余白に手書きで書き込んでも問題ありません。

7 ▶ 複文を使いこなし、文法の評価を上げよう

　複文とは、従属節と主節で構成されている文で、それぞれの節に〈主語＋動詞〉が含まれます。単文（〈主語＋動詞〉が1つだけ）よりも複雑なので、複文を作るには文法力を要します。

　単文：I recognised him.　　　　　**複文**：I recognised that he is my old friend.

　両者を比べると、複文の方ではthat節で詳細が書かれている一方で、単文は情報量が少ないのがわかるはずです。単文ばかりが続くと短い文の羅列となり、文と文のつながりも表現しにくいのです。

　複文の従属節は、よくbecause, as, whenなどの接続詞を使って構成しますが、ここでは書き言葉でよく使われる接続詞に絞って、複文の例を紹介しましょう。

whereas（〜であるのに）
　Men walked more for leisure at 20%, **whereas** only 16% walked for travel.
　（男性は移動のために歩いたのはわずか16パーセントだったが、余暇のために歩いたのはより多く、20パーセントだった）

although（〜だけれども）
　Automation in business will provide more advantages than disadvantages, **although** it can potentially take over jobs from people.
　（ビジネスにおける自動化は人々の仕事を奪いうるが、短所より長所を多くもたらすだろう）

> 実はスピーキングテストにおいても、複文の構成力が文法のスコアUPにつながります。テストは便宜上、4技能に分かれていますが、求められる能力には共通しているものが多いのです。それぞれを個別に考えるよりは、総合力を上げるべく取り組んでいきましょう。

8 ▶ 適切な接続表現（cohesive devices）でまとまりのあるエッセイに

　接続表現は、文と文をつなぐ役割を果たし、エッセイ全体のまとまりを出すために欠かせないものです。ライティングテストの評価基準である〈一貫性とまとまり〉で、**接続表現の運用力がチェックされています**。ここでタスク1、2のエッセイの一部を読み、接続表現への理解を深めましょう。

タスク1
In the early stages of the brick making process, **firstly**, the raw clay is extracted from a quarry by a large digger. **Then** it is refined by separating large pieces from smaller ones using a metal grid. **Finally**, this refined clay is conveyed via a belt on rollers to be mixed with sand and water.
　煉瓦が作られる工程を説明するエッセイの一段落で、下線が順序を示す接続表現です。

タスク2
There are many good reasons for having zoos in our cities. **Most importantly**, they attract tourists and make money for the city. Visitors get a chance to see wild animals that they would not see **unless** they travelled far away. **Therefore**, we cannot underestimate the economic and educational importance of zoos.

動物園に関するエッセイの一段落で、下線が接続表現です。

　注意すべきなのは、エッセイの中にとにかく接続表現を詰め込めば、スコアUPするわけではない点です。本書に掲載しているエッセイの中の主な接続表現には、下線が引いてあります。実際のエッセイでどのように接続表現を使えばいいのかエッセイを読みながら研究し、接続表現を自分のものにしましょう。

9 ▸ アカデミック・ライティングの基本ルールに従おう

ライティングテストでは、アカデミック・ライティングのルールに従いましょう。

短縮形はNG

アカデミック・ライティングでは、短縮形は避けましょう。

　　　don't → do not　　　　can't → cannot（cannotは1語扱い）

数字の表記

10未満の数字はスペルアウトします（1 millionなど、桁が大きい場合を除く）。

　　There are **seven** steps in the process for making wine.

％の前の数字は、スペルアウトせずにアラビア数字で表記します。ただし、文頭の場合はThirty percent of men walked ...のようにスペルアウトできると望ましいです。

　　8%（× eight%）（eight percentはOK）

正確な数値が読み取れないときは、「おおよそ」を意味する語句を使いましょう。

　　about / approximately（約）　　almost（ほとんど）　　roughly（おおよそ）　　nearly（〜近く）
　　just over〜（〜強）　　just under〜（〜弱）

スペルの統一

スペルはアメリカ式、イギリス式のどちらでも問題ありませんが、混在させないようにしましょう。

10 ▸ アカデミックな語彙で書こう

「アカデミックな語彙で書こう」と言われても、ピンとこない方が多いかもしれません。そんな方に参考にしていただきたいのがThe Academic Word List（AWL）です。これは、英語を母国語としない学習者が、英語での高等教育を受けるにあたり必要となるアカデミックな語彙をまとめたリストです（リストはインターネット上で閲覧可能：https://www.wgtn.ac.nz/lals/resources/academicwordlist）。

　AWLの例を動詞で挙げると、abandon / identify / illustrate / suspend ...などで、「アカデミックな語彙＝難解な単語ばかり」ではなく、皆さんが日常的に使う単語も含まれます。したがって必要以上に気負うことはありません。「アカデミックな語彙で書こう」の裏を返せば、カジュアル過ぎる語彙は使わない方がよいといえます。**スラングや口語的表現を使って書くのはやめましょう。**

Task 1 対策

段落構成　基本のフォーマット

本書では、タスク1での段落構成として、次の図で示したものを推奨しています。

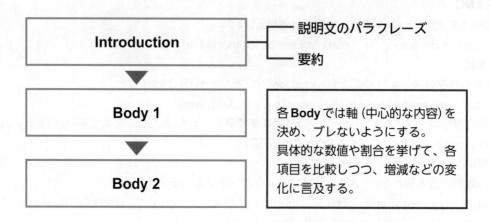

Introduction ── 説明文のパラフレーズ
　　　　　　　　 └─ 要約

Body 1

Body 2

各**Body**では軸（中心的な内容）を決め、ブレないようにする。
具体的な数値や割合を挙げて、各項目を比較しつつ、増減などの変化に言及する。

1 ▶ Introduction

Introductionは「説明文のパラフレーズ」と「要約」から成ります。**どちらか1つでも抜けてしまうと減点になるので**、気をつけましょう。

》》》 説明文のパラフレーズ

問題文中に、グラフや図が何を表すのか説明している文があるので、それを言い換えて冒頭に書きます。ここで、どんなトピックのエッセイなのかを明確に伝えます。
Point
- 説明文をすべて書き写すと、語数にカウントされないので注意

パラフレーズのコツ

説明文は、必ず〈**The＋グラフや図の種類＋show(s) ...**〉の構文で書かれています。一番簡単なパラフレーズは、動詞のshowを同義語で言い換える方法です。

illustrate（〜を描写する）

The table **illustrates** employment numbers in Australia over a 30-year period from 1971 to 2000.
（この表は1971年から2000年までの30年間にわたる、オーストラリアにおける雇用人数を描写している）

compare（〜を比較する）

The chart **compares** the number of cars that were made in France, Germany and Norway over a decade from 2000 to 2009.

（このグラフは、2000年から2009年の10年間に、フランス、ドイツ、ノルウェーで製造された自動車の数を比較している）

present（〜を示す）

The graph **presents** data from Ireland showing cinema attendance in major cities in 2016.

（このグラフは、アイルランドが作成した、主要都市における2016年の映画鑑賞者のデータを示している）

〉〉〉 要 約

　要約では全項目の変化に触れる必要はなく、次の例のように、主な特徴に言及しつつ全体をまとめた文が求められます。

Overall, it can be seen that there were significantly more men and women in part-time studies. Increases were seen across the board except fewer men were studying part-time.

（全体的に見ると、パートタイムの学習者で、［フルタイムよりも］かなり多くの男女がいたことがわかる。パートタイムで学ぶ男性が少なくなった点以外は、一律で増加傾向が見られた）

Point

- 主な特徴を説明する文で、1〜2文あれば十分
- Overall（全体的に）、In brief（まとめると、要するに）、In summary / To summarise（要約すると）、It can be clearly seen that S＋V.（SVということが明らかだ）などの表現で書き出すことが多い
- 具体的な数値（32%など）には言及しなくてよい
- many（多い）、a few（少ない）、increase（増える、増加）、decrease（減る、減少）など、数値の大小や変化を描写する表現を使う
- 内容が次の例1、2のように抽象的になり過ぎないようにする
  例1：Overall, it can be seen that there were some differences between the cities.
  例2：There were some changes and some similarities.
- 「2種類のグラフや表が与えられる問題」では、両方の主な特徴に言及する必要がある

2 ▶ Body

　Bodyとはエッセイの本題にあたり、多くの場合、Bodyの数は2〜3ほどです。具体的な数値や根拠を示して数の増減を描写したり、**項目同士を比較したりします。**特に以下の点に着目して、グラフや図の特徴を描写してください。

- 急に増加／減少したもの
- 変化がない、一定なもの
- 最高点／最低点に到達したもの
- 最大値／最小値
- 変動が激しいもの

　以上がタスク1の段落構成です。実際は、先生や参考書によって推奨する段落構成は異なります。

　例えば、Introductionで要約を書かず、最後のBodyの後に「要約の段落」を作る方法もあります。こちらも正しいのですが、この方法だと時間切れで要約を書けなくなるおそれがあり、その場合〈課題の達成度〉の評価が下がります。したがって本書では、**初心者の方でも書きやすく、スコアを稼ぎやすいものとして、図の段落構成を推奨しています。**

Task 1 攻略ルール

1 ▶ 主観的な意見は不要！

タスク1で書く内容は、IntroductionでもBodyでも「グラフや図から読み取れる客観的な情報」であるべきです。I think ...などの書き出しで、自分の意見を書くのは避けるべきで、I assume ...やI guess ...など、推測するような表現も不要です。

誤った例

Oil is the most used energy source in this town, and I assume that the most power is required for domestic cooling due to hot summers.　（この町では石油が一番多く使われているエネルギー源であり、夏が暑いため、そのほとんどの電力が家屋の冷房のために必要なのだと予想する）

よい例

Oil is the most used energy source in this town and the most power is required for domestic cooling.　（この町では石油が一番多く使われているエネルギー源であり、そしてそのほとんどの電力は家屋の冷房のために必要とされている）

2 ▶ 高得点を狙うなら、Bodyで全項目の数値にまで言及しよう

イラストの円グラフには、3つの項目（Dogs, Cats, Birds）があります。このグラフをもとにエッセイを書くとして、もし高得点を狙いたいなら、全3項目の数値を取り上げ、比較しながら構成比を伝えてください。このとき、数値を羅列しただけの箇条書きにならないよう気をつけましょう。

棒グラフ、折れ線グラフで横軸の項目が時期（西暦や月）の場合は、項目数が多く、すべてに言及するのが難しいこともあります。こういったときは、**最低限、最初と最後の項目の数値に言及するのがマスト**です。加えて**特徴的な数値を示している時期の項目があれば、そこにも触れましょう**。下の棒グラフの場合、2000年、2003年に加えて、特徴的である2002年の数値にも言及するべきです。

➡ Dogs, Cats, Birds の
　数値に言及

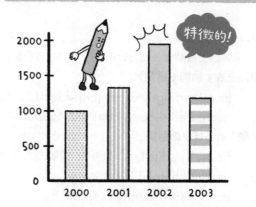

➡ 2000年, 2002年, 2003年の
　数値に言及

3 ▶ Task 1に特有の表現をマスターしよう

　タスク1のうち、「棒グラフ、折れ線グラフの問題」では、「増加／減少した」といった増減を表すのが必須です。加えて「表の問題」でも、増減の表現を使うことがあります。語彙のバリエーションを示せるほどスコアUPになるので、以下の例を参考にしてください。

〉〉〉 増減を表す表現（棒グラフ、折れ線グラフ、表）

増加を表す

[基本表現] **increase / rise / grow**（増加する）

　Sales **increased** significantly **from** $100 million in 2003 **to** $500 million in 2005.
　Sales **rose** considerably **from** $100 million **to** $500 million between 2003 and 2005.
　Sales **grew** dramatically **from** $100 million in 2003 **to** $500 million in 2005.

[応用表現] **skyrocket / surge**（急上昇する）

　Sales **skyrocketed to** $500 million in 2005.
　Sales **surged to** $500 million in 2005.

減少を表す

[基本表現] **decrease / fall / decline / drop**（減少する）

　Sales **decreased slightly from** $450 million in 1995 **to** $430 million in 1997.
　Sales **fell moderately to** $480 million in 2007 **from** a high of $500 million in 2005.
　Sales **declined from** $500 million in 2005 **to** $480 million in 2007.
　There was a slight drop in sales **from** $500 million in 2005 **to** $480 million in 2007.（この文の
dropは名詞）

[応用表現] **plummet**（急落する）**/ reduction**（減少）

　Sales **plummeted from** $400 million in 1998 **to** $100 million in 2000.
　There was a considerable reduction in sales **from** $400 million in 1998 **to** $100 million in 2000.

　なお、増減を表すときは、「どれほど」「どれくらいの速さで」増加／減少したのかといった情報を加えた方が具体的で自然な表現となります。次のような副詞や形容詞を加えましょう。

〈増減を表す動詞＋副詞〉

　increased significantly [considerably, dramatically]　（大幅に増加した）
　decreased slightly　（わずかに減少した）

よく使われるほかの副詞

　slowly [gradually]　（次第に、段階的に、徐々に）
　rapidly [sharply]　（急激に）
　steadily [constantly]　（絶えず）

〈形容詞＋増減を表す名詞〉

　a significant [considerable, dramatic] increase　（大幅な増加）
　a slight decrease　（わずかな減少）

変化していないことを表す

基本表現 **remain**（〜のままである）

Sales **remained stable** at $480 million between 2007 and 2009.

Sales **remained low** between 2000 and 2003.

応用表現 **level off**（横ばいになる）

Sales grew constantly until 2015 reaching a high of $600 million but **levelled off** after that.

変動的であることを表す

基本表現 **fluctuate**（変動する）

Sales **fluctuated** between 2018 and 2021 falling to $500 million in 2021.

応用表現 **variation**（変動）

From 1995 to 2021, **there was a huge variation** in sales, ranging between $100 million and $600 million.

》》 さらにスコアUPにつながる表現

高得点を目指す方は、以下の表現も意識して使えるようにしましょう。

倍数表現

「増加／減少した」というシンプルな表現に加えて、倍数を用いた表現も織り交ぜられると、語彙力のアピールになります。

halve（〜に半減する）

Sales **halved to** $100 million in 2000.

double to 〜（〜に倍増する）

Sales **doubled to** $500 million in 2005.

twofold（2倍の［に］）

Sales increased more than **twofold** between 2004 and 2005.

two times（2倍）

Sales increased by more than **two times** between 2004 and 2005.

最高値・最低値

最高値と最低値は、要約やBodyで特筆すべき特徴の1つです。以下の表現を覚えておきましょう。

最高値　reach a peak of 〜（〜で最高値に達する）

Sales steadily increased, **reaching a peak of** $600 million in 2015.

類似表現：peak at 〜 / reach a highest point at 〜

最低値　hit the lowest point at 〜（〜で最低値を記録する）

Sales continued to decline and **hit their lowest point at** $100 million in 2000.

類似表現：fall to the bottom at 〜 / hit a bottom

>>> 割合や構成を示す表現（円グラフ、表）

「円グラフの問題」や一部の「表の問題」では、割合や構成を表現する必要があります。次の動詞（句）はすべて「〜を占める」「〜を表す」といった意味で、特に「円グラフの問題」で重宝する表現です。

account for 〜（〜を占める）など

Sport
- accounts for
- represents
- makes up
- comprises

29% of all physical activities undertaken by males in the UK.

割合

「割合」に当たる英語には、percentageとproportionがあります。同じ語句を何度も繰り返さないように、バランスよく使いましょう。

A larger percentage of men did sport, which was 29%, compared with only 17% of women who participated in the same activity. Men generally cycled much more than women. Ten percent cycled for leisure and 5% did so for travelling. Lastly, **the proportion of** men who did fitness training was exactly the same as women.

分数

割合を挙げるときは「何%」と表の数値をそのまま書いても問題ありませんが、分数を使って語彙力をアピールする方法もあります。

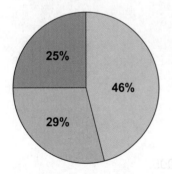

46%（約半分）: nearly half / less than half / a little under a half

25%（4分の1）: a quarter / one-fourth

29%（約3分の1）: approximately one-third / just less than a third

>>> 「地図の問題」で使える表現

この問題タイプでは、ある街の昔と今を表す地図が与えられ、その変化を描写する課題が多く、次のような表現が役立ちます。

描写するときは「誰がマンションを建設した」「誰が線路を拡張した」などの「誰が」に当たる「主語」は重要ではないので、受動態がよく使われるのも特徴の1つです。

変化を表す動詞（句）表現

追加される	変化する	なくなる
put up, **develop**, erect, construct, set up, establish, introduce	**extend**, replace, relocate, expand, renovate, **convert**, merge, connect, join, transform, separate	demolish, knock down, eliminate, **no longer exist**, get rid of, clear away

The forest **was developed** into a campsite.
The main road **was extended** and became a large interstate highway.
The old warehouse **was converted** into an art gallery.
Both the mill and the shipbuilding facility **no longer exist**.

位置や方角を表す表現

　この問題タイプでは、地図上の「どこで」変化が起きたのか伝えるために、位置や方角を表す語彙も使いこなす必要があります。

to the east [west / north / south] of 〜 （〜の東側［西側／北側／南側］には）
to the left [right] of 〜 （〜の左手［右手］には）
on the other side of 〜 / opposite to 〜 （〜の反対側には）
in the middle [centre] of 〜 （〜の中心には）
behind （後ろに）　between （〜の間に）　next to 〜 / by （〜の隣に）
in front of 〜 （〜の前に）　beyond （〜の先に）　beside （〜の横に）
facing （〜に向かって）

>>> 「工程を表す図の問題」で使える表現

　この問題タイプでは、工程を順序立てて明確に説明することがマストです。

順序を示す表現

初めに：　first / first of all / firstly / to begin with
続いて：　after that / after / next / then / secondly / thirdly / followed by
　　　　　/ once (that's done)
同時に：　while / whilst / at the same time / during
最後に：　lastly / finally

>>> どのグラフや図でも使える表現

対比、比較する表現

　タスク1の問題文の指示には、必ず make comparisons where relevant（関連がある箇所を比較しなさい）と書かれています。これは評価基準の〈課題の達成度〉に関わる重要な指示なので、以下の表現を活用して、

関連があるデータを比較しましょう。

whereas (〜であるのに)

Thirty-three percent of women walked for leisure, **whereas** 20% did so for travel.

while (〜の一方で)

Men walked more for leisure at 20%, **while** only 16% walked for travel.

on the other hand (他方で)

On the other hand, initially the proportion of men in part-time studies was significantly higher than women.

compared to [with] 〜 (〜と比較すると)

A larger percentage of men did sport, which was 29%, **compared with** only 17% of women who participated in the same activity.

ほかに、in contrast(対照的に)、conversely(逆に)などの表現もあります。

出題されるグラフ、表、図を知ろう

> **task type-1** > 円グラフの問題　Pie chart　　　　　　　　>>> サンプル問題

書くべきこと　比較しつつ構成比を伝える

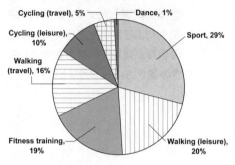

Physical Activities: UK Males 2017

Cycling (travel), 5% — Dance, 1%
Cycling (leisure), 10%
Sport, 29%
Walking (travel), 16%
Fitness training, 19%
Walking (leisure), 20%

- 円グラフ＝項目の構成比を視覚的に比較しやすくまとめたもの
- 各項目の構成を描写したり、項目ごとの割合を比較したりすることが求められる

> **task type-2** > 棒グラフの問題　Bar chart　　　　　　　　>>> 実践1

書くべきこと　増減などの変化を伝える

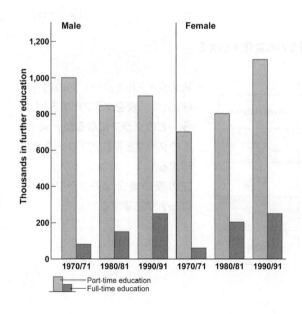

Male　　　　Female

1,200
1,000
800
600
400
200
0

Thousands in further education

1970/71　1980/81　1990/91　1970/71　1980/81　1990/91

Part-time education
Full-time education

- 棒グラフ＝横軸の項目におけるデータを棒の高さで表現したもの
- 頻出なのは、横軸の項目に時期（例：2000年、2005年 …）を配置したもので、その場合、時系列による変化を描写していく
- 基本的には横軸の全項目の数値に言及する
- 横軸の項目が時期で、項目数が多い場合、最低限、最初（一番左）と最後（一番右）の項目に言及する。加えて特徴的な変化や数を示す項目があれば、その数値も挙げる

折れ線グラフの問題 Line graph　　　　>>> 実践2

書くべきこと　増減などの変化を伝える

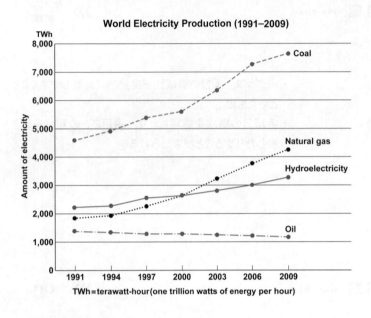

World Electricity Production (1991–2009)

TWh=terawatt-hour(one trillion watts of energy per hour)

- 折れ線グラフ＝横軸の項目におけるデータの推移を折れ線で表現したもの
- 棒グラフと同様に、横軸の項目に時期を配置したグラフが多く、時系列による変化を描写する。横軸の項目が時期で、項目数が多いときの書き方は棒グラフと同じ

task type-4　表の問題 Table　　　　>>> 実践3

書くべきこと　比較しつつ構成比を伝える、または増減などの変化を伝える

Method of travel to work in Australia (2016)

	Drive	Public transport	Walk / Bicycle	Work at home
Sydney	65.5%	21%	6%	7.5%
Melbourne	74.5%	13.5%	4.5%	7.5%
Adelaide	80%	8%	4%	8%
Hobart	76%	5.5%	8%	10.5%

- 表のタイトルと、行と列の内容を確認し、「**表をグラフ化するとしたら、どのグラフになるか**」考え、そのグラフと同じアプローチで描写する
- 左の表の場合は円グラフのアプローチで描写する

書くべきこと　過去と現在における変化を伝える

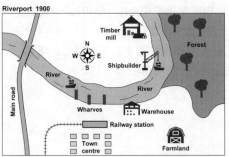

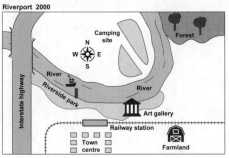

- 典型的な問題は、ある街の過去と現在の地図が与えられ、変化を描写するタイプ
- 数値の変化ではなく「マンションが建設された」「緑地が減った」といった変化を描写する
- 高得点を狙うのであれば、すべての変化した点と変化していない点に言及しよう

> task type-6 〉 工程を表す図の問題 Process & Diagram　　　　>>> 実践5

書くべきこと　順序立てて、工程を説明する

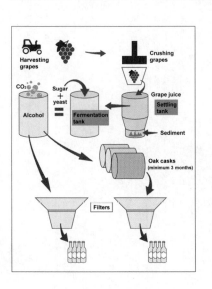

- 製品の製造過程や、機械の使用手順など、物事の工程を表すフローチャートが与えられる
- **全工程を漏らさずに順序立てて描写する**必要がある

Writing

2種類のグラフや表が与えられる問題
Multiple graph

Daily water consumed by household appliances in the US (2010)

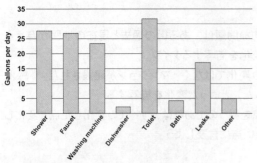

Total gallons daily water consumed in the US (per person)

1985	98 gallons per day
1990	102 gallons per day
1995	105 gallons per day
2000	112 gallons per day
2005	118 gallons per day
2010	110 gallons per day

- 「棒グラフと表」「折れ線グラフと円グラフ」など、2種類のグラフや表が与えられる
- 両者の中に相関関係を見出し、分析したうえで描写する必要があるので、難易度が高い
- 両者を比較しながら描写するのが難しい場合は、別々のBodyに分けて個別に描写しよう

Task 1 エッセイ 完成までの4つのSTEP（サンプル問題）

　では、サンプル問題として、「円グラフの問題」のエッセイを書いてみましょう。以下の4つのSTEPを踏んで完成させていきます。

エッセイ 完成までの4つのSTEP	
STEP 1	問題を分析する
STEP 2	構成を組み立てる
STEP 3	エッセイを書く
STEP 4	見直しをする

サンプル問題

You should spend about 20 minutes on this task.

① **The charts below show the most popular physical activities for males and females in the UK in 2017.**

② **Summarise the information by selecting and reporting the main features, and make comparisons where relevant.**

→問題文の文章は2つの要素から成る
①説明文（何のグラフや図なのかを説明する文）
②指示文（この指示文はタスク1で共通）

Write at least 150 words.

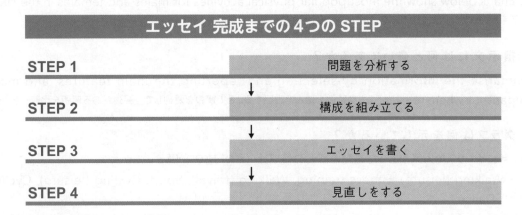

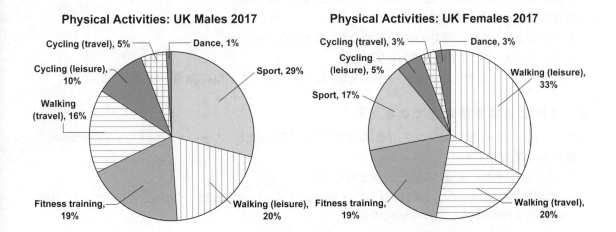

Physical Activities: UK Males 2017

Physical Activities: UK Females 2017

109

STEP-1　問題を分析する

問題を分析するときは、具体的に次のチェックポイントを押さえていきましょう。

☑ 説明文には何と書いてあるか？

The charts below show the most popular physical activities for males and females in the UK in 2017.（下記のグラフは、2017年のイギリスで男性と女性に最も人気のある運動を示している）

☑ 指示文には何と書いてあるか？

Summarise the information by selecting and reporting the main features, and make comparisons where relevant.（主な特徴を選んで説明することで情報を要約して、関連がある箇所を比較しなさい）

☑ グラフは何を示しているか？

2017年にイギリスで人気があった運動の割合の構成比（左の円グラフが男性、右が女性）
項目＝ Walking (leisure), Fitness training, Walking (travel), Sport, Cycling (leisure), Cycling (travel), Dance
→項目の訳は、それぞれ、ウォーキング（余暇）、フィットネス、ウォーキング（移動）、スポーツ、サイクリング（余暇）、サイクリング（移動）、ダンス。

☑ どの時制で書くべきか？

2017年のデータなので過去形

STEP-2　構成を組み立てる

ここがスコアを大きく左右する重要なSTEPです。書き出す前のプランニングをしていきましょう。
STEP 2では「指示文にある主な特徴(the main features)とは何か。項目を分類、整理しながら、それをどのように描写するか」を掘り下げて考えなければいけません。

☑ 主な特徴は何か？

• 男女ともに、余暇と移動を合算した場合、ウォーキングの割合が一番高く、女性の方がより高かった
• ダンスは女性の割合の方が高かったが、男女ともに割合は低かった
• 男性の方が、スポーツの割合が高かった
• サイクリングは、余暇、移動ともに、男性の割合の方が高かった
• フィットネスは、男女で割合が変わらなかった
　→指示文には「主な特徴」とあるが、高得点を狙いたいなら、Bodyで全項目の数値にまで言及しよう。

☑ 項目は分類や整理ができるか？

• ウォーキング（余暇）とウォーキング（移動）はグラフでは違う項目だが、ウォーキングとしてまとめられるので、同じBody内で描写する
• サイクリングも同様に余暇と移動をまとめて描写する
　→この問題は項目が多いので、1項目ずつを個別に描写していくとエッセイが間延びしてしまうが、このように分類、整理ができれば、読みやすいエッセイになる。

☑ 各Bodyにおける軸は何か?

Body 1の軸:最大値と最小値(ウォーキングとダンス)

Body 2の軸:そのほか(スポーツ、サイクリング、フィットネス)

→**軸とは、各Bodyで書く中心的な内容**のこと。このエッセイでは、最大値のウォーキングと最小値のダンスをまとめてBody 1の軸として、そのほかをBody 2にまとめている。〈一貫性とまとまり〉の評価を上げるには、軸を持って書くことが必須。なお、「最大値と最小値を同じBodyにまとめる」のも、分類や整理のよい例。

☑ 構成をメモにまとめる

メモの例

---

1 ▸ Intro
- パラフレ
- Overall
- ・Sport: men > women　・Cycle: men > women
- ・women = more walking / #1 both　・Fitness = equally

2 ▸ Body 1
- Walk : men (20% L / 16% T) < women (33% L / 20% T)
- Dance: women (3%) > men (1%) = least popular

3 ▸ Body 2
- Sport: men (29%) > women (17%)
- Cycle: men (10% L / 5% T) > women (5% L / 3% T) = nearly half
- Fitness: men = women (19%)

→メモにまとめるときは、STEP 3でスムーズにエッセイを書くために、具体的な語句で書こう。

STEP-3　エッセイを書く(約15分)

いよいよエッセイを書き始めます。段落の構成は、Introduction→Bodyでした。本エッセイのBodyの数は2つです。タスク1全体にかける時間が20分として、STEP 3に15分ほどかけられるように、うまく時間配分をしていきましょう。

1 ▸ Introductionを書く

Introductionは「問題文中の説明文のパラフレーズ」と「要約」から成ります。

≫≫「説明文のパラフレーズ」を書く

エッセイ冒頭では「何についてのグラフなのか」、説明文を言い換えて表現します。先に述べたように、**説明文を丸写しすると語数にカウントされないので、必ずパラフレーズしましょう。**

Writing

111

The charts below show the most popular physical activities for males and females in the UK in 2017.

The pie charts illustrate the physical activities of British men and women in 2017.

→ パラフレーズ charts ⇄ pie charts / show ⇄ illustrate / males and females ⇄ men and women / the UK ⇄ British

>>> 「 要 約 」を書く

パラフレーズに続いて、グラフが示す主な特徴を要約として書きます。

Overall, it can be seen that men played significantly more sport than women. They also cycled much more. In contrast, women were more likely to go walking and this was the most popular activity for both sexes. They participated in fitness training equally.

[要約で書いていること]
• 男性の方が女性よりスポーツをしていた
• サイクリングも男性の方が多いが、女性の方が歩いており、ウォーキングは男女ともに一番人気のあった活動
• フィットネスは男女で同じように参加していた
→要約に割合まで入れると必要以上に細かい説明になり減点となるので要注意。また、ダンスには言及していないが、要約では全項目を網羅する必要はなく、問題ない。

2 ▶ Body 1を書く

Bodyでは、グラフに掲載されている具体的な割合を盛り込んで詳細を説明していきます。Body 1では、最大値であるウォーキングと、最小値であるダンスに言及します。

Body 1

Twenty percent of males walked for leisure and 16% did so out of necessity. The numbers were higher for women, and they walked more for leisure. This figure stood at nearly a third, and 20% of women walked for travelling. Dancing was the least popular activity for both men and women. Women preferred dancing more than men, but this percentage was still very small at only 3%, representing a mere 2% difference between them.

[Body 1で書いていること]
- ウォーキング：女性の方が割合が高い
- ダンス：女性の方がダンスを好むが、割合は低く、最も人気のない活動

3 ▶ Body 2を書く

Body 2は、ウォーキングとダンス以外、つまりスポーツ、サイクリング、フィットネスの3つに軸を定め、展開していきます。

Body 2

A larger percentage of men did sport, which was close to a third, compared with only 17% of women who participated in the same activity. Men generally cycled much more than women, 10% cycled for leisure and 5% did so for travelling. Conversely, only 5% of women cycled for leisure and 3% for travel, which is about half as much as their male counterparts. Lastly, the proportion of men who did fitness training was exactly the same as women (19%).

[Body 2で書いていること]
- スポーツ：男性に人気で、男女間で大きな開きがある
- サイクリング：男性の方が女性よりはるかにしている
- フィットネス：男女で割合が同じ

STEP-4 見直しをする

エッセイを書き上げたら、それで完成ではありません！次の点に気をつけて、必ず見直しをしましょう。

☑ 課題を達成できているか
（→Introductionに「説明文のパラフレーズ」と「要約」はあるか。Bodyで「主な特徴」（高得点を狙うなら全項目の名称と数値）に言及しているか）
☑ 段落構成はわかりやすいか
☑ 同じ単語を繰り返さず、幅広い語彙力を示せているか
☑ 接続表現を使い、わかりやすく展開できているか
☑ 複文を織り交ぜ、正しい構文を使えているか
☑ 時制は適切か
☑ グラフや図を客観的に読み取り、個人的な意見を挟まずに描写できているか
☑ スペルや文法のミスはないか（冠詞や三単現sのつけ忘れに注意）
☑ 体裁は整っているか（段落の区切りは1行空けるなど）
☑ 150 words以上書けているか

次頁以降では、ここまで段落ごとに紹介してきた「上級者のエッセイ」の全文とともに、「中級者のエッセイ」も紹介していきます。両者を比較することでスコアUPするにはどうすればいいか見えてくるはずです。

これから紹介するサンプルエッセイには、スペルミスや文法ミスはありません。しかし、「中級者のエッセイ」には、スコアUPの妨げとなる「受験者によく見られるミス（「課題の指示を満たしていない」などのミス）」をあえて入れ、皆さんが同じミスを犯さないように解説しています。
なお、サンプルエッセイのスコアの目安は、**「中級者のエッセイ」が6.5以上、「上級者のエッセイ」が8以上**です。両者のよい点、使える表現や語彙を参考にして、皆さんのライティング力を磨いてください！

受験者の皆さんから「エッセイを書くときに、スペルは英米のどちらにすればいいですか」と質問を受けることがあります。答えは、**イギリス式／アメリカ式のどちらでも構いません。**
というのもIELTSは国際的な試験なので、どちらでも問題ないのです。両者が混在することでスペルミスとみなされ、減点の要因になることはありません。ただし体裁を整えるために、どちらかに統一するのが望ましいです。
スペルの違いにはいくつかルールがあるので、ここで代表的なものを紹介しましょう。

イギリスとアメリカのスペルの違い

-tre 🇬🇧 と -ter 🇺🇸
centre, center / metre, meter

-bour 🇬🇧 と -bor 🇺🇸
favourite, favorite / labour, labor / colour, color

-se 🇬🇧 と -ze 🇺🇸
organise, organize / recognise, recognize

ほか、語尾のl（エル）の前に母音を持つ動詞が進行形や過去形になるとき、イギリス英語ではlを重ねます。
travel → travelling, travelled 🇬🇧 / traveling, traveled 🇺🇸

中級者のエッセイ

[Introduction]

パラフレーズ The chart shows the physical activities of men and women in the UK in 2017.

要約 Overall, women walked more than men. The figure was 53% for women and only 36% for men. I think that this must be the case because women don't work as much as men, so they have more time to go walking.

[Body 1]

Men walked more for leisure at 20% and only 16% walked for travel. Nineteen percent of men did fitness training, which was equal to the number of women who did so. Twenty-nine percent of men did sport. Meanwhile, 10% of men did cycling as a leisure activity and 5% cycled for travel.

[Body 2]

Whereas 33% of women walked for leisure, 20% did so for travel. Women walked more than men. Nineteen percent of women did fitness training. Seventeen percent did sport, while 3% did dancing as a leisure activity, and only 5% of women cycled for leisure. Females don't seem to like doing physical activity but they like dancing more than men.

(167 words)／※下線＝〈一貫性とまとまり〉のスコアに関わる接続表現

受験者によく見られるミス！ 〜「中級者のエッセイ」の注意点〜

- Introduction の要約で数値を入れている。要約では、具体的な数値は必要ない
- データを主観的にとらえている。タスク1では、主観的な意見や解釈は不要（p.117参照）！

Writing

上級者のエッセイ

[Introduction]

パラフレーズ The pie charts illustrate the physical activities of British men and women in 2017. 要約 Overall, it can be seen that men played significantly more sport than women. They also cycled much more. In contrast, women were more likely to go walking and this was the most popular activity for both sexes. They participated in fitness training equally.

[Body 1]

Twenty percent of males walked for leisure and 16% did so out of necessity. The numbers were higher for women, and they walked more for leisure. This figure stood at nearly a third, and 20% of women walked for travelling. Dancing was the least popular activity for both men and women. Women preferred dancing more than men, but this percentage was still very small at only 3%, representing a mere 2% difference between them.

[Body 2]

A larger percentage of men did sport, which was close to a third, compared with only 17% of women who participated in the same activity. Men generally cycled much more than women, 10% cycled for leisure and 5% did so for travelling. Conversely, only 5% of women cycled for leisure and 3% for travel, which is about half as much as their male counterparts. Lastly, the proportion of men who did fitness training was exactly the same as women (19%).

(211 words)／※下線＝〈一貫性とまとまり〉のスコアに関わる接続表現

〉〉〉 上級者エッセイの構成

Introduction —— 説明文のパラフレーズ＋要約
Body 1 —————— 最も人気なウォーキングと人気のないダンスの割合、男女比較
Body 2 —————— 男性に人気のスポーツと、ほかの項目(サイクリング、フィットネス)の男女比較

〈課題の達成度〉

[Introduction]

中級 要約ではウォーキングのみに言及しており情報不足。また、要約に53%などの数値は不要。I think ... の文は、主観なのでカットすべき。

[Body]

中級 女性のサイクリング（移動）にまったく言及しておらず、男性のダンスの割合も漏れている。高得点を狙うなら、Bodyで全項目の数値まで出して説明しよう。

フィットネスの記述が、Body 1と2に散在しているなど、軸がブレている。

最終文のseem to 〜は「〜のようだ」と、主観的な判断を表すため、タスク1では不適切。

〈語彙力〉

上級 グラフ内の語句を巧みに言い換えている（travel ⇄ out of necessityなど）。また、グラフ内の数値を分数で表現している（33% ⇄ nearly a third / 29% ⇄ close to a third）。

〈文法知識と正確さ〉

中級 文法的なミスはないが、Twenty-nine percent of men did sport. などは、単文で細切れな印象。一方で、Nineteen percent of men did fitness training, which ... は、関係代名詞（which, who）を使った複文の好例。

上級 Body 2の1文目で、関係代名詞の非制限用法（, which）を用いた高度な複文を書けている。ほか、中級に比べて比較表現の幅が広い。

┤ **Vocabulary** ├

中級

□ **physical activity** 　身体活動、運動
□ **case** ［名］実情
□ **for leisure** 　余暇のため
□ **whereas** ［接］〜であるのに

上級

□ **significantly** ［副］かなり、大幅に
□ **in contrast** 　対照的に
□ **be more likely to 〜** 　〜する傾向がある
□ **participate in 〜** 　〜に参加する
□ **necessity** ［名］必要性
□ **stand at 〜** 　（数値が）〜を示す
□ **prefer** ［動］〜をより好む
□ **represent** ［動］〜に相当する
□ **mere** ［形］ほんの
□ **compared with 〜** 　〜と比べて
□ **generally** ［副］一般的に
□ **conversely** ［副］反対に、逆に
□ **proportion of 〜** 　〜の割合

Task 1 実践問題

棒グラフの問題

You should spend about 20 minutes on this task.

> *The chart below shows the number of men and women in further education in Britain in three periods and whether they were studying full-time or part-time.*
>
> *Summarise the information by selecting and reporting the main features, and make comparisons where relevant.*

Write at least 150 words.

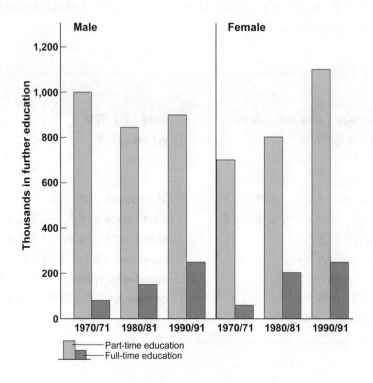

You should spend about 20 minutes on this task.

The graph shows the global electricity production by four types of sources from 1991 to 2009.

Summarise the information by selecting and reporting the main features, and make comparisons where relevant.

Write at least 150 words.

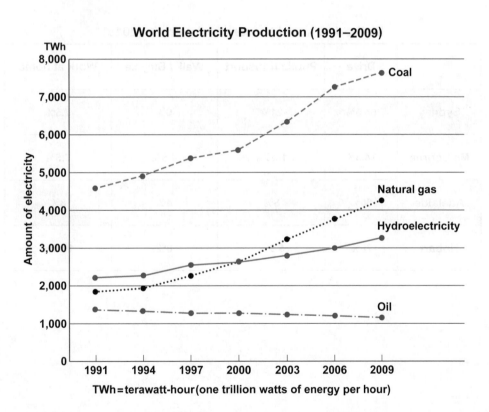

World Electricity Production (1991–2009)

TWh = terawatt-hour (one trillion watts of energy per hour)

Source: Our World in Data based on BP Statistical Review of World Energy & Ember (2021) Retrieved from: https://ourworldindata.org/grapher/electricity-production-by-source

You should spend about 20 minutes on this task.

> **The table below shows the usual method of travel to work for people in four Australian cities in 2016.**
>
> **Summarise the information by selecting and reporting the main features, and make comparisons where relevant.**

Write at least 150 words.

Method of travel to work in Australia (2016)

	Drive	Public transport	Walk / Bicycle	Work at home
Sydney	65.5%	21%	6%	7.5%
Melbourne	74.5%	13.5%	4.5%	7.5%
Adelaide	80%	8%	4%	8%
Hobart	76%	5.5%	8%	10.5%

You should spend about 20 minutes on this task.

The maps below show the town of Riverport in 1900 and 2000.

Summarise the information by selecting and reporting the main features, and make comparisons where relevant.

Write at least 150 words.

Riverport 1900

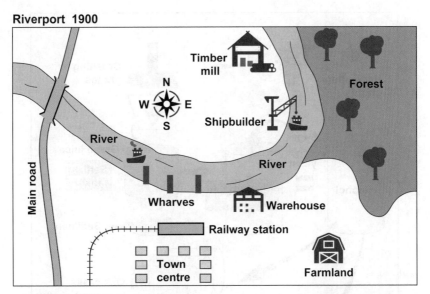

Riverport 2000

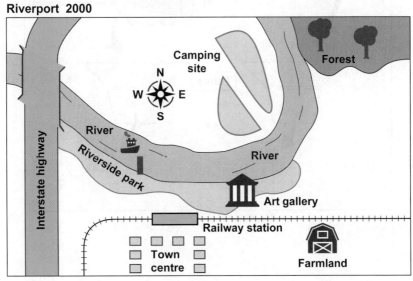

Writing

You should spend about 20 minutes on this task.

The diagram below shows the process by which white wine is made.

Summarise the information by selecting and reporting the main features, and make comparisons where relevant.

Write at least 150 words.

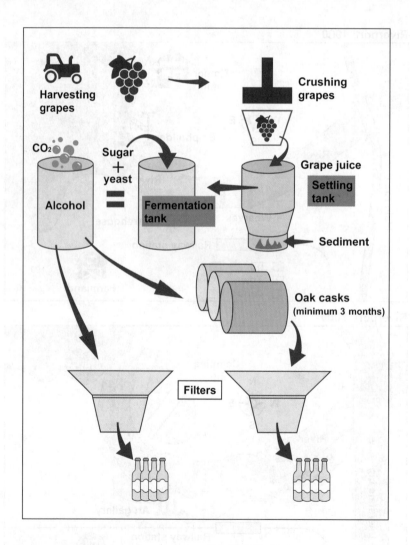

You should spend about 20 minutes on this task.

> *The bar graph indicates the average amount of water used by different household appliances each day in the United States. The table shows how many gallons of water were consumed per person in the United States over a 26-year period.*
>
> *Summarise the information by selecting and reporting the main features, and make comparisons where relevant.*

Write at least 150 words.

Daily water consumed by household appliances in the US (2010)

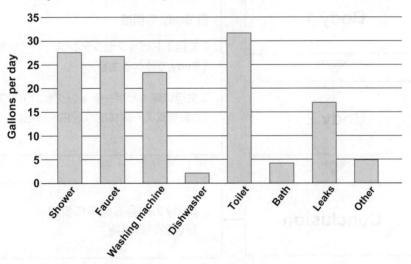

Total gallons daily water consumed in the US (per person)

1985	98 gallons per day
1990	102 gallons per day
1995	105 gallons per day
2000	112 gallons per day
2005	118 gallons per day
2010	110 gallons per day

Task 2 対策

段落構成　基本のフォーマット

タスク2の段落構成は、下の図のようになります。

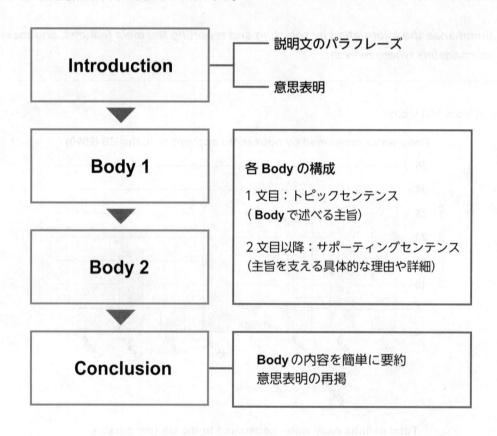

Introduction → 説明文のパラフレーズ
意思表明

Body 1

Body 2

各 Body の構成

1 文目：トピックセンテンス
（Body で述べる主旨）

2 文目以降：サポーティングセンテンス
（主旨を支える具体的な理由や詳細）

Conclusion → Body の内容を簡単に要約
意思表明の再掲

1 ▸ Introduction

Introduction は「説明文のパラフレーズ」と「意思表明」から成ります。**どちらか1つでも抜けてしまうと減点になる**ので、気をつけましょう。

》》》 説明文のパラフレーズ

どんなトピックかを簡単に紹介する文で書き出します。問題文中の説明文に書いてある情報をもとに、パラフレーズさせましょう。

Point

- 説明文をすべて書き写すと、語数にカウントされないので注意

》》》 意思表明

自分の考えや立場を明確に表明します。エッセイの序盤で意思表明をすることで、主張が伝わりやすいエッセイを展開していきます。

Point

- I (personally) think ... や In my opinion, ... などの書き出しで始めることが多い

2 ▸ Body

ここは、Introduction の意思表明に関して、**具体的な主張や裏付けをする本論です。**大半の場合、1文目は主旨を表すトピックセンテンスで書き出します。2文目以降では、主旨を支える具体的な理由や詳細を挙げて論理的にまとめましょう。

Point

- 多くの場合、Bodyの数は2〜3ほど
- 原則は「1つのBodyには1つの主旨」を書く
- 各Bodyの構成は、トピックセンテンスとサポーティングセンテンスから成る

3 ▸ Conclusion

Conclusion では、Bodyの内容を簡単に要約し、Introductionの意思表明を再度行います。このとき、Introduction や Body で使った文をそのまま使うのではなく、語句や構文を変えてください。繰り返すと単調になりますし、言い換えることで語彙力や文法力のアピールにもなります。なお、**Conclusionがないと減点になる**ので、時間切れで書けない事態にならないように時間配分に注意してください。

Point

- Introductionの意思表明を読み返したうえで、意思表明の再掲を行う
- 再掲だが、同じフレーズを繰り返すのではなくパラフレーズする
- 「まとめ」なので、**新しい話は持ち出さない**

Task 2 攻略ルール

1 ▸ 主観的な意見を述べるのがマスト

先に「タスク1では主観的な意見は不要」という話をしました。では、タスク2ではどうでしょうか。実は、タスク2では主観的な意見を述べなくてはいけません。具体的には、**Introductionで意思表明をするとき**と、**Conclusionで意思表明の再掲をするときに、主観的な意見を展開**します。

一方で、タスク2のBodyでは、自分の意見をサポートする客観的な理由や詳細を中心に展開するので、主観的な表現はあまり使いません。

2 ▸ 断定を避ける表現を使おう

アカデミック・ライティングでは、十分なデータや証拠がないことに対して断言しません。タスク2のライティングでは、大半の場合、断言できるほどのデータや証拠を用意できないので、断定的な表現を避けて論を展開することが多くなります。

断定的な表現

Over-consumption of fast food makes young people obese.
（ファストフードの食べ過ぎは、若者を肥満にする）

改善例

Over-consumption of fast food **could** make young people obese.
〜しうる

Over-consumption of fast food **tends to** make young people obese.
〜する傾向がある

It is often stated that over-consumption of fast food makes young people obese.
SVとよく言われている

In many instances, over-consumption of fast food makes young people obese.
多くの場合

Generally speaking, over-consumption of fast food **can** make young people obese.
一般的には　　　　　　　　　　　　　　　　　　　　　　　　　　　　　〜しうる

3 ▶ 使い古された決まり文句や慣用句は、使用しない

タスク2では、使い古された決まり文句（cliche）や慣用句を使うと語彙力のアピールになると誤解して、積極的に使ってしまうミスが時々見られます。スピーキングテストでは、話の流れの中でこういった表現を自然に使えていれば評価されますが、ライティングテストではむしろ逆効果です。次に挙げたような表現を暗記して使うよりも、文脈に合ったシンプルで明確な表現で書きましょう。

悪い例		よい例
crux of the discussion	→	The main [key] issue is ...
（議論の核心）		（重要な点は...である）
a double-edged sword	→	This solution can also cause issues as S＋V.
（両刃の剣）		（SVなので、この策は問題を起こす可能性もある）
Every coin has two sides.	→	There are both advantages and disadvantages.
（どのコインにも表と裏がある）		（長所と短所の両方がある）

4 ▶「特定分野の語彙」は、文章の中で学んでいこう

特にタスク2は「教育」「テクノロジー」「健康・医療」「環境」など、出題範囲が広く、各トピックの語彙をエッセイの中で適切に使えると評価されます。例えば、「医療」の分野だと、vaccination（ワクチン接種）、health care workers（医療従事者）、acute（急性の）などが「特定分野の語彙」に当たります。

習得するときは「特定分野の語彙」の単語や語句だけを丸暗記しても語彙の運用力はあまり上がりません。それよりも、**生きた文章の中で学び、語彙を増やす方が、語句の使い方やコロケーションも学べるため、力がつくのです。**

例えば、「健康・医療」分野の語彙を強化したいなら、BBCやCNNのサイトに行き、Healthのタブをクリックしましょう。そうすれば、すぐに記事にアクセスでき、自然な文章の中で語彙を学べます。

もっと手軽なのは、本書に掲載されている**リーディング・パッセージを活用する**方法です。例えば、リーディングの章の練習4、5にGrey Workersと題した問題がありますが、このパッセージを読むと、early retirement（早期退職）、seniority-based pay scales（年功序列の給与体系）、piece-rate（出来高払い）など、エッセイを書く際に役立ちそうな「特定分野の語彙」が多く登場します。

「特定分野の語彙」は、社会的なトピックが出題されるスピーキングテストのパート3でも必要不可欠です。やはり「ライティングのスコアだけを上げる勉強」と思わずに、「特定分野の語彙」を学ぶ中で「リーディングの読解力が上がる」「スピーキングでも武器になる」と、総合力を上げていくのが得策です。

5つの問題タイプを知ろう

　タスク2でよく出題される問題タイプを紹介していきます。実際には、これらの質問が組み合わされた形で出題される問題など、さまざまなパターンがあります。

　実は、タスク2で大切なのは、問題タイプを暗記することではなく、その問題が**「言及すべき」と要求しているポイントを理解し、それらを漏れなくエッセイの中で描写する**ことです。本書ではこのポイントを［要求ポイント］と呼んでいます。

〔要求ポイント〕を
全部エッセイに盛り込む！

> **task type-1** > 賛成か反対かを述べる問題　Agree / Disagree　　　》》》 サンプル問題

例：The use of chemical sprays in agriculture has increased food production but greatly reduced the number of insects there are in the world. For this reason, some people believe that the use of chemicals in agriculture should be immediately stopped.

To what extent do you agree or disagree with this opinion?

（この意見に対して、どの程度賛成もしくは反対するか）

［要求ポイント］→1つ
　①自分の意見（賛成もしくは反対）の主張

> **task type-2** > 対立する2つの見解を論じ、自分の意見を述べる問題　Discussion　　　》》》 実践1

例：Some people believe that having fewer children is the best way to preserve the world's limited resources. Others believe that technology is the answer, and that population control is unnecessary.

Discuss both views and give your own opinion.

（両者の見解を論じ、あなた自身の意見を述べなさい）

[要求ポイント]→3つ

　①限られた資源を維持するため出生数を減らすのが最善という見解

　②技術が答えで、人口管理は不要という見解

　③自分の意見

task type-3 問題の原因、解決策を述べる問題 Problem / Solution ≫≫ 実践2

例：Many young people are motivated and successful at high school. Many others, however, lack motivation and see high school as irrelevant to their interests and needs.

Why is this? What could be done to help all students succeed?

（これはなぜか。生徒全員の成功を手助けするために何ができるか）

[要求ポイント]→2つ

　①原因：多くの若者は士気が高く、高校でうまくやっている一方で、士気に欠け、高校に興味がなく必要性を感じていない者も多い。それはなぜか

　②解決策：すべての生徒がうまくやっていくために、何ができるか

task type-4 長所と短所を比較する問題 Advantage / Disadvantage ≫≫ 実践3

例：Social media has become a very effective method of communication. At the same time, there is concern about its impact on the individual and society.

Do the advantages of social media outweigh the disadvantages?

（ソーシャルメディアの長所は短所を上回るか）

[要求ポイント]→2つ

　①ソーシャルメディアの長所

　②ソーシャルメディアの短所

　→「短所が長所を上回る」見解の場合は、長所の数より短所を多く書き、「長所が短所を上回る」見解の場合は、短所より長所を多く書くことで、自分の意見を明確にする。

task type-5 肯定的か否定的かを答える問題 Positive / Negative ≫≫ 実践4

例：Nowadays, people expect that automation in business will rapidly take over jobs from people.

Why do people think this? Is this a positive or negative development?

（なぜ人々はそう思うのか。これは肯定的もしくは否定的な発展か）

[要求ポイント]→2つ

　①ビジネスにおける自動化が人々の仕事を奪うという見方があるが、なぜ人々はそう思うのか

　②この発展は肯定的か否定的か（自分の意見）

タスク2では、**問題タイプごとに［要求ポイント］の数が固定しているわけではないので、個々の問題ごとに、問題文をよく読み解き、その都度判断する力が求められます。**
例えば、以下の「問題の原因、解決策を述べる問題」の場合、a) の［要求ポイント］は2つです。一方で、b) は、個人と政府の両方に言及すべきなので、［要求ポイント］は3つになります。

a) Why is this? What should **individuals** do to stop air pollution?

b) Why is this? What should **individuals** and **the government** do to stop air pollution?

このように、同じ問題タイプでも［要求ポイント］の数が異なることもあるので、書き始める前に、問題を注意深く分析する時間を取りましょう！

Tips **Two-question essayとは？**

Two-question essayとは、**問題文の中に2つの疑問文が登場するエッセイ**で、ここまで紹介したtask typeの例の中では、task type 3と5が該当します。ただし、task type 3、5なら必ずTwo-question essayになるわけではありませんし、ほかのtask typeでもTwo-question essayになることはあります。その点は注意してください。
実際にTwo-question essayにどう取り組むかですが、疑問文が1つの問題のときと基本的な対策は変わりません。つまり、ライティングテストでは、あくまでも**［要求ポイント］の数と内容を把握し、それらを漏れなくエッセイに盛り込むことが大切**なのです。
ただし、段落の構成面では注意が必要で、**各質問の回答に1つのBodyを使い、明確に分けるべき**です。
疑問文の内容に関して言うと、Two-question essayでは多くの場合、最初の質問で「原因」を聞いてきます。「原因」といってもWhyで始まらない疑問文もあるので、次の例を参考にしてください。

例1 : In many countries, people have more health problems because they live an unhealthy lifestyle. What do you think are the causes of this? What solutions can you suggest?

例2 : Children spending too much time on digital devices is becoming a major problem worldwide. What are the reasons for this? How could this problem be tackled?

Task 2 エッセイ 完成までの4つのSTEP(サンプル問題)

では、「賛成か反対かを述べる問題」(Agree / Disagree)をサンプル問題として、以下の4つのSTEPを1つずつ押さえていきながら、エッセイを完成させてみましょう。

エッセイ 完成までの4つの STEP

STEP 1	問題を分析する
↓	
STEP 2	構成を組み立てる
↓	
STEP 3	エッセイを書く
↓	
STEP 4	見直しをする

サンプル問題

You should spend about 40 minutes on this task.

Write about the following topic:

> ① *The use of chemical sprays in agriculture has increased food production but greatly reduced the number of insects there are in the world. For this reason, some people believe that the use of chemicals in agriculture should be immediately stopped.*
>
> ② *To what extent do you agree or disagree with this opinion?*
>
> →問題文の文章は2つの要素から成る
> ①説明文（トピックを説明する文）
> ②指示文（具体的な課題の提示）

Give reasons for your answer and include any relevant examples from your own knowledge or experience.

Write at least 250 words.

　まずは問題文を読んで、課題は何かを把握します。このSTEPでの最大のポイントは［要求ポイント］の数と内容を正確につかむことです。

☑　**問題文には何と書いてあるか？**

The use of chemical sprays in agriculture has increased food production but greatly reduced the number of insects there are in the world. For this reason, some people believe that the use of chemicals in agriculture should be immediately stopped.

To what extent do you agree or disagree with this opinion?

（農業で農薬噴霧液を使用することで食糧生産量は増えてきたが、世界中の昆虫の数は大幅に減ってきた。こういった理由で、農業における薬剤の使用はすぐに中止すべきだと考える人がいる。この意見にどの程度、賛成もしくは反対するか）

☑　**問題タイプは？**

「賛成か反対かを述べる問題」（Agree / Disagree）

☑　**［要求ポイント］の数と内容は？**

［要求ポイント］→1つ

　　①自分の意見（賛成もしくは反対）の主張

　問題を分析できたら、構成を練っていきます。どんな問題でも、書いている途中で意見がブレないように、自分の意見を必ずメモに書き出してください。Bodyに書く理由や詳細は、できる限り具体的な語句で書いて、STEP 3につなげていきます。

☑　**「賛成と反対」どちらの意見で書くか？**

「農業における薬剤の使用はすぐに中止すべき」という意見に、**部分的に賛成する**立場

☑　**構成をメモにまとめる**

メモの例

> 1 ▶ Intro
>   - growing population → chemical sprays = key role
>   - partially support → some should be allowed
>
> 2 ▶ Body 1
>   - safeguard humans / earth
>   · careful　ex. only pesticides / herbicides = not remain
>   · prevent permanent poisoning
>   · cause cancer = not allowed

```
3 ▶ Body 2
   - can't eliminate
      · recent study → no chemicals = half of crops die
      · not enough food → higher food prices / hungry
      · larger land → detrimental effect on environment

4 ▶ Conc
   - some negatives / but necessary
   - partially support →  use cautiously = min. harm to enviro
```

STEP-3 エッセイを書く（約30分）

いよいよエッセイを書き始めます。タスク2の構成は、Introduction → Body → Conclusion でした。本エッセイのBodyの数は2つです。タスク全体で40分かけるとして、STEP 3で30分ほどの時間を確保できるようにしましょう。

1 ▶ Introductionを書く

Introductionは「説明文のパラフレーズ」と「意思表明」から成ります。

〉〉〉「説明文のパラフレーズ」を書く

まずは読み手にトピックを説明します。問題文中の説明文を再びよく読み、必ずパラフレーズしながら自分の言葉で書き出しましょう。先に述べた通り、説明文を流用すると、その部分は語数にカウントされないため、減点につながります。

問題文中の説明文

The use of chemical sprays in agriculture has increased food production but greatly reduced the number of insects there are in the world. For this reason, some people believe that the use of chemicals in agriculture should be immediately stopped.

説明文のパラフレーズ

To provide sufficient food to the growing world population, chemical sprays play a key role in controlling pests. Nevertheless, there are those who think that we should refrain from using pesticides as they kill too many insects and adversely affect the natural environment.

→問題文中の説明文の内容は「農業で農薬噴霧液を使用することで食糧生産量は増えてきたが、世界中の昆虫の数は大幅に減ってきた。こういった理由で、農業における薬剤の使用はすぐに中止すべきだと考える人がいる」。これをエッセイでは「増加する世界の人口に十分な食料を供給するためには、農薬噴霧液は害虫駆除において重要な役割を果たす。しかし、過剰な殺虫や環境へ悪影響から使用を控えるべきと考える人もいる」と言い換えてまとめている。

パラフレーズ greatly reduced the number or insects ⇄ kill too many insects / some people believe ⇄ those who think / be ... stopped ⇄ refrain from using

>>> 意思表明を書く

ここで自分の意見や立場を明確にします。タスク2で要求されていることの中で、最も重要な点の1つです。

I cannot fully agree with this view because completely stopping the use of chemicals may lead to food shortages and have a very negative impact on the world.

[意思表明で書いていること]
- 農薬噴霧液が禁止されるべきという見解に、完全に賛成することはできない（＝部分的に賛成）
- 食糧不足や世界に悪影響を及ぼす可能性があるから
  →意思表明に加えて、簡単に理由も添えることで、Bodyへスムーズに移行できる

2 ▶ Body 1を書く

Bodyでは「大方反対する立場」を支持する、具体的な理由や詳細を展開します。
　まず、Body 1では「最も配慮すべき点は、人々と地球の安全を守ること」という主旨を掲げ、環境や人に害をもたらす一部の薬剤は使用を中止すべきだと主張していきます。

Body 1

トピック The most important consideration should be to safeguard humans and the earth. Since chemicals can kill insects such as bees, which are generally important to the environment, farmers should be careful about which chemicals they use. For example, they should only use pesticides and herbicides that do not remain in the environment for a long time. This will prevent permanently poisoning the natural environment, including our precious water resources. In addition, certain chemical sprays that can be poisonous to humans, and even potentially cause cancer, should not be allowed.

[Body 1で書いていること]
- [トピックセンテンス] 最も配慮すべき点は、人々と地球の安全を守ること
- [理由・詳細1] 薬剤は環境に重要な蜂などの虫を殺すことがあるので、どの薬剤を使うか慎重になるべき（残存しない薬剤を使用すれば、水資源などの環境も汚染しない）
- [理由・詳細2] 薬剤の中には人にも悪影響があるものがあり（発がん性の疑い）、そういったものは禁止されるべき

3 ▶ Body 2 を書く

続く Body 2 では、「それでも薬剤の使用をやめるべきではない」という使用推進派としての主張を全面に出して展開していきます。

Body 2

トピック Chemicals, however, cannot be eliminated entirely. A recent study warned that if chemicals are not used on farms, half of the crops in the world may die because of diseases or insects. This means that farmers may not be able to produce enough food on existing farmland, resulting in higher food prices and people going hungry. Furthermore, if farmers had to use a larger area of land to grow food, this could potentially have a detrimental effect on the environment.

[Body 2で書いていること]

- [トピックセンテンス] 薬剤の使用は完全に中止するべきではない
- [理由・詳細1] 研究結果の紹介：薬剤を使用しない場合、病気や虫のために半分の作物がだめになり、食物価格の上昇や飢餓につながる
- [理由・詳細2] 薬剤使用を中止すれば、今より広い農業用地が必要で、環境への悪影響が出る可能性がある

4 ▶ Conclusion を書く

Conclusion では、Bodyの内容を簡単に要約しつつ、Introductionで表明した自分の意見を再掲し、まとめとします。

Conclusion

In conclusion, although using chemicals in agriculture does come with some negatives, their use is necessary to sustain the level of food production required. Therefore, I only partially support the view of restricting the use of chemicals in farming. I believe some chemicals should be allowed as long as they are used cautiously, minimising their harm to the environment.

[Conclusionで書いていること]

- 農業における薬剤使用は負の要素もあるが、食料の十分な生産を維持するためには不可欠
- 薬剤の使用を制限することに部分的にしか賛成できない
- 環境への害を最小限に抑え、注意深く薬剤を使用することは許容されるべき
  - →Introductionでの意思表明の文をそのまま流用するのではなく、変化をつけよう。語彙力の幅と、構文力をアピールする機会なので、最後まで気を抜かないように！

Introductionでの意思表明

    I cannot fully agree with this view ...

Conclusion：意思表明の再掲

    I only partially support the view of ...

エッセイを書き終えたら、必ず見直しをしましょう。

- ☑ 課題を達成できているか
  （→Introduction に「説明文のパラフレーズ」と「意思表明」はあるか。各 Body は主旨を示し、論理的な主張ができているか。Conclusion で全体をまとめ、「意思表明の再掲」をしているか）
- ☑ 同じ単語を繰り返さず、幅広い語彙力を示せているか
- ☑ 段落構成はわかりやすいか
- ☑ 接続表現を使い、わかりやすく展開できているか
- ☑ 複文を織り交ぜ、正しい構文を使えているか
- ☑ スペルや文法のミスはないか（冠詞や三単現 s のつけ忘れに注意）
- ☑ 時制は適切か
- ☑ 体裁は整っているか（段落の区切りは1行空けるなど）
- ☑ 250 words 以上書けているか

サンプル問題 中級者と上級者のエッセイを比較しよう

中級者のエッセイ

[Introduction]

パラフレーズ Controlling pests on farms with chemical sprays increases the amount of food we can produce. However, some people think that we should stop using chemical sprays. They say they kill insects and affect the environment too much. 意思表明 I mostly disagree with this view.

[Body 1]

Firstly, it is true that chemicals can kill insects such as bees. Bees are important to the environment. トピック I think that we should be careful about the chemicals farmers can use. For example, we should use chemical sprays that do not last for a long time. This way, the chemicals will not poison the environment, especially water. Also, we should immediately stop using chemicals that can cause cancer.

[Body 2]

トピック However, we cannot stop using chemicals entirely. In university, I read a study that said if we do not use chemicals on farms, half of the crops in the world will die because of diseases or insects. This means that farmers will not make enough food, and therefore people will suffer from hunger. If we stop using chemicals, it may also increase the cost of food. So, farmers might have to grow food on a larger area of land, which could be bad for the environment.

[Conclusion]

Chemical sprays are necessary to produce enough food for the world. For the reasons I discussed, I do not agree that we should stop using chemical sprays. If we did, it could become a very bad situation for us. However, we should be very careful with chemicals. They must not cause too much harm to the environment.

(254 words)／※下線＝〈一貫性とまとまり〉のスコアに関わる接続表現

[Introduction]

パラフレーズ To provide sufficient food to the growing world population, chemical sprays play a key role in controlling pests. Nevertheless, there are those who think that we should refrain from using pesticides as they kill too many insects and adversely affect the natural environment. 意思表明 I cannot fully agree with this view because completely stopping the use of chemicals may lead to food shortages and have a very negative impact on the world.

[Body 1]

トピック The most important consideration should be to safeguard humans and the earth. Since chemicals can kill insects such as bees, which are generally important to the environment, farmers should be careful about which chemicals they use. For example, they should only use pesticides and herbicides that do not remain in the environment for a long time. This will prevent permanently poisoning the natural environment, including our precious water resources. In addition, certain chemical sprays that can be poisonous to humans, and even potentially cause cancer, should not be allowed.

[Body 2]

トピック Chemicals, however, cannot be eliminated entirely. A recent study warned that if chemicals are not used on farms, half of the crops in the world may die because of diseases or insects. This means that farmers may not be able to produce enough food on existing farmland, resulting in higher food prices and people going hungry. Furthermore, if farmers had to use a larger area of land to grow food, this could potentially have a detrimental effect on the environment.

[Conclusion]

In conclusion, although using chemicals in agriculture does come with some negatives, their use is necessary to sustain the level of food production required. Therefore, I only partially support the view of restricting the use of chemicals in farming. I believe some chemicals should be allowed as long as they are used cautiously, minimising their harm to the environment.

(299 words)／※下線＝〈一貫性とまとまり〉のスコアに関わる接続表現

〉〉〉 上級者エッセイの構成

Introduction ── 説明文のパラフレーズ＋意思表明（農薬噴霧液の禁止に完全には賛成できない）
Body 1 ── 最も配慮すべき点は、人々と地球の安全を守ること
Body 2 ── 薬剤の使用自体はやめるべきではない
Conclusion ── Bodyの要約＋意思表明の再掲

>>> 解 説

〈課題への回答〉このエッセイで書くべき [要求ポイント]
①自分の意見（賛成もしくは反対）の主張
[Introduction]
上級 全面的には賛成できない理由も簡潔に述べてBodyに上手くつなげている。

〈一貫性とまとまり〉
中級 howeverが3回繰り返されているなど、上級に比べて限定的。
中級 Body 1ではトピックセンテンスが段落の1文目にない。そういうライティング形式もあるが、テストにおいて試験官にわかりやすく提示するためには上級の構成の方がよい。

〈語彙力〉
「中級→上級」で語彙力に差がある。
stop → refrain from / be eliminated / restricting
water → precious water resources
bad → a detrimental effect

〈文法知識と正確さ〉
中級 関係代名詞などで複文を構成できている一方で、Bees are important to the environment. など単文も見られる。全体的に、上級より単純な文法を使っている。

Vocabulary

中級
- [ ] **control pest** 害虫を駆除する
- [ ] **chemical spray** 農薬噴霧液
- [ ] **chemical** [名] 薬剤
- [ ] **poison** [動] ～を汚染する
- [ ] **crop** [名] 作物
- [ ] **suffer from ～** ～に苦しむ

上級
- [ ] **play a key role in ～** ～で重要な役割を果たす
- [ ] **pesticide** [名] 駆除剤、殺虫剤
- [ ] **adversely** [副] 不利に、反対に
- [ ] **food shortage** 食糧難
- [ ] **safeguard** [動] ～を保護する
- [ ] **herbicide** [名] 除草剤
- [ ] **permanently** [副] 永久に
- [ ] **be poisonous to ～** ～に有害である
- [ ] **eliminate** [動] ～を削除する
- [ ] **detrimental effect** 悪影響
- [ ] **as long as S＋V** SVする限り
- [ ] **cautiously** [副] 慎重に
- [ ] **minimise** [動] ～を最小化する

Task 2 実践問題

対立する2つの見解を論じ、自分の意見を述べる問題

40 min.

You should spend about 40 minutes on this task.

Write about the following topic:

> *Some people believe that having fewer children is the best way to preserve the world's limited resources. Others believe that technology is the answer, and that population control is unnecessary.*
>
> *Discuss both views and give your own opinion.*

Give reasons for your answer and include any relevant examples from your own knowledge or experience.

Write at least 250 words.

指示文(Discuss both views and give your own opinion.)を読んで、エッセイの中で書くように要求されている課題の数と内容([要求ポイント])を把握しましょう。

実践 **2** ▶ **問題の原因、解決策を述べる問題**

40
min.

You should spend about 40 minutes on this task.

Write about the following topic:

> *Many young people are motivated and successful at high school. Many others, however, lack motivation and see high school as irrelevant to their interests and needs.*
>
> *Why is this? What could be done to help all students succeed?*

Give reasons for your answer and include any relevant examples from your own knowledge or experience.

Write at least 250 words.

問題文の指示の中に、2つの質問がある形式（Two-question essay）です。
この形式でも、基本的なアプローチは変わりません。
［要求ポイント］の数と内容を把握しましょう。

Writing

You should spend about 40 minutes on this task.

Write about the following topic:

> *Social media has become a very effective method of communication. At the same time, there is concern about its impact on the individual and society.*
>
> *Do the advantages of social media outweigh the disadvantages?*

Give reasons for your answer and include any relevant examples from your own knowledge or experience.

Write at least 250 words.

You should spend about 40 minutes on this task.

Write about the following topic:

> *Nowadays, people expect that automation in business will rapidly take over jobs from people.*
>
> *Why do people think this? Is this a positive or negative development?*

Give reasons for your answer and include any relevant examples from your own knowledge or experience.

Write at least 250 words.

高得点ホルダーの勉強法を公開！②

Y.Tさん　男性　25歳／オーバーオール：7.0
（リスニング：7.0、リーディング：6.5、ライティング：6.0、スピーキング：7.5）

リスニング

- YouTubeでTED Talksを聞いた
- 数か月の間、毎日、海外ドラマを英語字幕つきで見た
  →アクセントに苦手意識のある国がないのは、**普段からジャンルを問わずいろいろな内容のものを聞いていたからだ**と思う。

リーディング

- 英語のニュースで、興味のある記事を読んだ
- まずは問題タイプに慣れるため、**問題タイプごとの練習問題がある教材を解いた**

> English Innovationsに在籍しているほかの生徒さんの学習法も紹介しましょう。「間違えた問題を分析してノートにまとめる」「同じパッセージの問題を毎週解く」など、時間をかけて取り組んでいる方が多いようです。**IELTSのリーディングに太刀打ちできる読解力は、短期的に身につくものではないので、長い目で取り組んでいきましょう！**

ライティング

- 段落の基本構成を学んだうえで、同じ接続詞を繰り返し使わないようにして書く練習を積んだ
- 書く時間が取れない場合は「タスク1のグラフや図を見て分析する」「タスク2のテーマに対して意見や展開例を考える」など、時間がないなかでできることをした

スピーキング

- 問題集の模範回答を使って、シャドーイングをたくさんした
- 自然な抑揚やフレーズを身につけるために、**海外ドラマを見ながらセリフを真似して話した**

> 海外ドラマを見ながらセリフを言うのは、あまり勉強らしくないと思うかもしれませんが、実は効果的な方法です。**IELTSのスピーキングは、堅い面接ではなく、カフェでリラックスして話すような感覚**で臨んでください。この感覚を日本にいながら身につける効果的な方法が、海外ドラマなのです。

Speaking

About Speaking

スピーキングテストは試験官との一対一の面接形式で行われ、3つのパートで構成されています。試験時間の合計は11〜14分で、次の図の流れで進みます。
パート1とパート3は質疑応答形式で、パート2は2分間、1人で話し続けるテストです。パート2は「長い時間1人で話す力をアピールする機会」であり、本書ではロングターンと呼んでいます。

Introduction	本人確認	30秒

フルネームを聞かれ、本人確認のためにパスポートを提示する(テストのスコアには反映されない)。

Part 1	身近なトピック：会話形式	4.5〜5分

仕事、学業、趣味、家族など、身近なトピックに関する質問に答える。多くの場合、2つのトピックが出題される(1つのトピックにつき4つほどの質問がある)。

Part 2	2分間のロングターン	3〜4分

トピックとメモ用紙、筆記用具が渡される	トピックには身近なことに関する質問が印字されている。

1分間で準備をする	トピックを読み、話す内容をメモにまとめる。

2分間、話し切るつもりでロングターンを始める	2分を超えると試験官が中断するが、スコアに響かないので気にする必要はない。

1、2問、短い質問に答える	試験官がロングターンの内容に関する質問をするので、1文程度で簡潔に答える。

Part 3	一般的・社会的なトピック：ディスカッション	4〜5分

Part 2に関連した議題でディスカッションをする。Part 1, 2のように個人的で身近なことではなく、一般的な意見を展開する。多くの場合、2つのトピックが出題される(1つのトピックにつき4つほどの質問がある)。

評価基準

1〜9のバンドスコア（0.5刻み）で評価されます。評価基準は〈流暢さと一貫性〉〈語彙力〉〈文法力〉〈発音〉の4つで、それぞれ1〜9のスコアが与えられます。4つの平均値が、スピーキングテストのバンドスコアです。

基準	内容
流暢さ 一貫性	・不自然な間が空いたり、言いよどんだりせずに話せるか ・適切な接続詞やディスコース・マーカーを使い、理路整然と話せるか ・繰り返しや言い直しが多過ぎず、自然な速さで話せるか
語彙力	・幅広い語彙や熟語を正確に使用できるか
文法力	・正しい構文を使って話せるか ・複雑な構文も使いこなせるか ・文法上の間違いがないか
発音	・聞き取りやすく、明快な発音で話せるか ・自然なリズム、イントネーションで話せるか

では、この評価基準に沿って、6レベルを取るために必要なことを具体的に確認しましょう。

基準	必要なこと
流暢さ 一貫性	・時々繰り返し、言い直し、ためらいがあるため、一貫性に欠けることはあるが、積極的に話し続ける姿勢がある ・幅広い接続詞やディスコース・マーカーを使っているが、適切に使えないこともある
語彙力	・与えられたトピックについて詳しく話すために必要な幅広い語彙力があり、時折間違った使い方もするが、意味は通じる ・概ね正しくパラフレーズ（言い換え）ができる
文法力	・単文と複文の両方を使いこなせているが、柔軟性に欠ける ・複文では間違いが多いが、意味は通じる
発音	・幅広い発音の特性（イントネーション・強弱・リズムなど）を意識した話し方がある程度できているが、安定していない ・概ね理解するのに支障はないが、単語の発音を間違えることがある

このように、6レベルであれば、どの評価基準でも、ある程度の間違いや不安定さは許容されています。その上の7や8レベルでも、伝えたい意図がしっかり伝われば、時折うっかりミスをしても、スコアにさほど影響しません。大切なことは間違えることを恐れず、まずは積極的に話すことです！

実際にどのようにすれば評価基準を満たせるのかは、次ページ以降で詳しく説明していきます。

なお、ディスコース・マーカーは聞き慣れない言葉かもしれません。これは特にパート2で使いこなすことが必

須なので、パート2の中で解説して、具体的なフレーズも紹介します。

本書では、主に〈流暢さと一貫性〉〈語彙力〉〈文法力〉の3つを中心に解説しています。

〈発音〉に関しては、音声DLを聞き、適切なリズムやイントネーション（抑揚）をつかんでください。

最近では、パソコンへの吹き込み式でスピーキングテストを実施する試験が増えてきましたが、IELTSは試験官と受験者の1対1のリアルなコミュニケーションを通して、スピーキング力を測ります。

普段の会話では、相手の言っていることがわからなかったら聞き返したり、相手が答えに詰まっていたら、ちょっと待ってあげたりするはずです。IELTSのスピーキングテストでも同様で、受験者が質問を聞き返しても大丈夫ですし、試験官が受験者に考える時間を与えることもあります。普段の会話の感覚で、安心して臨んでくださいね。

Speaking 攻略ルール

1 ▶ 必要なのは「英語力＋内省」と「英語力＋見識」

パート1、2では身近なトピックが出題されます。特にパート2では「思い出に残っているイベント」「付き合いの長い親友について」などと、過去を詳しく説明させる質問もあるので、今だけでなく**過去の自分も深掘りしておく必要**があります。

一方で、**パート3ではベクトルを外へ**向けましょう。「労働問題」や「環境問題」、「幸福とは何か」など、抽象的、一般的、社会的なトピックが出題されるので、普段から時事情報に触れ、さまざまな問題に対する見識を深めておくように。とりわけパート3は英語力だけあっても太刀打ちできません。各トピックに関する知識はもちろん、**自身の意見を持ち、それを理路整然と説明する力**が求められるので、相応の準備が必要となります。なお、どのような意見を発言するか、内容自体は評価基準に含まれません。

2 ▶ 日本語訛りに悩まないで！ We hear your accent!

スピーキングテストとなると、ご自身のアクセント（訛り）を気にする方が多いようです。「Rの音を完璧に発音するべき」「ネイティブのような発音を習得するべき」...これは本当でしょうか。

We hear your accent.（我々はあなたのアクセントを聞けますよ）

これはIELTSのスピーキングテストにおける方針です。あなたの英語を判断するのはコンピューターではなく、試験官。さらに言うと、彼らは全員、英語を母国語としない人に英語を教えた経験があり、**非ネイティブのアクセントに慣れている**のです。

もちろん、カタカナ英語はもってのほかですが、アクセントを気にし過ぎる必要はありません。単語を極力正しく発音する努力をするとともに、**英語特有のリズムやイントネーション（抑揚）、強弱の習得に注力する**とよいでしょう。

3 ▶ ネイティブスピードを目指す必要はない

話すスピードは速過ぎても遅過ぎてもいけません。「ネイティブのように話さなきゃ」と思いがちですが、テストの目的はネイティブ並みの速さで話すことではありません。本書の音声DLでは、スピーキングのみ日本人の音声を収録しています。音声を聞いて音読もすることで、適切な感覚をつかんでください。実際に**ストップ**

Speaking

ウォッチを使って、**本書の回答例や自分の回答を読み上げる**のもいいでしょう（ただし回答例の丸暗記はNG!）。特にパート2では「2分」の感覚を体に染み込ませるためにも有益です。

4 ▶ ボキャブラリー・マインドマップで語彙を増やそう

　本書では、パートごとに頻出のトピックを紹介しています（パート1：p.156／パート2：p.167／パート3：p.176）。それらをもとにマインドマップを作れば語彙力が上がるのはもちろん、回答を作成する際の助けになります。次のTravelの例をまねて、自身のオリジナルを作り、語彙のストックを増やしましょう！

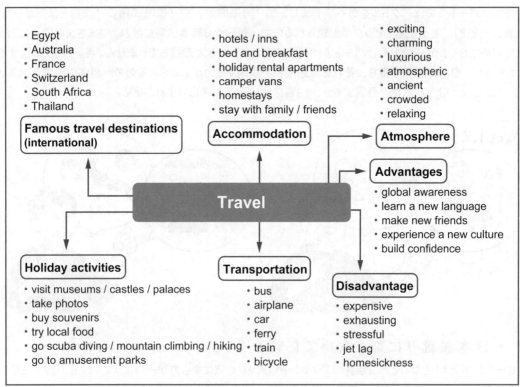

5 ▶ 曖昧なまま答えないで！ 質問してOK

　先に述べた通り、スピーキングテストでは試験官が対面で評価します。これはあなたが最大限の力を出すサポートをするためでもあります。単語や質問の意味がわからないときは、堂々と質問してください。曖昧なまま答えるよりも、**聞き直したうえで回答する方が、いい印象を与える**でしょう。全体を通じて数回聞き直すことでスコアダウンすることはありませんので、安心してください。

　パート1では、聞けば同じ質問を繰り返してもらえます。パート3では、質問をわかりやすい言葉で言い換えてくれます（パート2では質問が印字されたトピックが配られる）。ただし、質問の内容自体は変更できません。

質問するときのフレーズ例

　　　Sorry, I didn't catch that. Could you repeat it, please?
　　　（申し訳ないです、聞き取れませんでした。繰り返していただけますか）

　　　Sorry, could you say that again? （申し訳ないです、もう一度言っていただけますか）

Sorry, I didn't understand the question. Could you rephrase it, please?
（申し訳ないです、質問を理解できませんでした。言い換えていただけませんか）

6 ▸ 語 句 や 構 文 の 過 度 な 「 繰 り 返 し 」 は 避 け よ う

同じ単語や構文を繰り返し過ぎないように、同義語に言い換えていきましょう。

E ＝ Examiner（試験官）　　C ＝ Candidate（受験者）

E　Do you prefer to go shopping **alone** or with friends?

C　I prefer to go shopping **by myself** because I shop quickly and don't like window shopping .

　この場合、試験官が言ったaloneをby myselfに言い換えています。自然な会話の中で**多少の繰り返しは起こりますが、これが多過ぎると単調な印象になる**ので注意しましょう。言い換えることで語彙力の幅も示せます。

7 ▸ f i l l e r w o r d s （ 間 を 埋 め る 語 句 ） で 沈 黙 知 ら ず

　英語を話していて、言おうとしている単語が出てこなかったり、構文を組み立てるのに時間がかかったりして、不自然な間が空いて焦った経験はありませんか。

　そのとき、5秒、10秒と沈黙が続くと〈流暢さと一貫性〉の評価に響くので、こういうときは、間を埋める「とっさの一言」で切り抜けましょう。filler wordsをうまく使えば自然な英語になります。ただし、eh / uh / em / er / you knowといったfiller wordsは意味を持たないので、なるべく避けてください。

よいfiller wordsの例

　　Let me see. / Let's see. / Well … / Let me think.　（えっと、そうですね）

　　I'm not sure if this is the right way to put it, but …　（この言い方で合っているか自信がありませんが…）

　　That's a difficult[an interesting]question.　（それは難しい［興味深い］質問ですね）

　　Honestly, I've never thought about that.　（正直なところ、それについて考えたことが一度もありませんでした）

　なお、**沈黙がネガティブな印象を与えるのは、留学先や国際的なビジネスの場でも同じです。**英語圏では、考えがまとまらなくても話し始め、活発な議論を交わすのがスタンダード。話しながら考え、「沈黙を作らない癖」をつけましょう。

8 ▶「アカデミック英語」より、カフェで友だちと話す感覚で

　スピーキングでは、アカデミック・モジュールとジェネラル・トレーニング・モジュールで共通の問題が出題されます。これはどういうことかと言うと、IELTSとしては、あなたに**大学の講義のようなアカデミック英語ではなく、日常的で自然な英語を話してもらい、その中で評価したい**のです。ここで言う「日常的で自然」とは、BBCのキャスターが話す英語ではありません。下の例文を参考に、普段カフェで友だちと過ごすときの会話をイメージしてください。

アカデミック英語

　According to recent research by the Japanese government, the fitness level of today's youth is declining. （日本政府による最近の研究によると、今日の若者の健康状態は低下しています）

日常的で自然な英語

　Many people say young people in Japan nowadays are less fit than before.
（多くの人々が最近の日本の若者は、昔より健康的ではないと言っています）

　時々「IELTSのスピーキングテストでは、アカデミック英語で話して！」というアドバイスを耳にすることがあります。確かに、スコア8〜9レベルを目指すのであれば、適切な箇所でアカデミック英語も織り交ぜながら話す能力が求められます。しかし、7レベルを目指す段階でアカデミック英語を意識し過ぎると、次のような失敗を招きがちです。

- 日常的な語彙の中に変にアカデミック英語が混ざり、ちぐはぐで不自然な印象になる
- アカデミックな語彙をアウトプットしようと考えて間が空く結果、流暢ではなくなる

　では、ここで「カフェで友だちと話すときの日常的で自然な英語」とは何か、深掘りしていきましょう。

- 罵り言葉は使わない。敬語を多用する必要はないが、丁寧に話す
- スラングは使ってよい。ただし、全世代に浸透しているものがよく、失礼な言い回しや、差別表現はNG。判断が難しいものは避ける

　特に**日本人は、試験官や先生、上司に敬語で話すのが習慣になっており、英語で話すときも過剰にフォーマル**になりがちです。英語圏の国ではどうでしょうか。**彼らは、目上の相手でもフラットにカジュアルに話すことが多く、それが彼らの文化**です。普段から海外ドラマや映画で、学生と教授、職場での会話に触れておくのも「日常的で自然な英語」をイメージするのに有効です。

9 ▶ 暗記力より瞬発力を磨こう

特にパート1では、仕事や学業など、ある程度質問が予想できるので、想定問答集を作る受験者が多いはず。これは対策としては一定の効果がありますが、暗記回答を忠実に再現するのにこだわり、変な間が空いたり、質問から脱線した内容を答えていては、元も子もありません。

試験官はプロなので暗記して話しているとすぐに気づきます。**暗記文をロボットのように話しても、スコアUPにつながらず、むしろスコアが下がる**ことも。彼らが求めているのは杓子定規の回答ではなく自然な英語です。

彼らは、さまざまな角度から、時には想定外の質問も投げかけますが、これは受験者の知識の深さを評価するためではありません（知識があれば話を展開しやすくはなるが、評価対象ではない）。彼らは、**突発的な質問に英語でどれだけ対応できるかを測りたい**のです。これはパート3で顕著ですが、パート1でもWhy?やWhy not?と聞き返されることがよくあり、瞬発力が試されていると言えます。

10 ▶ 適切な時制を使おう

試験官の質問をよく聞き、適切な時制で答えましょう。過去のことを語るときは過去形で、未来の質問がきたら仮定のifや未来形で答えます。これは簡単そうですが、意外とミスをする受験者が多く、差がつくポイントです。

現在形	What **do** you study?
	- I'm **studying** science at university. / I **study** science at university.
過去形	What **did** you study?
	- I **studied** science when I was at university.
未来形	What **will** you study?
	- I'm **planning** to study science in the future.
現在完了形	**Have** you ever **been** abroad?
	- Yes, I **have been** to Australia on a study tour.

11 ▶ 文法スコアUPの秘訣は、複文の運用力とバラエティ!

単文だけではなく、複雑な構文を使いこなせると高評価につながります。単文とは、〈主語＋動詞〉が1組のみのシンプルな文です。対して複文は、従属節と主節から成り、どちらの節にも〈主語＋動詞〉があります。

複文の例

> **While** there are lots of negatives, there are also some positive points.
> （多くの否定的な側面がある一方で、肯定的な点もいくらかあります）

次に、評価基準の〈文法力〉の中で「複文の運用と正確性」をどれくらい達成すればいいのか、スコア別に目安を示しました。ポイントは、**ミスゼロを目指す必要はない**点。6〜7レベルを目指すのであれば、多少の間違いは許容で、むしろ複文で話すことに気をとられ過ぎて流暢さが失われるとマイナスです。複文を取り入れながら、自分の意見を明確に、テンポよく伝えられたら、6〜7は十分目指せるので一緒に頑張りましょう。

スコア	複文の運用と正確性
7	ある程度の柔軟性を持って、幅広く複文を運用できているが、まだ間違いはある
6	単文と複文の両方を運用できているが、複文は間違いが多い
5	単文が中心で、複文の運用は限定的

　また、仮定法、関係代名詞などは構造が複雑なので、いざ正確にアウトプットしようとすると難しいものです。口をついて出てくるように練習を積みましょう。

-if（条件）
　パート3では、一般的な問題について問われたり、その解決策について問われたりします。その際に、If節で条件を表す文が役立ちます。

If the government does not increase restrictions, many more people will suffer as a result.
（政府が規制を増やさないと、結果的にさらに多くの人々が苦しむでしょう）

-if（仮定法）
　この文は仮定法過去を使っています（仮定法の解説はp.185を参照）。

If I **had** the choice, **I'd** prefer to live in the countryside as I generally prefer a slower pace of life.
（選べるならば、全体的にゆっくりした暮らしが好きなので、好んで田舎に住むでしょう）

- 関係代名詞

People **who** eat healthy food and exercise tend to live longer.（主格）
（健康的な食生活を送り、運動をする人々は、長生きする傾向があります）

The thing **that** I especially like is the activity and energy in the little streets in the old quarter.（目的格）
（私が特に好きなことは、旧市街の小さな通りに満ちた活気です）

- 現在完了形

Sadly, I **haven't had** the opportunity to revisit Hanoi for some time, but I hope to do it next year.
（残念ながら、しばらくハノイを再訪する機会がなかったのですが、願わくば来年再訪したいです）

- 助動詞

　助動詞は、特にパート3で一般的な事柄について意見を述べるときに有効です。以下に、例として助動詞を使った文を作る際の組み立て方をまとめました。

主語	助動詞	動詞（＋目的語など）	目的を表す副詞句
• The government 　（政府） • Parents 　（親） • Teachers 　（教師たち） • Local 　authorities 　（地方公共団体）	• must 　（〜しなければならない） • have to 　（〜しなければならない） • should 　（〜すべきだ） • could 　（〜しうる） • may be able to 　（〜できるかもしれない）	• take action 　（策を講じる） • take measures 　（策を講じる） • find ways 　（方法を見つける）	• to reduce the problem 　（問題を減らすために） • to solve the issue 　（問題を解決するために） • to improve the situation 　（状況を改善するために） • to reduce this worrying trend 　（この憂慮すべき傾向を減らすために）

上記の要素を組み合わせると、いろいろな文が作れます。

　The government should take action to improve the situation, so all students can enjoy their studies at high school more.

　（政府は、全高校生が学習をもっと楽しめるように、その状況を改善するために策を講じるべきです）

　以上が、スピーキングテストのパート1〜3に共通する「攻略ルール」です。
　1対1の対面形式となると、どうしても緊張しがちですが、肩の力を抜いて、友だちに意見や経験を聞いてもらうつもりで臨みましょう。試験官は、あなたがスピーキング力を発揮するのを助けてくれるサポーターです。**緊張をほぐして、マインドセットをするのが攻略のカギ**ですよ。

Part 1 対策

　パート1では、仕事・学業、家族、出身地など、身近な話題について質問されます。パート1全体で2つのトピックが出題されることが多く、1つのトピックにつき質問は4問ほどです。ただし、受け答えの長さや会話の展開によっては、3つ目のトピックが提示されることもあります。

　パート1の本題に入る前に、イントロダクションとして、最初にフルネームを聞かれ、その後に本人確認のためにパスポートの提示が求められます。ほんの数十秒しかないやり取りですが、ここで聞き取りやすい明確な発音で話し、よいスタートを切りましょう。

イントロダクションの例

E＝Examiner（試験官）　C＝Candidate（受験者）

E　Good afternoon. My name is Ruby Brown. Can you tell me your full name, please?
C　I'm Mika Suzuki.
E　Can I see your identification, please?
C　Here you are.
E　Thank you. Now, in this first part, I'm going to ask you some questions about yourself.

E　こんにちは。ルヴィ・ブラウンと申します。フルネームをお聞きしてもよいですか。
C　鈴木美香と申します。
E　身分証明書を拝見できますか。
C　こちらです。
E　ありがとう。では最初のパートでは、いくつかあなたについてご質問をします。

頻出トピック

　パート1の中で最も頻出で必ず押さえるべきトピックは、普段していること（**Job・Study**）と、住まいに関して（**House・Apartment / City**）です。

　これら以外では、Fashion / Shopping / Travelling / Food / Music / Books / Family / Friends / Hobbies / Sports / Future plans / Weatherなどもよく出題されます。

Part 1 攻略ルール

1 ▸ 長々と話す必要はない。リラックスして臨もう

　パート1では長く話す必要はありません。**1つの質問に対して、1〜3文ほどで答えられたら十分**です。パート1は最も易しいパートと言われています。よいスタートダッシュを切って次のパートにつなげられるように、試験官とのやり取りを楽しむ感覚で臨みましょう！

2 ▸ Yes / Noの後に、理由・例・経験などを必ず追加する

　質問をされたらYes / Noで終わらせないように。その後に、理由・例・経験などの詳細情報を加えてください。自分の意見を加えるのも手です。もし回答が短い場合は、試験官がWhy?など話を膨らませるための質問を追加しますが、その前に詳細情報を続けられるのがベストです。

追加するフレーズの例

理由を述べる

> It's because S＋V.　（それはSVだからです）
> The reason for this is ...　（この理由は...です）
> because of 〜　（〜のために）

例を挙げる

> For example[instance],　（例えば）
> such as 〜　（〜のような）

経験を話す

> Once　（かつて）
> I remember when S＋V.　（SVしたときを思い出します）
> I don't remember exactly when, but ...　（正確にいつかは思い出せませんが...）
> Just the other day　（つい先日）
> Not so long ago　（この間、少し前）
> In my childhood,　（子どもの頃に）
> When I was very young,　（とても若いときに）
> I used to 〜.　（以前はよく〜していました）

意見を表明する

> I think S＋V. / I believe S＋V. / I guess S＋V. / I suppose S＋V.　（私はSVだと思います）

　考えを表すときの最も一般的な語はthink。believeはthinkに比べて話者の確信が高い。guess, supposeはともに確信は低めで、「〜かなと思う」という推測のニュアンスが出てくるが、guessの方が口語的。

Speaking

3 ▶ Yes / Noのバリエーションを持つ

　実際のやり取りでは、試験官からのすべての質問に白黒はっきりYes / Noで答えられるわけではありません。全肯定することもあれば、「まぁ、部分的にそうですね」と軽く肯定する場合もあるでしょう。受け答えにバリエーションがあれば語彙力をアピールできます。

　次のリストでは、Certainly. / Definitely. / Yes.は全肯定で、下に行くほど肯定の度合いが下がります。

Certainly. （もちろん）/ Definitely. （絶対に）/ Yes. （はい）

Without a doubt, yes. / Of course, yes. （〔両者ともに〕もちろん、そう）

By and large, yes. / For the most part, yes. （〔両者ともに〕大体は、そう）

That's partly true. （部分的に、そう）

Yes and No. （何とも言えない）

At times, yes. / On occasion, yes （時折、そう）

I'm not so sure about that. / I'm not so certain if that's correct.

（〔両者ともに〕あまり確信がない）

That's rarely true. （めったに当てはまらない）/ Not likely. （まずそうはならない）

Not precisely. / Not really. （〔両者ともに〕そうではない、あまり）

Not at all. （絶対に違う）/ Absolutely not. （絶対に違う）/ No. （いいえ）

以上が、パート1の攻略ルールです。このパートは、長く話すことが目的ではないので、気負わず臨みましょう。その上で、答えの後に、理由・例・経験を加える癖をつけられたら高得点が見えてきます!

最頻出トピックの回答例

▶ **Job**

TRACK

16

What is the best thing about your job?

My co-workers are very friendly, and my workplace is clean and ₁well-organised. Also, I think my salary is a bit better compared to my previous jobs.

Is there anything you'd like to change in your workplace?

₂Hmmm, let me think ... Oh yes, our company's computers.

Why?

Well, they are very slow. In order to work more efficiently, we need better computers. ₃The same goes for the Wi-Fi. So, we often have technical issues.

Do you think you will be doing the same job for a long time?

Yes, because it's my dream job. Also, I have a good relationship with my co-workers and my company is generally a good place to work.

>>> 解説

1 ——— well-organisedは「よく整理された」。仕事のトピックは頻出なので、同僚や職場を表す形容詞を覚えておこう。同僚なら、friendly（友好的な）、sociable（社交的な）、hardworking（勤勉な）、supportive（協力的な）、down-to-earth（地に足がついた）、職場ならclean（きれいな）、old（古い）、spacious（広々とした）、accessible（行きやすい）、convenient（便利な）、organised（整理された）など。

2 ——— すぐに質問に答えられないときは、間を埋めるfiller wordsで切り抜けよう。

3 ——— Also, our Wi-Fi is very slow. と言っても通じるが、回答例だとslowの繰り返しを避けられる。**繰り返しが多過ぎると単調になるので注意**しよう。

Speaking

159

▶ Study

What is the best thing about the subjects you study?

₁One subject that I especially like is History. I'm currently studying it at university. The great thing about history is that I can learn about past events and other cultures at the same time.

Is there anything you'd like to change about your university?

Yes, the buildings are very old and so is the heating system. In the winter, it is too cold to study comfortably ₂on campus. I think the management should really try to improve this.

Do you think you will be studying the same subject for a long time?

₃Yes.

₃Why?

That's because I want to keep on researching and studying history for many years, and maybe become a history teacher at my university or abroad.

>>> 解説

1 ———— シンプルな答えだが、目的格の関係代名詞を使っており、文法力を示せている。

2 ———— on campusをin the buildingsとしても通じるが、前の文でbuildingsを使っているので、繰り返しを避けて同義語に言い換えた方が語彙力のアピールにもなる。

3 ———— 質問のDo you think you will ...?の後にWhy?と聞かれているわけではないが、**常に「なぜなのか」、詳細まで答える心意気で臨もう**。この場合Yes.とだけ答えたので、試験官は詳細を聞き出そうとWhy?と追加で聞いている。

▶ House・Apartment / City

TRACK 18

Would you say your area is a good place to live?

Yes, I think so. Since I am a student, it's great because it's so conveniently located. ₁However, families would probably not think so.

Why not?

Because it's noisy and doesn't have enough parks for children. If I had kids myself, I would choose to live somewhere else.

₂Do you live in a house or an apartment?

I live in an apartment. ₃I have been living in this apartment for five years. It is very comfortable and sunny, and the neighbours are also nice.

Do you think the area where you live has changed ₄very much recently?

Yes, ₃it has changed ₄a lot in the last few years. There is more public transportation available and shops as well. I feel it has become more convenient.

>>> 解説

1 ── 自分のことだけで話がもたないとき、立場が違う人の考えを推測して述べてもいい。〈S＋would probably ...〉で「おそらく ...だろう」。

2 ── この質問は、住まいや街に関する質問の中でも特に頻出。

3 ── 現在完了形で聞かれていないが、「5年間住んでいる状態が続いている」ことを表したいので、現在完了進行形で答える。liveのような状態動詞も、現在も続いていることを強調したいときには進行形にできる。続く質問は、質問の時制に合わせてit has changedで答えている。

4 ── very muchをa lotに言い換えている。試験官の言葉を繰り返しても問題ないが、このように細かい点でも語彙力の幅をアピールしよう。

Speaking

161

▶ Fashion

E = Examiner（試験官）　　C = Candidate（受験者）

E ₁Would you say you are interested in fashion?

C Actually, ₂not much. Of course, I choose clothes to wear every morning before going out, to look nice and neat. However, I'm not interested in reading about fashion in magazines or the internet.

E What was your favourite piece of clothing when you were a child?

C ₃Hmmm... It was such a long time ago, but I am sure it was my baseball jacket. The reason why it was my favourite was because I ₄used to play baseball a lot and it had a logo of the team I loved.

E Do you like wearing very colourful clothes?

C No, not really. Personally, I like to wear basic colours, especially black and white.

E Why?

C I think they are easy to match to any colour. I feel uncomfortable when I see myself in bright colours in the mirror.

E Are the colours you wear now different from what you used to wear when you were younger?

C When I was younger, I ₄used to wear more colourful clothes because my mother would dress me and she wasn't very fashionable!

⟩⟩⟩ 解説

1 ——— 〈Would you say (that) S＋V?〉は、意見を聞く表現。ここでは「ファッションに興味はありますか」。

2 ——— No. だと興味ゼロだが、not much だと 20〜30 パーセント。Yes / No 以外の答え方を身につけよう。

3 ——— 過去のことを聞かれても急に答えられないが、沈黙は避けたい。間をうまく埋めている。

4 ——— **過去の習慣的動作を表す used to 〜（よく〜したものだった）は、「現在ではそうではない」というニュアンスを含む**。特にパート 1、2 で過去のことを話すときに重宝する。

▶ Shopping

E Who does most of the shopping for your family?

C ₁Usually, my mother, because she stays at home and my father is too busy on weekdays. My sister and I also ₁sometimes help with the shopping, but ₁not often.

E ₂Is shopping online popular in your country?

C Yes, for sure it has become very common recently. Especially, in the last five years as more people have smartphones and the delivery service is quick, even in the countryside.

E   Do you prefer to go shopping alone or with friends?

C   I prefer to go shopping by myself because I shop quickly and don't like window shopping. Even my friends and family say that they don't like going shopping with me.

>>> 解 説

1 ────usually, sometimes, not oftenで頻度の違いを表現している。頻度を表す副詞には、頻度が高い →低い順に、always, usually, frequently, often, sometimes, occasionally, seldom, rarely, neverなどがある。

2 ────パート1では身近な質問が多いが、これはin your countryなので一般論を聞かれている。頻度は 少ないが、こういう場合もある。

▸ Travelling

E   How often do you use trains?

C   I use trains three to five times a week to go to work. It depends on how many times I need to go to the office. I would like to use them less frequently if I could.

E   Is there anything you don't like about public transport in your city?

C   Yes, a few things. ₁First, it's too crowded during rush hours. ₁Second, it's confusing as there are so many different types of services: local, semi-rapid, rapid, ₂and so on. I think it can be quite stressful, particularly if you are in a big city like Tokyo.

E   Do you prefer to travel alone or with friends?

C   ₃I like to travel alone rather than travelling with friends. My hobby is taking photos, and I am not very interested in food and social activities.

>>> 解 説

1 ────理由が複数あるときはFirst, ... Second, ...と順序立てると簡潔。Firstly, ... Secondly, ...でも可。

2 ────「など」を表す、少しフォーマルな表現だが使っても問題ない。

3 ────Do you prefer to ～?と聞かれているので、I prefer to travel alone.と答えてもよい。

▸ Food

E   Do you like to eat sweet things?

C   Yes, I do, especially, baked goods like chocolate cake or cookies. However, I cannot eat a lot. I don't know why, but I feel dizzy afterwards.

E   What was your favourite food ₁when you were a child?

C   My favourite food was sushi. It's a traditional Japanese dish made with raw fresh fish and rice. ₁In fact, it is still my favourite food. Generally, I like eating fish more than meat.

E ₂Why do you think people like eating at restaurants?

C ₂I think people like to go to restaurants instead of eating at home because if the family is not big, it's convenient and might be cheaper than eating at home. It's also interesting to try ₃new kinds of dishes that may be difficult to cook, and we can also get some cooking inspiration ₄while eating out.

>>> 解説

1————子どもの頃の話や好みを聞く問題は頻出。最初はもちろん過去形で答えているが、過去の話だけだと続かない場合、In fact, ...のように現在の話につなげるのも手。

2————パート1にしては珍しく、主語がpeopleで一般論を聞いている問題。I think people ...と一般論で答えている。

3————「調理が難しいかもしれない新しい料理」。主格の関係代名詞で、that ... cookの部分がnew kinds of dishesを修飾している。

4————このwhileは「〜の一方で」ではなく、「〜している間」という意味。**whenが特定の一時点を表すのに対して、whileは長さを持った期間**を表す。もともとは、while we are eating outだが、we areが省略されている。主節と主語が同じ（＝we）で、while節の動詞がbe動詞の場合、このような省略がよく起こる。

▶ Music

E What sort of music do you like to listen to?

C Instrumental music, ₁especially guitar or piano solos. I usually get tired of listening to vocals and I don't like pop or rock music either, so instrumental music is perfect for me.

E Is there any type of music that you don't really like?

C ₂I really haven't liked pop idols' music since when I was younger.

E Why not?

C ₃I honestly don't know the reason, but ₂I have never liked any of their songs.

E Is the music you like also popular with the rest of your family?

C We have totally different preferences. They listen mostly to recently trending songs on TV, but I am not interested in TV and recent music.

>>> 解説

1————Instrumental music（器楽曲）だけだと漠然とするので、especially以下で詳細を述べている。

2————質問は現在形だが、アイドルの音楽を好まないのは若い頃から続いている感情なので、現在完了形の継続用法で答えている。続くI have never likedも同様で、過去の一時点から現在までの継続を表す。

3————パート1ではYes / Noの後に理由や例を述べるべきだが、ときに明確な理由がないこともあるはず。

▶ 練習問題

パート1のまとめとして、2つのトピックに関して試験官が質問します。音声DLを聞いて、実際に声に出して答えてみましょう。

なお、**実際の試験では、質問が印字されたメモは配られないので注意してください。**

Where you live

• Is there anything special about the town or city where you live now? [Why? / Why not?]

• Do you have many friends who live nearby? [Why? / Why not?]

• Does your city have many places for people to exercise? [Why? / Why not?]

Being bored

• What things do you find boring? [Why?]

• When was the last time you felt very bored? [Why?]

• What do you do to prevent boredom? [Why?]

• Do you think that people are more bored nowadays than in the past? [Why? / Why not?]

パート1では、まずは、日常に関する簡単な質問から始まりますが、次に「なぜ?」と理由を問う質問で深掘りされ、難易度が上がっていくことが多いです。

例えば「どんな服を着るのが好きですか」という質問には「Tシャツとジーンズを着るのが好きです」などと、答えやすいですよね。しかし、そこから「なぜ好きなのですか」と聞かれたら、言葉に詰まってしまうかもしれません。

IELTSを受験する皆さんは、日頃から「なぜ?」と自問する習慣をつけるといいでしょう!

Speaking

165

Part 2 対策

　パート2では、与えられたトピックの指示に従って2分間話し続けるロングターンを行います。初めにパート2の流れを確認しておきましょう。

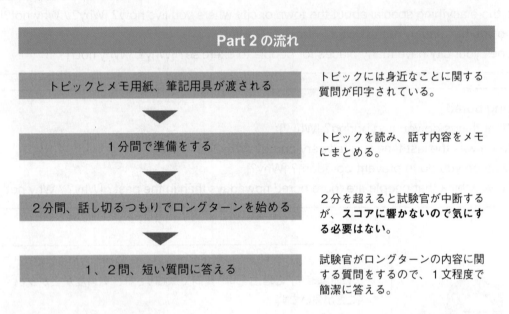

Part 2 の流れ	
トピックとメモ用紙、筆記用具が渡される	トピックには身近なことに関する質問が印字されている。
1分間で準備をする	トピックを読み、話す内容をメモにまとめる。
2分間、話し切るつもりでロングターンを始める	2分を超えると試験官が中断するが、**スコアに響かないので気にする必要はない。**
1、2問、短い質問に答える	試験官がロングターンの内容に関する質問をするので、1文程度で簡潔に答える。

　準備時間が終わると、試験官がCan you start speaking now, please?と、ロングターン開始の合図を出してくれます。

トピックの例

> **Describe a happy event that you have attended and which you remember well.**
> 　　　**You should say:**
> 　　　　　**when the event was**
> 　　　　　**where it was**
> 　　　　　**who was there**
> **and explain why you remember it well.**

（よく記憶している幸せなイベントについて説明しなさい。いつのイベントだったか、どこで行われたか、そこに誰がいたかを話すこと。そしてなぜよく記憶しているのかを説明しなさい）

頻出トピック

パート2でも日常に関わるトピックが出題されます。以下に、代表的なものをまとめました。こうした頻出トピックに関しては、普段から考えをまとめておき、語彙を増やしておきましょう。

質問内容が子どもの頃のことまで遡ることもあります。現在のことだけではなく、**過去の思い出や趣味、好きだったことや人間関係なども整理しておく**とよいでしょう。

カテゴリー	トピック例
人	Best friend / Neighbour / Older people / Teacher / Famous person
場所	Popular place / Room / Workplace / Restaurant / Park / Garden / Café / Building
イベント	Sports event / Festival / Birthday
生活	Meal / Food / Shopping / Housework / Clothes
旅行・移動	City / Town / Country / Foreign travel / Transport
メディア	Book / TV / Social media / Newspaper / Film・Movie / News / Website
余暇・娯楽	Holiday / Sport / Weekend / Music
そのほか	Animal / Pet / Problem / Pollution / Gift

実際には、次のように質問されます。

Best friend → Describe a best friend you have known the longest.
（一番付き合いの長い親友について説明してください）

Popular place → Describe a popular place in your city.
（あなたの街で人気のある場所について説明してください）

Meal → Describe a meal that is famous in your country.
（あなたの国で有名な食事について説明してください）

Country → Describe a country you would like to visit.
（行ってみたい国について説明してください）

Movie → Describe a movie you have recently watched.
（最近見た映画について説明してください）

Part 2 攻略ルール

1 ▶ パート2は、お堅いスピーチやプレゼンテーションではない！

　パート2をかしこまったスピーチ、プレゼンテーションと捉えてしまうと、「堅い単語で話した方がいいの？」「最後はコンクルージョンでまとめるべき？」などと構えてしまいがちです。

　しかし実際のところ、先に述べた通り、**スピーキングテストでは日常的な英語を使っていいのです**。プレゼンテーションで言うコンクルージョンにあたる**「まとめ」も必要なわけではありません**（「まとめ」を話してもいいが、時間切れになって話せなくても気にしなくていい）。

　こういうわけで、本書ではパート2を**ロングターン**（試験官に長い時間1人で話す力をアピールする機会のこと）と呼んでいるのです。パート1と同じように、試験官にあなたの身近な話を楽しんで聞いてもらう感覚で、肩の力を抜いて臨みましょう！

2 ▶ 適切なスピードで、2分間駆け抜けよう！

　パート2では2分間話し切るのがベストです。2分になると試験官が話を止めます。たとえ話にまとまりがなく終わってしまっても、そのことがスコアに影響することはないので心配ありません。むしろ2分も話せた自分を褒めてあげてください。重要なのは、**試験官が評価する参考材料となる英語をたくさん話すこと**です。

　ロングターンでは受験者だけが話し続けるので、緊張して早口になりがちです。そうすると話すつもりだったことを1分以内に出し切って、時間が余って困ることになりかねません。もし話が1分に届かなかった場合、試験官はあなたが再開するのを待ち続けるか、もしくは、ほかに話すことがあるか聞くはずです（そのときの返事は必ずYes.）。いずれの場合も、試験官はあなたが与えられた時間の中で、幅広い語彙や文法を使えているか、詳細な話を展開できる能力があるか判断したいのです。動揺せずに次のように話を再開しましょう。

> Oh, I still have more time left! Well, to describe it in more detail, the size is quite large and...
> （まだ時間がありましたね！　もっと詳細を説明すると、サイズはとても大きく...）

3 ▸ 詰まったときは、打開するフレーズで乗り切ろう

パート2を苦手とする受験者から「どうしても途中でネタが尽きてしまいます」「混乱して言葉が出てこなくなるんです」といった話を聞くことがあります。ここでは、回答に詰まった場合に、特にパート2で使える語句を紹介しましょう。

> What else can I say about that? Oh, yes ...
> （それについてほかに言えることは何でしょうか。あっ、そういえば…）
> Well, another thing that I can remember is ...　（えっと、覚えているほかのことは…です）
> That reminds me about another time (that) I ...　（それでほかに私が…したときのことを思い出しました）

4 ▸ ディスコース・マーカーで伝わりやすいロングターンに

ディスコース・マーカーという言葉をご存知ですか。これは簡単に言うと、論理的な展開にするために、文と文、語句と語句を適切な形でつなぐ役割を果たすものです。ほかに、話し手がこれから話す内容を事前に示すサインとして機能するものもあります。全パートで使えますが、ほかのパートよりも1人で話し続けるパート2では特に重宝します。

> The food I ate last night probably gave me food poisoning, **so**, **unfortunately**, I've been up all night.
> （昨晩食べたもののせいでたぶん食あたりになりました、だから残念なことに一晩中寝ていないのです）

so＝結果を表すディスコース・マーカー

The food ... food poisoning で「食あたりを起こした**原因**」を述べ、soを入れて「一晩中寝られなかった**結果**」につなげている。

unfortunately＝意見・感情を表すディスコース・マーカー

話し手にとって寝られなかったことはネガティブな事実だが、I've been up ...と言う前にunfortunatelyを挿入することで、聞き手としては、これから残念な話が続くと予想できる。

代表的なディスコース・マーカー
順序立てる

> First, / First of all, / To begin with,　（はじめに）
> Then ...　（次に）/ The next point is ...　（次の点は…）
> Firstly, ... Secondly, ... Thirdly, ...　（最初に…2番目に…3番目に…）
> Subsequently,　（続いて）
> Finally,　（最後に）

情報を追加する

> Another thing that comes to mind is ....　（ほかに頭に浮かんだのは…です）
> also　（また）　　　besides / Additionally,　（その上）

文修飾などで意見・感情を表現する

      Unfortunately,　（残念なことに）　　　　　　Sadly,　（残念ながら）

      I'm afraid (that) S＋V.　（残念ながらSVです）　Actually, / In fact,　（実際には）

      To be honest,　（正直に言うと）　　　　　　If you ask me,　（私の考えでは）

      Basically,　（基本的に）　　　　　　　　　Clearly,　（明らかに）

      Thankfully,　（ありがたいことに）　　　　Seriously,　（真面目な話）

同列に並べる

      Similarly,　（同様に）　　　　　　In the same way,　（同じ方法で）

      Likewise,　（さらにまた、同様に）

逆接を表す・譲歩する

      however　（しかしながら）　　　　although[though] S＋V　（SVだけれども）

      despite 〜　（〜にもかかわらず）

結果を示す

      so ...　（だから、結果...）　　then ...　（それから、それで...）

      as a result of this　（この結果）

ロングターン 完成までの4つのSTEP（サンプル問題）

　では、サンプル問題を解いていき、実際にどのようにメモを取って回答につなげればよいか、解説していきましょう。

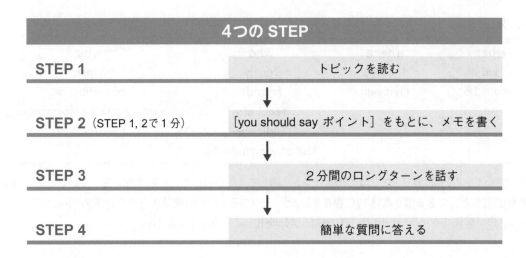

4つの STEP	
STEP 1	トピックを読む
STEP 2（STEP 1, 2で1分）	［you should say ポイント］をもとに、メモを書く
STEP 3	2分間のロングターンを話す
STEP 4	簡単な質問に答える

STEP-1　トピックを読む

> **Describe a happy event that you have attended and which you remember well.**
> 　　**You should say:**
> 　　　　① **when the event was**
> 　　　　② **where it was**
> 　　　　③ **who was there**
> ④ **and explain why you remember it well.**

　まずは、Describe ...の文を読んでトピックを把握し、何について話すか決めます。本問は**よく記憶している幸せなイベントについて説明する**問題です。

STEP-2　［you should sayポイント］をもとに、メモを書く

　トピックカードの［you should sayポイント］（①②③④の内容）をロングターンに組み込みましょう。話す順番は、①→④である必要はありません。
　ここで1つ注意すべき点があります。you **should** sayという指示があるものの、実のところ、4項目のすべてを盛り込まなくても、トピックに沿った話をすれば高得点を取ることは可能だということです。
　したがって、「何が何でも4つのポイントを入れなければ」と神経質になる必要はありませんが、**4つのポイントを入れることを意識すれば、おのずと詳細で具体性のあるロングターンになります**。そのため、本書の回答例では4つのポイントを盛り込んだものを紹介しています。

Speaking

サンプル問題の ［you should say ポイント］

①**when the event was**（いつのイベントだったか）

②**where it was**（どこで行われたか）

③**who was there**（そこに誰がいたか）

④**why you remember it well**（なぜよく記憶しているのか）

メモの例

when	where	who	why
kid	theatre	family	happiest
about 12	civic hall	friends	big influence
		teachers	quite a few performances
		audience	Theatre Arts
		the other students	

　文を書いている時間はないので、4つのポイントに関して、思いついたことを語句で書いていきます。このとき、**年数や名前など、できる限り具体的に書きましょう**。そうすることで臨場感のあるロングターンにつながります。メモは自分が解読できればいいので、長い単語は簡略化しても問題ありません。

STEP-3　2分間のロングターンを話す

ロングターンの最初に、Describe a happy event ... の文を言い換えて、話すトピックを試験官に伝えます。

　　Describe a happy event that you have attended and which you remember well.
　　例1　I'm going to talk about a happy event that I attended when I was a kid ...
　　例2　I'd like to tell you about an event that occurred when I was a kid ...

▶ 回答例

TRACK
20

　　Well, I'd like to tell you about an event that occurred ①when I was a kid. I was very shy back then, but for some reason I decided to try out for the school play. ①I think I must have been about 12. Anyway, I got selected for one of the main parts and there were lots of lines to remember. There were rehearsals after school and every Saturday ... it was a big thing.

　　On the night of the performance, ②we went to the theatre within the civic hall, where even professionals performed. The theatre was packed with ③our families, friends and teachers and we could hear them chatting away in the audience. ③Myself and all of the other students performing were all dressed up with our makeup on and everyone was excited and on edge. Initially, I was very nervous but as soon as I got my cue and walked onto stage and said my first line, then my next line, it suddenly all became very easy and natural. When the play finished, the audience was applauding madly, and I was hooked. ④It was the happiest I'd ever been and the experience had a big influence on me so I remember it well.

　　Since then, I've been in quite a few performances, and I love it every time. That's why I'm planning to study Theatre Arts in Canada next year ... And by the way, I'm still shy, but not when I've got a costume and makeup on!

⟩⟩⟩ 解説

　　12歳くらいのときに学校の劇で主要な役に選ばれ、緊張しつつもやり遂げた話と、それ以後、経験を積み、現在はシアター・アーツを学ぼうとしていることまでを、そのときどきの感情を表現しながら話せている。

　　適切な関係代名詞や接続詞を入れることで複雑な構文を作っている。Vocabulary に挙げた on edge や be hooked は口語的な表現だが、これくらいカジュアルでも問題ない。

[you should say ポイント]

　　ロングターンの下線部分（①〜④）で、以下の①〜④に言及している。
① **when the event was**（いつのイベントだったか）
② **where it was**（どこで行われたか）
③ **who was there**（そこに誰がいたか）
④ **why you remember it well**（なぜよく記憶しているのか）

□ **for some reason**　どういうわけか　　　□ **try out**　試してみる

□ **be packed**　（会場などが）満席である　　□ **on edge**　緊張して、ピリピリして

□ **be hooked**　夢中になる　　　　　　　　□ **have an influence on ～**　～に影響を与える

□ **quite a few ～**　かなり多数の～

STEP-4　簡単な質問に答える

　ロングターンが終わると、試験官が短い質問をします。回答は1文で十分で、理由など詳細情報を加える必要はありません。

E　Thank you. Do other people remember this event well?

C　I don't think so, but I remember it well like it happened yesterday.

練習問題

パート2のまとめとして、練習問題に挑戦しましょう。

パート2では以下のようなトピックが配られます。これをもとに、1分間メモを使って構成を練った後に、2分間のロングターンを始めてください。

Describe a place where you wish you could spend more time.

    You should say:

        where this place is

        how you know about this place

        what this place looks like

and explain why you wish you could spend more time there.

話すべきポイントをメモにまとめた後にロングターンを始めよう。

Part 3 対策

　いよいよ最後のパートです。パート3ではパート2のトピックに関連した質問が出題されます。ただし**パート3の質問は抽象的かつ一般的**。例えば、パート2で「先生」について出題されたら、パート3のトピックとしては「教育」が考えられます。

　身近なトピックが中心となるパート1、2とは違い、パート3では**社会的な内容が多く出題される**のも特徴です。論理的に意見を言い、考察する力も必要となり、より高度な英語力が求められます。

　次の図を見て、パート2のトピックが、パート3ではどのように抽象化されるのか確認しましょう。

頻出トピック

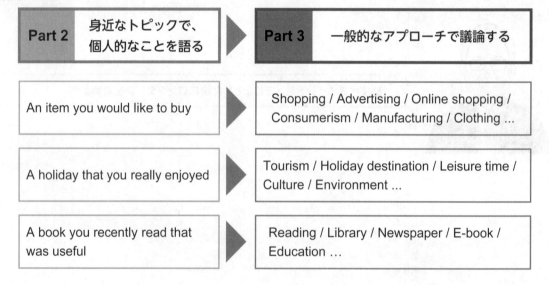

　実際には、次のように質問されます。

Advertising →	Do you think advertising influences what people buy? （広告は人々が買うものに影響すると思いますか）
Online shopping →	Why do you think online shopping is popular these days? （なぜ最近オンラインショッピングが人気だと思いますか）
Leisure time →	How do you think leisure activities have changed over the last 10 years? （過去10年で余暇の活動はどう変化してきたと思いますか）
Tourism →	What kind of valuable experiences can people gain from travelling? （旅をすることで得られる貴重な経験は何だと思いますか）

Part 3 攻略ルール

1 ▸ 個 人 的 な 話 よ り も 一 般 的 な 議 論 を !

> **E** How do you think social media will change in the future?
>
> **C** I am confident that social media will be more and more important in the future. **It already has a lot of effect on our lives**. For example, **in America's presidential election**, some social networking services were the fastest way to know the latest information ...

この回答例を読むと、個人的な話ではなく一般的な話を展開しているのがわかるはずです。具体的には「**私たちの生活に多くの影響を与えてきた**」「**アメリカの大統領選では**」と、スケールの大きい話をしています。

では、パート3で個人的なことは一切話してはいけないのでしょうか。実際には、**意見を述べるサポートとして、個人の経験や考えを述べても問題ありません**。ただし、パート2のように、自身の身近なものや経験を深掘りして詳細まで伝えるのは避けましょう。

一般的な話をするときのフレーズ

> Generally, （一般的には）
>
> In most cases, （ほとんどの場合）
>
> In my country most people believe (that) S＋V.
> （私の国ではほとんどの人がSVと考えています）
>
> There are a lot of examples of this in my country.
> （私の国では、これに関してたくさんの例があります）
>
> It is often said (that) S＋V. （SVということがよく言われています）

2 ▸ 知 識 不 足 は 素 直 に 認 め た う え で 答 え よ う

いくら準備していても、ときにはまったく知識のない分野に関する質問や、どう答えていいかわからない質問にあたることもあるでしょう。そうしたときは、知ったかぶりをして無理に話して結果的に言葉に詰まるよりも、**正直に打ち明けて、わからないなりに言葉をつないでいく方がよいでしょう**。こういう場合は確信を持って意見を言いにくいため、**推測するフレーズを使って話す**と展開しやすいです。

推測するフレーズ

> I have never thought about this but I suppose (that) S＋V.
> （それについて考えたことがありませんでしたが、私はSVだと推測します）
>
> I'm not confident I can speak well about this topic but let me try my best.
> （このトピックについてうまく話せるか自信がないですが、最善を尽くさせてください）
>
> I don't have much knowledge about this but I would imagine (that) S＋V.
> （これについてあまり知識がありませんが、私はSVだと推測します）

3 ▶ 論理的な議論を展開するフレーズを使おう

　次に挙げたフレーズは、意見を言ったり、賛成したり、言いたいことを相手に円滑に伝えるときの助けになります。もちろんパート1、2でも役立つものですが、一貫性を保ち、論理的な議論を展開するべきパート3では、特に欠かせません。

　なお、「意見を表明する」「理由を述べる」「例を挙げる」は、パート1の「攻略ルール」でも紹介していますが、パート3によりふさわしいフレーズを足しています。

論理的な議論をするうえで役立つフレーズ

意見を表明する

　　　I think (that) S＋V. / I believe (that) S＋V. /
　　　I guess (that) S＋V. / I suppose (that) S＋V. 　（私はSVだと思います）
　　　In my opinion, 　（私の意見では）
　　　I have no doubt (that) S＋V. 　（SVに疑いがありません）
　　　I am confident (that) S＋V. / I am sure (that) S＋V. 　（SVを確信しています）

理由を述べる　　becauseでつなげる以外にも、いろいろな表現方法があります。

　　　It's because S＋V. 　（それはSVだからです）
　　　The reason for this is ... 　（この理由は...です）
　　　I think the main reason is ... 　（主な理由は...だと思います）
　　　Another reason might be 〜. 　（ほかの理由は〜かもしれません）
　　　The biggest reason is ... 　（最大の理由は...です）
　　　due to 〜 　（〜のために）

例を挙げる

　　　For example[instance], 　（例えば）　　　Take 〜 for example, 　（〜を例に挙げると）
　　　such as 〜 　（〜のような）

賛成する

Absolutely, I wholeheartedly agree with that. （絶対にそうです。それに心から賛成します）

No doubt about it. （疑いようがありません）

反対する

I'm afraid (that) I disagree. （残念ながら反対です）

That's not always the case. / That's not always true. （いつもそうとは限りません）

I'm not so sure about that. （それは少し確信できかねます）

I don't think so. （そうは思いません）

比較する

prefer 〜 to ... （...より〜を好みます）　　　more 〜 than any other ... （ほかのどんな...よりも〜）

be not as ... as 〜 （〜ほど...ではありません）

be similar to 〜 （〜に似ています）

対比する

compared to 〜 （〜と比較すると）　　　in contrast to 〜 （〜と対照的で）

On one hand ... On the other hand ... （一方では...。他方では...）

while S＋V （SVの一方で）

推測する

My guess is (that) S＋V. （私の推測ではSVです）

I expect (that) S＋V. （私はSVだと思います）

I would imagine (that) S＋V. （私はSVだと推測します）

It seems (that) S＋V. （SVのようです）

It's probably 〜. （おそらく〜です）

I'd say (that) S＋V. （SVでしょう）

It's possible (that) S＋V. （SVはありえます）

It might[may] 〜. （〜かもしれません）

Well, if I think about 〜 （えっと、〜について考えると）

結果を示す　定番のsoやthenに加えて、以下のフレーズも使えるとよいでしょう。

As a result, （結果として）

Therefore, （それゆえに）

Consequently, （結果として）

Speaking

サンプル問題の回答例

　パート2のサンプル問題はDescribe a happy event that you have attended and which you remember well. でした。この場合、パート3ではhappy times, being happyといった抽象的なトピックでの出題が予想されます。

TRACK 22

We've been talking about a happy event that you have attended and remember well, and I'd like to discuss with you one or two more general questions related to this. Let's consider first of all family events. In your country, do families gather to celebrate special occasions?

Of course, most families get together at least once a year to celebrate festivals and holidays.

Are there any specific events that families celebrate together?

Yes, certainly. Weddings are one of the happy occasions that families celebrate together.

What are some other happy occasions that occur in the family home?

Well, I expect that most families enjoy celebrating festivals like New Year or Christmas in the family home. Apart from that, usually, families come together for occasions such as birthdays, anniversaries, housewarmings, and so on. Nowadays, we have small families, so we don't have a lot of family events.

How do families celebrate these happy occasions?

₁Let me see... every family is different, but usually families eat, drink, and exchange gifts to celebrate. ₂Some families also invite friends and neighbours if the occasion is really special.

₃Are the ways that young people celebrate different to how older people celebrate?

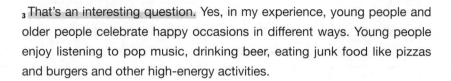 ₃That's an interesting question. Yes, in my experience, young people and older people celebrate happy occasions in different ways. Young people enjoy listening to pop music, drinking beer, eating junk food like pizzas and burgers and other high-energy activities.

 ₄What about older people? How do you think they like to celebrate?

₅I'd say older people like to have more peaceful celebrations. They like to relax with the family, eat traditional meals, and do activities that are relaxing rather than tiring, such as talking and listening to soft music.

 ₆Do you think people in the countryside have more or fewer opportunities for having fun than people in the cities?

₆Hmmm ... I guess it depends on the person. People in the countryside celebrate various local festivals and get together as a community often. ₇On the other hand, city people frequently go out with friends and co-workers to drink or to watch movies. ₈I'm sure that people can have fun wherever they are as long as they have good company.

 Right, let's move on to think about being happy. What types of people are the happiest, do you think?

₉Ah, I'm not sure what to say about it ... I feel it's impossible to say for sure that one type of person is the happiest, but it seems that people who are active and social are usually happy.

 Do you think a good social life is important for staying healthy?

In my opinion, a good social life is necessary to keep me healthy because if I don't have friends around, I will have fewer opportunities to laugh. I really think smiling is the key to keeping my mental health in good condition. Mental health is connected to physical health, so a good social life is important for this reason.

Speaking

Do you mean people who have a lot of friends are happier?

Precisely. I believe that people with a lot of friends have a positive attitude, and that's why they can make friends easily. If we are optimistic, we don't give up even when things are not going well. As a result, other people are attracted to our personality and want to be around us.

Is being sad always a bad thing?

₁₀Hmmm ... let me see, is being sad always bad? I guess not. Being sad or happy is a natural part of life. Sometimes, we can be sad remembering happy moments.

Why is that?

₁₁Personally speaking, I often miss my grandmother who's passed away and feel sad, but then I also remember the happy times I spent with her when I was a child, and it brings me joy. ₁₁Therefore, occasionally, ₁₂things that make us sad are also things that make us happy.

Thank you very much. That is the end of the Speaking Test.

>>> 解 説

1 ——— filler wordsを挟み「家族によって異なるが、たいていは...」とつなぐ。パート3の一般論は、断定しづらいことが多いが、ここではusuallyを使って断定を避けている。

2 ——— **断定しづらいとき、Some people ...（...の人もいる）は重宝するフレーズ。**ここではSome families ...で、一例を挙げている。

3 ——— 質問は「若者の祝い方は、高齢者とは違いますか」。すぐに答えられない内容なので、That's an interesting question.で時間を稼ぐ。

4 ——— 若者の祝い方しか具体的に説明しなかったので、試験官は高齢者のことも話させようと、What about older people?と質問している。最初の質問の後に、双方の祝い方を一気に話せるのが理想的だが、追加の質問は試験官からの助け舟だと思って話を展開しよう。

5 ——— 〈I'd say (that) S＋V.〉（SVだろう）は、控えめな意見表明。

6 ——— 質問は「田舎の人は都会の人よりも楽しむ機会が多いと思うか、少ないと思うか」。断言しづらい質問なので、I guess ...と推測で答える。it depends on 〜（〜による）も汎用性が高い表現。

7 ——— 〈田舎の人の楽しみ方＋On the other hand, ＋都会の人の楽しみ方〉の構造で対比させている。

8 ——— whereverは複合関係副詞で「どこにいようとも」という譲歩を表す。「人々は気の合う仲間がいる限りは、どこにいても楽しめると思います」

9 ——— 答えづらい質問なので、まずは時間を稼ぎ、その後「どんな人が幸せか断言できない」と前置きしたうえで、自分の意見に移っている。〈It seems (that) S＋V.〉（SVのようだ）も、断定を避けるフレーズ。

10 ── このように**試験官の質問を質問で返した後に、自分の意見を続ける**手もある。

11 ── パート3では一般的なことを述べる比重が高くなるが、個人的な体験を述べてもいい。その場合は、「個人的な話をすると」と、サインになる挿入句を使うとよい。その後のTherefore, 以降は、うまく一般論でまとめている。

12 ──「私たちを悲しませるものは、私たちを幸せにもします」。that make us sadとthat make us happyが、それぞれ直前のthingsを修飾する主格の関係代名詞節。

Vocabulary

- □ **apart from that** さておき、それとは別に
- □ **as long as S＋V** SVである限り
- □ **precisely** ［副］そのとおり
- □ **pass away** 亡くなる
- □ **housewarming** ［名］新築祝い
- □ **be connected to 〜** 〜に関係がある
- □ **that's why S＋V** そういうわけでSVである

Tips 日本特有の名詞には、説明を加えよう

スピーキングテストでは、自分の国のことについて問われることがよくあります。日本独自の食べ物、地名、習慣などを挙げるときには、説明を加えてください。試験官は日本文化に詳しいとは限らないので、説明することで相手の理解が深まります。同時に話を広げることができ、語彙力や流暢さを示すよい機会にもなります。

例：My favourite food is okonomiyaki.
→My favourite food is okonomiyaki, a popular Japanese savory pancake.

また、日本特有の休日で英語になっているものも、同様に補足するとよいでしょう。
例：I recently celebrated my Coming of Age Day.
→I recently celebrated my Coming of Age Day, a traditional Japanese event to welcome youth into adulthood.

頻出トピックの回答例

ここではさまざまなトピックや質問パターンを知っていただくために、頻出のトピックから、質問と回答のセットを1つずつ紹介します。

▶ Labour

E＝Examiner（試験官）　C＝Candidate（受験者）

E　Do you think young people have more job opportunities than older people?

C　₁I guess many companies prefer younger people to older people. ₂There are several reasons. Companies want to pay as little salary as possible to make bigger profits. Younger people usually have less work experience than older people, so basically, their salary is lower. ₂Also, young people can work longer at the same company. It means the company can make a longer human resource plan and maintain its workforce.

>>> 解説

▶2つの事柄やものを比較させる質問です。

1―――guessは「～ではないかと思う」と推測しつつ意見を言うときの表現で、口語的。

2―――〈（There are several reasons. 理由1）＋（Also, 理由2）〉の構成で、順序立てて説明している。Companies ... Young(er) people ...と大きな主語で語っており、一般論を通している。

▶ Family

E　How has the size of the family changed recently in your country?

C　Family size ₁has changed recently in my country, ₂especially in the last 2 to 3 decades. ₃Before, there used to be a total of 5 to 7 people in one family—grandparents, parents, and 2 to 3 children. ₃However, nowadays, most of the families are nuclear families with usually 1 to 2 kids. ₄This is generally because of the economic situation and smaller houses in the urban areas.

>>> 解説

▶ある事柄に関して、過去と現在を比較させる質問です。

1―――過去から今までの変化を述べているので、現在完了形がふさわしい。

2―――recentlyだけだと曖昧なので、その後に具体的な年数を述べて詳細を伝えている。

3―――〈（Before, 昔の家族）＋（However, nowadays, 最近の家族）〉の対比構造。

4―――典型的な昔の家族と現在の家族について伝えた後、最終文で理由も述べており説得力がある。This is generally because ofの部分は、generallyを入れて「一般的な」理由であることを強調。

▶ Living

> **E** Some people think it is better to live alone. What do you think about that?
>
> **C** ₁I completely agree with the statement ₁because I don't like sharing space either and prefer to spend time alone. ₂I think people like me don't want anyone to bother them, also ₂they want to keep a private lifestyle. ₂Personally, I don't mind living with my family but I would say living alone would definitely be better.

〉〉〉 解 説

▶考え、意見を問う質問です。

1 ——— I completely agree with 〜. で強い同意を表す。**意見を聞かれたら、最初の文で立場を明確にし**よう。この場合〈賛成と表明＋理由〉が端的に述べられている。

2 ——— 一般論だけではなく、Personally, ... と個人的な意見や詳細が入ることもある。ただしパート3で個人的な話ばかりするのは避けるべき。この場合は、主語をIだけにせず、I think people like me ..., they ... にして一般論化している。

▶ Robots

> **E** If all the jobs were done by robots, would it be good for the society?
>
> **C** No, I don't think so. Robots are helpful in making people's lives easier, but ₁if all the jobs were done by robots, humans would become lazy and unhealthy. ₂In addition, people would have no motivation to invent new things or create art. As a result, the society would become dull and unhappy.

〉〉〉 解 説

▶仮定的な質問です。

1 ——— 仮定法過去の基本的な文型〈If＋主語＋過去形 ..., 主語＋would 〜.〉（もし...だったら、〜だろう）を使って答えている。

ifを使った文は紛らわしいので、ここで整理しておこう。

直説法：現実に起こりえる条件（単に条件を挙げているだけなので仮定法ではない）

  If you practise hard, you will win the game.

  （もし一生懸命練習すれば、試合に勝つだろう）

仮定法過去：話者が実現可能だと思っていない、実際にそうではないこと

  If you **practised** hard, you **would win** the game.

  （一生懸命練習したら、試合に勝つだろう＝一生懸命練習しないので勝てない）

仮定法過去完了：話者が実現可能だったと思っていない、実際にそうならなかったこと

  If you **had practised** hard, you **would have won** the game.

  （一生懸命練習していたら、試合に勝てていただろうに＝一生懸命練習しなかったので勝てなかった）

2 ——— Noである理由を付加的に述べている。後に名詞相当語句を続ける場合は、in addition to 〜（〜に加えて）を使おう。

練習問題

パート3のまとめとして、練習問題を解きましょう。

この問題のトピックは、パート2の練習問題（Describe a place where you wish you could spend more time.）と連動した内容になっています。

なお、実際のパート3では、**質問内容が印字されたメモは配られない**ので注意してください。

Places to visit

- In cities, where do people like to go to relax?
- Why do you think natural places like forests or the seaside are pleasant to be in?
- Some people prefer to stay in their homes rather than go out and visit beautiful places. Why is that?

City living

- What are some of the things that governments can do to make cities better places to live?
- How can local people improve their neighbourhoods?
- In modern cities, do you think it's difficult for people to find time to be alone?
- How important is it to find time alone?

質問に対して一言答えるだけだと足りないので、意見や根拠を加えましょう。
回答は、IELTSに長年携わっているエキスパート陣で何度も話し合い作成しました。是非参考にしてください。

Part 1-3 実践問題

最後に実践問題として、パート 1 から 3 を一気に解いてみましょう。
実際の試験では、**質問が印字されたトピックが配られるのはパート 2 のみ**なので注意してください。

Part 1

Hometown
- What kinds of jobs do people in your hometown do? [Why?]
- In which part of your hometown do most people live? [Why?]
- Where did you play in your hometown when you were a child? [Why?]

Neighbours
- How often do you see your neighbours? [Why?]
- Do you invite your neighbours to your home? [Why? / Why not?]
- Do you think you are a good neighbour? [Why? / Why not?]
- Has a neighbour ever helped you? [Why? / Why not?]

The weather
- What kind of weather did you like best when you were a child? [Why?]
- Does the weather affect your mood? [Why? / Why not?]
- What is the best weather for studying or working? [Why?]
- Would you like to live in a country that has very hot or very cold weather? [Why? / Why not?]

Speaking

Part 2

Describe something you were given that was very useful.
    You should say:
        what this thing was
        who gave it to you
        why it was useful
and explain how you felt when you used it.

Part 3

Giving

- What are some examples of popular birthday gifts that people give to each other in your country?
- When giving something, how important is it that the gift is wrapped up beautifully?
- Some say that giving a person your time, that is, listening to them or helping them, is the best gift. What do you think about that?

International aid

- When there are natural disasters such as earthquakes, floods, or tsunamis, what sort of help will the victims need from their own country or from other countries?
- Some people say that it is better to build local infrastructure, for example, bridges and dams, than to just give money to poor countries. What do you think about that?
- Some say that rich countries give aid to poor countries as a way of spreading their influence in the region rather than actually helping people. What do you think?

Practice Test 1

WRITING

WRITING TASK 1

You should spend about 20 minutes on this task.

> *The maps below indicate the changes to the downtown area of a town called Hamford over a 50-year period.*
>
> *Summarise the information by selecting and reporting the main features, and make comparisons where relevant.*

Write at least 150 words.

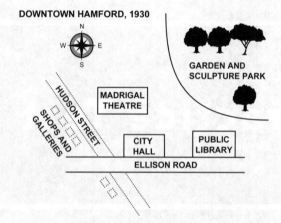

DOWNTOWN HAMFORD, 1930

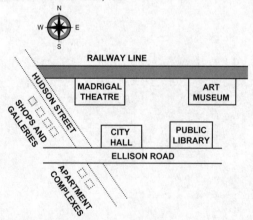

DOWNTOWN HAMFORD, 1980

WRITING TASK 2

You should spend about 40 minutes on this task.

Write about the following topic:

> *Many people believe that the best response to high levels of violent crime is to increase the length of prison sentences. Others believe that long prison sentences do nothing to prevent crime.*
>
> *Discuss both views and give your own opinion.*

Give reasons for your answer and include any relevant examples from your own knowledge or experience.

Write at least 250 words.

READING PASSAGE 1

You should spend about 20 minutes on **Questions 1–13**, which are based on Reading Passage 1 below.

Fermented Foods for Babies

Malnutrition during weaning age—when breast milk is being replaced by semi-solid foods at a time when milk alone is inadequate for growth—is highly prevalent among children of households in many poorer regions of the world. While there can be many factors leading to malnutrition, the immediate causes are recognised as feeding at less than adequate levels for child growth and development, and recurrent infections, including diarrhea, resulting mainly from ingestion of contaminated foods. As a result, many young children, particularly from six months to two years of age, experience weight loss and impaired growth and development.

Foods become contaminated mostly because of pathogens in food, on utensils, in water, and on the hands of the preparer. The problems are aggravated when food has to be stored at high ambient temperatures because of the lack of refrigeration. For infant foods, the heavy workload of mothers and lack of regular supplies of food, water and fuel may prevent the preparation of fresh food for each meal of the day.

Studies in various countries that have concentrated on traditional food preparation methods have resulted in offering cheap and practical answers to these problems based on familiar, indigenous and culturally acceptable home processing practices. One important answer that has arisen is cereal fermentation. It has been proved to reduce the risk of contamination under the existing inappropriate conditions for food preparation and storage in many households.

The practice has been a traditional way of food preservation in many parts of the world and has been used since ancient times. The antimicrobial properties of fermented foods and their relative higher safety—documented since the early 1900's—have been indicated in a number of studies. Some common examples of fermented foods include soy sauce, *tempeh* (Indonesia), some kinds of cheese, *kimchi* (Korea), *miso* (Japan), *sauerkraut* (Germany), and vinegar. In Africa, such as in Ghana it is common to ferment maize dough before cooking it as porridge. In Kenya, cereal-based porridge and milk are traditionally fermented. Preserving milk in the form of yoghurt is known to many households living in hot climates.

What are the underlying mechanisms by which fermentation processes help to prevent or reduce contamination? A possible answer suggests that during the fermentation process foods become more acidic. This explains why diarrhea-causing bacteria are not able to grow in fermented foods as rapidly as in unfermented ones. It is also hypothesized that some of the germs present in the foods are killed or inhibited from growing through the action of antimicrobial substances produced during fermentation. The fermented foods can, therefore, be kept for a longer time compared to fresh ones. It has been shown that while contamination levels in cooked unfermented foods increase with storage time, fermented foods remain less contaminated.

Whatever the underlying mechanisms, the fact is that the fermentation process reduces contamination without adding to the household cost both in terms of time and money. Its preparation is easy. The cereal flour is mixed with water to form a dough which is left to ferment; the addition of yeast, or mixing with a small portion of previously fermented dough is sometimes needed. The dough can then be cooked into porridge for feeding to the child.

Although beneficial, unfortunately the practice is going out of fashion. A study on the use of fermented foods for young children in Kenya demonstrated that while foods are still frequently fermented at home for child feeding, their use is becoming less popular, particularly in urban areas where commercial products are more available. There is, of course, a great deal of promotion of commercial products, though there is generally little to show that these products are ultimately better for child growth, and indeed in less than sanitary conditions, the dangers are well evidenced.

And quite apart from the improved food safety, we now know that fermented foods also have a wide range of other benefits. The transformation of sugars and starches enhances the natural, beneficial bacteria in food. These bacteria, known as probiotics or 'good' bacteria, are thought to help with a multitude of health issues, specifically digestive health. Fermented foods are also easier to digest. For example, fermentation breaks down the lactose in milk to simpler sugars—glucose and galactose—which, if you are lactose intolerant, can make products such as yogurt and cheese potentially easier to consume. Fermentation can also increase the availability of vitamins and minerals for our bodies to absorb as well as assist the beneficial bacteria in your gut to manufacture B vitamins and synthesise vitamin K. Your immune system is made more robust. Finally, fermented foods often lose the more unpalatable flavour of foods in their original state and are reported to be more appetizing.

Clearly fermented foods now need to be promoted in poorer countries, and might even help provide better nutrition in developed economies as well.

Questions 1–8

Complete the summary below.

*Choose **NO MORE THAN TWO WORDS** from Reading Passage 1 for each answer.*

Write your answers in boxes 1–8 on your answer sheet.

Fermented Foods for Babies

Malnutrition is caused by inadequate **1** .... and by infection due to contamination of food. This contamination is caused by **2** .... and by improper storage. One traditional solution is **3** ....

Fermentation kills pathogens because food becomes more acidic and because of the **4** .... action in the fermentation process. Because of lower levels of contamination, fermented foods can also be **5** .... longer.

Now fermented foods are less in demand, partly because of the availability of **6** ....

This is unfortunate because fermented foods also: have more **7** ....; are easier to digest; help the body absorb vitamins and minerals; help boost the **8** ....; are more appetizing.

Questions 9–10

*Choose the correct letter, **A, B, C,** or **D.***

Write the correct letter in boxes 9–10 on your answer sheet.

9 What is the main reason that the fermentation of food is being investigated?

    A It can improve the nutritional value of food.

    B It is a traditional method of food preparation which is becoming less popular.

    C It both inhibits food contamination and enhances storability.

    D It is popular all over the world.

10 Contamination of food is not caused by

    A the water used for cooking.

    B storage of food for too long at high temperatures.

    C too much acid in the food.

    D lack of hygiene in the kitchen.

Questions 11–13

Do the following statements agree with the claims of the writer in Reading Passage 1?

In boxes 11–13 on your answer sheet, write

YES   *if the statement agrees with the claims of the writer*

NO   *if the statement contradicts the claims of the writer*

NOT GIVEN   *if it is impossible to say what the writer thinks about this*

11 Fermented foods are free of contamination.

12 Traditional fermented foods tend to be less popular in cities.

13 Fermented foods often taste better.

READING PASSAGE 2

*You should spend about 20 minutes on **Questions 14–26**, which are based on Reading Passage 2 below.*

A short history of tall buildings: the making of the modern skyscraper

From the legendary Tower of Babel to the iconic Burj Khalifa, humans have always aspired to build to ever greater heights. Historically, tall buildings were often built by religions to inspire, and for almost six centuries from the early 14th century, the world's tallest building was always a church or a cathedral. The 160-metre-tall Lincoln Cathedral was finished in 1311, but the spire collapsed in 1549. Subsequently the record was held by various churches/cathedrals in Europe until the Ulm Minster was finished in 1890.

Yet these grand historical efforts are overshadowed by the skyscrapers of the 20th and 21st centuries. Looking out from the top of today's tallest buildings, cities lie below like toy models, a densely packed mass of streets and high-rise buildings.

For almost all of the 20th century, the world's tallest building was always in the United States. The famous Empire State Building in New York at 380 metres held the record for the longest period, about 40 years from 1931, and considering the pace of change these days it is unlikely any building will ever hold the record for quite so long again. In 1998, the distinction moved to the Eastern Hemisphere, where Malaysia was the first country to break the United States' record of constructing the tallest buildings in the world when the Petronas Twin Towers were completed (452 metres). Taiwan's Taipei 101 (509 metres) was the next building to hold the record, beginning in 2004, until the Burj Khalifa (828 metres) took over in 2010.

So how did we make this great leap upwards? We can trace our answer back to the 1880s, when the first generation of skyscrapers appeared in Chicago and New York. The booming insurance businesses of the mid-19th century were among the first enterprises to exploit the technological advancements which made tall buildings possible. Constructed in the aftermath of the great fire of 1871, Chicago's Home Insurance building—completed at the end of 1884 by William Le Baron Jenney—is widely considered to be the first tall building of the industrial era, at 12 storeys high.

Architects Louis Sullivan and Dankmar Adler first coined the term 'tall office building' in 1896. Their definition denoted that the first two storeys are given over to the entrance way and retail activity, with a service basement below, repeated storeys above and an attic storey to finish the building at the top. Vertical ducts unite the building with power, heat and circulation. This specification still largely applies today.

The American technological revolution of 1880 to 1890 saw a wave of new inventions that helped architects to build higher than ever before; Bessemer steel, formed into I-sections in the new rolling mills, enabled taller and more flexible frame design than the cast iron of the previous era; the newly-patented sprinkler head allowed buildings to escape the strict 23-metre height limit, which was imposed to control the risk of fire; and the patenting of AC electricity allowed elevators to be electrically powered and rise to ten or more storeys.

Early tall buildings contained offices. The typewriter, telephone and US universal postal system also appeared in this decade, and this new technology revolutionised office work and enabled administration to be concentrated in individual high-rise buildings within a city's business district. On the other hand, residential buildings in the crowded cities of the pre motor car age, such as Paris, London, and Manhattan, remained mostly low-level terraced houses, notable exceptions being a few high-rise mansion blocks around Central Park in New York, and nine storey blocks in ultra-dense Hong Kong.

Early office towers filled their city blocks entirely, with buildings enclosing a large light and air-well, as a squared U, O or H shape. This permitted natural light and ventilation within the building, but didn't provide any public spaces. Nor did it permit much variation in appearance. Chicago imposed a height limit of 40 metres in 1893, but New York raced ahead with large and tall blocks.

As a consequence, in 1915, following the completion of the 40-storey Equitable building on Broadway, there was such alarm at the darkening streets that New York introduced 'zoning laws' that forced new buildings to have a stepped frontage in order to bring daylight down to street level. This 'ziggurat' design meant that while the base still filled the city block, every few storeys the frontage would step back while the rest of the tower continued to rise. This was a radical change in the shape of tall buildings, and the second generation of skyscrapers. The ziggurat style became the most recognizable architectural symbol of the Art Deco movement of that time.

The mania for profit-driven tall development got out of hand in the late 1920s, however, and culminated in 1931 with the Chrysler and the Empire State buildings. The oversupply of office buildings, the depression of the 1930s and World War II brought an end to the Art Deco boom. There were no more skyscrapers until the 1950s, when the postwar era summoned forth a third generation: the International Style, the buildings of darkened glass and steel-framed boxes, with air-conditioning and plaza fronts with retreated facades that we see in so many of the world's cities today. They remained largely rectangular in style until well into the 1970s.

Questions 14–19

Complete the sentences below.

Choose **ONE OR TWO WORDS** from Reading Passage 2 for each answer.

Write your answers in boxes 14–19 on your answer sheet.

14 For a period of about six .... the tallest buildings were churches or cathedrals.

15 The Empire State Building had the record of highest building for the .... in the
    20th century.

16 In the modern era, the first country other than the US to have the tallest building was
    ....

17 Companies could begin building big offices downtown because of ....

18 Early office towers didn't have ....

19 The ziggurat style was a .... from previous designs.

Questions 20–26

Do the following statements agree with the information given in Reading Passage 2?

In boxes 20–26 on your answer sheet, write

TRUE   if the statement agrees with the information

FALSE   if the statement contradicts the information

NOT GIVEN   if there is no information on this

20 All of the tallest buildings in the 1880s were built by insurance companies.

21 The tallest building in 1884 was 12 storeys high.

22 The basic concept of tall buildings hasn't changed since 1896.

23 The main reason they could start building taller buildings was the invention of elevators.

24 There was a big early demand for tall buildings for housing.

25 Hong Kong competed with New York to build the highest office buildings.

26 New York put a height limit on buildings in 1915 because of dark streets.

READING PASSAGE 3

*You should spend about 20 minutes on **Questions 27–40**, which are based on Reading Passage 3 below.*

Coffee: 60% of wild species are at risk of extinction due to climate change

A ———What kind of coffee do you drink? If it's a high-quality brew, it's almost certainly made with beans from the Arabica species (*Coffea arabica*), which is known for its finer flavours. Examples would be Javan coffees, Ethiopian sidamo, and the expensive Jamaican blue mountain. If you like instant blends, it's probably from a different species, Robusta (*Coffea canephora*), known for its harsher taste but cheaper price. Robusta is sometimes openly mixed with Arabica in commercial products—and is often secretly used to adulterate '100% Arabica' products to reduce costs. A third species, *Coffea liberica*, which is native to west and central Africa, is widely grown for local use in tropical countries but is not globally traded because of its more bitter taste. A fourth species *Coffea eugenoides was* originally bred with Robusta to give rise to Arabica, which is a crossbreed.

B ———There are actually more than 100 species of coffee in the wild. Apart from the four mentioned above, another 38 closely related species are known or assumed to have fertile pollen transfer with commercial coffees. There are a further 82 species which are more distantly related to the commercial breeds, but scientists could interbreed them with commercial coffees in a lab. The range of species is important because they could help to protect coffee, as all these relatives can help enhance the genetic diversity of commercial coffee species, making them more adaptable to environmental changes.

C ———One threat is coming from climate change as changing temperatures and rainfall patterns affect plant growth and endanger coffee yields. The changing climate may also be leaving plants more vulnerable to disease. All major commercial coffee-growing countries have been badly affected by 'coffee leaf rust', which spread across Africa and into Asia during the early 20th century, then to South America, becoming entrenched globally by the turn of the millennium. The Central American coffee rust outbreak that began in the 2011–2012 harvest season affected 70% of farms in the region, resulting in over 1.7m lost jobs and US$3.2 billion in damage and lost income.

D ———As an example of how cross-breeding can help, Robusta varieties, which are resistant to leaf rust, have been key to developing resistance in Arabica varieties. But as climate change and disease risks escalate, wild coffee species offer a crucial resource for maintaining the world's coffee supply in the face of other threats and challenges. Arabica has tightly limited geographic ranges in which it grows well, and Robusta is vulnerable to diseases other than leaf rust.

E ———A recent study led by the UK's Kew Royal Botanic Gardens set the value of this variety in wild coffee species in context: over 60% of coffee species are threatened with extinction. Coffee species are particularly vulnerable to extinction because they thrive in small numbers in specific geographic ranges—such as pockets of wild Arabica populations between certain altitude ranges in the Ethiopian highlands. Wild coffee species—and wild varieties of the commercial species—are almost all in decline due to competition for land use and overharvesting of the coffee plant for timber or firewood. A number of wild coffee relatives haven't been spotted for many decades and may be extinct.

F ———One species, the *Cafe marron*, from the remote island of Rodrigues in the Indian Ocean, was known from only one sighting in 1877. A century later, a schoolboy drew an 'unusual' tree while exploring and showed it to a teacher, and it was recognised as a surviving *Cafe marron*. The sole surviving specimen of that wild coffee has inspired wider forest conservation on Rodrigues. It is also being cultured in lab collections at Kew.

G ———Sadly, there may be less hope for other species. Coffee seeds don't store well, unlike wild relatives of other crops such as wheat or maize. So we can't rely on storage in seed banks to conserve coffee diversity and resilience. Freezing plant matter in labs or growing samples in test tubes might be an alternative, but not one that has been explored beyond existing commercial strains.

H ———Preserving different coffee varieties in botanic gardens isn't really a viable solution for protecting genetic diversity either. Coffee species readily fertilise each other, 'contaminating' the resource you're trying to conserve. While some experts suggest we preserve coffee diversity in collections, the Kew Gardens study argues that the sustainability of coffee depends on conservation of these species wherever they grow, in protected areas and working with communities throughout their native distribution in Africa and Asia.

I ———Conserving genetic diversity should be included in existing approaches for sustainable coffee production, such as Fair Trade and Rainforest Alliance certifications. Ensuring the continuity of the coffee trade means protecting the ecosystems coffee comes from and the livelihoods of people across the bean to coffee cup economy. We can also expect new flavours and even coffees with naturally low or zero caffeine content.

Complete the notes below.

*Choose **NO MORE THAN TWO WORDS OR A NUMBER** from Reading Passage 3 for each answer.*

Write your answers in boxes 27–33 on your answer sheet.

Coffee

Coffee species

· Four main ones and another **27** .... commonly interbreed naturally

· The range is important to protect coffees from **28** ....

· **29** .... is not very affected by coffee leaf rust

Threats to coffee species

· Climate change + diseases

· Many species naturally appear only in certain small **30** ....

· Competing land use

· Overharvesting for timber/firewood

· Coffee beans are difficult to **31** ....

The future

· Cannot just keep coffee varieties in botanical gardens

· There must be **32** .... of species wherever they grow

· Must work with local **33** ....

· Genetic diversity should be one of the criteria for sustainable coffee production

---

Questions 34–37

Reading Passage 3 has nine paragraphs, **A–I**.

Which paragraph contains the following information?

Write the correct letter, **A–I**, in boxes 34–37 on your answer sheet.

34 an example of the effects of climate change

35 a recommendation from Kew Royal Botanic Gardens

36 a comparison of better-known coffee varieties

37 a species that has re-surfaced

Questions 38–40

Choose the correct letter, **A**, **B**, **C**, or **D**.

Write the correct letter in boxes 38–40 on your answer sheet.

38 Robusta is mixed with Arabica to

    A improve the quality of Arabica.

    B save money.

    C produce a new coffee product.

    D produce a different taste.

39 Crossing different varieties of coffee

    A produces a new variety which is prone to disease.

    B has led to the outbreak of coffee rust.

    C depends on temperatures and rainfall.

    D produces a better variety adaptable to change.

40 Which one is not true about the coffee rust?

    A It has affected all key areas where coffee is grown.

    B It has existed for about a century.

    C It has impacted on farmers' earnings.

    D It has affected all coffee varieties equally.

LISTENING

PART 1 *Questions 1–10*

Questions 1–6

Complete the booking form below.

Write NO MORE THAN THREE WORDS AND/OR A NUMBER *for each answer.*

Glen Rent-a-Car: Driver details	
Surname: 1	First name: Richard
Age: 2	
Nationality: British	
License Number: 3	
Pick up	
Date: 3rd November	
Time: 4	
Location: City office	
Return	
Date: 5	
Time: 5 pm	
Location: 6	

Questions 7–10

Complete the notes below.

Write NO MORE THAN TWO WORDS AND/OR A NUMBER *for each answer.*

OPTIONS

Type of car: **7** ....

Transmission: **8** ....

Extras: –

Plan: **9** ....

Tax: **10** ....

PART 2   Questions 11–20

Questions 11–17

Complete the table below. **Write ONE WORD AND/OR A NUMBER** for each answer.

What does the London Coffee Festival feature?	celebration of London's coffee scene coffee and gourmet food stalls coffee **11** ...., and demonstrations by international baristas themed areas for live entertainment and music
What does the ticket include?	learn to make & brew coffee meet your favourite barista enjoy **12** .... food & street food markets
Additional info for visitors	children under 16 must be **13** .... wheelchair-accessible **14** .... are not allowed
When?	2–5 April
How to get there?	walk or go by **15** .... or bus
Where?	15 Brick Lane, London Some of the festival zones have the same names as famous **16** .... in London.
What are the two important events?	- **17** .... Days: from Thursday to Friday 2nd–3rd April, that include workshops, seminars, product tastings, etc. - Public celebrations: from Friday afternoon to Sunday, free tastings, street food, coffee-based cocktails, etc.

Questions 18–20

Answer the questions below.

Write **NO MORE THAN TWO WORDS AND/OR A NUMBER** for each answer.

18 How much of all ticket sales goes to charity?

19 In which country was Project Waterfall set up?

20 Besides ticket sales, how did the London Coffee Festival raise funds in 2017?

PART 3   Questions 21–30

Questions 21–24

*Choose the correct letter, **A, B** or **C**.*

21 To climb Kilimanjaro, beginners

    A need a guide.

    B still have to carry their equipment.

    C can take any of six official routes.

22 The difficulty of the route is mostly determined by

    A the landscape.

    B the weather.

    C distance of the route.

23 What advice was given about special fitness training?

    A You need to exercise every day.

    B You should diversify your workouts.

    C You should exercise for more than one month.

24 When climbing Kilimanjaro

    A you need to carry extra water.

    B you need to carry a range of pills.

    C you may experience altitude sickness.

Complete the itinerary below.

Write **ONE WORD AND/OR A NUMBER** *for each answer.*

Machame Route Itinerary

Day 1

· Start from the Kilimanjaro National Park office.

· Climb through a **25** .... most of the day.

Day 2

· Walk beside a river.

· Go up a steep **26** ....

· Spend the night at Camp Shira.

Day 3

· Need to get used to the altitude.

· Have lunch at Lava Tower.

· Camp at a plateau with large rocks.

· Can see a wonderful **27** ....

Day 4

· Have to climb over difficult ground.

· Travel **28** .... kilometres.

Day 5

· At this altitude, the landscape resembles a **29** ....

· You can clearly see other mountaintops from this point.

Day 6

· Climb in **30** ....

· Reach the summit in time to see the sunrise.

· Spend the night down at Camp Mweka.

Test-1

PART 4   *Questions 31–40*

Complete the notes below.

Write **NO MORE THAN TWO WORDS AND/OR A NUMBER** *for each answer.*

Denmark: A Happy Country

What makes Danish people happy?

· Education and public health care are free.

· The rate of **31** .... is low.

· The country has a high level of **32** .... and community spirit.

Danes are happy to pay taxes

· As much as **33** .... of their earnings go to taxes.

· They believe higher taxes can support the **34** .... to ensure social safety net

for children, the elderly and ill people.

· They pay taxes to help jobless people for almost **35** ....—although these

people have to try to find jobs.

Trust and safety

· Honesty is important. They have a secure government and low levels of corruption among

36 .... and in business.

· Safety level is high. Young children are able to travel **37** .... using public

transport.

'Hygge'

· 'Hygge' means to enjoy life by getting away from the **38** ....

· 'Hygge' was added to the Oxford Dictionary in 2017.

· During winter it is practised **39** .... where people play board games, etc.

· 'Hygge' in the summer means spending time in small holiday homes where they take care

of their **40** ...., and throw parties.

Empowerment is the key to happiness

· There is a strong link between happiness and empowerment.

· People are given freedom to do what they desire in life.

SPEAKING

実際の試験では、印字された冊子が配布されるのはパート2のみです。

PART 1

TRACK (31)

Study
- What are some of the everyday tasks you do when you study? [Why?]
- How did you choose your college?
- Tell me about one of the things that surprised you when you first started at your college. [Why?]

Running
- How often do you run? [Why?]
- Do you run more or less now than when you were a child? [Why? / Why not?]
- Do you think everybody should run at least once a week? [Why? / Why not?]
- Is using a running machine in a gym as good as running outdoors? [Why? / Why not?]

Insects
- What are the most common insects where you live? [Why?]
- Do you find anything about insects interesting? [Why? / Why not?]
- Do you have a favourite insect? [Why? / Why not?]
- Do you think that we should protect insects in the same way as we protect bigger animals?
  [Why? / Why not?]

PART 2

TRACK (32)

Describe a time when you felt very tired.
> **You should say:**
>> **what made you tired**
>> **where it was**
>> **who was there**

and explain how you felt about being tired.

PART 3

Being tired
- On what occasions do people commonly feel tired?
- What are some of the different ways that people deal with tiredness?
- Do you think most people get enough sleep nowadays?

Work and leisure
- What makes some people work hard, while others don't work hard?
- Why do you think that some people like to do physically exhausting activities such as long-distance running as a form of leisure activity?
- Do men and women have different ways of relaxing?

Practice Test 2

WRITING

WRITING TASK 1

You should spend about 20 minutes on this task.

The graph below shows the average audience size per performance at four Canadian theatres from 2000–2014.

Summarise the information by selecting and reporting the main features, and make comparisons where relevant.

Write at least 150 words.

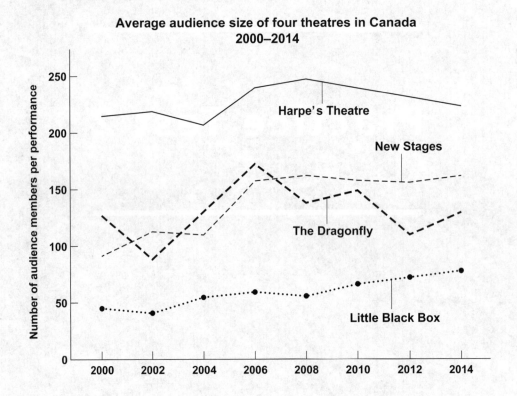

Average audience size of four theatres in Canada
2000–2014

WRITING TASK 2

You should spend about 40 minutes on this task.

Write about the following topic:

> *Technology that will allow cars to function automatically, without a human driver is currently being developed. When the technology for self-driving cars has been perfected, these vehicles will replace cars operated by humans.*
>
> *Is this a positive or a negative development?*

Give reasons for your answer and include any relevant examples from your own knowledge or experience.

Write at least 250 words.

READING

READING PASSAGE 1

*You should spend about 20 minutes on **Questions 1–13**, which are based on Reading Passage 1 below.*

We judge incomplete faces as more attractive

A recent study has suggested that when people see incomplete faces in photographs—for example, faces that are partially obscured—they perceive the subject to be more physically attractive than they would have if they had seen the complete photograph. In other words, people fill in the missing information to imagine the faces to be more attractive than they really are.

Positive Bias

Positive bias is common in human cognition. When people consider themselves, for example, they are often unrealistically positive—they might believe they have more control over their environment than they in fact do, or they might think that the opinions they have are held by many more people than is the case. When people compare themselves with others, the so-called *better-than-average* effect suggests that people perceive themselves to be more attractive, more kind, and more sincere than the average person. These positive illusions, or positive biases, help to promote psychological well-being by creating a positive self-image.

There are good reasons to believe that people may have unrealistic expectations when perceiving others as well. The literature has shown that people tend to have an optimistic impression about others' personalities when they have limited information about them. But do these biases also apply to physical appearance? Do we perceive others as better-looking when we are presented with incomplete information about their faces?

Physically Attractive

The question is important because positivity bias can have profound implications on our social interactions. People that we perceive as more attractive are also perceived as more sociable, happier, healthier and wealthier, academically brighter, and as having more expertise and better job qualifications. This *halo-effect* for attractive people plays an important role, not only on how we perceive others but also on how we behave towards them. Indeed, we tend to give more attention, and offer more help and care to people that we perceive as more attractive. People thought to be attractive can even be given milder court sentences by judges.

It is also important because these days we often judge the appearance of others using incomplete information. Such is the case when we see someone for the first time from far away or in poor light conditions. Similarly, most online encounters involve aesthetic judgements based on small, incomplete, or partially obscured profile pictures. These online personas are important. For example, organisations are increasingly using social media to gather information about job candidates, and any incompleteness of online images could therefore bias the first impressions of employers about potential employees. Also note the popularity of modern dating apps, where people post various photos of themselves.

The Present Study

In the present study, participants in the first experiment were asked to judge the attractiveness of 96 human faces in four types of photographs: photographs with complete faces, small photographs, photographs with only one-third of the face visible, and blurred photographs. In the second experiment the effect was replicated with one new modification: groups of pixels, accounting for a third of the total image, were randomly removed from the photographs so that only 66% of the face was visible, and the missing parts were from all around the face.

When the attractiveness ratings of the 96 faces across the four conditions were compared, it was found that participants judged small, one-third, and blurred faces as more attractive than the complete photographs. The version depicting one-third of faces led to the largest positivity bias, and the small-size version led to the smallest (but still significant) bias. Similar results were found in the second experiment, with a definite positivity bias for the incomplete images compared with the complete ones.

Discussion

Overall, these findings support the hypothesis that when perceiving incomplete faces people fill in the missing information with positive details. It seems that, presented with incomplete human faces and instructed to judge their attractiveness, participants resort to what they know about faces (structure and features) and their representation of a prototypical face in their memories to generate new holistic representations. Interestingly, it was seen that the bias is more pronounced in male participants. Also, the bias is specific to aesthetic judgments, but generalises to other dimensions (e.g. the person's character) when the bias is strong enough.

Being positively biased about the attractiveness of strangers might have been a mechanism which was important in human evolution, as it might have facilitated social interactions. However, the impact of this bias might only apply to impressions and interactions in first encounters. It is known that first impressions get diluted as we get to know and acquire more information about a person. Thus, an interesting question for future research is the influence of the positivity bias on subsequent interactions with the target person.

And it should be noted that one limitation of the study is that all experiments were performed online. While there is research showing that data from online experiments is comparable to data from lab-based experiments, these conclusions need to be replicated in the laboratory and in contexts where the implications of the research might be directly relevant (e.g., social media, recruitment, fashion industry, entertainment, advertisement, and marketing).

Questions 1–7

Complete the notes below.

*Choose **ONE OR TWO WORDS** from Reading Passage 1 for each answer.*

Write your answers in boxes 1–7 on your answer sheet.

Study on attractive faces

Positive bias for attractiveness

· we tend to see ourselves as more attractive than we are

· having a favourable self-impression leads to better **1** .... health

Attractiveness is important

· we think attractive people have many other positive qualities

· we **2** .... more positively toward attractive people

The study

· used complete photos compared to small/one-third/blurred photos

· also used photos with some **3** .... removed

Results

· the one-third photos had the biggest **4** ....

· people match incomplete faces with faces in their **5** ....

· more positive bias was applied by **6** ....

Limitations

· bias may only apply to **7** ....

· the study was only done online

Questions 8–13

Do the following statements agree with the information given in Reading Passage 1?

In boxes 8–13 on your answer sheet, write

TRUE	if the statement agrees with the information
FALSE	if the statement contradicts the information
NOT GIVEN	if there is no information on this

8 We can fairly accurately predict how many people agree with our opinions.

9 Positive biases about ourselves help us to feel better.

10 We think attractive people are also more friendly.

11 Attractive people cannot get better treatment in the justice system.

12 We should only show one-third of our faces on dating apps.

13 There might be an evolutionary reason for this positive bias.

READING PASSAGE 2

You should spend about 20 minutes on **Questions 14–26**, which are based on Reading Passage 2 on pages 219 and 220.

Questions 14–20

Reading Passage 2 has nine paragraphs, **A–I**.

Choose the correct heading for each paragraph from the list of headings below.

Note the headings for paragraphs A and B have already been done.

Write the correct number, **i–xii**, in boxes 14–20 on your answer sheet.

List of Headings

i	The role of the slave trade
ii	Sugar in the Mediterranean
iii	After slavery
iv	Where it started
v	A closely related product
vi	Solutions
vii	Why sugar is important today
viii	Significance of the history of sugar
ix	Early processed sugar
x	Larger-scale sugar industries
xi	Impacts today
xii	The addictiveness of sugar

Paragraph **A**		*vii*
Paragraph **B**		*iv*
14	Paragraph **C**	....
15	Paragraph **D**	....
16	Paragraph **E**	....
17	Paragraph **F**	....
18	Paragraph **G**	....
19	Paragraph **H**	....
20	Paragraph **I**	....

A history of sugar—the food nobody needs, but everyone craves

A ——It seems as though no other substance occupies so much of the world's land, for so little benefit to humanity, as sugar. According to the latest data, sugarcane is the world's third most valuable crop after cereals and rice, and it occupies 26,942,686 hectares of land across the globe. Its main output—apart from commercial profits—is a global public health crisis, which has been centuries in the making. The obesity epidemic—along with related diseases including cancer, dementia, heart disease and diabetes—has spread across every nation where sugar-based carbohydrates have come to dominate the food economy. So at this time, it pays to step back and consider the ancient origins of sugar, to understand how it has grown to present an imminent threat to our landscapes, our societies and our health.

B ——Human physiology evolved on a diet containing very little sugar and virtually no refined carbohydrates. In fact, sugar probably entered into our diets by accident. It is likely that sugarcane was initially a 'fodder' crop, used to fatten pigs, and then humans later began to chew on the stalks. Evidence from plant remnants and DNA suggests that sugarcane evolved in Southeast Asia. Researchers are currently hunting for early evidence of sugarcane cultivation at the Kuk Swamp in Papua New Guinea, where the domestication of related crops such as taro and banana dates back to approximately 8000 BC. The crop spread around the Eastern Pacific and Indian Oceans around 3,500 years ago, carried by Austronesian and Polynesian seafarers.

C ——The first chemically refined sugar appeared on the scene in India about 2,500 years ago. From there, the technique spread east towards China, and west towards Persia and the early Islamic worlds, eventually reaching the Mediterranean in the 13th century. Cyprus and Sicily became important centres for sugar production. Throughout the Middle Ages (500 to 1500 AD), it was considered a rare and expensive spice, rather than an everyday condiment.

D ——The first place to cultivate sugarcane explicitly for large-scale refinement and trade was the Atlantic island of Madeira, during the late 15th century. Then, it was the Portuguese who realised that new and favourable conditions for sugar plantations existed in Brazil, where a slave-based plantation economy was established. When Brazilian sugarcane was introduced in the Caribbean, shortly before 1647, it led to the growth of the industry which came to feed the sugar craze of Western Europe.

E ——This food—which nobody needed, but everyone craved—drove the formation of the modern world. There was a huge demand for labour to cultivate the massive sugar plantations in Brazil and the Caribbean. This need was met by transatlantic slave trade, which resulted in around 12,570,000 humans shipped from Africa to the Americas between 1501 and 1867. And of course, goods such as copper and brass, rum, cloth, tobacco and guns were needed to purchase slaves from the African elites. These were secured through the expansion of industrial production, particularly in the English Midlands and southwest regions. Modern-day banking and insurance can also trace their origins to the 18th-century transatlantic slaving economy.

F ————When slaves were finally emancipated in 1834 in the British Empire, it was the slave owners who were fully compensated—not the slaves. Much of this money was used to build Victorian infrastructure, such as railways and factories. Meanwhile, many former slaves were forced to continue to work for their former owners under an 'apprenticeship' system.

G ————In many ways, the story of sugar and tobacco are closely aligned. Both products were initially produced through slave labour, and were originally thought to be beneficial to health. And although both sugar and tobacco have ancient origins, it was their sudden, mass consumption from the mid-17th century onwards that created the health risks we associate with them today. The idea of 'industrial epidemics' of non-communicable diseases, being driven by the profit motives of major corporations, rings true for both. And while tobacco is widely acknowledged to be addictive, sugar can also drive behavioural responses that are indistinguishable from addiction.

H ————But in the 21st century, the grip of sugar is stronger than comparable scourges like tobacco, or even alcohol. Sugar is not only ubiquitous—it is potentially responsible for approximately 20% of the caloric content of modern diets—but also central to the world's economy and cultural heritage. Perhaps a better comparison is our reliance on fossil fuels. Fossil fuels are not just a vice or bad habit but central to the way we live, and to the geography and politics of the territories where they are sourced. Likewise, the rise of sugar has been key to global trade and socioeconomic development, slavery and the African Diaspora and modern cultural norms.

I ————The evolutionary and historical origins of sugarcane may hold insights into why sugar dominates modern culture, and what we can do to mitigate its malign influence. Like many great challenges of the 21st century, such as climate change, the science identifying the problem seems clear. What is lacking is the public and political will to address it, in ways such as the proposed sugar tax and prominently displayed health warnings. With sugar still deeply part of our food system—in 2013, sugar crops made up 6.2% of world's agricultural yield and 9.4% of its total monetary value—such bold socioeconomic measures are needed to make the necessary changes possible.

Questions 21–25

Do the following statements agree with the information given in Reading Passage 2?

In boxes 21–25 on your answer sheet, write

> **TRUE**　　　　　*if the statement agrees with the information*
>
> **FALSE**　　　　*if the statement contradicts the information*
>
> **NOT GIVEN**　*if there is no information on this*

21 Obesity is only a problem in countries where sugar-based carbohydrates dominate the food economy.

22 In the beginning, humans gave sugarcane to pigs and also ate it themselves.

23 Refined sugar was once expensive.

24 The large-scale sugar industry began in Portugal and Brazil.

25 Sugar is known to be addictive.

Question 26

*Choose the correct letter, **A**, **B**, **C** or **D**.*

Which of these was not said to be related to the slave trade?

A large-scale production in Madeira

B production of copper

C banking

D Victorian infrastructure

READING PASSAGE 3

*You should spend about 20 minutes on **Questions 27–40**, which are based on Reading Passage 3 below.*

Ötzi the Iceman
Scholars continue to be amazed by the ancient man found frozen in the Alps.

A————In 1991, a group of hikers exploring the Ötztal Alps on the Austrian-Italian border came across the mummified corpse of a person half-entombed in ice. Because the find was at an elevation of 10,530 feet, the group initially suspected that the remains belonged to a lost mountaineer. Local officials brought in to examine the scene further floated the possibility that it was the body of an Italian soldier lost during one of the World Wars.

B————Only after archaeologists had a chance to examine Ötzi, so-named for the mountain range where he was discovered, did the stunning truth of his age come to light. Using radiocarbon dating, scientists determined that he had perished in the Alps an astounding 5,300 years earlier. His condition was remarkable, with his brain, internal organs, and even one of his eyeballs all completely intact. In the time since his discovery, Ötzi has become an authentic celebrity of the scientific world—providing insights and blowing away assumptions about the ancient world. Below are just a few of the secrets researchers have uncovered from the Iceman, his possessions, and the circumstances surrounding his unusual death.

C————Living links to the Iceman have now been revealed by a new DNA study. Gene researchers looking at unusual markers on the Iceman's male sex chromosome report that they have uncovered at least 19 genetic relatives of Ötzi in Austria's Tyrol region. The match was made from samples of 3,700 anonymous blood donors in a study led by Walther Parson at Innsbruck Medical University. Sharing a rare mutation, 'the Iceman and those 19 share a common ancestor, who may have lived 10,000 to 12,000 years ago', Parson said.

D————The finding supports previous research suggesting that Ötzi and his ancestors were of farming stock. The study used Y-chromosome markers that are passed from father to son to trace the Neolithic migrations that brought farming to Europe via the Alps. Ötzi belonged to a Y-chromosome group called haplogroup G, which is rooted, like farming, in the Middle East.

E————Another area that has been closely investigated is Ötzi's health. The findings don't make pretty reading as he had more than 40 complaints including worn joints, hardened arteries, and gallstones. He likely had Lyme disease (caused by the bites of deer ticks); he had alarming amounts of arsenic in his system (probably due to working with copper extraction) and his gut contained the eggs of parasitic worms. Interestingly, he had a kind of medical kit for the worms as he carried birch fungus, which is known to kill intestinal parasites.

F————Ötzi was also in need of a dentist—an in-depth dental examination found evidence of advanced gum disease and tooth decay. His teeth were well worn, probably due to a diet of milled grain products, and there was a bluish tinge to his teeth, which no one has been able to explain. He lacked wisdom teeth and had a gap between his two front teeth, known as a diastema.

G ——He had a range of tattoos, numbering over 50 in total. These weren't produced using a needle, but by making fine cuts in the skin and then rubbing in charcoal. They were all covered by clothing, so were unlikely to have been used for purposes of identification by other tribes, and must have had some inner meaning. It is likely that the designs marked the passage from youth to manhood, something done by older cultures the world over.

H ——Ötzi was well prepared for the alpine chill. His basic garment was an unlined fur robe made of patches of deer, chamois, and ibex skin. Though badly repaired at many points, the robe had been cleverly stitched together with threads of plant fibre, in what appears to be a mosaic-like pattern, belying the previous image of cavemen in crude skins. For further protection, he wore a woven grass cape over the garment similar to those worn by Tyrolean shepherds as late as the early part of the 20th century. His well-worn shoes were made of leather and stuffed with grass for warmth.

I ——He carried a grass net, probably serving to hold the things he took with him, and amongst his tools there was a fur quiver (or arrow holder) with several feathered arrows carved from viburnum and dogwood branches. A dozen of them were as yet unfinished, but two were primed for shooting, with flint points and feathers. The feathers had been affixed with a resin-like glue at an angle that would cause spin in flight and help maintain a true course, so we can conclude that ballistic principles were known and applied.

J ——The bow, which had not yet been notched for a bowstring, was made of yew which is the best wood in Central Europe for bow-making and the wood the famous English longbows were made of. Yew is relatively rare in the Alps, so clearly some effort had been made to find the best material.

Questions 27–31

Reading Passage 3 has ten paragraphs, **A–J**.

Which paragraph contains the following information?

*Write the correct letter, **A–J**, in boxes 27–31 on your answer sheet.*

NB *You may use any letter more than once.*

27 something that Ötzi ate

28 how Ötzi may have used natural medicines

29 something still puzzling scientists about Ötzi

30 how well Ötzi's body was preserved

31 where Ötzi's ancestors originally came from

Questions 32–36

Complete the sentences below.

*Choose **ONE OR TWO WORDS** from Reading Passage 3 for each answer.*

Write your answers in boxes 32–36 on your answer sheet.

32 His modern 'relatives' were identified because they had the same ....

33 Working with metal caused high levels of ....

34 His clothes were mainly made from animal skins sewn with ....

35 He probably carried his belongings in a ....

36 The design of his arrows showed some understanding of ....

Questions 37–40

Do the following statements agree with the information given in Reading Passage 3?

In boxes 37–40 on your answer sheet, write

> **TRUE**   *if the statement agrees with the information*
>
> **FALSE**   *if the statement contradicts the information*
>
> **NOT GIVEN**   *if there is no information on this*

37 Tattoos were probably used to indicate which tribe Ötzi belonged to.

38 Ötzi's clothes were skillfully made.

39 Ötzi made his own arrows.

40 The wood used in Ötzi's bow was actually rarely used for bows.

PART 1   *Questions 1–10*

Complete the notes below.

Write **NO MORE THAN TWO WORDS AND/OR A NUMBER** *for each answer.*

A FLIGHT BOOKING

Personal Information

· Full name: **1** .... Adams   · Nationality: Canadian

Booking Details

Ticket type: **2** ....

Departure date: **3** .... August

Class: **4** ....

Disadvantage of the schedule: a long **5** ....

Arrival time in Christchurch: **6** ....

Payment

Advantage of making a payment by credit card: there is no **7** ....

Total fare: $ **8** ....

Card expiry date: **9** ....

Special requirements: **10** .... diet

PART 2   *Questions 11–20*

Questions 11–14

The speaker mentions four things that make Budapest a good place to visit.

*Choose **FOUR** letters, **A–H**.*

A   The city is ideal for people who like specialty beers.

B   It is a good place for walking.

C   The riverbank is the best part of the city.

D   There are many famous modern buildings.

E   Most attractions can be reached by public transport.

F   Shopping is very cheap.

G   The city has two very different halves.

H   There is plenty of wildlife outside the city.

Questions 15–20

Complete the itinerary below.

Write **NO MORE THAN TWO WORDS** *for each answer.*

Day	Places to visit	Details
1–3	Castle District	- Go there by funicular railway. - Start early in the morning when the roads are **15** ....
	Hungarian National Gallery	- Visit Hungarian National Gallery with works of art, including **16** .... from the Middle Ages and impressive modern paintings.
	Matthias Church and Fishermen's Bastion	- You will find seven towers representing nomadic tribes' settlement in Hungary over a millennium ago.
	Danube River	- Take the cruise so as not to miss great views from the river such as the **17** .... building. - Take a sunset tour on a SUP for a more exciting journey.
	Downtown Pest	- Váci Street is the most important street featuring shops where you can buy everything. - If you're feeling hungry, visit the lovely historic cafés, famous for coffee and **18** ....
4–5	Pécs	- a university city with special historical heritage, including UNESCO-listed sites like the ancient burial **19** ....
	Villány	- a village famous for its strong **20** ....

PART 3 *Questions 21–30*

Questions 21–24

Choose the correct letter A, B or C.

Paper on the Great Migration

21 Why did Cindy choose the topic of the Great Migration?

    A She is originally from the city of Chicago.

    B She particularly liked a book on the topic.

    C Many of her classmates were interested in the Great Migration.

22 What does Cindy think Isabel Wilkerson was mistaken about?

    A Migrant statistics.

    B The fact that there were two migrations.

    C The dates when the migration happened.

23 According to Cindy, why did the number of migrants shoot up?

    A America experienced post-World War II prosperity.

    B People wanted to avoid serving in the army.

    C New York was no longer the only destination for migrants.

24 Why was Cindy surprised about migration to Los Angeles?

    A There were not many African-American migrants to Los Angeles.

    B Hollywood attracted many African-American workers.

    C Her previous ideas about the culture of Los Angeles were wrong.

Questions 25–30

Which statement is related to which city?

Write the correct letter, A, B or C, next to Questions 25–30.

Cities
A Los Angeles
B New York
C Chicago

The Great Migration

25 Most African-American migrants began arriving at the start of World War II.

26 It had a large African-American community before the Great Migration.

27 Most of its African-American migrants arrived from Mississippi and Louisiana.

28 African-American migrants transformed its culture.

29 African-Americans found early success here.

30 It drew many African-American migrants from the Carolinas.

Complete the notes below. Write ONE WORD AND/OR A NUMBER for each answer.

The Bajau People: Sea Nomads

· The Bajau people of Southeast Asia are known as 'Sea Nomads'.

The lifestyle of the Bajau

· The Bajau spend their lives almost entirely at sea.

· They visit land only to escape storms and buy **31** ....

· They travel the seas between several countries.

· Most of them do not have a **32** ....

Extraordinary diving skill

· The Bajau are remarkable underwater divers.

· They can spend up to **33** .... minutes underwater.

· Young Bajau sometimes deliberately tear their **34** .... so that diving is easier.

The Bajau spleen

· Other **35** .... that spend a long time underwater have large spleens.

· The spleen may help when blood supply is low because it acts as a kind of blood

  36 ....

· A large spleen may be a benefit for divers.

A comparison with other groups

· Scientists compared the Bajau with a **37** .... tribe—the Saluan.

· Bajau spleens were much larger.

· Scientists also conducted **38** .... of the genome of Bajau and other

  ethnicities.

Is it really natural selection?

· Some researchers believe that evolution has played a part in the different physique of the

  Bajau.

· Other researchers have **39** .... relating to the influence of natural selection.

· We are not yet sure whether the Bajau are evidence of evolution in **40**........................ .

PART 1

Where you live
- Which room in your home would you most like to improve? [Why?]
- Would you say where you live is noisy or quiet? [Why?]
- Would you say your neighbourhood is a good place for young people to live? [Why? / Why not?]

Colours
- Are there any colours you really don't like? [Why? / Why not?]
- Has your choice in the colour of your clothes changed very much since you were younger? [Why? / Why not?]
- Is the colour of personal goods, like mobile phones, for example, important to you? [Why? / Why not?]
- Do you think the colours that people wear tell us anything about their personality? [Why? / Why not?]

Keeping animals in zoos
- Do you think that every city should have a zoo? [Why? / Why not?]
- When did you last visit a zoo? [Why?]
- Who likes zoos the most, young people or older people? [Why?]
- Do you think that zoos will become more or less popular in the future? [Why? / Why not?]

PART 2

Describe a person you know who has a special skill.

> **You should say:**
>> **how you know this person**
>> **what their skill is**
>> **how they learnt this skill**

and explain how you feel about this person.

PART 3

Learning a skill

- What do you think is the best way to learn a new skill?
- Do you think anyone can learn anything, or do you need some natural talent to begin with?
- Do young people learn new skills more easily than older people?

Rewarding skills

- Society rewards some skills, like sporting talent, for example, much more than other skills. Why is that?
- How does being good at something influence a person's life?
- As technology advances, what sorts of new skills will young people have to learn in the future?

ライティング評価基準 ― タスク1

(A) アカデミック　(G) ジェネラル・トレーニング

段階評価	課題の達成度	一貫性とまとまり	語彙力	文法知識と正確さ
9	・課題の要件を完全に満たしている ・詳細説明を含む回答が明確に記述されている	・目立つことなく自然に接続詞を使用している ・段落分けをうまく行っている	・幅広い語彙を単語の特徴を生かして自然かつ洗練された方法で使用でき、軽微な誤りがまれに「うっかり起こる」	・様々な構文を非常に柔軟かつ正確に使いこなすことができまれに軽微な誤りが「うっかり起こる」
8	・課題の要件を十分にカバーしている ・明確かつ適切に重点／要点を記述、強調、説明できている	・情報や意見を論理的に配置している ・全ての観点から文章を上手にまとめている ・段落分けを十分かつ適切に行っている	・正確な意味を伝達するために幅広い語彙を流暢かつ柔軟に使用できる ・一般的でない語句をうまく使用できるが、単語の選択や組み合わせに時おり不適切さがみられる ・単語のスペルや語形成（またはその両方）に間違いがほとんどない	・様々な構文を使用できる ・総じて間違いのない文章を書くことができる ・間違いや不適切さがまれに見られる
7	・課題の要件をカバーしている ・(A) 主要動向、差異、段階の明確な要旨が記述されている ・(GT) 意図が明確に記述されており、統一性のある適切な文調になっている ・重点／要点が明確に記述され、強調できているが、詳述の余地がある	・情報や意見が論理的に整理されており、全体を通じ明確な連続性がある ・適切に様々な接続詞を使用しているが、使用の仕方に過不足がみられる	・十分に幅広い語彙を使用でき柔軟性や正確さも認められる ・一般的でない語句を使用でき、表現や組み合わせにも拝領している ・単語の選択・スペルや語形成（またはその両方）に間違いが散見される	・様々な複雑な構文を使用できる ・間違いの全くない文章を書けることが多い ・文法と句読点をうまく使いこなすが、依然として間違いが存在する
6	・課題の要件に取り組めている ・(A) 適切に選択された情報を含む要旨が記述されている ・(GT) 文調に統一性が見られない場合もあるが、概ね明確に意図を記述している ・重点／要点を記述し、十分に強調できているが、詳細部分が関連性を欠いたり、不適切であったり、不正確であったりする	・情報や意見の配置に一貫性があり、概ね明確な連続性がある ・接続詞を効果的に使用しているが文書中や文章間（またはその両方）の接続詞が機能していなかったり、機械的であったりする ・参照が明確でなかったり、適切でなかったりする	・課題に対する十分な範囲の語彙を使用できる ・一般的でない語句の使用を試みるが、不正確さが見られる ・単語の選択・スペルや語形成（またはその両方）に間違いが散見されるが、コミュニケーションを阻害するほどではない	・簡単な構文と複雑な構文の両方を使用する ・文法と句読点に間違いもあるがコミュニケーションに支障の出るようなことはめったにない
5	・課題の要件に大体取り組めてはいるが、所々の書式が不適切であったりする ・(A) 明確な要旨がなく機械的に詳細を記述し、記述を裏付けるデータが含まれていない ・(GT) 手紙は時おり不明瞭であるが意図が記述されている、文調に統一性がなく、不適切な箇所もある ・重点／要点を記述しているが、十分にカバーしきれておらず、詳細にこだわる傾向がある場合もある	・情報がある程度整理されて記述されているが、全体的な連続性を欠く ・接続詞の使用が、不十分であったり、不適切であったり、多用しすぎであったりする ・参照や置換が不十分なために重複が見られる場合もある	・語彙の使用範囲は限定的であるが、課題に最低限必要なレベルである ・スペルや語形成（またはその両方）にかなりの間違いが見られ、読み手の理解が困難な場合もある	・複雑な構文の使用は限定的である ・複雑な構文の使用も試みるが、簡単な構文と比較して不正確になるきらいがある ・文法や句読点の間違いが多く、間違いのため読みづらいこともある
4	・課題の要件に取り組もうとしているが、重点／要点をカバーしておらず、書式が不適切であったりする ・(GT) 手紙の意図を明確に説明できておらず、文調が不適切な場合もある ・重点／要点と詳細を区別できていない場合もあり、不明瞭、無関連、重複、不正確な部分がある	・情報や意見は記述されているが一貫性を持って配置されておらず、回答に明確な連続性を欠く ・基本的な接続詞が使用されているが、不正確であったり、重複していたりする	・基本的な語彙のみを重複して使用したりし、課題に不適切な場合もある ・スペル、語形成（またはその両方）の使用は限定的である ・間違いが読み手に負担を与える場合がある	・極めて限定的な構文の使用で複文構成はめったにない ・正確な構文もあるが、間違いが多見され、句読点にもしばしば間違いがある
3	・課題の要件に取り組めておらず、課題を全く理解できていない場合もある ・十分に意見を記述できておらず、大半が関連性がないか重複である	・意見を論理的に整理できていない ・接続詞の使用は非常に限定的で使用している場合でも、意見間に明確な関連性を示すことができていない	・使用する語彙と表現が極めて限定的で、語形成やスペル（またはその両方）をうまく操作できない ・間違いによってメッセージが大きく歪曲される	・文章の構成を試みるが、文法と句読点の間違いが多見され意味が歪曲されてしまう
2	・回答がほとんど課題と関連性がない	・文章を整理する能力がほとんどない	・極端に限定的な語彙で、基本的に語形成やスペル（またはその両方）をうまく操作できない	・暗記しているフレーズ以外に文章構成ができない
1	・回答が課題と全く関連性がない	・メッセージが伝わらない	・片言の言葉しか使用できない	・文章構成が全くできない
0	・暗記した回答を記述している			

ライティング評価基準 ― タスク2

段階評価	課題への回答	一貫性とまとまり	語彙力	文法知識と正確さ
9	・課題の全ての部分に完全に取り組んでいる ・回答に対し、関連性のある詳細で十分な裏づけのある理由を提示し、確固とした見解を示すことができる	・目立つことなく自然に接続詞を使用している ・段落分けをうまく行っている	・幅広い語彙を単語の特徴を生かして自然かつ洗練された方法で使用でき、軽微な誤りがまれに「うっかり起こる」	・様々な構文を非常に柔軟にかつ正確に使いこなすことができ、まれに軽微な誤りが「うっかり起こる」
8	・課題の全ての部分に十分取り組んでいる ・回答に対し、関連性のある詳細で十分な裏づけのある理由を提示し、熟考された回答ができている	・情報や意見を論理的に配置している ・全ての観点から文章を上手にまとめている ・段落分けを十分かつ適切に行っている	・正確な意味を伝達するために幅広い語彙を流暢かつ柔軟に使用できる ・一般的でない語句をうまく使用できるが、単語の選択や組み合わせに時おり不適切さがみられる・単語の選択や語形成(またはその両方)に間違いがほとんどない	・様々な構文を使用できる ・総じて間違いのない文章を書くことができる ・間違いや不適切さがまれに見られる
7	・課題の全ての部分に取り組んでいる ・回答を通じ終始明確な見解を示すことができている ・主旨を示し、詳細と理由を提示できるが、一般化しすぎたり理由の論旨が明快ではなかったりする(またはその両方である)	・情報や意見を論理的に整理しており、全体を通じ明確な連続性がある ・様々な接続詞を適切に使用しているが、使用の仕方に過不足がみられる ・各段落には明確な中心主題が存在している	・十分な幅の語彙を使用でき、柔軟性や正確さも認められる ・一般的でない語句を使用でき、表現方法や組み合わせにも配慮している ・単語の選択・スペルや語形成(またはその両方)に間違いが散見される	・様々な複雑な構文を使用できる ・間違いの全くない文章を書けることが多い ・文法と句読点をうまく使いこなすが、エラーは依然として存在する
6	・課題の全ての部分に取り組んでいるが、詳述されている部分とそうでない部分がある ・関連性のある見解を示すことができるが、結論もしくは論点は重複していたりする ・関連性のある主旨を示すことができるが、詳細に欠けたり、不明瞭であったりする	・情報や意見の配置に一貫性があり、概ね明確な連続性がある ・接続詞を効果的に使用しているが、文書中や文章間(またはその両方)の接続が機能していなかったり、機械的であったりする ・参照が明確でなかったり、適切でなかったりする ・段落分けがされているが、必ずしも論理的ではない	・課題に対する十分な範囲の語彙を使用できる ・一般的でない語句の使用を試みるが、不正確さが見られる ・スペルや語形成(またはその両方)に間違いが散見されるが、コミュニケーションを阻害するほどではない	・簡単な構文と複雑な構文の両方を使用する ・文法と句読点に間違いもあるが、コミュニケーションに支障の出るようなことはめったにない
5	・課題の一部にのみ取り組んでおり、所々の書式が不適切であったりする ・見解を表明してはいるが、展開が不明瞭であったり、結論が記述されていないこともある ・要旨が記述されているが、限定的であり、展開が不十分で、無関係な詳細が含まれていることもある	・情報がある程度整理されているが、全般的な連続性を欠く ・接続詞の使用が不十分であったり、不適切であったり、多用しすぎであったりする ・参照や置換が不十分なために重複が見られる ・段落形式で記述されていなかったり、されていても不十分であったりする	・語彙の使用範囲は限定的であるが、課題に最低限必要なレベルである ・スペルや語形成(またはその両方)にかなりの間違いが見られ、読み手の理解が困難な場合もある	・複雑な構文の使用は限定的である ・複雑な構文の使用も試みるが、簡単な構文と比較して不正確になるきらいがある ・文法や句読点の間違いが多く、間違いが理由で読みづらいこともある
4	・課題の要件には最低限しか取り組んでしておらず回答が的外れで、形式も不適切であったりする ・見解を記述しているが不明瞭である ・要旨を記載しているが、特定することが困難であったり、重複、無関係、理由づけが不十分であったりする	・情報や意見は記載されているが、一貫性を持って並べられておらず、回答に明確な連続性を欠く ・基本的な接続詞が使用されているが、不正確であったり、重複していたりする ・段落形式で記述されていなかったり、されていても混沌としている	・基本的な語彙のみを重複して使用したりし、課題をこなすには不十分である ・スペルや語形成(またはその両方)の使用は限定的である ・間違いにより読み手が負担を感じる	・極めて限定的な構文の使用で複文構成はめったにない ・正確な構文もあるが、間違いが多見され、句読点にも間違いがある
3	・課題のどの部分にも十分取り組んでいない ・明確な見解を示していない ・ほとんど意見の記載がなく、多くが詳細と関連性を欠く	・意見を論理的に整理できていない ・接続詞の使用は非常に限定的で、使用している場合でも、意見と意見の間に論理的な関連性を示すことができていない	・使用語彙と表現が極めて限定的で、語形成やスペル(またはその両方)をうまく操作できない ・間違いにメッセージが大きく歪曲される	・文章の構成を試みるが、文法と句読点の間違いが多見され、意味が歪曲されてしまう
2	・課題にほぼ回答していない ・見解を示していない ・意見をひとつふたつ記載しようと試みているが、詳細が記載されていない	・整理する能力がほとんどない	・極端に限定的な語彙で、基本的に語形成やスペル(またはその両方)を操作できない	・暗記しているフレーズ以外に文章構成ができない
1	・回答は課題と全く関連性がない	・メッセージが伝わらない	・片言の言葉しか使用できない	・文章構成が全くできない
0	・受験していない ・課題に取り組んでいない ・暗記した回答を記載している			

スピーキング評価基準

段階評価	流暢さと一貫性	語彙力	文法知識と正確さ	発音
9	・繰り返しや言い直しをほぼすることなく流暢に話し、言いよどむ際は、言葉や文法を考えるというより、話す内容について考える場合のみである ・最も適切な接続詞を使用して理路整然と話すことができる ・テーマを幅広く適切に展開できる	・全てのテーマにおいて、非常に柔軟かつ正確に語彙を使用できる ・熟語を自然かつ正確に使用できる	・様々な構文を自然にかつ適切に使いこなすことができる ・ネイティブスピーカーの会話に見られるような「うっかり」を除き、総じて正確な構文が使用できる	・幅広い発音の特性を正確かつ巧妙に使用できる ・特性を一貫して柔軟に使用できる ・無理なく理解できる
8	・時折繰り返しや言い直しをするが流暢に話し、言いよどむ際は、言葉や文法を考えるというより、話す内容について考える場合のみである ・テーマを理路整然と適切に展開できる	・正確な意味を伝達するために幅広い語彙をすぐに柔軟に使用できる ・不正確さも散見されるが、一般的でない熟語もうまく使いこなすことができる ・必要に応じ言い換えができる	・様々な構文を柔軟に使用できる ・不適切さや軽微な/非体系的な間違いがまれに見られるが、総じて間違いのない文章を話すことができる	・幅広い発音の特性を使用できる ・特性を柔軟に使用できるが、時おりうっかり間違うこともある ・無理なく理解でき、母語のアクセントが明瞭さに与える影響はほぼない
7	・目立った努力を行わずもしくは一貫性を失わずに詳細に話すことができる ・言葉が理由で時折言いよどむことがあり、繰り返しや言い直しがある ・幅広い連結詞や談話標識（文と文との論理的関係を示すことば）を柔軟に使用できる	・様々なテーマを論じる際に柔軟に語彙を使用できる ・一般的でない熟語も使用でき、表現や単語同士の組み合わせにも適切な選択をする場合もある ・必要に応じ効果的に言い換えを行える	・ある程度の柔軟性を持って幅広い複雑な構文を使用できる ・間違いの全くない文章を話せることも多いが、文法の間違いは依然として存在する	・バンド6の全てのプラスの特徴と、バンド8のプラスの特徴を部分的に備えている
6	・時折繰り返し、言い直し、ためらいが見られ、そのため一貫性を失うことがあるものの、すすんで詳細に話す ・幅広い連結詞や談話標識を使用できるが、不適切な使用もある	・テーマについて詳細に論じることができる幅広い語彙力を持っており、不適切な場合でも意味を明確にすることができる ・概ね正しく言い換えができる	・柔軟性に欠けるが、簡単な構文と複雑な構文の両方を使用できる ・複雑な構文では間違いも多いが、理解に支障の出るようなことはめったにない	・幅広い発音の特性を使用できるが、コントロールは不安定 ・特性を効果的に使用できる場合もあるが、一定していない ・概ね理解しやすいが、個々の単語の発音の間違いや不明瞭な音が時おり混じる
5	・通常は途切れることなく話せるが、繰り返し、言い直しや、ためらいが見られ、かつ/または、話し続けようとするとスピードが落ちる ・特定の連結詞や談話標識を過度に使用する ・簡単な話は流暢だが、複雑なコミュニケーションとなると流暢さに問題がみられる	・身近なテーマ、そうでないテーマについても話すことができるが、語彙の使用は柔軟性に欠ける ・言い換えが正しくできるときとそうでないときがある	・ある程度の正確さで基本的な構文を作成できる ・複雑な構文の使用は限定的で、たいてい間違いが含まれており、理解の支障となることもある	・バンド4の全てのプラスの特徴と、バンド6のプラスの特徴を部分的に備えている
4	・顕著な間隔なしには受け答えができず、話す速度が遅く、繰り返しや言い直しが多々ある ・基本的な文章をつなげることはできるが、簡単な連結詞を多用し、一貫性が維持できない	・身近なテーマについては話すことができるが、そうでないテーマは基本的な意味のみ伝えることができ、言葉の選択にも間違いが多い ・言い換えはめったにしない	・基本的な構文を作成でき、単純な文章には間違いがないが、複文構成はめったにない ・間違いも多く、誤解につながることもある	・発音の特性の使用は限定的 ・特性をコントロールしようとするが、よく失敗する ・発音の間違いが多く、聞き取りが困難な場合もある
3	・途切れ途切れに話す ・簡単な文章をつなげる能力に限界がある ・簡単な受け答えのみができ、基本的なメッセージを伝えることさえもできないことが往々にしてある	・個人的情報を伝える際に簡単な語彙を使用できる ・あまり身近でないテーマについては、語彙不足である	・基本構文を試みても困難であったり、明らかにうろ覚えの表現に頼ってしまう ・暗記表現以外は、間違いが非常に多い	・バンド2のいくつかの特徴と、バンド4のプラスの特徴を部分的に備えている
2	・言葉の前にたいてい長い間隔があく ・コミュニケーションがほとんど取れない	・片言もしくは暗記した言葉のみを話す	・基本構文を作成できない	・話し言葉が不明瞭なことが多い
1	・コミュニケーションが全く取れない ・評価できる言語を発しない			
0	・受験をしていない			

IELTSは、British Council、IDP：IELTS Australia、Cambridge English Language Assessmentの共同所有です。

BRITISH COUNCIL **idp** **Cambridge Assessment English**

IELTS Reading Answer Sheet

Candidate Name

Candidate No.

Centre No.

Test Module ☐ Academic ☐ General Training

Test Date Day Month Year

Reading Reading Reading Reading Reading Reading Reading

Marker use only

1		1 ✓ ✗
2		2 ✓ ✗
3		3 ✓ ✗
4		4 ✓ ✗
5		5 ✓ ✗
6		6 ✓ ✗
7		7 ✓ ✗
8		8 ✓ ✗
9		9 ✓ ✗
10		10 ✓ ✗
11		11 ✓ ✗
12		12 ✓ ✗
13		13 ✓ ✗
14		14 ✓ ✗
15		15 ✓ ✗
16		16 ✓ ✗
17		17 ✓ ✗
18		18 ✓ ✗
19		19 ✓ ✗
20		20 ✓ ✗

Marker use only

21		21 ✓ ✗
22		22 ✓ ✗
23		23 ✓ ✗
24		24 ✓ ✗
25		25 ✓ ✗
26		26 ✓ ✗
27		27 ✓ ✗
28		28 ✓ ✗
29		29 ✓ ✗
30		30 ✓ ✗
31		31 ✓ ✗
32		32 ✓ ✗
33		33 ✓ ✗
34		34 ✓ ✗
35		35 ✓ ✗
36		36 ✓ ✗
37		37 ✓ ✗
38		38 ✓ ✗
39		39 ✓ ✗
40		40 ✓ ✗

Marker 2 Signature:

Marker 1 Signature:

Reading Total:

BRITISH COUNCIL

idp

Cambridge Assessment English

IELTS Listening Answer Sheet

685427 1086

Candidate Name

Candidate No.

Centre No.

Test Date   Day   Month   Year

Listening   Listening   Listening   Listening   Listening   Listening   Listening

#	Marker use only	#	Marker use only
1	1 ✓ ✗	21	21 ✓ ✗
2	2 ✓ ✗	22	22 ✓ ✗
3	3 ✓ ✗	23	23 ✓ ✗
4	4 ✓ ✗	24	24 ✓ ✗
5	5 ✓ ✗	25	25 ✓ ✗
6	6 ✓ ✗	26	26 ✓ ✗
7	7 ✓ ✗	27	27 ✓ ✗
8	8 ✓ ✗	28	28 ✓ ✗
9	9 ✓ ✗	29	29 ✓ ✗
10	10 ✓ ✗	30	30 ✓ ✗
11	11 ✓ ✗	31	31 ✓ ✗
12	12 ✓ ✗	32	32 ✓ ✗
13	13 ✓ ✗	33	33 ✓ ✗
14	14 ✓ ✗	34	34 ✓ ✗
15	15 ✓ ✗	35	35 ✓ ✗
16	16 ✓ ✗	36	36 ✓ ✗
17	17 ✓ ✗	37	37 ✓ ✗
18	18 ✓ ✗	38	38 ✓ ✗
19	19 ✓ ✗	39	39 ✓ ✗
20	20 ✓ ✗	40	40 ✓ ✗

Marker 2 Signature:

Marker 1 Signature:

Listening Total:

BRITISH COUNCIL

idp

Cambridge Assessment English

IELTS Writing Answer Sheet

Candidate Name

Candidate No.

Centre No.

Test Module ☐ Academic ☐ General Training

Test Date   Day   Month   Year

If you need more space to write your answer, use an additional sheet and write in the space provided to indicate how many sheets you are using: Sheet   of

Writing   Writing   Writing   Writing   Writing   Writing   Writing

Do not write below this line

Do not write in this area. Please continue your answer on the other side of this sheet.

PROUD CO-OWNER OF IELTS

🔊 音声 DL付き

4 技 能 対 策 ＋ 模 試 2 回

IDP Education
IELTS
公認問題集

IDP Education / イングリッシュイノベーションズ 共著

別 冊 解 答・解 説

Ⓚ 桐原書店

Reading

Reading

練習1 ▶ **図 を 完 成 さ せ る 問 題**　　　　　　　　　　　　　　　本冊P.36

解答　**1** ▶ South African　　**2** ▶ French　　**3** ▶ Spanish

▶ **解説**

全文を読まずにスキャニングだけで解ける問題。問題を解き始める前に図や選択肢リストに目を通そう。

1, 2　図の数字がキーワード。パッセージ中の数字20, 30付近から種を特定できる。

3　段落2の中盤、The shallowest tunnels belong to a much smaller Spanish speciesから解く。

▶ **問題文の訳**

Questions 1-3　ボックス内の単語を使い、以下の図に描かれたトンネルに名前をつけなさい。解答用紙の1〜3の欄に解答を記入すること。　　　　　　　　　　　　　　　　　　※図版の訳は省略しています

糞虫の種類	
フランス種	スペイン種
地中海種	南アフリカ種
オーストラリア原種	南アフリカ・フンコロガシ

▶ **パッセージの訳**

注目すべき甲虫

糞虫を牧草地に放つのは簡単な作業だ。およそ1500匹が、一度に手でつかめる数ずつ牛の放牧地に落とされたばかりの牛糞に撒かれる。糞虫はすぐにその下に姿を消し、穴を掘ってトンネルを掘り、そしてこの新しい環境にうまく適応すれば、すぐにこの土地の生態系に永続的で自立的な存在として組み込まれる。やがて彼らは繁殖し、3、4年以内にはその牧草地への恩恵がはっきりと現れてくる。

糞虫はフンの内側で活動するので、鳥やキツネなどの捕食者から守られる。ほとんどの種は地面に穴を掘り、フンをその真下にあるトンネルに埋めるので、フンは内側から空洞になる。フランスに固有のいくつかの大型種は、牛糞の下30センチメートルくらいの深さまでトンネルを掘る。そうした糞虫は、トンネルに沿ってソーセージのような形をした育房を作る。最も浅いトンネルを掘るのは、はるかに小型のスペインの種で、梨の木の枝から果実がぶら下がっているように見える育房にフンを埋める。南アフリカの糞虫は、フンの表面からおよそ20センチメートル下まで細いトンネルを掘る。南アフリカの種を含む、地表に生息する糞虫の中には、フンを完全な球体に切り取り、それを転がして植物の根元に貼りつけるものもいる。

[語彙]　1. dung：動物のフン、排泄物　2. cow pats：牛糞

練習2 ▶ **フ ロ ー チ ャ ー ト を 完 成 さ せ る 問 題**　　　　　　　本冊P.37

解答　**1** ▶ glucose　　**2** ▶ free radicals　　**3** ▶ preservation

▶ **解説**

練習1同様に全文を読まずにスキャニングだけで解ける問題。問題を解き始める前にフローチャートのキーワードを特定しよう。

1 段落3の2文目にある minimises the amount がチャートの less と一致する。または、チャート内の CR mimetic と processed をキーワードに、段落2の1文目 by interfering with the way cells process glucose を見ると、interfering with が less につながるので答えを導ける。

2, 3 段落3中盤以降で「ブドウ糖処理とATP生成を阻害することがなぜ老化を遅らせるか」に関して2つの説が紹介されている。One possibility relates ... constrain the damage. と Another hypothesis suggests ... and reproduction. は、それぞれチャートの Theory 1 と Theory 2 に対応している。

2 空欄前後から可算名詞の複数形が入ると予想がつく。段落3後半の should limit their production の their は free radicals のこと。パッセージ ⇄ チャートの順で、limit ⇄ fewer / production ⇄ are emitted / thereby constrain the damage ⇄ less damaged のパラフレーズから判断する。

3 Theory 2 の内容を表す Another hypothesis ... 以降を読もう。 パラフレーズ emphasises ⇄ focus on

▶ 問題文の訳

Questions 1-3 以下のフローチャートを完成させなさい。それぞれの答えとして、文章より2語以内の語句を選ぶこと。解答用紙の1〜3の欄に解答を記入すること。

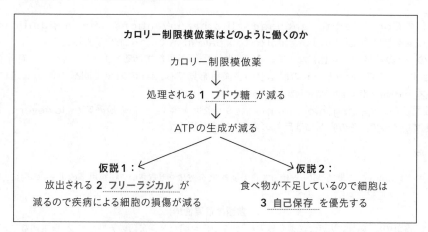

カロリー制限模倣薬はどのように働くのか

カロリー制限模倣薬

↓

処理される **1 ブドウ糖** が減る

↓

ATPの生成が減る

仮説1：
放出される **2 フリーラジカル** が減るので疾病による細胞の損傷が減る

仮説2：
食べ物が不足しているので細胞は **3 自己保存** を優先する

▶ パッセージの訳

アンチエイジング薬の本格的な探求

現在、市場で手に入るどのような治療薬でも、人の老化を遅らせることができると証明されたものはない。しかし、1つの治療的な措置、すなわち低カロリーでありながら栄養的にバランスの取れた食事は、さまざまな種類の動物において寿命を延ばし、健康を長期間保ってくれるなど、驚くほどの効果を発揮している。このような発見は、摂取カロリーの制限が人間の場合でも老化を遅らせ、寿命を延ばす可能性があることを示している。しかし、人に食べる量を実際に減らすよう強いることなく、食べる量を減らしたときと似た生理学的影響を生み出す錠剤「カロリー制限模倣薬」を作り出せるとしたらどうだろう。

カロリー制限模倣薬の候補として最もよく研究されている2DG（2-デオキシ-D-グルコース）は、細胞によるブドウ糖の処理を阻害することによってその機能を発揮する。動物実験では一定の量で毒性を示すことが実証されているため、人間には使用できない。しかし、化学物質によってカロリー制限の効果を再現できることが示された。ポイントは適切な化学物質を見つけ出すことである。

細胞は食物に含まれるブドウ糖を使ってATP（アデノシン三リン酸）を生成する。これは体内の多くの活動のエネルギー源となる分子である。食物の摂取が制限されてカロリーが減少すると、細胞に入るブドウ糖の量が最小限に抑えられ、ATPの生成が減少する。普通の量の餌を食べている動物に2DGを投与すると十分な量のブドウ糖が細胞に届けられるが、この薬によってそのほとんどが処理されなくなるので、ATPの合成も低下する。研究者らは、ブドウ糖の処理とATPの生成を阻害することで、なぜ老化を遅らせることができるのか、いくつかの説を唱えている。1つの可能性は、ATP生成機構によるフリーラジカル（遊離基）の放出に関連している。このフリーラジカルは、細胞に損傷を与えることによって、老化だけでなく、がんなどの加齢性疾患の原因になると考えられている。この機構の働きを低下させるとその生成が減り、そのような損傷も抑制される。もう1つの仮説が示唆しているのは、ブドウ糖の処理が減少することで、食物が不足していることを（実際にそうでなくても）細胞に伝え、成長や生殖などの「贅沢なもの」よりも、生命体の自己保存を優先するアンチエイジング・モードに移行するように誘導するのではないか

ということである。

*calorie（カロリー）：食品のエネルギー換算値

| 練習3 | 要約を完成させる問題 | 本冊P.39 |

| 解答 | **1 ▸ E　　2 ▸ G　　3 ▸ B　　4 ▸ F** |

▸ 解説

実際に問題を解き始める前に、必ず要約のタイトルと要約に目を通そう。本問の場合、パッセージタイトルよりも要約タイトルの方が具体的なので、主旨をつかむうえで役立つ。

1 要約冒頭のwheelから段落1の2文目へ。パッセージ ⇄ 要約の順で、have transformed ⇄ has had a major impact onに加え、existence ⇄ lifeのパラフレーズを見抜けるかがポイント。existence＝「暮らし方、生活」

2 段落1中盤のCompared to language, all other inventions pale in significanceに注目。significanceを言い換えたfundamentalを選ぶ。pale in 〜で「〜において劣る」。

3 空欄文中のyetの前後で、対比になっている。後半は言語が単純であると述べているので、前半には反対の内容がくるはず。一方で、パッセージの段落2の2文目を見ても、yetの前後で同様の対比構造になっている。
　　パラフレーズ extraordinary sophistication ⇄ very complex

4 こちらも段落2の2文目、ingenious simplicityから答えを導く。要約の最終文がHowever ...と言語の複雑さに言及しているので、その直前には反対の内容がくると予想できる。

▸ 問題文の訳

Questions 1-4　下のA〜Gの単語リストを使って次の要約文を完成させなさい。解答用紙の1〜4の欄に、A〜Gの正しい文字を記入すること。

言語の重要性

車輪は生活の **1　物質的な**　側面に大きな影響を与えてきた1つの発明だが、言語の影響ほど **2　根本的な**　ものは、ほかにない。言語はとても **3　複雑な**　ものだが、限られた数の音で構成されている。言語は使うのが **4　簡単に**　思える。しかしながら、その複雑さは、しばしば見落とされがちである。

A 難しい　B 複雑な　C 独特な　D 称賛された　E 物質的な　F 簡単な　G 根本的な

▸ パッセージの訳

このすばらしい発明

人類による数々の発明の中で、言語は最高の地位にあるに違いない。そのほかの発明——車輪、農業、スライスした食パン——は、私たちの物質的な暮らし方を変えたかもしれないが、言語の誕生こそが私たちを人間らしくしたものである。言語に比べると、ほかのどの発明も重要性で劣るが、それは私たちがこれまでに成し遂げてきたあらゆることが言語に依存し、言語から生まれたからである。言語が存在しなければ、私たちは、ほかのすべての動物、さらには自然界そのものに対する圧倒的な力を獲得するまでに登りつめることはできなかっただろう。

しかし、言語が最も重要なのは、単にそれが出発点だからではない。言語は、それ自体が非常に高度な道具でありながら、巧妙な単純さという発想に基づいている。つまり「言語は25種類から30種類の音を組み合わせて無数の表現を生み出す、すばらしい発明なのである。そして、その表現自体は私たちの心の中にあるものとはまったく異なっているが、その秘密のすべてを他者に開示し、私たちの心に入り込めない人たちに、私たちが思い浮かべるあらゆること、私たちの魂のあらゆる動きを伝えることを可能にしてくれる」。このような形で、1660年にベルサイユの近くにあるポール・ロワイヤル修道院の高名なフランスの文法学者たちが言語の本質を導き出し、それ以後、言語の功績の大きさをこれほど雄弁に称賛した者は誰もいない。とはいえ、こうした賛美の数々にはたった1つだけ欠陥がある。というのも、言語の類まれな成果への敬意の裏には、単純ながら重大な矛盾が隠されているからである。言語は人類の最大の発明だが、当然ながら、それは（意図して）作り出されたものではないという

ことだ。この明らかな逆説こそ、私たちが言語に対して魅力を感じる核の部分であり、その秘密の多くを宿しているのである。

練習4 ▶ 複数の選択肢から選ぶ問題　　　　　　　本冊P.40

解答 1, 2 ▶ B, G（順不同）　　　3, 4 ▶ C, E（順不同）

▶ 解説

問題文に目を向けると、1, 2では高齢労働者を雇用するメリットを、3, 4では若年労働者を雇用するデメリットを選択する問いだとわかる。前者は主に段落1で、後者は段落2で列挙されている。事前に情報収集して目的意識を持ってスキャニングしよう。

選択肢にはもっともらしいものもあるが、**パッセージに書かれていないなら不正解**。自分の知識や常識に惑わされないようにしよう。

1, 2　段落1中盤のgood management, such as ... 以下で高齢者のよい点が具体的に挙げられている。... an ability to handle people diplomaticallyがGで、are more skilled in personal relationshipsに言い換えられている。また、spot a problem before it blows upとBが一致する。spotはpredictのパラフレーズ。spot ＝ deal withではないのでDは不正解。

3, 4　段落2の中盤their education standards are much better than those of today's young high-school graduatesがEと一致。段落2の終盤young people tend to switch jobs so frequentlyの部分がCに言い換えられている。

▶ 問題文の訳

Questions 1-2　A～Gの中から2つを選びなさい。解答用紙の1と2の欄に正解となる文字を記入すること。筆者が言及している高齢労働者を雇用することの2つのメリットはどれか。

- **A**　彼らは不注意による事故に巻き込まれる可能性が低い。
- **B**　彼らは将来的に問題となりそうなことを予測できる。
- **C**　彼らは若い労働者を訓練することができる。
- **D**　彼らは予期しなかった問題に対処できる。
- **E**　彼らの方が良心的である。
- **F**　彼らはより低い給料でも働く用意がある。
- **G**　彼らは対人関係のスキルがより高い。

Questions 3-4　A～Fの中から2つを選びなさい。解答用紙の3と4の欄に正解となる文字を記入すること。筆者が言及している若年労働者を雇用することの2つのデメリットはどれか。

- **A**　彼らは自分のスキルを過信している。
- **B**　彼らは、けがをする可能性がある。
- **C**　彼らは1つの会社であまり長く働かない。
- **D**　彼らの訓練は、理論に偏り過ぎていた。
- **E**　彼らは高齢の労働者ほど高い教育を受けていない。
- **F**　彼らはより高い給料を要求する。

▶ パッセージの訳

白髪の労働者①

当然のことだが、高齢者が負荷の多い肉体労働をすると、その年齢のせいで生産性が低下する場合がある。しかし、それ以外のスキル、例えば如才なく他人に対応する能力、会議を取り仕切る能力、問題の発生を予見する能力など、優れた管理に必要不可欠なさまざまな能力は年齢とともに高まるかもしれない。高齢化の政策的含意に関するOECDの研究を統括するピーター・ヒックス氏によると、多くの調査では高齢者の方が（労働力として）価値が高いために、より多くの報酬が支払われている。

また、若者であることの価値は誇張されているのかもしれない。「高齢の労働者を雇用し続けている少数派の企業は、彼らには

5

優れた判断力があり生産性も申し分ないと感じている」と、高齢化の影響に関する本を最近出版したピーター・ピーターソンは語っている。「そのうえ、彼らの教育水準は、今の若い高卒者よりもはるかに高い」。企業は、高齢の労働者は職業生活を間もなく終えようとしているのだから、訓練をする価値がないと言うかもしれない。実際には、若者は頻繁に転職をする傾向があるので、彼らを訓練しても、その見返りはこの上なく低い。雇用主による訓練の対象年齢の中央値は40代後半から50代前半であり、そうした訓練は主に管理職を対象としている。

*OECD：経済協力開発機構

練習5 　複数の選択肢から選ぶ問題 　　　　本冊P.42

解答 　1 ▶ A 　　2 ▶ C 　　3 ▶ D 　　4 ▶ B

▶ 解説

1 選択肢 A, B, C に共通するキーワードである pay から段落1中盤の Take away seniority-based pay scales, へ。これがAと一致する。 パラフレーズ Take away ⇄ abolishing / seniority-based pay scales ⇄ schemes that are based on age
Bのキーワード piece-rates は、段落終盤に manual workers on piece-rates often earn less as they get older と事実が述べられているだけで筆者の主張はない。C, D に当てはまる記述はない。

2 問題文の Skill Team から段落2へ。Aは for 88% of his last IBM salary、Bは up to the age of 60 に反する。
Cが段落最終文の allowing it to retain access to some of the intellectual capital と一致する。
パラフレーズ the intellectual capital ⇄ the expertise
「スキルチーム」は早期退職者向けの会社であり、若者に関係がないのでDは不正解。

3 'bridge' jobs から段落3へ。Aは、it is the best-paid and worst-paid who carry on working に反する。
本文で言及されていないのでBは不正解。
アメリカで実施された研究が紹介されているだけで「橋渡し」の仕事がアメリカ発祥とは書かれていないのでCは不正解。
Dの distinct groups of が、two very different types of と一致する。

4 David Storey's から最終段落へ。Aにあたる記述はない。
Bの内容が、70% of businesses started by people over 55 survived と一致。started, survived の2単語の意味が、Bの are good at running に集約されている。
C, D は、自営業の高齢者や若手経営者の数や数の推移に言及した箇所はないので不正解。

▶ 問題文の訳

Questions 1-4 　A, B, C, または D のうち正解となる文字を選びなさい。解答用紙の1～4の欄に正しい文字を記入すること。

1 第1パラグラフで、筆者は企業が（ 　　 ）を検討できると示唆している。
　A 　年功序列型の給与体系の廃止
　B 　出来高制に基づいた賃金の回避
　C 　高齢労働者の賃金の引き上げ
　D 　高齢労働者に新しいスキルを身につけさせること

2 「スキルチーム」は（ 　　 ）会社の一例である。
　A 　高齢労働者にもっと高い給料を提供する
　B 　社員が望むだけの期間、働き続けることを認める
　C 　高齢労働者の専門知識を活用することを可能にする
　D 　高齢労働者と若年労働者を平等に扱っている

3 筆者によると「橋渡し」の仕事は、（ 　　 ）。
　A 　中程度の給与所得者を引きつける傾向がある

B いくつかのフルタイムの仕事よりも給料が高い

C アメリカで誕生した

D 高齢労働者の中の特定の人たちにとって魅力的である

4 デビッド・ストーリー氏の調査で（　）ということがわかった。

A 人は年を取るにつれて仕事に要求することが多くなる

B 高齢者は自分の会社を経営することに長けている

C ますます多くの高齢者が自営業者になっている

D 自分の会社を経営している若者はほとんどいない

▶ パッセージの訳

白髪の労働者②

一般的には、高齢の労働者は、生産性が高いからではなく、それが高くないにもかかわらず、より多くの報酬を得ていると思われている。雇用者がコスト削減の圧力にさらされたときに、55歳の人に早期退職を促すのは、それが1つの理由なのかもしれない。年功序列型の賃金体系を廃止すれば、高齢の労働者は今よりもっと魅力的な雇用対象になるかもしれない。しかし、ほとんどの雇用主と多くの労働者は、年を重ねた後で賃金を下げるという考えに違和感を持っている。もちろん、出来高制の肉体労働者の場合は、年を取るにつれて収入が減ることがよくあるけれども。したがって、高齢の労働者の雇用を維持することは、異なる方法で彼らを雇い続けることになるのかもしれない。

1つの新方式がIBMベルギーによって考案された。人件費を削減する必要に迫られ、削減の対象を55歳から60歳の社員に絞り込むことにしたとき、IBMは「スキルチーム」という名称の別会社を設立し、同社は60歳まで働き続けることを希望する早期退職者を再雇用した。55歳のときに5年契約でスキルチームに入社した社員は、定年まで働いた場合の時間の58パーセントだけ働き、IBMで最後に得た給料の88パーセントが支払われる。同社はIBMにサービスを提供するので、同社がなければ失っていたであろう知的財産が引き続き利用できるようになった。

高齢者に仕事を続けるように促す最善の方法は、そのような「橋渡し」の仕事、すなわちフルタイムの仕事から退職までの段階的な移行を実現するパートタイムもしくは一時的な雇用を基にすることなのかもしれない。いくつかの研究によると、アメリカでは、中年でフルタイムの仕事に就いていたすべての男女の半数近くが、勤労生活が終わる頃にそのような「橋渡し」の仕事に転職している。一般的には、仕事を続ける人たちは最高賃金労働者と最低賃金労働者である。「橋渡し」の仕事をしている人たちには、まったく異なる2つのタイプがあるようだ。働かなければならないから働き続ける人たちと、引退する余裕はあるけれど仕事をしたいから働き続ける人たちである。

もし雇用市場がもっと柔軟になれば、高齢者は自分に合ったもっと多くの仕事を見つけられるかもしれない。しばしば、彼らは自営業者になるだろう。自分の会社を始める人もいるかもしれない。ウォーリック大学のデビッド・ストーリー氏の調査によると、イギリスでは55歳以上の人たちが始めた企業の70パーセントが存続できたのに対し、国全体の平均では、それはわずか19パーセントだった。しかし、彼らがどのような雇用の形を選んだとしても、今後数年間のうちに、こうした「（白髪の）高齢労働者」が持つスキルはますます評価され、報われなければならないだろう。

練習6	特定する問題	本冊P.44

解答	**1 ▶ NO**	**2 ▶ NO**	**3 ▶ NOT GIVEN**	**4 ▶ YES**	**5 ▶ YES**

▶ 解説

1 段落1の前半のsome people wanted a new semicircular ...と、その後のBut thankfully ...以下を読むと、半円形を推す意見があったが、首相が長方形のデザインを維持したことがわかる。thankfullyに筆者の意見が集約されている。

2 段落1の終盤、seeming to think that a restricted space added urgencyに注目する。urgencyが問題文のrelaxedと噛み合わない。パラフレーズ a restricted space ⇄ a small debating chamber

3 段落2の2文目 It is based on ... では、behaviour, moodと並列されており、どちらの影響が大きいかまでは述べられていない。パラフレーズ influence ⇄ affected

4 キーワードである Pruitt-Igoeから段落3、4へ。段落3最終文のdecayed through neglectと、段落4の2文目 led to chronic neglectが、not cared for properlyにつながる。

5 段落4の最終文で、Pruitt-Igoeの環境の悪化が人々の精神状況を悪化させたという記述がある。feeling distressed ... psychological problemsが問題文のmental healthと一致する。

▶ 問題文の訳

Questions 1-5 以下の文は、文章に記載されている筆者の見解と一致しているか。解答用紙の1～5の欄に、次のように記入すること。

文が筆者の見解と一致する場合はYES
文が筆者の見解と矛盾する場合はNO
筆者がどう考えているか判断できない場合はNOT GIVEN

1 庶民院のデザインは半円形の方が優れていた。
2 チャーチルは、狭い議場の方が討論はより落ち着いたものになると考えていた。
3 環境は人々の行動よりも気分に影響を及ぼした。
4 プルーイット・アイゴー団地が失敗したのは、適切に管理されなかったためだった。
5 プルーイット・アイゴーでは、環境と心の健康の間に関係があった。

▶ パッセージの訳

環境心理学―― 物理的な環境が私たちにとって重要である理由①

私が初めて建物が人の心理に及ぼす影響に興味を持ったのは、第二次世界大戦後に再建された英国議会の庶民院について読んでいたときのことでした。当時は、現在のヨーロッパの多くの議会で好まれているような半円形の馬蹄形の新しいデザインにし、議場も拡張することを望んでいた人もいました。しかし、幸いなことに、ウィンストン・チャーチル首相は、政党が互いに向かい合って座る方が二大政党制に適していると言って、伝統的な長方形のデザインのままにするように議員たちを説得したのです。チャーチルはまた、議場の拡張に反対しましたが、それは狭い空間が議場の雰囲気に緊張感を与えると考えたためのようです。賢明にも、彼はこう語っています。「私たちは建物の形を決めるが、その後で建物が私たちの行動を形作る」

私たち人間と、私たちの周囲の物理的な世界との関係についての研究は、環境心理学と呼ばれています。それは、私たちが占めている空間が、私たちの行動、気分、心の健康に影響を与える可能性もあるという考え方に基づいています。それはハロルド・プロシャンスキーが『環境心理学：人間とその物理的環境』を出版した1970年に広く認知される分野となりました。プロシャンスキーの主張によると、私たちの心理状態は、従来の心理学が教えていたような生い立ちだけでなく、私たちがその中で暮らし、活動する建物のデザインによっても影響を受けるのです。

当時、環境心理学をアメリカにおける深刻な住宅問題に適用しようとするいくつかの試みがありました。中でも最もよく知られている失敗例は、セントルイスでのプルーイット・アイゴープロジェクトでした。同市の数千人もの貧困層の人たちを住まわせるために1954年に建設されたプルーイット・アイゴー団地は、33棟の高層アパートで構成されていました。その建設当時、同団地は新たな入居者から「砂漠のオアシス」と称えられ、それまで住んでいた非常に貧弱な居住環境に比べてよい評価を得ていました。しかしながら、16年も経たないうちに、プルーイット・アイゴー団地全体が管理不足によって急速に荒廃し、取り壊す必要に迫られました。

さて、こうした問題には、いくつかの原因があったことは明らかです。プルーイット・アイゴー団地では、共有スペースの存在と私的なスペースの不足が慢性的な管理不足をもたらしました。設計者らは、共有スペースがあることで誰もが住環境に気を配るようになるだろうと期待していましたが、実際には誰もそれに責任や個人的な満足を感じていませんでした。住環境の悪化により、そこに住む人々は不安を感じ、犯罪行為や精神的な問題が高率で発生するようになりました。

解答	1 ▶ purchase probability　2 ▶ mystery
	3 ▶ (shopping) malls　4 ▶ wasting time

▶ 解説

文を完成させる問題

1　問題文の、emotional, producedなどのキーワードを頼りに段落1の2文目produce specific emotional effects ... を特定する。
　　パラフレーズ effects ⇄ impact / enhance ⇄ increase

2　4原則が述べられている段落2から答えを探す。問題文のカンマより前半は4原則のThe third ...の内容を言い換えているので、後半はthe fourth ...の内容を答えると予想できる。
　　パラフレーズ interested ⇄ not bored

3　principlesの話題なので段落2へ。最終文が問題文の言い換えになっている。
　　パラフレーズ reflected ⇄ shown / today's ⇄ modern

4　問題文は段落3の中盤にあるCasinos deliberately remove ... in a casino.を言い換えたもの。パッセージの文は事実を述べる文だが、問題文では仮定法に言い換えられており、難易度が高め。

▶ 問題文の訳

Questions 1-4　以下の文を完成させなさい。それぞれの答えとして、文章の中から1語または2語を選ぶこと。解答用紙の1〜4の欄に解答を記入すること。

1　店舗のデザインが人の感情に及ぼす影響によって、消費者による　購入の確率　が上がるかもしれない。
2　人が退屈しないように、建物の内部はある程度複雑でなければならず、　ミステリー　の要素もあるべきだ。
3　「アトモスフェリックス」の原則は、多くの最新式の　（ショッピング）モール　の設計に反映されている。
4　カジノに窓や時計があると、人は自分が　時間を浪費している　と思うかもしれない。

解答	5 ▶ C　6 ▶ C　7 ▶ B

▶ 解説

特徴を組み合わせる問題

casinoとhospitalに関しては、それぞれ段落3、4で言及しているので重点的に見ていこう。

5　段落3、段落4のそれぞれ最終文で照明がカジノと病院に影響を与えることが書かれている。
6　段落3の中盤Sound is also manipulated ...と、段落4の最終文Background music ... also have a positive effect.が一致。
7　段落4の最終文にhigh ceilings ...とあるので病院は該当する。
　　パラフレーズ ceilings ⇄ The height of indoor spaces

▶ 問題文の訳

Questions 5-7　この文章によると、次のA〜Cに当てはまるのは以下の記述のどれか。解答用紙の5〜7の欄にA〜Cの正しい文字を記入すること。注意：いずれの文字も何度でも使ってよい。

場所
A カジノのみ　B 病院のみ　C カジノと病院の両方

5　照明は人の精神状態において役割を果たしている。
6　音は、人の精神状態に影響を与えるうえで重要である。

9

7　屋内スペースの高さは、何らかの影響を及ぼす。

▶ パッセージの訳

環境心理学——物理的な環境が私たちにとって重要である理由②

環境心理学は、フィリップ・コトラーが『The Journal of Retailing』誌に発表した論文で「アトモスフェリックス＝雰囲気」という用語を作り出した1973年になって、初めて別の文脈で適用されました。彼は「アトモスフェリックス」を「消費者が商品を購入する可能性を高める特定の感情に影響するように、買い物の環境を設計すること」と定義しました。コトラーは、場合によっては販売する商品よりも店の雰囲気の方が重要であり、消費者はその空間にいることが快適だというだけでその店に引き寄せられる可能性があると主張しました。

彼は4つの原則を定めました。1つ目は「統一性」でした。基本的に、これは色や形、音などの要素がうまく連動することを意味していました。2つ目は「わかりやすさ」で、建物は人が移動しやすいことを条件にしていました。3つ目の「複雑さ」は、建物の内部も、人がその中を移動することに興味を持ち続けられるよう変化のあるものでなければならないと定めました。これに関連した4つ目の原則は「ミステリー」でした。次の角を曲がったら何があるのかまったくわからない、ということでした。これはずっと飽きずにいたいという消費者の欲求を満たすものでした。これらの原則はすべて、今日の多くのショッピングモールの設計に反映されています。

現代において、最新式のカジノほど、設計者が消費者に影響を与えるために、いかに大きな努力を払っているのかを示すビジネスはありません。ラスベガスの典型的なカジノの内部は、独特の雰囲気を持っています。壁には窓も時計もありません。時間を感じさせるものがないのです。カジノは、通常の時間の経過を感じさせる手がかりをすべて意図的に排除し、客に自分がカジノで「無駄な時間を過ごしている」ことを忘れさせるようにします。音響もカジノの経営者によって操作されます。絶え間なく流れる背景音が、時間が止まったような雰囲気を保つ一方で、誰かが大当たりを出すたびに響くコインの流れ落ちる音が、人に成功への期待を与え続けます。ある意味、カジノのフロアは「わかりやすい」ものではありません。カジノの設計者は、あなたに、いわば迷子になって現実の世界を忘れてほしいからです。しかし、彼らはあなたが本当に迷子になっていると「感じて」ほしくはありません。なぜなら、それではあなたが不安を感じるからです。そういうわけで、照明とカーペットの模様が、カジノの経営者があなたに行ってほしい場所に無意識的に導くのです。

今日、環境心理学の応用は以前よりもはるかに細かく複雑になっています。例えば、病院の建物については、安心感を高め、ひいては患者の回復の助けになることを目的に研究が進められています。多くの国々で行われている研究によると、病院に「緑地」を設けるだけで患者の気分が晴れるだけでなく、実際に手術してから回復するまでの時間が短縮され、慢性疾患の場合には、はるかに望ましい結果が得られています。背景音楽、高い天井、そして患者に照明の調節ができるようにすることもまた、プラスの効果があります。

環境心理学をさらに洗練させることによって、私たちの生活はあらゆる面で改善されつつあり、今後も生活環境にさらなる多くの向上が期待できるでしょう。

実践問題

| 実践1 | 情報を組み合わせる問題
文の前半と後半を組み合わせる問題
要約を完成させる問題 | 本冊P.48 |

解答 　1 ▶ G 　2 ▶ B 　3 ▶ F 　4 ▶ D 　5 ▶ E

▶ 解説

情報を組み合わせる問題

1 future がキーワード。スキミングすると、本パッセージは特に段落A〜Eまでは過去の出来事を述べていることがわかり、除外できる。段落Gの最初の文と「未来の出来事に関する警告」がマッチする。

2 the destruction of a village と、段落Bの後半 obliterating the small community of Tambora のパラフレーズを見抜こう。

3 問題文にある climate change は段落Fに登場する global warming のこと。suggestion から、過去の出来事に言及した段落A〜Eではないと推測できる。
[パラフレーズ] tackle the problem of global warming ⇄ addressing climate change

4 噴火が芸術に与えた影響に触れているのは段落Dのみ。painted landscapes, novel を拾えたら解きやすい。

5 キーワードは social unrest。段落Eでは噴火が気候に与えた影響に言及している。本段落を読み進めると「気候変動→凶作→価格高騰→社会不安」と話が展開する。
[パラフレーズ] riots, arson, and looting ⇄ social unrest

▶ 問題文の訳

Questions 1-5 　この文章には、A〜Gの7つの段落がある。次の情報が含まれている段落はどれか。解答用紙の1〜5の欄にA〜Gの正しい文字を記入すること。

1 未来の出来事に関する警告
2 集落が破壊されたことへの言及
3 気候変動に対処するための提案
4 芸術の世界への影響に関する説
5 社会不安への言及

解答 　6 ▶ B 　7 ▶ H 　8 ▶ F 　9 ▶ E 　10 ▶ A

▶ 解説

文の前半と後半を組み合わせる問題

6 文の前半の ash cloud がパッセージ段落Bの最終文で ash shroud になっている。
[パラフレーズ] stench ⇄ bad stink

7 文の前半の Wood and ash in the sea から段落Cの2文目へ。
[パラフレーズ] formed floating islands ⇄ formation of huge rafts

8 tsunami から段落Cへ。3、4文目A medium-sized tsunami hit ...と一致する。

9 段落D, E, F で stratosphere が出てくるが、EとFは気候変動に関する内容。段落D中盤のWinds spread the fine particles around the globe, creating incredible optical phenomena.と一致する。
[パラフレーズ] optical ⇄ visual

10 Bad harvests から段落E中盤のThe crops were so poor ...へ。demonstrations in front of grain markets and bakeries, followed by riots, arson, and looting were common からAを選ぶ。同じ段落の後半にtyphusやcholeraが出てくるが、これらはドイツの話ではない。短絡的にDを選ばないように。

Questions 6-10　後半部分として正しいものを以下のA〜Hから選んで各文を完成させなさい。解答用紙の6〜10の欄にA〜Hの正しい文字を記入すること。

6　直後に発生した火山灰雲は（ バタビアの空気中の悪臭 ）をもたらした。
7　海に流れ出た木材と灰が一緒になって（ 巨大な漂流物の形成 ）をもたらした。
8　津波は（ モルッカ諸島での死者 ）をもたらした。
9　成層圏の微細な灰が（ 劇的な視覚効果 ）をもたらした。
10　凶作が（ 社会不安と抗議運動 ）をもたらした。

> A　社会不安と抗議運動
> B　バタビアの空気中の悪臭
> C　火砕流
> D　ドイツの諸都市における疫病の流行
> E　劇的な視覚効果
> F　モルッカ諸島での死者
> G　気候学者の間での激しい議論
> H　巨大な漂流物の形成

解答	11 ▶ cost　　12 ▶ ozone　　13 ▶ rainfall 14 ▶ mega-eruption / eruption / disaster

▶ 解説

「要約を完成させる問題」 は、パッセージの全体ではなく一部の段落を要約していることが多い。まずはタイトルと要約文をざっと読んで、パッセージのどこの要約なのか見当をつけてから取り掛かろう。ここでは段落FとGの一部をスキャニングすれば解ける。空欄前後を読んで、品詞など文法的な予想をしておくのも忘れずに。

11　直前にtheがあるので、空欄には単数か不可算名詞が入ると判断する。段落Fの2文目と要約2文目が一致する。パラフレーズ reasonable ⇄ acceptable

12　段落Fの後半のReduction in the ozone levelと、要約の... and there might be loss of 13　ozone　in the atmosphere.が一致する。パラフレーズ Reduction ⇄ loss of

13　geoengineering, rise sharplyを頼りに段落Fの最終文に行き着く。
パラフレーズ should ⇄ if / be stopped all at once ⇄ a halt suddenly

14　段落Gの1文目と要約の最終文の主節が一致する。パラフレーズ critics ⇄ Pessimists

▶ 問題文の訳

Questions 11-14　以下の要約文を完成させなさい。それぞれの答えとして、文章から1語を選ぶこと。解答用紙の11〜14の欄に解答を記入すること。

地球工学的手法に関する懸念

気候変動を克服する方法として、地球工学的手法が提案されている。二酸化硫黄を成層圏に取り入れることは効果的かもしれず、その**11　コスト**　は許容できるものだろう。しかし、そのような対策には不都合な点もいくつか出てくるかもしれない。粒子は呼吸器疾患を持つ人たちに害を及ぼす可能性があり、大気中からは**12　オゾン**　が減少するかもしれない。また、この地球工学的手法が突然停止された場合、**13　降雨量**　と気温が急激に上昇するだろう。悲観論者は、私たちが歴史を案内人と見なしたなら、もう次の**14　（大）噴火／災害**　を迎える時期が来ていると指摘している。

▶ パッセージの訳

タンボラ火山

A　その爆発音は2600キロメートル離れた所でも聞こえた。灰は少なくとも1300キロメートル離れた地点にも降り注いだ。1815年にインドネシアのスンバワ島にあるタンボラ火山が、有史以来最大の規模となる噴火で山頂部を吹き飛ばしたとき、

その直接的な影響は壊滅的なものだった。スンバワ島そのものと、すぐ近くのロンボク島やバリ島では、数千人もの人命が失われた。長期的な影響は、遠くヨーロッパやアメリカを含め世界中で感じられた。今日でも、現行の気候変動との闘いに関わっている気候学者の間では、タンボラ山の噴火の気象学的影響は引き続き議論の的となっている。

B　タンボラ山は1815年4月5日に火山活動が活発になった。翌朝、火山灰が東ジャワに降り始め、4月10日まで小規模の爆発音が風に乗って聞こえてきた。その日のうちに噴火は激しさを増し、山腹全体が流れる液状の火の塊に変わり、火砕流が斜面を海まで流れ下ってタンボラ島の小さな集落を完全に破壊した。火山灰の幕はバタビア（現代のジャカルタ）にまで及び、そこでは亜硝酸の悪臭が辺りに漂い、酸性の激しい雨が数日間降り続いた。

C　スンバワ島の植生はすべて失われた。倒れた木々は軽石混じりの灰とともに海に押し流され、幅5キロメートルにもなる浮島が生まれた。中規模の津波がインドネシア諸島のいくつかの島々の沿岸を襲い、遠く離れた場所で人命の犠牲と破壊を引き起こした。東ジャワとモルッカ諸島では、津波の高さは2〜3メートルに達した。推定される死者数は参照する記録によって異なる。すべての主な情報源を考慮すると、火砕流によって引き起こされた直接の死者数は1万人と計算される。その後スンバワ島では1万8000人が餓死し、ロンボク島では約1万人が飢えとそれに関連する病気で死亡した。全体では、インドネシア諸島で10万人が、この噴火の直接的および間接的な影響で亡くなったと考えられている。

D　タンボラ山の噴火は、43キロメートル以上の高さの成層圏にまで火山灰を噴き上げた。氷床コアに残された痕跡によると、この高密度の塵は上空10〜30キロメートルの高さで地球の大気中に数か月から数年の間とどまっていた。風がこの微粒子を世界中に拡散し、目を見張るような光学現象を生み出した。ロンドンでは鮮やかな色の夕日が頻繁に観測され、それがあの有名なJ. M. W. ターナーの鮮烈な色彩の風景画に影響を与えたとする説もある。暗くなった空はまた、小説『フランケンシュタイン』が生み出されるきっかけになったとも言われている。

E　非常に大量の二酸化硫黄（SO_2）が成層圏に放出されたため、それが気候に大きな影響を与えた。1816年という年は1400年頃以降、北半球で2番目に寒かった年で、1810年代は記録に残っている限り最も寒い10年間であることが今ではわかっている。1816年は「夏のない年」として知られるようになった。歴史家たちは、ヨーロッパでは、この大幅な寒冷化により9万人の命が失われたと推定している。ヨーロッパ各地でも例年の冬より嵐が多く発生し、気温が低く大雨が降ったため、イギリスからアイルランドにかけて凶作になった。ドイツではひどい凶作のために食料の価格が急騰し、穀物市場やパン屋の前でのデモや、それに続く暴動、放火、略奪行為が多くの都市で頻発した。それはこの国にとって、19世紀で最悪の飢饉だった。気候の変動はまた、1816年から1819年までヨーロッパの南東部と地中海の東岸沿いで起きたチフス大流行の原因とされている。インドでは、それがモンスーンの発生を乱して3回にわたる凶作を引き起こし、新種のコレラの蔓延をもたらして、これらが数千万人の死につながった。

F　近年、一部の科学者たちは地球温暖化の問題に対処するために、タンボラ山の噴火のような冷却効果を人工的に生み出すことができないかどうか検討し始めている。ミサイル発射装置や飛行機を使って成層圏に二酸化硫黄を注入することは、合理的なコストで実行でき、地球の気温を下げるのに十分に効果があると提案されている。しかし、この種の地球工学的手法は議論を引き起こしている。これに反対する人たちはいくつかのリスクを指摘している。まず健康被害の懸念がある。硫酸塩の粒子が大量に地面に落ちてきた場合、それが喘息患者やそのほかの呼吸器疾患を持つ患者に害を及ぼすだろう。オゾン濃度の低下は、もう1つの考えられる副作用である。また、地球工学的な措置をいきなり中止すると、地球温暖化の5倍から10倍のスピードで気温と降雨量が急増すると指摘する科学者もいる。

G　こうした批判者らは、タンボラ山の噴火の効果を再現しようとすることよりも、そのような規模で本物の噴火が再び起こることをもっと心配する必要があるとつけ加えている。過去の気象データによると、この種の大噴火は、平均すると2世紀に1回、世界のどこかで起こってきた。タンボラ火山が噴火してから200年以上が経過している。そのような災害が現在のような相互に結びついた世界に与えるであろう経済的、社会的、環境的な影響を考えれば、私たちは身震いするしかないのである。

解答	1 ▸ v	2 ▸ x	3 ▸ ii	4 ▸ iv	5 ▸ i	6 ▸ vi

▶ 解説

「**段落に合う見出しを選ぶ問題**」では、各段落のトピックセンテンスを読んで主旨を把握すればよい。トピックセンテンスは段落の最初にくることが多いが、最初にない場合は、最後の文→中盤にも目を通す必要がある。

1 段落Bのトピックセンテンスは1文目だが、これだけでは答えを導けないので注意。Bの最終文が根拠になる。選択肢vのThousands of time zonesが「すべての町が独自のタイムゾーンを持っていました」につながる。

2 段落Cの1文目が主旨を表す。主旨＝「鉄道移動と電信通信によって（公式の）タイムゾーンの必要性が高まった」。Cの最終文も根拠に答えを導こう。

3 段落Dはフレミングの具体的な話から始まっており、1文目がトピックセンテンスではない。後半にさしかかるFleming's plan is now 150 years old ...の文がトピックセンテンスで、それがA long-lasting systemと結びつく。

4 段落Eのトピックセンテンスは2文目。「タイムゾーンを再び不要とする動き＝another change」。ixのThe impact of the internetは主旨ではなく、インターネットは不要論の勃興のきっかけの1つにすぎないので不適当。

5 段落Fのトピックセンテンスは1文目。選択肢iのfuture change＝「世界時の導入」。段落中のThe benefits, positive psychological impactなどから世界時の利点を列挙している段落だとわかる。また、仮定的なwould が多用されており、未来について書かれていると判断できる。

6 段落Gのトピックセンテンスは1文目で、後半のUniversal Time would take a long time to grow used to とviが結びつく。主旨＝「世界時に慣れるのは容易ではないかもしれない」

▶ 問題文の訳

Questions 1-6 この文章にはA〜Gの7つの段落がある。以下の見出しリストから段落B〜Gにふさわしい見出しを選びなさい。段落Aは、すでに解答が与えられている。解答用紙の1〜6の欄にi〜xの正しい番号を記入すること。

※解答欄の訳は省略しています

> **見出しリスト**
> i 将来的な変更がもたらす利点
> ii 長く続いているシステム
> iii 1つの国に5つのタイムゾーン
> iv 再び変更が必要なとき？
> v 何千ものタイムゾーン
> vi 慣れるのに時間がかかる？
> vii 経済的ないくつかの利点
> viii 現代生活でおなじみのこと
> ix インターネットの影響
> x タイムゾーンが必要になる

解答	7 ▸ NOT GIVEN	8 ▸ TRUE	9 ▸ TRUE	10 ▸ FALSE
	11 ▸ FALSE	12 ▸ FALSE		

▶ 解説

特定する問題

7 問題文の19th century, horse, 100 kmを頼りに段落Bへ。Bの中にも100 kmと記述があるが「馬乗りが1

日100kmしか移動できなかった」に当てはまる／反する情報はないのでNOT GIVENが正解。

8 問題文のTrain travelから段落Cへ。Cの最終文から答えを導く。

9 問題文に固有名詞Flemingがあるので段落Dを特定しやすい。Dの中盤Fleming took that as his starting pointのthatはGMTで、この部分が問題文と一致する。

10 段落D後半のcertain countries have elected to distinguish themselves by 30 minutesに反する。

11 段落Eでは、空の旅で移動時間が短縮してタイムゾーン不要論が浮上した内容が書かれている。

12 段落F中盤The benefits ... 以降で、世界時の利点が述べられている。Fの終盤The problems due to ... 以降で健康上の利点に言及している。

▶ 問題文の訳

Questions 7-12　以下の文は、この文章に記載されている情報と一致しているか。解答用紙の7〜12の欄に、次のように記入すること。

記述が情報と一致する場合はTRUE

記述が情報と矛盾する場合はFALSE

それに関する情報がない場合はNOT GIVEN

7 19世紀に馬で移動した人は、1日あたり100キロメートルしか移動できなかった。

8 列車の旅は、公式なタイムゾーンが必要となるきっかけとなった。

9 フレミングは、彼の方式を既存の慣例に基づいて生み出した。

10 すべてのタイムゾーンは、お互いの間に少なくとも1時間の間隔がある。

11 空の旅によって、タイムゾーンがさらに必要となった。

12 世界時には健康上の利点はない。

解答 | **13 ▶ C**

▶ 解 説

複数の選択肢から選ぶ問題

13 世界時に言及しているのは段落E, F, G。段落Fの最終文と選択肢Cが同義。

パラフレーズ positive psychological impact ⇄ feel better psychologically / keeping exactly the same time ⇄ Universal Time

A→段落FのBusinesses ... save money. に反する。

B→太平洋諸島への影響が述べられているが、ほかに日本やロサンゼルスの例もあるので一致しない。

D→パッセージ中に書かれていない内容。

▶ 問題文の訳

Question 13　正解となるA, B, CまたはDの文字を選びなさい。解答用紙の13の欄に正しい文字を記入すること。世界時は、

A 経済的な恩恵はもたらさないだろう。

B 主に太平洋諸島に影響を及ぼす。

C 人々を心理的に楽にしてくれる。

D 地域によって変更されることがある。

▶ パッセージの訳

タイムゾーン（時間帯）はなぜあるのか

A あなたがいる場所では、今、何時でしょうか。例えば、あなたがシンガポールでこれを読んでいて、月曜日の夜の19時24分だと想像してみましょう。太陽は沈んだばかりです。あと30分ほどで、家族と一緒に夕食のテーブルに着くのかもしれません。世界のほかの場所では、それよりも時間が早かったり遅かったりします。ロンドンでは午前の中頃です。ニューヨークでは6時24分で、早起きの人なら朝のコーヒーを飲んでいるところです。ニュージーランドのオークランドでは、すでに火曜日になっています。今では、私たちは世界が複数のタイムゾーンに分割されていることを当然のように思っています。私たちはこうした考え方に十分になじんでいるので、タイムゾーンという考えそのものが、人類の歴史の中で比較的新しいもので

あることに気づいていないのかもしれません。

B 200年前には、タイムゾーンは存在しませんでした。19世紀半ばに電信装置が発明される前、すなわち馬に乗るよりも速く移動する方法がなかった時代には、公的なタイムゾーンなどは必要ありませんでした。当時、わずか100キロメートル離れた町では何時なのか、ましてや地球の裏側が何時なのか誰も気にせず、各自治体がそれぞれの時間を設定していただけでした。太陽が空の最高点に達すると、誰もが自分の時計を正午に合わせ、そこから1日の時間を割り出しました。その結果として、すべての町が独自のタイムゾーンを持っていました。

C それがすべて、鉄道移動と電信通信の発明とともに一変しました。人々の移動がより活発になると、遠くの町では何時なのかが問題になり始めました。あなたがその町を出発する乗り継ぎ列車に乗る予定ならば、その列車に乗り遅れてしまうかもしれません。みんなの腕時計が異なる時間を示していたら、国の鉄道網はどうして機能できるでしょうか。ヨーロッパでは、19世紀半ばまでに大陸間の鉄道網が発達し始め、まもなくそれにアメリカの大陸横断鉄道が続きました。標準時というものがなければ、このようなシステムは運営できるはずはありません。

D 1876年のある日、サンドフォード・フレミングというスコットランド系カナダ人の技師が列車に乗り遅れてしまい、腹立たしさを感じました。彼は世界を24のタイムゾーンに分割するという案を思いつきました。1855年以来、イギリスはグリニッジ標準時（GMT）として知られる古い航海用の基準時間に基づいて「鉄道時間」と呼ばれる標準時を使っていました。フレミングはそれを出発点として、全世界をGMTと関連づけて24の区域に分割することを提案しました。グリニッジの東側の地域の時間はより早く、西側の地域はより遅くなります。例えば、イスタンブールならGMTプラス3時間、ブエノスアイレスならGMTマイナス3時間となります。フレミングの案は、今では150年の歴史があり、グローバルなコミュニケーションやビジネスの基本的な一部分となっています。実際には、現在の状況は24のタイムゾーンとはなっていません。一部の国々は時間を30分単位で区切ることにしたため、実際には全体で39のタイムゾーンがあります。アメリカには東部、中部、山岳部、太平洋の4つのタイムゾーンがあります。ただし、中国のタイムゾーンは、その地理的な広がりからすると本来なら5つくらいあるべきですが、1つしかありません。

E しかし、これで話は終わりではないかもしれません。空の旅が移動の時間をさらに短縮し、インターネットが世界をさらに近いものにしたため、なぜタイムゾーンが必要なのかと疑問を投げかける人が出てきました。なぜ私たちは世界中のどこでも共通の時間を持っていないのでしょうか。リチャード・コン・ヘンリーとスティーブ・ハンケという2人のアメリカの大学教授は「世界時」を提案しています。それによれば、私たちは皆、かつてGMTと呼ばれていたロンドンの時間に時計の時刻を設定するだけでよいのです。このようなことは、すでにいくつかの分野で起こっています。金融トレーダーは、一部の国の軍隊と同様、自分がどこにいようと時計をGMTに設定することが多くなっています。

F ヘンリーとハンケは、時計の時刻は人間が人工的に作り出したものなので、私たち全員がまったく同じ方針に従うことはできないとする科学的な根拠はないと指摘しています。ニューヨークの9時が東京、カラチ、オークランドでも9時だったら、事はもっと単純ではないでしょうか。その利点は、即効性があり大きなものになるだろうと2人は強調しています。生活はもっと単純になるでしょう。世界のほかの場所で今何時なのかを計算する必要はなくなり、長距離旅行の計画は今よりずっと簡単になるでしょう。企業や政府機関はコストを節約できるでしょう。睡眠不足や心臓病の高い発生率など、人為的に強制された現行のタイムゾーンが原因だとされている問題は、各地域が独自の予定表を設定することで解消されるかもしれません。何よりも、全人類がまったく同じ時間を共有することの長期的で好ましい心理的影響は計り知れません。

G しかしながら、これを批判する人たちは、これに心理的に慣れるのはそれほど簡単ではないかもしれないと指摘しています。例えば、日本に住んでいる場合、新しい1日はいつも午前中の中途半端な時間に始まります。ロサンゼルスでは、新しい1日は午後遅くに始まることになります。太平洋のいくつかの島々では、太陽が高く昇る時間に日付が変わります。人は金曜日に目を覚まし、土曜日に就寝することになるでしょう。そのため「世界時」に慣れるまでには長い時間がかかり、そのほかにもいくつかの欠点があるでしょう。「午前2時までパーティーをする」「9時5時（定時）の仕事をしている」などの文化的な表現は意味をなさなくなります。いずれにしても、私たちが長距離便に乗るときはいつでも、時差ぼけには悩まされ続けることでしょう。

Listening

Part 1 〉 対策

練習1 〉 表を完成させる問題 　　　　　　　　　　　　　　　　本冊P.68 / track 1

解答
1 ▸ 16[sixteen]　　2 ▸ classes　　3 ▸ $1.75　　4 ▸ Equipment Only
5 ▸ cardio

▶ 解説

1 　accessには「利用」の意味もあり、音声ではuseにパラフレーズされている。
2 　First, there is The Full Service Membership. を聞き逃さないように、表におけるType 1: Full Service Membershipの内容が流れるサインとなっている。
3 　ディストラクターのUS$ 2に注意。
4 　Ashleyの発言、And the other type?により、次に解答が来ると予想できる。
5 　問題文のmachines for strength andを読めば、空欄には、ほかの用途の機器を表す語句が来ると予想できる。

▶ 問題文の訳

Questions 1-5　以下の表を完成させなさい。それぞれの解答として、2つ以下の単語か1つの数字、もしくはその両方を記入すること。

ビレッジ・ウェルネス・クラブ　　　　　会員契約	
会員資格の最低年齢条件：	
ジムの利用：1　16　歳	会員契約者：18歳
タイプ1：フルサービス会員	
利用範囲：すべての機器と2　レッスン	
個人プログラム：運動と減量の専門家の指導	
料金：3　1.75ドル　／日	
タイプ2：4　マシン限定　会員	
個人プログラムはありません	
利用範囲：筋力トレーニングと5　カーディオ　用のマシン、およびフリーウェイト	
料金：1日1ドル	

▶ スクリプトと訳

You will hear a conversation between a staff member at a wellness centre and a woman who wants to become a member. First, you have some time to look at Questions 1 to 5.
Now listen carefully and answer Questions 1 to 5.
A = Ashley 🇬🇧　R = Receptionist 🇺🇸

ウェルネスセンターのスタッフと入会をしたい女性の会話が聞こえてきます。まず、設問1〜5を見る時間があります。では、音声を注意深く聞いて設問1〜5に答えなさい。
A=アシュリー　　R=フロント係

A　Hi, I'd like some information about joining the Village Wellness Club.
R　Sure. What exactly can I help you with?
A　I'd like to know about the membership contract.

こんにちは。ビレッジ・ウェルネス・クラブへの入会について少し教えてほしいことがあるのですが。
かしこまりました。具体的に、どのようなことでしょうか。
会員契約のことを知りたいんです。

R First of all ₁you must be over **16** years of age to use the Gym, and must be at least two years older, that is 18, to agree to a membership contract. May I see your ID card?	まず、ここのジムを利用するには16歳以上である必要があり、会員契約を結ぶには少なくともその2歳年上、つまり18歳である必要があります。あなたの身分証を拝見できますか。
A Sure. Here it is.	ええ。これです。
R You were born on 21st of January 2001—yes, you're eligible. For your information, there are two types of membership.	あなたは2001年1月21日のお生まれですね。はい、入会資格はおおありです。ご参考までに、会員には2つのタイプがあります。
A Can you tell me what they are?	それがどういうものか教えてください。
R First, there is the Full Service Membership. ₂You can use all the equipment at any time, and you can also join any **classes**. And not only that, you'll get the services of our exercise and weight loss professionals who can help you design your own personalised programme and teach you how to perform each exercise.	まず、「フルサービス会員」があります。いつでもすべての運動機器が利用でき、また、どのレッスンでも参加できます。さらに、自分に合ったプログラムを作ったり、個々の運動のやり方を教えてくれたりする運動と減量の専門家の指導を受けられます。
A Wow I like that. How much do I have to pay for that one?	わあ、それはいいですね。それには、どれくらいの費用がかかりますか。
R It's quite cheap! ₃Less than US$2 per day—to be exact **US$1.75.** If you work with a personal trainer like this at other clubs, it could cost thousands of dollars.	とてもお手頃ですよ！1日あたり2米ドル足らず、正確には1.75米ドルです。ほかのクラブでそうした個人トレーナーがついて運動するとしたら、数千ドルかかるかもしれません。
A That's great... And the other type?	それはすばらしいですね…それで、もう1つのタイプは？
R ₄It's the **Equipment Only** Membership. It's recommended for those who are not interested in taking classes or working with the staff.	それは「マシン限定会員」です。これは、レッスンを受けたり、スタッフの指導を受けて運動をしたりすることには興味がない方におすすめです。
A Equipment only ... so ... no classes?	マシン限定…ということは…レッスンがないのですね。
R No... This membership is designed for those who just want to use our wide range of equipment. There are three main kinds of equipment available, ₅machines for developing strength, for **cardio**, and the free weight equipment. This is, of course priced much cheaper—only at around a dollar a day.	ええ…。この会員は、当クラブにあるいろいろな機器を使いたいだけの方が対象です。利用できる機器には、大きく分けて3種類あります。筋力を鍛えるためのマシン、カーディオ（有酸素運動）用のマシン、そしてフリーウェイトです。こちらは当然ながら、はるかに低額で、1日あたりわずか1ドルくらいです。

練習2 ▶	フォームを完成させる問題	本冊P.69 ／ track 2

解答	1 ▶ Mkere 2 ▶ Westall 3 ▶ BS8 9PU 4 ▶ 0.75 m[metre(s) / meter(s)] (wide) 5 ▶ 0.5 m[metre(s) / meter(s)] (high[deep]) 6, 7 ▶ (some) books, (some) toys（順不同） 8 ▶ 1,700

▶ 解説

1 は人名、**2** は大学名、**4, 5** は長さなど、各々に入る語を予想しておこう。

3 本問の郵便番号はイギリス式。なお、オーストラリアは4桁、アメリカは5桁の数字で表記される。郵便番号は複数の数字や文字が含まれても、1つの数字とみなされる。

6, 7 clothesのような荷物を表す名詞が入ると判断できる。音声中のclothesの後に集中する。

Questions 1-8　以下の記入用紙を完成させなさい。それぞれの解答として、3つ以下の単語か1つの数字、もしくはその両方を記入すること。

※フォームの一部分を省略しています

パッカム運輸　お客様　お見積もりフォーム	
お名前：	ジェイコブ**1**　ムケレ
集荷住所：	**2** ウェストオール　カレッジ、ダウンランズ・ロード
町：	ブリストル
郵便番号：	**3** BS8 9PU
荷物のサイズ：	縦 1.5m　横 **4** 0.75m　高さ **5** 0.5m
中身：	衣類 **6** （何冊かの）本　**7** （いくつかの）おもちゃ　（順不同）
総評価額：	**8** £ 1700

▶ スクリプトと訳

You will hear a telephone conversation between a customer and an agent at a company which ships large boxes overseas. First, you have time to look at Questions 1 to 8.

Now listen carefully and answer Questions 1 to 8.

A = Agent 🇬🇧　　C = Customer 🇬🇧

大きい荷物を海外に郵送する業者とその顧客が電話で交わしている会話が聞こえてきます。最初に、設問1～8を見る時間があります。では、音声を注意深く聞いて設問1～8に答えなさい。

A＝業者　　C＝顧客

A　Good morning, Packham's Shipping Agents. Can I help you?

C　Oh yes, I'm ringing to make enquiries about sending a large box, a container, back home to Kenya from the UK.

A　Yes, of course. Would you like me to try and make some quotations for you?

C　Yes, that'd be great, thank you.

A　Well first of all, I need a few details from you.

C　Fine.

A　Can I have your name?

C　It's Jacob **₁Mkere**.

A　Can you spell your surname, please?

C　Yes, it's **₁M-K-E-R-E**.

A　Is that 'M' for mother?

C　Yes.

A　Thank you, and you say that you will be sending the box to Kenya?

C　That's right.

A　And where would you like the box picked up from?

C　From my college, if possible.

A　Yes, of course. I'll take down the address now.

C　It's **₂Westall** College.

A　Is that **₂W-E-S-T-A-L-L**?

おはようございます。パッカム運輸です。どのようなご用件でしょうか。

ああ、はい。大きな箱を，段ボール箱なんですが、イギリスから私の出身国であるケニアに送ることについて問い合わせをしたくてお電話しました。

はい、わかりました。費用のお見積もりをいたしましょうか。

はい、そうしていただけるとありがたいです。お願いします。

それではまず、お客様からいくつか詳しいことをお聞きする必要があります。

どうぞ。

お名前は何とおっしゃいますか。

ジェイコブ・ムケレです。

名字のつづりを教えていただけますか。

はい、M-K-E-R-Eです。

それはmotherの「M」ですか。

はい。

ありがとうございます。それで、その荷物をケニアに送られるということですね。

そのとおりです。

そして、その荷物はどこで引き取りをご希望ですか。

できれば私の大学で。

ええ、大丈夫です。ではそのご住所を書き留めます。

ウェストオール・カレッジです。

それはW-E-S-T-A-L-Lですか。

C	Yes, ... college.	はい...そして「カレッジ」です。
A	Westall College. And where's that?	ウェストオール・カレッジですね。そして、その所在地は?
C	It's on Downlands Road, in Bristol.	ブリストルのダウンランズ・ロードです。
A	Sure, thanks. And the postcode?	ありがとうございます。それから郵便番号は?
C	It's ₃**BS8 9PU**.	BS8 9PUです。
A	Right ... and I need to know the size.	わかりました...それからサイズをお聞きする必要があります。
C	Yes, I've measured it carefully, and it's 1.5m long ...	ええ、私は慎重に測りました。長さが150cmで...。
A	Right.	はい。
C	₄**0.75m** wide ...	幅が75cmで...。
A	OK.	なるほど。
C	And it's ₅**0.5m** high or deep.	高さ、もしくは深さが50cmです。
A	Great. So I'll calculate the volume in a moment and get you some quotes for that. But first can you tell me, you know, very generally, what will be in the box?	けっこうです。では、今すぐ容積を計算して、その見積額を計算することにします。ただ、その前に、あのですね、大まかけっこうですので、その箱の中に何が入っているのか教えていただけますか。
C	Yes, there're mostly clothes.	はい、ほとんどは衣類です。
A	OK. [writing down]	なるほど。[書き留める]
C	And there're ₆,₇**some books**.	それから何冊か本が入っています。
A	OK, good. Um ... Anything else?	わかりました。けっこうです。...ほかに何かありますか。
C	Yes, there's also ₆,₇**some toys**.	はい、おもちゃがいくつか入っています。
A	OK and what is the total value, do you think, of the contents?	わかりました。それで、中の品物の合計価格はどれくらいだと思われますか。
C	Well the most valuable items are the clothes and the books—they'll be about £1,500 but then, the toys are about another two hundred— so I'd put down £₈**1,700**.	そうですね、一番価値があるのは衣類と本なのです。1500ポンドくらいですが、おもちゃが200ポンドほどなので、1700ポンドというところです。

| 練習1 〉 | 制限内の語数で答える問題 | 本冊P.72 / track 4 |

解答

1 ▶ 2[two] days　　2 ▶ wine tasting　　3 ▶ Saturday evening
4 ▶ town tour　　5 ▶ online

▶ 解説

1　質問文のHow long ... event?から、イベントの期間を答えさせる問題だと判断できる。日数など期間を表す数字や表現に注意して聞こう。

2　What ... doingと、Saturday morningがキーワード。Saturday morningが、音声では、At around 10 am on Saturdayにパラフレーズされている。

3　the feature activity（質問文）⇄ the highlight of the event（音声）のパラフレーズを見抜ければ、あとは質問文のWhenをもとに、日時、曜日など時を表す表現を聞き取ればよい。

4　[パラフレーズ] suitable for kids ⇄ family-friendly ... stroller-friendly。stroller＝「ベビーカー」

5　after the 1st of Marchが重要なキーワード。[パラフレーズ] buy ⇄ order

▶ 問題文の訳

Questions 1-5　以下の設問に答えなさい。それぞれの解答として、2つ以下の単語か1つの数字、もしくはその両方を記入すること。

1　「テイスト・オブ・ナイアガラ・オン・ザ・レイク」のイベントは全体でどれほどの長さか。
2　土曜日の午前中に、何をすることになっているのか。
3　目玉となるイベントは、いつ行われるのか。
4　子ども向けのアクティビティはどれか。
5　3月1日以降は、どうすればチケットを購入できるのか。

▶ スクリプトと訳 🍁

You will hear a man called Thomas Brandy, talking on a radio about a well-known event in Canada. First, you have some time to look at Questions 1 to 5. Now listen carefully and answer Questions 1 to 5.

トーマス・ブランディという男性がラジオでカナダの有名なイベントについて話しているのが聞こえてきます。まず、設問1〜5を見る時間があります。では、音声を注意深く聞いて設問1〜5に答えなさい。

Good morning everyone. My name is Thomas Brandy, I'm here to tell you about one of the most well-known annual events in Canada, which is happening quite soon—it's called 'A Taste of Niagara-on-the-Lake'. I also hope my explanation will answer some questions related to the event that I've received by email.

皆さん、おはようございます。私の名前はトーマス・ブランディといい、カナダで最も有名な毎年恒例のイベントをご紹介するために参りました。これは間もなく開催されますが「テイスト・オブ・ナイアガラ・オン・ザ・レイク」と呼ばれるものです。私のご説明が、このイベントについてこれまでにメールでいただいていたいくつかのご質問への答えになってくれたらよいと思います。

Now let's start with what 'A Taste of Niagara-on-the-Lake' is. During the festival, we're highlighting local restaurants and wineries. ₁It is a unique event that's

それでは「テイスト・オブ・ナイアガラ・オン・ザ・レイク」とは何かというご説明から始めましょう。このフェスティバルの期間中、私たちは地元のレストランやワイン醸

held over **two days**, taking guests on a bus tour to five restaurants in the heart of the town and providing a five-course meal with wine pairings. I'm going to explain that in detail in a minute.

Alright, let's start with the activities during your visit. Your adventure begins on Friday evening with 'Wine & Cheese Get-together' at Navy Hall. You will join your fellow dining partners here. ₂At around 10 am on Saturday, you will discover the best **wine tasting** experiences. The local Niagara winemakers will share their knowledge and skills during the tour. Make sure you don't miss ₃the highlight of the event, which will take place on **Saturday evening**. You will experience a five-course gourmet dining and wine pairing adventure served in a progressive manner. Chefs and wine experts from five of the top wineries will thrill your palate—so make sure you don't miss it. Then your adventure concludes on Sunday with ₄a **town tour**, which is a more family-friendly tour and stroller-friendly too.

I'm afraid that there're only a limited number of seats left, so you'd better hurry now as the tour only has space for about 130 customers. You can buy tickets by calling 1-905-468-5157 ₅before March 1st. After that date, you can only buy them **online**. Tickets are $160 per person, inclusive of all the activities and all taxes. If you have any questions or comments about 'A Taste of Niagara-on-the-Lake', please feel free to contact us at ⋯⋯⋯⋯⋯ (fading)

造所を前面に押し出します。これは、2日間にわたり、お客様をバスツアーで町の中心部にある5軒のレストランへお連れし、5品のコース料理とそれに合ったワインを楽しんでいただくというユニークなイベントです。詳細については、この後すぐにご説明いたします。

では、皆さんが観光中にすることからお話ししましょう。皆さんの冒険は金曜日の夜にネイビーホールで開かれる「ワインとチーズの宴」から始まります。皆さんは、一緒に食事をする仲間たちとここで出会います。土曜日の午前10時頃に、皆さんは最高のワイン試飲体験をすることになります。地元のナイアガラのワイン醸造所が、見学中にその知識と技術を披露してくれます。土曜日の夜に行われるこのイベントの目玉を、お見逃しなく。皆さんは、斬新な調理法で提供される5品のグルメディナーとそれに合うワインという冒険を体験するのです。シェフと5軒の一流ワイン醸造所からのワインの専門家が、皆さんの味覚をこの上なく刺激してくれるので、この機会をけっして逃してはいけません。その後、皆さんの冒険は、日曜日で終了します。これは、どちらかと言えば家族向けのツアーで、ベビーカーの使用にも対応しています。

残されている席数に限りがあることをご了承ください。このツアーにはおよそ130名のお客様しか受け入れられませんので、急がれた方がよいでしょう。チケットは、3月1日までならば1-905-468-5157に電話をしてご購入できます。その日以降は、オンラインでのみ購入することができます。チケットはお1人様160ドルで、すべての活動と税金が含まれています。「テイスト・オブ・ナイアガラ・オン・ザ・レイク」について、ご質問やご意見がございましたら、どうぞご連絡は……(音声が次第に小さくなっていく)

| 練習2 | 地図を完成させる問題 | 本冊P.73 / track 5 |

| 解答 | 1 ▶ A | 2 ▶ F | 3 ▶ C |

▶ **解説**

「地図を完成させる問題」では、必ず現在地を確認し、音声を聞きながら線を引こう。冒頭の We are standing here at the entrance. You can see it at the bottom of the map. In front of us, you can see the tall flagpole を聞き逃さないように。

なお、空欄のBはカンガルー、Dはサル、Gはシマウマ、Hはワニが該当する。

▶ **問題文の訳**

Questions 1-3 以下の地図中に名前をつけなさい。正解をA～Gの文字から選ぶこと。

※地図の日本語訳は省略しています

23

▶ スクリプトと訳

You will hear a talk by a guide at a zoo talking to a group of tourists about the animals they can see at the zoo. First, you have some time to look at Questions 1 to 3.
Now listen carefully and answer Questions 1 to 3.

動物園のガイドが観光客に園内で見られる動物について話しているのが聞こえてきます。最初に、設問1～3を見る時間があります。では、音声を注意深く聞いて設問1～3に答えなさい。

Let's take a look at the map before we enter the zoo itself. We are standing here at the entrance. You can see it at the bottom of the map. In front of us, you can see the tall flagpole with the Australian flag fluttering in the wind. That's a good landmark. If you get lost, just look up and the flag will show you where the entrance is.

実際に動物園に入る前にこの地図を見てみましょう。私たちは入り口のここに立っています。地図の一番下を見てください。私たちの目の前には、風でたなびくオーストラリアの国旗を掲げている長いポールが見えます。それはよい目印です。もし迷子になったら、見上げさえすれば、その旗が入り口の場所を教えてくれます。

I imagine many of you who are visiting from abroad are keen to see some of our iconic Australian wildlife. To do that, you need to go straight ahead past the flagpole, walk past the café on your left and at the end of the path, right in front of you, you will see the emu section. To the right of the emus is the kangaroo area, and ₁to the left of the emus, you can find the koalas.

海外からお越しの皆さんの多くは、ここオーストラリアを代表する野生生物をとても見たがっていることと思います。そのためには旗のポールの先をまっすぐ進み、左側のカフェの横を通り過ぎる必要があり、その道の突き当たりで、すぐ目の前にエミュー舎が見えます。エミューの右側にはカンガルー舎があり、エミューの左側にはコアラがいます。

Now let's turn our attention to the carnivores of Asia. We tend to keep them separate from the cute Aussie marsupials for obvious reasons. To visit the carnivore area, instead of going straight, at the flagpole, turn right, and go past the shops. On your right, you will see the reptile house, full of snakes and lizards, and then ₂at the corner, there is a large crocodile swamp. The next pen after that is where the tigers can be seen. Then, beyond the tigers, there's a pen holding Komodo dragons from Indonesia.

次にアジアの肉食動物に注目してみましょう。私たちは、その動物たちをかわいらしいオーストラリアの有袋類とは別にするように配慮していますが、その理由は明らかですね。この肉食動物ゾーンに行くには、旗のポールの先を直進するのではなく、右に曲がっていくつかのショップを通り過ぎます。すると右側には、たくさんのヘビやトカゲがいる爬虫類館が見えてきて、次の曲がり角にはワニがいる大きな沼があります。そして、その次の獣舎ではトラを見ることができます。そしてトラの先には、インドネシアのコモドオオトカゲがいる獣舎があります。

Now, one of our most popular attractions is the African elephant show. The kids especially love this one. To get there you need to turn left at the flagpole and walk down that path toward the giraffe area at the end. You'll pass a large pen on your left containing some other African mammals, such as zebras. Keep on walking around the corner to your right, past the first aid station and the monkey enclosure on your right, and then, ₃just past the monkeys, that's where you'll find the African elephant show.

今、ここで一番人気のあるアトラクションの1つはアフリカゾウのショーです。これは特に子どもたちに大人気です。そこに行くには、旗のポールの所で左に曲がり、その通路を突き当たりのキリン舎に向かって歩く必要があります。左側の、シマウマなどアフリカの別の哺乳類が入っている大きな獣舎の前を通り過ぎます。曲がり角を右に折れて歩き続け、右側の救護所とサル山の前を通り、サルたちを通り過ぎた所で、アフリカゾウのショーが見られます。

Now, before you run off to explore, I should mention that you should not feed any of the animals in the zoo.

さて、皆さんが探索に出かける前に、動物園ではどの動物にも餌を与えてはいけないと言っておかなければなりません。

解答	1 ▶ H	2 ▶ G	3 ▶ D	4 ▶ B	5 ▶ F

▶ 解説

まずは、So here we are at the entrance to the town library. を聞いて、現在地を特定しよう。

1 音声の opposite this の this は、Librarian's desk を指す。
2 beyond は前置詞で「〜の向こう側に」。where 以降に注意して聞こう。
3 fiction, non-fiction の説明の後に3の説明がくる。
4 音声の next door to that の that は、Seminar room を指す。
5 子ども用図書室を説明した後に Then が流れるが、これが話を転換するサインとなっている。

▶ 問題文の訳

Questions 1-5 以下の平面図中に名前をつけなさい。囲みの中から5つの答えを選び、解答欄の1〜5にA〜Iの正しい文字を記入すること。

※平面図の日本語訳は省略しています

A	美術品展示室
B	子ども用図書室
C	コンピューター
D	地域の歴史書
E	会議室
F	マルチメディア室
G	定期刊行物
H	参考図書
I	観光情報

▶ スクリプトと訳 🇺🇸

You will hear the librarian of a new town library talking to a group of people who are visiting the library. First, you have some time to look at Questions 1 to 5.
Now listen carefully and answer Questions 1 to 5.

新しく完成した町立図書館の図書館員が、そこを訪れている人たちに話しているのが聞こえてきます。最初に、設問1〜5を見る時間があります。では、音声を注意深く聞いて設問1〜5に答えなさい。

OK, everyone. So here we are at the entrance to the town library. My name is Ann, and I'm the chief librarian here, and you'll usually find me at the desk just by the main entrance right here. So, I'd like to tell you a bit about the way the library is organised, and what you'll find where ... and you should all have a plan in front of you. Well, as you can see, my desk is just

では、皆さん。私たちが今いる所が町立図書館の入り口です。私の名前はアンでここの主任司書ですが、たいてい私はこの正面玄関のすぐ近くの席にいます。では、この図書館の中がどのような配置になっていて、どこに何があるのか少しご説明したいと思います...それで、皆さんのお手元には館内の見取り図があるはずです。さて、ご覧のとおり、私の席はここを入ってすぐ右側にあり、その反対側の

Listening

on your right as you go in, and **₁ opposite this, the first room on your left has an excellent collection of reference books,** and is also a place where people can read or study peacefully. **₂ Just beyond the librarian's desk on the right is a room where we have up-to-date periodicals** such as newspapers and magazines, and this room also has a photocopier in case you want to copy any of the articles. If you carry straight on, you'll get to a large room, and this is the main reading area. There is fiction on the shelves on the left, and non-fiction materials are on your right, and **₃ on the shelves on the far wall there is an excellent collection of books relating to local history.** We're hoping to add a section on local tourist attractions too, later in the year. Through the far door in the library, just past the fiction shelves, is a seminar room that can be booked for meetings or talks. And **₄ next door to that is the children's library,** which has a good collection of stories and picture books for the under elevens. **₅ Then, there's a large room to the right of the reading area—that's the multimedia collection.** This is where you can borrow videos and DVDs and so on, and we also have CD-ROMs you can borrow to use on your computer at home. It originally held an art collection but that's been moved to another building. Well, that's about it.

左側の最初の部屋には充実した参考図書が収められていて、利用者が静かに読書したり勉強したりすることのできる場所にもなっています。司書の席のすぐ先の右側には、新聞や雑誌などの最新の定期刊行物が置かれた部屋があり、この部屋には記事をコピーしたいときに使えるコピー機もあります。そのまま進むと広い部屋に入りますが、そこが主たる読書室です。左側の棚にはフィクション、右側の棚にはノンフィクションの本があり、奥の壁ぎわの棚にはこの地域の歴史に関する充実した蔵書があります。年内には、この地域の観光名所についてのコーナーも設けたいと思っています。フィクションの棚のすぐ先にある読書室のドアの向こう側には、会議や講演用に予約することができるセミナー室があります。そして、その隣には子ども用の図書室があり、11歳未満の児童向きの物語や絵本を豊富に取り揃えてあります。次に、読書室の右側に広い部屋がありますが、これはビデオやDVDなどを借りることができるマルチメディア室で、自宅のコンピューターで使うために借りることができるCD-ROMもあります。そこはもともと美術品の展示室でしたが、別の建物に移されました。ご説明は以上です。

練習1 〉 文 を 完 成 さ せ る 問 題　　　　　本冊P.77 / track 7

解答
**1 ▶ motivation　2 ▶ time(-)management　3 ▶ modules
4 ▶ summer school(s)**

▶ 解説

1 空欄には、demandの目的語として名詞が入ると予想しておく。パラフレーズ demanded a great deal of ⇄ needed to maintain a high level of

2 音声のgot very good at 〜（〜がとても上手になった）が、問題文のimprovedにリンクする。

3 空欄は前置詞inの後なので、名詞相当語句が入ると判断できる。パラフレーズ the course was structured in ⇄ the degree is made up of

4 同じく空欄は前置詞の後なので、名詞相当語句を探す。パラフレーズ meeting other students ⇄ meet all the other people

▶ 問題文の訳

Questions 1-4 以下の文を完成しなさい。それぞれの解答として、2つ以下の単語を記入すること。

1 通信制大学で学ぶには、かなりの　モチベーション　が必要だった。
2 学びながら仕事もすることで、レイチェルの　時間管理　のスキルが高まった。
3 コースが　単元　で構成されていることが助けになった。
4 彼女は　夏期講習　でほかの学生と出会えたのがありがたかった。

▶ スクリプトと訳

You will hear two friends, Rachel and Paul discussing about studying at the Open University. First, you have some time to look at Questions 1 to 5. *Now listen carefully and answer Questions 1 to 5.* P＝Paul 🇬🇧　R＝Rachel 🇬🇧	友人同士であるレイチェルとポールが通信制大学で学ぶことについて話し合っているのが聞こえてきます。最初に、設問1〜5を見る時間があります。では、音声を注意深く聞いて設問1〜5に答えなさい。 P ＝ポール　　R ＝レイチェル

P Hey Rachel, I've been meaning to ask you if you found it hard studying at the Open University.	ねえ、レイチェル、通信制大学で勉強するのは大変だったか聞こうとしていたんだ。
R You mean, because you're studying on your own, most of the time?	それって、ほとんど1人で勉強するからってこと？
P Mm.	うん。
R Well, it took me a while to get used to it. I found ₁I need to maintain a high level of **motivation**, because it's so different from school. There's no one saying, 'Why haven't you written your assignment yet?' and that sort of thing.	そう、それに慣れるのに少し時間がかかったよ。モチベーションを高く保つ必要があることに気づいたの。学校とはずいぶん違うから。「なぜ、あなたはまだ課題のレポートを書いてないの？」なんて言ってくれる人は誰もいないし。
P Oh dear.	ええっ。

27

R	You'll learn how to deal with it, Paul. Another thing was that ₂I got very good at **time-management** because I had to fit time for studying round a full-time job.	あなたも慣れるよ、ポール。もう1つ気づいたのは、時間の管理がとても上手になったこと。フルタイムの仕事の合間を縫って、勉強する時間を調整しなければいけなかったから。
P	Well, I'm hoping to change to working part-time, so that'll help.	ええと、僕はパートタイムで働くようにしたいと思っているんだ。それだったら楽だろうね。
R	₃What makes it easier is that the degree is made up of **modules**, so you can take time off between them if you need to. It isn't like a traditional three- or four-year course, where you've got to do the whole thing in one go.	楽な点は、コースがいくつかの単元から成っているから、必要なら単元と単元の間に休みを取れることだね。これは、すべて一気に終える必要のある普通の3年制や4年制のコースとは違うところだよ。
P	That's good, because I'd like to spend six months travelling next year.	それはいいね。来年、僕は半年を旅行して過ごしたいと思っているから。
R	Huh, it's all right for some; then even though you're mostly studying at home, remember you've got tutors to help you, and from time to time ₄there are **summer schools**, which usually last a week. ₄They're great, because you meet all the other people struggling with the same things as you. I've made some really good friends that way.	へえーっ、それでうまくいく人もいるけどね。それから、あなたはほとんど自宅で勉強することになるけれど、あなたには指導教官がいて、ときどき夏期講習があることを忘れないでね。それはたいてい1週間続くのよ。これがとてもすばらしいのは、自分と同じことで苦労している多くの人たちと出会えるからだよ。私は、そうしてとてもいい友だちを作ったの。
P	Sounds good. So how do I apply?	それはいいね。じゃあ、応募するにはどうすればいいの?

練習2	複数の選択肢から選ぶ問題	本冊P.78 / track 8

解答	1 ▶ C	2 ▶ B	3 ▶ C	4 ▶ A	5 ▶ B

▶ 解説

1 スクリプト中の下線1がCと一致する。Bのinnate（生得的な、先天的な）は、下線1や、But natural talent is certainly not the major component of creativity, so you don't need innate talent in order to be creative. と矛盾する。 パラフレーズ no matter how old you are ⇄ at any age

2 Bのenvironmentが、下線2でcontextにパラフレーズされている。

3 下線3の前にあるit's a good idea to design something new ... even if it is just re-designing or reworking old projects ...を読むとre-designingは推奨されており、Bは正答にならない。

4 有名なクリエイターと自分を比較することについて、Aは否定的で、BとCは肯定的。直接的な解答の根拠は下線4にあるが、その前の博士の発言、Ah ... I know what your problem is. 以降、否定的な意見が続くので、B、Cは消去できるはず。
パラフレーズ inhibit your creativity ⇄ diminish your own creative ability

5 Bのlearn from the expertsを具体的に言ったのが下線5。パート3では、抽象的な問題文の内容が、音声では具体的に言い換えられるパターンが多い。
パラフレーズ improve your creativity ⇄ boosting creativity

▶ 問題文の訳

Questions 1-5 正解を、A, BまたはCから選びなさい。

1 創造力は ....
   A まったく後天的なものである。

B　ほとんど先天的なものである。

C　たとえ何歳であっても伸ばすことができる。

2　創造力は、＿＿＿＿＿＿いれば、伸ばすことができる。

A　生まれつきの才能をたくさん持って

B　環境に恵まれて

C　すでに何かを発明して

3　もし＿＿＿＿＿＿と、創造力は衰えるだろう。

A　あなたの家庭環境が協力的過ぎる

B　以前の制作物をデザインし直す

C　人と違った考え方をすることが認められない

4　自分を創造力が豊かな著名人と比べることで、＿＿＿＿＿＿

A　あなたの創造性が発揮できなくなるかもしれない。

B　あなたはもっと創造的になるよう励まされるかもしれない。

C　あなたはより多くのグラフィックデザインを生み出せるかもしれない。

5　あなたの創造力を伸ばす方法の1つは＿＿＿＿＿＿

A　ロゴや名刺などを集めることである。

B　専門家から学ぶことである。

C　ほかのデザイナーたちと一緒に作業をすることである。

 Listening

▶ スクリプトと訳

You will hear two design students, called Huan and Kumiko talking to their professor Dr Kennedy about how they can develop their creative skills. First, you have some time to look at Questions 1 to 5.
Now listen carefully and answer Questions 1 to 5.
H = Huan 🇺🇸　　K = Kumiko 🇨🇦
D = Dr Kennedy 🇨🇦

2人のデザイン専攻の学生であるフアンとクミコが、教授のケネディ博士と、創造力のスキルの磨き方について話しているのが聞こえてきます。最初に、設問1〜5を見る時間があります。では、音声を注意深く聞いて設問1〜5に答えなさい。
H ＝フアン　K ＝クミコ
D ＝ケネディ博士

H Sometimes, I regret doing graphic design ... I don't seem to get any creative ideas. Creativity is not in my blood, I think. Do you feel the same, Kumiko?

K Well, some days I can be super creative, but today, I feel like I lack creativity. Do you have any suggestions for us, Dr Kennedy? Maybe, we are just not naturally creative.

D People sometimes wonder whether creativity comes from *nature* or *nurture*, whether you are born with it or you have to learn it. Let me tell you that ₁ creativity is, in fact, basically the latter. It's a skill—not a gift—that can be learned and mastered at any age, Huan.

H But aren't some people naturally born creative? They start creating and inventing things all by

僕はときどき、グラフィックデザインをしていて後悔することがあります。独創的なアイデアが何も浮かびそうもないんです。自分には生まれつき創造力がないのだと思います。クミコ、君も同じように感じませんか。

そうですね、すごく創造的になれる日もあるけど、今日は自分の創造力が十分じゃない気がします。ケネディ博士、私たちに何かアドバイスがありますか。たぶん、私たちは生まれつき創造力を持っていないだけなのかもしれません。

人は誰でも、創造力は生まれか育ちなのか、つまり、それを持って生まれたのか、それとも学んで身につける必要があるのかと疑問を抱くことがあります。私に言わせてもらえれば、創造力というものは、実は基本的には後者なのです。それは才能ではなく技術であって、どの年齢でも学んで習得できるものなのですよ、フアン。

でも、生まれたときから自然に創造的な人もいるのではないですか。そうした人たちは、自分の力だけでいろいろな

themselves.

D Well, it's true that everyone—adults and children alike—has a creative streak. But natural talent is certainly not a major component of creativity, so you don't need innate talent in order to be creative.

K I agree. I read there was research to prove that ₂everyone's basic creativity can be improved when it is encouraged and cultivated.

D Yes that's true. So, ₂very creative people are more likely to have been raised in a context where their basic creativity was able to develop.

H And if the circumstances are not supportive of creativity?

D Then the reverse is true. Firstly creativity is likely to suffer when it is not practised and encouraged. For example, if you're a designer, it's a good idea to design something new every day, even if it is just re-designing or reworking old projects that you have.

K Hmm ... That's what I'm afraid of.

D And secondly ₃a reduction in creativity is also frequently experienced in the workplace and in families where the culture does not encourage people to think differently and does not support new ideas.

H Hmm ... I think that's what's happened to me in my family but I really wanted to be like Milton Glasser, that famous graphic designer.

D Ah ... I know what your problem is. It just might be that the main reason you think you're not creative is because you compare yourself to others who are famous for their creativity.

K Hmm ... Sometimes, I compare myself to my mom, who's a very good graphic designer ...

D ₄When you're in a comparison mindset, you inadvertently diminish your own creative ability. One path to progress is to stop comparing yourself to an ideal and instead zoom in on you. When you are trying to enhance your creative skills, then, as a graphic artist, the most important thing is to focus on your own work such as to create some new brands or letterheads, logos, mock websites or even business cards.

H That's very doable. I never thought about that.

K Hmm ... I'd rather learn from other designers.

D ₅That's another important way of boosting creativity. You should always speak to the ones who are better than you, who are more

ものを創造したり、発明するようになったりします。
確かに、大人も子どもも、誰でも創造性の素質を持っています。ただし、生まれつきの才能は明らかに創造性の重要な要素ではないので、創造力を発揮するためには生まれながらの才能は必要ないのです。

私もそう思います。どこかで読んだのですけど、誰もが持つ基本的な創造力は、人からほめられたり、訓練したりすることで伸ばせることを示した研究がありました。
はい、そのとおりです。ですから、非常に創造的な人たちは、基本的な創造力を発達させることのできる環境で育てられた可能性が高いと言えるでしょう。
では、環境が創造力を伸ばしてくれない場合はどうなりますか。
そうなると、逆のことが起こります。まず、創造力は、それが使われたり促進されたりしていないと弱まってしまうかもしれません。例えば、あなたがデザイナーであれば、毎日何か新しいものをデザインするといいでしょう。たとえ、それがすでに存在する古い制作物を改良したり、やり直したりするだけであってもね。
ええと...それが私の心配していることなんです。
そして次に、創造力の低下は、人が異なる考え方を持つことに消極的で、新しいアイデアを受け入れない土壌がある職場や家庭でよく起こります。

なるほど、それが僕の家庭で起きたことなんだと思いますが、僕はどうしても、あの有名なグラフィック・デザイナーのミルトン・グラッサーのようになりたかったんです。
ああ、あなたの問題がわかりました。自分が創造的でないと思う一番大きな理由は、単に創造力が豊かで有名な他人と自分を比べるせいなのかもしれません。

うーん...私は、自分をとても優れたグラフィック・デザイナーである母と比べてしまうことがあって...。
いつも自分を人と比べてばかりいると、気づかないうちに自分の創造力を弱めてしまいます。進歩への1つの道筋は、自分を理想像と比べるのをやめて、その代わりに自分のことだけに専念することです。創造的な技術を高めようとするなら、グラフィック・アーティストとして最も大切なことは、自分の作業に集中して、何か新しいブランドやレターヘッド、ロゴ、ウェブサイトの見本、あるいは名刺でもいいですから、デザインをしてみることです。

それはとても取り組みやすいですね。僕はそれをまったく思いつきませんでした。
ええと、私は、ほかのデザイナーから学ぶ方がいいです。
それも創造性を高めるもう1つの大切な方法です。あなたは常に自分よりも優れていたり、その分野でより多くの経験を持っていたりする人たちと対話をし、彼らから新しい

experienced in that area in order to learn some new skills from them. I know that it is hard to admit that there is someone better than you, but if you want to really move forward, you should accept it and try to get the best from them.

技術を学ぶ必要があります。自分より優れた人がいることを認めたくはないと思いますが、本当に進歩したいと思うならば、それを認めて、そうした人たちの一番よいところを学ぶよう努めるべきです。

練習3 ▶ マッチングする問題 　　　本冊P.79／track 9

解答	**1 ▶ B**	**2 ▶ F**	**3 ▶ E**	**4 ▶ A**	**5 ▶ C**

▶ 解説

話者が4人もいるので漫然と聞いていると混乱してしまう。実際には、会話の中心者は教授で、彼が順番に学生に話題を振っている。つまり**「教授と各学生の会話」がいくつか続く**と考えて冷静に聞こう。the first thing, a second idea ...など、「何番目のアイデアなのか」を示す語句を聞き取ろう。

2 Another idea is a change of scenery. だけだと抽象的だが、その次の文まで注意深く聞けば答えを導ける。選択肢Fの in the open air が音声では outside に言い換えられている。

3 バラフレーズ Move to an alternative indoor location ⇄ moving to a different room in my own house

4 選択肢の develop は「開発する」ではなく「設定する、設ける」というニュアンス。つまり、これが音声の set にリンクする。

5 選択肢の inviting は形容詞で「興味などを引きつける」という意味があり、この場合は「勉強のやる気が出るような」といったニュアンスになる。バラフレーズ Create an inviting environment ⇄ creating an atmosphere that encourages us to study

▶ 問題文の訳

Questions 1-5 オンライン学習に関して学生たちが提案している5つのアイデアは何か。囲みの中から5つの答えを選び、解答欄の1〜5にA〜Fの正しい文字を記入すること。

> **アイデア**
> **A** 厳しい毎日の日課を設ける
> **B** チームでオンラインで勉強する
> **C** やる気の出る環境を作る
> **D** 定期的な休憩を取る
> **E** 屋内の別の場所に移動する
> **F** 野外で勉強する

▶ スクリプトと訳

You will hear a lecturer called Professor West, talking to three students about how they deal with studying from home. First, you have some time to look at Questions 1 to 5.
Now listen carefully and answer Questions 1 to 5.
L ＝ Lynn 　W ＝ West
R ＝ Rick 　J ＝ Julie

講師のウェスト教授が、自宅学習の進め方について3人の学生と話をしているのが聞こえてきます。最初に、設問1〜5を見る時間があります。では、音声を注意深く聞いて設問1〜5に答えなさい。
L＝リン　　W＝ウェスト教授
R＝リック　J＝ジュリー

L	Hi Professor West.
W	Hi. Our online class starts in two hours. What are you all doing here?
R	We would like to submit our assignments.
W	But you can submit them online or by email.
J	Yes, we know, but we've felt a bit overwhelmed studying from home, and now that the restrictions have been lifted, we are taking the opportunity to get outside when we can.
W	Ah, I see.
R	Professor, it's been really difficult studying online. We really miss our face-to-face classes. We miss the real discussions.
W	Well, I hope you've been applying some strategies to help you with online study, as we're probably going to continue online for a while yet. Let's brainstorm some ideas together, and make a list to share with other students. Lynn, you start.
L	Well, I think ₁the first thing on the list should be forming an online study group. I use the free video chat option on one of the popular social media platforms, but there are also paid services you can use if you like. I set a designated time each week to meet my group online and we quiz each other. Much better than studying alone!
W	That sounds good. Can you add a second idea to our list?
L	₂Another idea is a change of scenery. I like to grab my laptop or my printed notes and find a quiet place to study outside; for example, a quiet picnic table in a sparsely populated park, or even my own backyard. I find that a greener environment can really make a difference.
W	Hmm, I like that, Lynn. I'm an outdoor person too. Rick, you're next.
R	OK. So, ₃point number three. Well, I don't like to go outside. But I find that just changing my study space inside—moving to a different room in my own house—can make a difference too. If you are just sitting at the same desk, and looking at the same things around you, you can become tired and bored more quickly.
W	A good suggestion, Rick. Can you add another point? ₄Point four?
R	Yes, ₄once I've found a schedule that works for me, I stick with it. I set a dedicated time to get up each morning, and some fairly regular times for meals, and for study, and for some exercise. I'm not sure that would suit everyone, but it helped me a lot.

こんにちは、ウェスト教授。

こんにちは。私たちのオンライン授業はあと2時間で始まります。皆さん、ここで何をしているんですか。

課題を提出したいと思っているんです。

でも、それならオンラインかメールで送れますよ。

はい、それはわかっているんですけど、みんな家で勉強するのに、ちょっとうんざりしていたんです。規制が解除されたので、この機会にできるときには外に出ることにしているんです。

ああ、なるほど。

教授、オンラインで勉強するのはとても大変でした。僕たちは対面式の授業がなくて本当に寂しいです。本物の議論がしたくて。

そうですね、皆さん、オンライン授業の対策を立ててきたかと思います。たぶん、まだしばらくオンライン授業を続けることになると思いますから。ここでアイデアを議論して、ほかの学生と共有するためにリストを作りましょう。リン、あなたから始めてください。

そうですね、リストの1つめは、オンライン学習グループを作ることじゃないかと思います。私は無料で利用できるある人気のソーシャル・メディア・プラットフォームのビデオチャット機能を使っていますが、お望みなら、有料で利用できるサービスもあります。私は毎週、決まった時間を設定してオンラインで集まり、みんながお互いにクイズを出し合います。1人で勉強するよりずっといいです！

それはいいですね。リストの載せる2つめのアイデアを加えてもらえますか。

もうひとつのアイデアは、風景を変えることです。私はノートパソコンやプリントアウトしたメモを手に持ち、外で静かに勉強できる場所を探します。例えば、人の少ない公園にある静かなピクニックテーブルなどですが、自宅の裏庭でもいいんです。緑の多い環境だと、本当に違うことに気づきました。

うーん、それはいいですね、リン。私もアウトドア派ですからね。リック、あなたが次です。

はい。ナンバー3ですね。そうですね、僕は外に出るのが好きではないので。でも、家の中でも勉強する場所を変えると——自宅の別の部屋に移動するだけでも——効果があると思います。ただずっと同じ机に座って、身の周りの代わり映えしないものを見ているだけだと、すぐに疲れたり退屈したりしてしまいそうです。

いい提案ですね、リック。ほかの点を加えてもらえますか。4つめです。

はい、僕は自分に合ったスケジュールがわかったら、それを通します。毎朝、決まった時間に起きることにして、食事や勉強、そして運動のために、きっちりとしたスケジュールを立てました。それが万人向けかはわかりませんが、僕にはとても役立ちました。

J　Hmm, I can't do what Rick does ... I need to have some freedom from a rigid timetable!

W　OK, we don't all have to do the same things. So, what are your suggestions, Julie?

J　My idea—so that's ₅point five on our list, isn't it?—is I think ₅we should try creating an atmosphere that encourages us to study.

W　What do you mean?

J　I think people should find out what it is that helps them concentrate. Is it their favourite music, or do they prefer complete quiet? What kind of lighting is best? Find the things that help you focus and set up your own super-study space. I have a plug-in coffee maker for long study sessions. I also like to use essential oils, as the smell helps me to concentrate.

W　That all sounds good too, Julie. Those are five excellent suggestions that are worth sharing. I'll put those up on our class page.

うーん、リックがやっていることは私には無理ですね…厳しいスケジュールから少し自由なることが必要だから！

そう、誰もが同じようにする必要はありませんからね。ジュリーの提案は何でしょうか。

私のアイデア、5つめのポイントですが、私たちは、勉強したくなる雰囲気を作るようにすべきだと思います。

どういうことですか。

自分の気持ちを集中させてくれるものを何か見つけるべきだと思います。自分の好きな音楽だったり。それとも完全な静けさかもしれませんね。どの照明が一番なのか。集中するのに役立つものを見つけて、自分にとって最適な学習環境を作り上げるんです。私は長時間の勉強に備えて差し込み式のコーヒーメーカーを用意しています。エッセンシャルオイルを使うのも気に入っています。その香りが集中しやすくしてくれるからです。

全部いいですね、ジュリー。共有する価値のある5つのすばらしい提案です。クラスページに上げておきます。

| 練習1 〉 | フローチャートを完成させる問題 | 本冊P.83 ／ track 10 |

| 解答 | 1 ▸ expectations　　2 ▸ (physical) symptoms　　3 ▸ decisions |
| | 4 ▸ memory[memories]　　5 ▸ actions　　6 ▸ danger |

▶ 解説

まず、フローチャートのタイトル（FOUR STAGES OF FEAR）と内容を把握しておこう。フローチャートは4つに分類でき、「恐怖の4段階」のそれぞれを要約した内容となっている。

1　空欄直後のareから、複数名詞を入れる問題だと判断できる。 パラフレーズ negative ⇄ not positive

2　フローチャートのa range of 〜(さまざまな〜) がポイント。下線2の後で、you start to hyperventilate, your heart beats fasterなど、さまざまな身体症状が列挙されている。 パラフレーズ generates ⇄ leads to

3　our minds don't function properly, and this is the third stage of fearが聞こえてきたら、フローチャートのOur minds don't work properlyの内容に入ったとわかるので集中しよう。

4　フローチャートのactivateが、音声ではkick inにパラフレーズされているのを見逃さないようにしよう。

5　音声のWe assume that the same thing will happen again, and our actions will follow.は、またネガティブなことが起こると想定して、行動がその想定に従って変わるということ。our actions will followが抽象的だが、その先のwe let this decide our actionsで具体的に述べられており、答えに確信が持てる。

6　We do this to avoid 6 .... to ourselves ⇄ we are trying to protect ourselves from dangerのパラフレーズに気づけると、「避ける」対象としてdangerを入れられる。

▶ 問題文の訳

Questions 1-6　2つ以下の単語を使い、以下のフローチャートを完成させなさい。

恐怖の4つの段階
それはすべて心の中で始まる。
- あなたは、さまざまなことを想像し始める。
- 私たちの**1　予想**　は、たいてい悲観的なものである。
　　↓

恐怖を感じる。
- 恐怖はさまざまな**2　（身体的な）症状**　を生み出す。
　　↓

思考が適切に働かない。
- **3　決定する**　ことができない。
- 無分別に行動し始める。
　　↓

私たちは4　記憶　を働かせる。
- 特に嫌な状況ほど、はっきりと記憶する。
- 以前の経験が私たちの**5　行動**　を決定づける。
- 私たちがそうするのは、自分にふりかかる**6　危険**　を避けるためである。

▶ スクリプトと訳 🇨🇦

You will hear part of a presentation by a psychology lecturer on the four stages of fear. First, you have some time to look at Questions 1 to 6.
Now listen carefully and answer Questions 1 to 6.

恐怖の４つの段階について、心理学の講師によるプレゼンテーションの一部が聞こえてきます。まず、設問１〜６を見る時間があります。では、音声を注意深く聞いて設問１〜６に答えなさい。

Good morning everyone, I'm Melissa May and today I'm going to talk about the four stages we experience when we feel fear.

皆さん、おはようございます。メリサ・メイです。では、今日は私たちが恐怖を感じるときに経験する４つの段階についてお話しします。

The first stage is imagination. Often when we begin to feel fear, we lose contact with what is really happening, and we start imagining things that might happen. The problem is that ₁our **expectations** are often not positive. The things we expect to happen are worse than the reality, and in this way we generate extra fear and anxiety for ourselves.

最初の段階は想像です。私たちが恐怖を感じ始めるときはたいてい、本当に起きていることを認識できず、起こりうることを想像し始めます。問題は、私たちの予想がしばしば楽観的ではないことです。私たちが起こると思うことは現実より悪く、このようにして、私たちは自ら余計な恐怖や不安を生み出します。

The second stage of fear is feeling the fear itself. We have already imagined what can happen, as I have said mostly in a negative way, and ₂now comes the fear. This leads to many **physical symptoms**. When fear arrives, you start to hyperventilate, your heart beats faster, your voice gets higher and your body fills with nerves. With these symptoms, you will find it more difficult to think and to act reasonably.

恐怖の第二段階は、恐怖そのものを感じることです。私たちはすでに何が起こりそうか、先ほど述べたように大概悲観的に想像しており、そうすると恐怖がやって来ます。これがいろいろな身体症状を引き起こします。恐怖が到来すると、呼吸が荒くなり、心臓の鼓動が速まり、声が上ずり、全身が緊張します。こういった症状が合理的に考え、行動することを、より困難にするのです。

Even when physical and emotional responses are in control, our minds don't function properly, and this is the third stage of fear. We may have a kind of mental paralysis where we can't think any more, and ₃we're unable to make **decisions** about what to do next. Alternatively, instead of paralysis, we may think and behave irrationally. An example is when we cover ourselves with bed sheets to hide from something or look in the closet for monsters.

心身の反応がコントロールされているときでさえ、私たちの思考は正常に機能しなくなり、これが恐怖の第三段階です。これ以上考えられなくなる一種の心的麻痺が起こったり、次に何をすべきか決定できなくなります。あるいは、麻痺に陥る代わりに、私たちは不合理に考え、行動するかもしれません。その例としては、何かから身を隠そうとしてベッドのシーツを自分にかぶせたり、クローゼットの中にいる怪物を探したりすることなどがあります。

Now, what's the last step in the chain of events associated with fear? ₄Our **memories** kick in. Everything is recorded in our minds, especially the events that were stressful or intensely emotional. And when we get into a similar situation in the future, we tend to recall those negative experiences. ₅We assume that the same thing will happen again, and our **actions** will follow. For example, if we had an unpleasant experience in a job interview, every

さて、恐怖が引き起こす一連の出来事の最後の段階は何でしょうか。私たちの記憶が働き始めます。特に強いストレスを感じたり、感情を激しく刺激したりする出来事が、私たちの心に記憶されます。そして将来同じシチュエーションになったら、このような悲観的な経験を呼び起こす傾向があるのです。私たちは同じことがまた起こると想定し、行動がそれに従います。例えば、仕事の面接で嫌な経験をしたら、同様の面接の度に前の記憶が呼び起こされ、それが私たちの行動を決定するでしょう。

time we have a similar interview, this previous memory will be recalled, and ₅ we let this decide our **actions**.

So, we are not rationally coming to a conclusion on what should be done, but instead we assume the situation is the same as it was on that last occasion, and that the result will be negative. In doing this, ₆ we are trying to protect ourselves from **danger**, but ultimately we end up with another negative result.

ですから、私たちはどうすべきか合理的に結論を出すことができなくなり、その代わりに、状況は前回に経験したときと同じで、悪い結果しかもたらさないと思い込んでしまうでしょう。そうすることで、私たちは自分を危険から守ろうとしているのですが、結局はまた同じような悪い結果となってしまうのです。

| 練習2 | 要約を完成させる問題 | 本冊P.84／track 11 |

| 解答 | **1 ▸ 7.2 million tonnes**　　**2 ▸ storage**　　**3 ▸ renewable energy**
4 ▸ organic matter　　**5 ▸ bad odours[odors]** |

▶ 解説

1　要約から音声の順で、それぞれeach year ⇄ every year / waste ⇄ discardなど、たくみにパラフレーズされているが、要約のIn the UKがそのまま音声で流れてくる。国名はパラフレーズされにくい語の1つ。

2　because ofの後に形容詞badがあるので、その後にはbadに修飾される名詞が続く。because ofとdue toのパラフレーズは、必ず押さえておこう。

3　要約の〈turn＋目的語＋into 〜〉から解答には名詞が来ると判断できる。音声のconvert the contents of our bins intoが、要約ではシンプルに turn food waste intoになっている。

4　要約の46 biogas generation plantsが、音声では46 plantsにパラフレーズされている。数字のキーワードは言い換えられないことが多く、大事なキーワード。
　　........ is broken down(要約) ⇄ micro-organisms break down organic matter(音声)と、受動態から能動態にパラフレーズされているので注意しよう。

5　空欄直前のproduceの目的語、空欄直後のthat can affect ...の先行詞となる名詞を探す問題。
　　パラフレーズ nearby homes ⇄ residential areas

▶ 問題文の訳

Questions 1-5　以下の要約を完成させなさい。それぞれの解答として、2つ以下の単語か1つの数字、もしくはその両方を記入すること。

英国では、レストランや食品業界が、実質的に毎年**1　720万トン**以上の食品を廃棄している。先進国が食品を廃棄しているだけでなく、発展途上国も、主に不適切な**2　保管**のために同様のことを行っている。食品廃棄物は、ほとんどが生物分解性である。この問題の解決策としては、食品廃棄物を**3　再生可能エネルギー**に変換できれば、それが大きな電力源になるかもしれない。これを行う方法の1つは、バクテリアや微生物による化学反応を利用することだ。英国には46のバイオガス発電施設があり、そこでは**4　有機物**が発電のために分解されており、今では年間およそ54メガワットを発電している。残念ながら、いくつかの問題があり、そのうちの1つは、処理施設が近隣の住宅地に影響を及ぼす**5　悪臭**を発生させることである。

You will hear a talk about the issue of food waste in the UK. First, you have some time to look at Questions 1 to 5.
Now listen carefully and answer Questions 1 to 5.

英国での食料の浪費問題について話しているのが聞こえてきます。まず、設問1〜5を見る時間があります。では、音声を注意深く聞いて設問1〜5に答えなさい。

The amount of food thrown away worldwide is staggering. One government-funded non-profit organisation, which was set up to encourage recycling and clamp down on food waste reports that ₁in the UK we discard more than **7.2 million tonnes** every year! Apparently, roughly equal amounts are generated from restaurants and from the food processing industry.

世界中で廃棄されている食品の量は膨大です。リサイクルを推進し、食品廃棄を取り締まるために政府の予算で設立されたある非営利団体の報告によると、英国では毎年720万トン以上が廃棄されているのです！どうやら、ほとんど同程度の量が、レストランや食品加工業から生じているようです。

In most developed countries, economic well-being somehow inevitably leads to poor use of resources, including food. ₂But developing countries also waste enormous quantities of food, and this is largely due to poor **storage**—one thing they commonly suffer from is a lack of refrigeration.

ほとんどの先進国では、経済的な繁栄は、どういうわけか必然的に食品を含む資源の浪費を引き起こしています。しかし、発展途上国もまた大量の食品を浪費していますが、これは主に不適切な保管が原因となっており、そうした国が共通して抱えている問題の1つは、冷蔵設備の不足です。

While we can try to reduce the quantity of food wasted, it will probably always happen, so the question is what to do with it. You firstly need to look at what food waste consists of. It typically contains carbohydrates such as potatoes and rice, proteins from meat and pulses, lipids such as animal fat and cooking oils, and water from washing and cooking. All of these are largely biodegradable. But dumped in the open or in landfill, they degrade to produce horrible smells and toxic liquids and gasses.

廃棄される食品の量を減らそうとすることは可能で、そうした努力はおそらく常に行われるでしょうが、問題は廃棄された食品をどう処理するかです。まず、食品廃棄物がどのようなもので構成されているのか考える必要があります。それは通常、ジャガイモや米などの炭水化物、肉や豆類などのタンパク質、動物性脂肪や食用油などの脂質、そして水洗いや調理の過程で出る水分が含まれています。そうしたものはみな、ほとんどが生物に分解されやすいのです。しかしそれが空き地や埋め立て地に投棄されると、分解の過程でひどい悪臭や有毒な液体やガスを発生させます。

So, what can be done about this? Well, rather than being considered a problem, ₃waste should be regarded as a high-quality, **renewable resource**. Rich in oils and starches formed from hydrocarbons, there is ample opportunity to convert the contents of our bins into **renewable energy** to power homes.

では、これをどうすればよいのでしょうか。そう、廃棄物を問題と見なすのではなく、むしろ高品質で再生可能な資源と見なすべきなのです。油分や、炭化水素から生じるデンプンが豊富なので、私たちのゴミ箱の中身を再生可能エネルギーに変えて、家庭に電力を供給できる可能性は十分にあります。

So, how can we turn waste into energy? One way is to use bacteria and microbes; the sort of chemical transformation that occurs naturally in anaerobic digestion or fermentation. Does that sound too technical? OK, let me explain further. Animal-based fertiliser, sewage sludge, food and plant waste are

では、どうすれば廃棄物をエネルギーに変えることができるでしょうか。1つの方法は、バクテリア（細菌）や微生物を使い、嫌気性消化もしくは発酵によって自然に起こる化学変換を活用するものです。これはとても専門的に聞こえますか。わかりました、では、もう少し詳しく説明させてください。動物由来の肥料、下水からの汚泥、不要に

Listening

collected, then treated using a natural process during which ₄micro-organisms break down **organic matter**. This is already being done in 46 plants in the UK. Each plant consumes from 150 tonnes to 150,000 tonnes of waste per year, and from this, they produce heat and power. At a total of 1.8 million tonnes per year, these plants digest 12% of the total annual food waste generated in the UK and are able to generate 54 megawatts of power.

But there are some limitations. The main issues are that the plants need a lot of space as the chemical processes happen in shallow pools over a large area, and secondly, the bugs won't eat just anything. They're not partial to fatty foods, which means a considerable amount of food waste has to be separated out and needs different treatment. Also the bugs are somewhat flatulent, and ₅this leads to **bad odours** often wafting away from the treatment plants to residential areas.

なった食品や植物を集めたら、微生物が有機物を分解する自然な働きを利用して処理するのです。これは、すでに英国内の46の処理施設で行われています。各施設は、年間150トンから15万トンの廃棄物を受け入れ、そこから熱と電力を生み出しています。こうした施設は、1年間の合計が180万トンという、英国で1年間に発生する総食品廃棄物の12パーセントを処理し、54メガワットの電力を生み出すことができます。

ただし、限界もあります。最も大きな問題は、この化学的処理が広い面積の浅い水槽で行われるため、施設が広い土地を必要とすることです。そして次に、微生物は何でも食べるわけではありません。それらは脂肪分の多い食品は好まないので、かなりの量の食品廃棄物を分別し、異なる処理を施す必要があります。また、微生物はいくらかのガスを発生させるので、しばしば悪臭が処理場から住宅街に流れ込むことがあります。

Part 1

解答	**1** ▸ Clery	**2** ▸ 205-864-739	**3** ▸ Australian	**4** ▸ 11(th)	**5** ▸ smoking

▶ 解説

フォームを完成させる問題

1 Maryなど一般的な名前以外は、普通1文字ずつスペルアウトされる。本問では4回も名前が登場するので、一度聞き逃しても根気強く聞き取ろう。

2 Can I have your passport number as well, please?が聞こえたら、聞き逃さないように集中しよう。なお、パスポートナンバーは、数字とアルファベットの組み合わせで出題されることが多い。

3 普通、**What's your nationality?**（国籍は?）と聞かれたら**I'm Japanese.**（日本人です）**と答える**。音声のI'm from Australia.から、Australia（オーストラリア）と国名を答えると間違いになるので要注意。

5 フォームのSpecial requestがキーワード。音声のDo you have any special requests?が、次に答えが流れるサインになっている。

▶ 問題文の訳

Questions 1-5　以下の予約カードを完成させなさい。それぞれの解答として、1つの単語か1つの数字、もしくはその両方を記入すること。

予約カード

名：シャーロット

姓：**1**　クレリー

パスポート番号：**2**　205-864-739

国籍：**3**　オーストラリア人

チェックイン：7月6日

チェックアウト：**4** 7月　11　日

特別な要望：**5**　喫煙可能な　部屋

解答	**6** ▸ High	**7** ▸ shuttle bus	**8** ▸ Beach Express
	9 ▸ 50[fifty] ¢[cents]	**10** ▸ basic	

▶ 解説

メモを完成させる問題

6 通りの名前を入れる問題。Maryland Guest Houseは固有名詞なので、音声でそのまま登場する可能性が高く、大切なキーワードになっている。

7 空欄前後から乗り物を表す名詞が入ると予想をつけておこう。

8 空欄直後のwritten on the frontが、空欄の語句を修飾する構造になっている。空欄には「バスの前面に書かれている内容」が来ると判断できる。

9 単位はスペルアウトしてもよいが、スペルミスを防ぐために記号で書く方がよい。

10 空欄に入るのはthingsを修飾する形容詞。品詞を絞って音声に集中しよう。 パラフレーズ sells ⇄ provide

Questions 6-10 以下のメモを完成させなさい。それぞれの解答として、2つ以下の単語か1つの数字、もしくはその両方を記入すること。

メリーランド・ゲストハウスの所在地：6　<u>ハイ・　ストリート</u>。

徒歩または7　<u>シャトルバス</u>　でバスターミナルに行く。

ビーチ行きのバスの前面には8　<u>ビーチ・エクスプレス</u>　と書かれている。

ビジネスセンターでの印刷料金は1ページあたり9　<u>50セント</u>　である。

ショップではテレホンカードやお菓子などの10　<u>雑貨品</u>　を販売している。

▶ スクリプトと訳

Part 1

You will hear a conversation between a hotel receptionist, and a guest who is checking into the hotel. First, you have some time to look at Questions 1 to 5.

Now listen carefully and answer Questions 1 to 5.

R = Receptionist 🇬🇧　G = Guest 🇦🇺

A = Anna 🇬🇧

R	Good evening, madam. How can I help you?
G	I've just arrived from Canberra. I have a reservation.
R	Of course, madam. Could I have your name, please?
G	Yes, Charlotte.
R	Okay—and your surname?
G	₁**Clery**.
R	How do you spell that?
G	₁**C-L-E-R-Y**.
R	Just a minute. Mrs Charlotte ₁**Clery**?
G	That's right.
R	Yes, that's fine. Okay, Mrs ₁**Clery**. Can I have your passport number as well, please?
G	Erm, just a minute. Yes, it's ₂**205-864-739**.
R	₂**205-864**-... yes?
G	...₂**739**.
R	Okay, and your nationality?
G	I'm from Australia.
R	So, you're ₃**Australian**. Right. According to your reservation, you're planning to stay for four nights. Is that right?
G	Yes, ... Oh, wait a minute, actually it's five nights.
R	Okay, so you have a reservation from the 6th, and you will be leaving on the ₄**11th**.
G	That's right.
R	Do you have any special requests?

パート1

ホテルのフロント係と、ホテルにチェックインしようとしている宿泊客との会話が聞こえてきます。最初に、設問1〜5を見る時間があります。では音声を注意深く聞いて、設問1〜5に答えなさい。

R ＝フロント係　G ＝宿泊客

A ＝アナ

こんばんは、お客様。おうかがいいたします。

私はキャンベラから到着したばかりなんです。予約はしてあります。

そうですか、お客様。お名前をお教えいただけますか。

ええ、シャーロットです。

わかりました。名字もお願いいたします。

クレリーです。

どのようなつづりですか。

C-L-E-R-Yです。

少々お待ちください。シャーロット・クレリー様ですね。

そうです。

はい、けっこうです。さて、クレリー様。パスポート番号も教えていただけますか。

ええと、ちょっと待ってください。はい、205-864-739です。

205-864-...そして？

...739です。

わかりました、そしてお客様の国籍は？

私はオーストラリア出身です。

では、あなたはオーストラリア人ですね。けっこうです。お客様のご予約によると、4泊されることになっています。それで正しいですか。

ええ...いや、ちょっと待ってください、実は5泊なんです。

わかりました。それでは6日からの予約で、11日にここを出られるのですね。

そうです。

何か特別なご要望はございますか。

G Umm...is it possible to have a ₅**smoking** room, please?	ええと…喫煙のできる部屋はありますか。
R Of course, madam.	かしこまりました、お客様。
G Thanks. Oh, I'd like to get some information about transport and the hotel services, if possible.	ありがとう。そうだ、できれば交通機関とこのホテルのサービスについて知りたいのですが。
R Certainly. You can talk to Anna, our Guest Relations Officer. There she is, she's standing at the concierge desk.	もちろんです。宿泊者案内係のアナとお話しください。彼女はあそこです、コンシェルジュ・デスクの所に立っています。
G That's great, thanks!	よかった、ありがとう！

Before you hear the rest of the conversation, you have some time to look at Questions 6 to 10.
Now listen and answer Questions 6 to 10.

会話の残りを聞く前に、設問6～10を見る時間があります。では、音声を聞いて設問6～10に答えなさい。

G Excuse me. The receptionist told me that I can find out about transport and hotel facilities here.	すみません。フロント係から、ここで交通機関やホテルの施設について聞けると言われたんですけれど。
A Yes, madam. How can I help you?	はい、お客様。どのようなご用件でしょうか。
G Do you have any brochures about public transport?	公共交通機関についての案内書のようなものはありますか。
A I'm sorry we don't have any. But it's a small town. May I ask where you'd like to go?	申し訳ありませんがございません。でもここは小さな町です。どちらに行かれたいのか教えていただけますか。
G I'm going to visit a friend at the Maryland Guest House. How do I get there from here?	メリーランド・ゲストハウスの友人を訪ねるつもりなんです。ここからのどのようにしてそこに行けますか。
A ₆Maryland Guest House ... umm ... it's on **High Street** ... Well, you'll have to get to the bus station first.	メリーランド・ゲストハウスですか…ええと…それはハイ・ストリートにあります…そうですね、お客様はまずバスターミナルに行かなければいけませんね。
G Hmm ... Is it far from here?	ふーん…ここから遠いのですか。
A ₇You can walk there from here in about 20 minutes, or take our **shuttle bus**. It's about a 5-minute journey.	ここから歩いておよそ20分ほどですが、当ホテルのシャトルバスもご利用いただけます。乗車時間はおよそ5分です。
G Hmm ... OK. I think I'll take the shuttle bus.	うーん…わかりました。シャトルバスに乗ろうと思います。
A The next shuttle is in 10 minutes. Is that OK?	次のシャトルバスは10分後の出発です。それでよろしいですか。
G That's fine. So, after I get to the bus station, which bus do I have to take?	けっこうです。それで，私がバスターミナルに着いたら、私はどのバスに乗る必要がありますか。
A At the bus station, catch the green bus to the beach. ₈Look for '**Beach Express**' on the front of the bus.	そのバスターミナルでビーチ行きの緑色のバスに乗ってください。バスの前面に「ビーチ・エクスプレス」とあるのが目印です。
G Right—let me just write that down ... green bus ... ₈'**Beach Express**'.	なるほど。ちょっとメモさせてください…緑のバス…「ビーチ・エクスプレス」ですね。
A Just ask for 'Maryland Guest House'. But it's only two kilometres from the centre of town, so you could walk it.	「メリーランド・ゲストハウス」で降りたいとだけ伝えてください。でも、そこは町の中心部からはわずか2キロメートルほどなので、歩いていくこともできるでしょう。
G OK. And one last thing, I need to print some documents rather urgently. Do you have a printer?	わかりました。それから最後に、私はいくつかの文書をかなり急いで印刷する必要があるんです。ここにプリンターはありますか。

A	Yes. We've got a business centre here in the hotel, with a printer and copier. It's down the corridor that way.	はい。当ホテルには、プリンターとコピー機を備えたビジネスセンターがあります。この廊下の先の方にあります。
G	And do you know how much it costs per page to print?	印刷料金は1ページあたりいくらなのかわかりますか。
A	I believe ₉it's **50 cents**.	50セントのはずです。
G	Fantastic. Is there a shop here in the hotel?	よかった。このホテルにショップはありますか。
A	Yes, ₁₀ we provide a few **basic** things, you know, phone cards and sweets, and other necessities.	はい、雑貨品をいくつか、例えばテレホンカードやお菓子、ほかの必需品を販売しています。
G	That sounds perfect. Thanks.	それで申し分ありません。ありがとう。
A	Have a lovely day, madam.	よい1日を、お客様。

That is the end of Part 1.
You now have one minute to check your answers to Part 1.

これでパート1は終わりです。
ここで1分間、パート1の解答を確認する時間があります。

Part 2

本冊P.86 / track 13

解答
11 ▸ classical music (concerts) / (classical) (music) concerts
12 ▸ (a) bookshop[book shop]　　13 ▸ planned
14 ▸ 1983　　15 ▸ (the) City Council　　16 ▸ 363

▶ 解説

メモを完成させる問題

11 メモのWell known forを言い換えたit's famous ...の文から解答を導こう。

12 concert rooms, theatres ...から、施設を表す名詞が入ると予想できる。また、16には日数が入ることも空欄の前後を見て、プレヴュータイム中に判断しておこう。

13 メモの前の行にある1940を音声で拾えるように集中しよう。空欄13の前にある1960sは、年代なので本来はパラフレーズされにくい語だが、本問では少し姿を変えてin the 60sで登場するので注意。

14 沿革を述べている部分で、Inの後に続く語を入れるとなると、空欄には年代が入ると判断できる。opened to publicがほぼそのまま音声で流れてくるので、サービス問題だと思って落とさないように。

▶ 問題文の訳

Questions 11-16 以下のメモを完成させなさい。それぞれの解答として、3つ以下の単語か1つの数字、もしくはその両方を記入すること。

国立芸術センター

有名な理由：**11** <u>クラシック音楽のコンサート</u>

施設の構成：コンサート会場

劇場

映画館

美術館

公共図書館

レストラン

12 <u>書店</u>

沿革：	1940年―この地域が爆撃で壊滅した	
	1960年代―文化センターが **13** <u>計画された</u>	
	14 <u>1983</u> 年に一般公開	
運営者：	**15** <u>市議会</u>	
営業日：	**16** 1年間に <u>363</u> 日	

解答	**17** ▸ (the) Garden Hall	**18** ▸ *Three Lives*	**19** ▸ £4.50
	20 ▸ *Faces of China*		

▸ **解説**

表を完成させる問題

17-20 各空欄の見出し（17→Venue, 18→Event …）を事前に確認することで、答えにどんな語が入るか予想しておこう。空欄以外の箇所、特に数字（TimeやTicket Price）は、音声内で言い換えられずに、そのまま流れる可能性が高いのでヒントになる。

▸ **問題文の訳**

Questions 17-20 以下の表を完成させなさい。それぞれの解答として、3つ以下の単語か1つの数字、もしくはその両方を記入すること。

曜日	時間	イベント	会場	チケット価格
月・火	午後7時30分	『魔笛』 （モーツァルトのオペラ）	**17** <u>ガーデンホール</u>	8ポンド〜
水	午後8時	**18** <u>スリー・ライブズ</u> （カナダ映画）	シネマ2	**19** <u>4.5ポンド</u>
土・日	午前11時〜 午後10時	**20** <u>中国のさまざまな顔</u> （美術展）	ギャラリー1	無料

▸ **スクリプトと訳** 🇬🇧

Part 2
You will hear a radio broadcast called 'Focus on the Arts'. First, you have some time to look at Questions 11 to 16.
Now listen carefully and answer Questions 11 to 16.

パート2
*Focus on the Arts*という題名のラジオ番組が聞こえてきます。最初に設問11〜16を見る時間があります。では音声を注意深く聞き、設問11〜16に答えなさい。

Hello and welcome to 'Focus on the Arts'. I'm your host, Dave Greene, and this is your very own local radio program. Every Friday evening, we put the spotlight on different arts and culture facilities and look at the shows and events that are on offer in the coming week, and today, the focus is on the National Art Centre. Now, if you don't already know it yourself, I'm sure you've all heard of it; **11** it's

こんにちは、Focus on the Artsにようこそ。司会のデイブ・グリーンです。そして、これは皆様だけの地域ラジオ番組です。毎週金曜日の夜に、さまざまな芸術・文化施設にスポットライトを当てて、翌週に開催される公演やイベントを取り上げていますが、今日は国立芸術センターに焦点を当てます。さて、あなたがまだここをよく知らないとしても、その名前は聞いたことがあると思います。ここは、クラシック音楽の重要な演奏会場の1つとして世界的に

famous throughout the world as one of the major venues for **classical music**, but did you know that it's actually much more than just a place to hear **concerts**?

The centre itself is a huge complex that caters for a great range of arts. Under a single roof, it houses concert rooms, theatres, cinemas, art galleries, and a wonderful public library, as well as service facilities including three restaurants and 12 **a book shop**. So, at any one time, the choice of entertainment there is simply enormous. So how did they manage to build such a big arts complex right in the heart of the city?

Well, the area was completely destroyed by bombs in 1940 during the war, so the opportunity was taken to create a Cultural Centre that they called 'the city's gift to the nation'. Of course, it took a while for such a big project to get started but 13 it was **planned** in the 60s, built in the 70s, and 14 eventually opened to the public in **1983**. Ever since then, it has proved to be a great success.

It's not privately owned like many art centres and is still in public hands. 15 It's run by **the City Council**. Both our National Symphony Orchestra and National Theatre Company were involved in the planning of the project and they are now based there, giving regular performances every week; And as 16 the centre is open **363** days of the year, there are plenty of performances to choose from.

Before you hear the rest of the broadcast, you have some time to look at Questions 17 to 20.
Now listen and answer Questions 17 to 20.

So, to give you some idea of what's on, and to help you choose from the many possibilities, we've made a selection of the star attractions. If you are interested in classical music, then we recommend you go along to the National on either Monday or Tuesday evening at 7:30 pm for a spectacular production of *The Magic Flute*; probably the most popular of all Mozart's operas. It's in 17 **the Garden Hall** and tickets start at only £8.00, but you'll have to be early if you want to get in at that low price. And remember, it's only on for those two evenings.

有名ですが、実はコンサートを聞くだけの場所ではないことをご存じでしたか。

このセンター自体は、さまざまな芸術活動に対応した巨大な複合施設です。1つの施設の中に、いくつかのコンサート会場、劇場、映画館、美術館、充実した公共図書館のほか、3つのレストランや書店などの店舗が集められています。ですから、いつでも、そこには実にさまざまな娯楽の選択肢が用意されています。では、どうして都市の中心部に、このような巨大な芸術複合施設を建設することができたのでしょうか。

そもそも、この地域は戦争中の1940年に爆撃で完全に破壊されてしまったため、それを機会に文化センターを作り、それをいわば「この街から国民への贈り物」にしようとしたのです。もちろん、このような大きなプロジェクトを始めるまでには、しばらく時間がかかりましたが、60年代に計画され、70年代に建設が始まり、ついに1983年に一般に公開されました。それ以来、このセンターは大きな成功を収めてきました。

ここは多くの芸術センターのように民間のものではなく、今でも公的な管理の下にあります。それは市議会によって運営されています。国立交響楽団と国立劇団の両方が、このプロジェクトの計画に加わり、現在はここを本拠地として、毎週、定期公演を行っています。また、このセンターは1年に363日開かれているので、豊富な公演から好みのものを選べます。

残りの放送を聞く前に、設問17～20を見る時間があります。では、音声を聞いて設問17～20に答えなさい。

ですから、今どのようなイベントが行われているのかお知らせし、数多くの候補から選びやすくするために、当番組が目玉となるイベントを絞り込みました。クラシック音楽がお好きなら、月曜日または火曜日の夜7時30分に国立芸術センターに行き、おそらくモーツァルトのオペラの中で最も人気のある『魔笛』の壮大な舞台を鑑賞することをおすすめします。それはガーデンホールで行われ、最も安いチケットはわずか8ポンドですが、その安い料金で入場したいのなら早めに行かなければなりません。そして覚えておいてください。公演は上記の2日の夜だけです。

For those more interested in the cinema, you might like to see the new Canadian film which is showing on Wednesday evening at 8:00 pm in Cinema 2. It's called 18 'Three Lives'. It's had fantastic reviews and tickets cost just 19 £4.50, which is a reduction on the usual price of £5.50, so it's really good value, especially for such a great movie.

But you can see the centre's main attraction at the weekend because on Saturday and Sunday from 11:00 am to 10:00 pm, they're showing a wonderful new exhibition that hasn't been seen anywhere else in Europe yet. It's a collection of Chinese art called 20 'Faces of China' that's in Gallery 1, and it has some really fascinating paintings and sculptures by leading artists from all over China. And the good news is that it's completely free. So, don't miss it!

So, why not go along to the National Art Centre next week for one or all of these great events? And you can always pick up a program and check out all the other performances and exhibitions on offer, or coming soon on almost every day of the year. Next week, we'll be looking at the new Museum of Science ...

That is the end of Part 2. You now have 30 seconds to check your answers to part 2.

映画の方が好きだという方は、水曜日の夜8時にシネマ2で上映される『Three Lives（スリー・ライブズ）』というタイトルのカナダの新作映画を見たいと思うかもしれません。この映画は高い評価を受けており、チケットの価格はわずか4.5ポンドで、通常価格の5.5ポンドから割り引かれていますから、このようなすばらしい映画なら特にお値打ちです。

ところで、週末にはこのセンターで大規模な催しを見ることができます。というのも、土曜日と日曜日の午前11時から午後10時まで、まだヨーロッパのほかのどの国でも見られたことがないすばらしい展覧会が初めて開催されるのです。それはギャラリー1での『Faces of China（中国のさまざまな顔）』と題された中国美術の作品展です。そこには中国各地の一流芸術家による非常に魅力的な絵画や彫刻があります。そして、ありがたいことにまったくの無料です。ですからお見逃しなく！

そういうわけで、来週はこうしたすばらしい催し物のどれか1つまたはすべてを目当てに、国立芸術センターに出かけてみませんか。それから、プログラムはいつでも手に入れることができますから、これら以外にも、1年間ほとんどどの日でも公開中、もしくは近日公開予定の公演や展覧会をチェックすることができます。なお来週は当番組では新しい科学博物館について詳しく見ていく予定で…

これでパート2は終わりです。30秒間、パート2での解答を確認する時間があります。

Part 3
本冊P.87 / track 14

解答	21 ▸ B	22 ▸ B	23 ▸ C	24 ▸ B	25 ▸ B

▶ 解説
複数の選択肢から選ぶ問題
21 ヴィッキーの新しい仕事に関する問だが、ティムの発言、You love music, right? が大きなヒントになる。銀行は彼女の現職なので、安易にAを選ばないように。
22 ティムの発言、This is what you should do ... First, ... から、仕事を変えるうえでの心得が数点述べられると予想する。
don't move suddenly into your new career からAは消去できる。BはJust slowly spend more time ... の内容と一致する。Cは、Don't bother making a complicated business plan at first. に反する。
23 音声中のmake a name for yourself は「有名になる、評判を高める」というイディオム。name につられてBを選ばないように。
24 Bのget even more skills が、音声ではobtain some deeper expertise にパラフレーズされている。その後にneed special training と流れるが、これは自身のためで、他人のためではないのでAは不正解。
25 音声のyou have to be prepared to wait が、Bのyou must be patient につながる。

Aの must always は「常に〜しなければならない」という強い表現で、こういう強意的な表現が含まれる選択肢には注意する。4年くらいかけて売れたバンドの例が挙げられているが、「全員が数年かかる」とは言っていない。

▶ 問題文の訳

Questions 21-25　正解を、A, BまたはCから選んで記入しなさい。

21　ヴィッキーは_____の分野で新しい仕事を始めたいと思っている。
　　A　銀行業
　　B　音楽
　　C　金融

22　新しい仕事への移行は_____行う必要がある。
　　A　いっぺんに
　　B　徐々に
　　C　自分の事業計画に厳密に従って

23　2人は「進め方を単純なものにする」ことについて話しているが、それは_____ということである。
　　A　ウェブサイトで使う言葉は読みやすいものでなければならない
　　B　自分の会社には簡単な名前をつけること
　　C　最初にすることは1つだけにし、それ以上は行わない

24　自分のビジネスを成長させようとするなら、_____ことも必要だ。
　　A　人のために特別なトレーニングを実施する
　　B　自分自身のために、さらに多くの技術を身につける
　　C　大きなグループで作業する

25　新しい仕事から収入を得る場合、_____。
　　A　常に数年間は待たなければならない
　　B　忍耐強くなければならない
　　C　すぐにお金を稼ぐ努力をすべきだ

| 解答 | **26** ▸ relax | **27** ▸ 7[seven] | **28** ▸ challenge | **29** ▸ perspective |
| | **30** ▸ shame | | | |

▶ 解説

文を完成させる問題

26 空欄部分に動詞の原形を入れて、「〜のために」と不定詞の副詞的用法にする。
27 空欄前後から「1週間に何日か」数字を入れる問題だとわかる。
28 an の後に emotional（形容詞）が続くので、空欄には名詞を入れる。
29 問題文の mirror が、音声では reflect に言い換えられている。ただし、reflect の目的語（you, who you are, and how you see things）は空欄に合わない。how you see things を1語で言い換えた perspective が正解。
30 feel の目的語として適当な名詞を入れる。 パラフレーズ not ... any 〜 ⇄ no 〜

▶ 問題文の訳

Questions 26-30　以下の文を完成させなさい。それぞれの解答として、1つの単語か1つの数字、もしくはその両方を記入すること。

26　自分の趣味を新しい仕事にするとき、趣味を　気分転換をする　ために使うことはできない。
27　1週間に　7　日間働く覚悟をしなければならない。

46

28 新しい仕事は重労働で、精神的にも　　試練　　になる可能性がある。

29 新しい仕事は、あなた自身の独特な　ものの見方　を反映するべきだ。

30 前の仕事に戻らなければならなくなっても、それを　　恥　　だと感じる必要はまったくない。

▶ スクリプトと訳

Part 3

You will hear a conversation between two friends about turning your hobby into your career. First, you have some time to look at Questions 21 to 25.

Now listen carefully and answer Questions 21 to 25.

V = Vicky 　T = Tim

パート3

2人の友人が自分の趣味を仕事にすることについて話しているのが聞こえてきます。音声を聞く前に、設問21～25を見る時間があります。では、音声を注意深く聞いて設問21～25に答えなさい。

V＝ヴィッキー　T＝ティム

V Hi, Tim. Do you have a few minutes?

T Hi, Vicky. Sure.

V You've turned your hobby into your career. I'm thinking of doing the same thing.

T And you'd like some advice?

V I would. I know you've done it with great success, and since I became a bank teller, I've never really enjoyed my job. Why not make a change, I thought. Do what Tim did.

T Well, it's a big decision, Vicky. It took me several months before I decided to quit. You have a good job at the bank. What if you're not happy with this new job one day?

V I'm sure I'll always be really happy doing what I love doing.

T ₂₁You love music, right?

V ₂₁Yes. And that's what I want to make my profession.

T Well, within the field of music you've got lots of options. This is what you should do ... First, make sure you have plenty of skills in the hobby, which I guess you do. Second, don't move suddenly into your new career. And third, at the same time, begin to cut down on your spending. Because you have to think about the finances. This will help you maintain a reasonable income from your current job while your new career is being consolidated. Don't bother making a complicated business plan at first. It is so hard to predict, and you will only get disappointed when it doesn't work out. ₂₂Just slowly spend more time on your new career and less time on your current career.

V OK. Got that.

T Most important of all, choose a hobby you're passionate about. Think about which aspect of

こんにちは、ティム。ちょっといい？

やあ、ヴィッキー。もちろんいいよ。

あなたって自分の趣味を仕事にしたじゃない。私も同じことを考えているの。

だから、何かアドバイスが欲しいってこと？

ええ、そう。あなたがそれで大成功したのを知っているから。そして、私は銀行の窓口係になってから、自分の仕事を心から楽しんだことがないの。ここで変化を求めたらどうかしらって思ったのよ。ティムを見習ってね。

そうだねえ、これは大きな決断だよ、ヴィッキー。僕はそれまでの仕事を辞めるって決めるまで数か月かかったんだ。君は銀行で安定した仕事をしているだろう。いつか、新しい仕事が嫌になったりしたらどうする？

自分がとても好きなことをしていれば、常に満足できると思うの。

君は音楽が好きだったね。

そう。で、それこそが私が自分の仕事にしたいことなの。

ええと、音楽業界だったら、いろいろな選択肢があるよ。君がすべきことはこうさ…まず、君がその趣味で十分な技術を持っていることを確認するんだ。君なら大丈夫だと思うけど。次に、いきなり新しい仕事に移らないこと。3番目に、それと同時に、出費を抑えるようにするんだ。経済状態に注意する必要があるからね。そうすれば、新しい仕事が軌道に乗るまで、今の仕事から十分な収入を確保することができるよ。最初から苦労して複雑な事業計画を立ててはいけない。将来を予測するのはとても難しいし、それがうまくいかないと失望するだけだからね。ただ、徐々に新しい仕事のための時間を増やし、今の仕事のための時間を減らしていけばいいのさ。

なるほど。わかった。

何よりも大切なのは、自分が情熱をもって打ち込める趣味を選ぶことだよ。その趣味のどんなところが、君の場合

your hobby, in your case music, really animates and excites you. Then, pursue a path to professionalism in that hobby.

V　OK, I'm into song writing, as you know, but I also love recording ...

T　Hmm, those are different things. You need to identify the one that excites you most.

V　To be honest, I'm not sure.

T　Well, in order to succeed, you have to start by keeping the process simple. 23 Simple is best at the beginning. You need to be well focused on one thing. Keep your eye on your goal and keep your aims clear. Don't try and do too many things at once—one is enough. It will be easier to make a name for yourself and market your services if you can put an explicit title on the service you offer.

V　Don't you think that simplifying things will limit my options for growth?

T　No, it shouldn't. There are plenty of opportunities out there, and if you remain focused on your main objective, you will get there faster and ultimately have more success in the end.

V　OK.

T　Also 24 obtain some deeper expertise. Even if you're passionate about your music, sometimes you need special training to ensure you can meet your full potential when you make that hobby your career. This special training depends on what sort of hobby you're interested in. If for you it is song writing, then maybe you need to know some extra musical theory or how to write for a large band ...

V　I see.

T　And don't worry if it takes time to see a reward. In fact, it usually does. Lots of people give up when they don't make money immediately, but that's a mistake. 25 It often takes time and you have to be prepared to wait. Again that's why you should make sure you have a separate income. The other day I heard about a pop band that spent years trying to get noticed and only after about four years did they get a big hit.

V　Got it. I hope it doesn't take me that long, though. Thanks for your advice Tim.

は音楽だけど、君を元気づけ、夢中にさせてくれるのか考えるんだ。そして、その趣味でプロになる道を追求するんだ。

ええ、知ってのとおり、私は作曲に夢中だけど、レコーディングも大好きだよ…。

うーん、その２つは違う分野だよ。君が一番夢中になれることに絞り込むんだ。

実は、決めかねているの。

だったら、成功するためには、進め方を単純なものにすることから始めるべきだね。最初は１つに絞るんだ。１つのことだけに集中し、自分の目標だけを見て、目的をはっきりさせておくんだ。一度にたくさんのことをしようとしないことだ。１つで十分さ。君が提供するサービスにわかりやすい呼び名をつけることができれば、人に知ってもらえて、そのサービスを売り込むのはずいぶん楽になるだろうね。

いろいろなことを１つに絞ると、成長のための選択肢が減ってしまうと思わない？

いや、そんなことにはならないよ。チャンスならいくらでもあるし、君が一番大切にしている目的にずっと集中していれば、それを早く達成できるし、結局はより大きな成功を手にできるだろうね。

そうね。

それから、専門知識も身につけるんだ。君が音楽に夢中になっていても、その趣味を仕事にするなら、自分の潜在能力を最大限に発揮できるようにするための特別なトレーニングが必要になる場合がある。この特別なトレーニングは、熱中している趣味の種類によって異なるけどね。君の場合は作曲だというなら、たぶん、音楽理論の知識を増やしたり、大人数のバンドのための作曲方法を知っていたりする必要があるかもしれない…。

なるほどね。

それから、収入を得るのに時間がかかっても、心配しなくていい。実際のところ、たいてい時間がかかるのだから。すぐにお金が稼げないからといって諦めてしまう人は多いけど、それは間違いさ。たいてい時間はかかるものだから、君は待つ覚悟をしなければいけない。繰り返すけど、だから君は別の収入源を確保しなければならないんだ。つい最近、何年も注目を集める努力をして、４年くらい経ってやっと大ヒットを飛ばしたポップバンドの話を聞いたよ。

わかった。でも、そんなに長くはかかってほしくないけど。アドバイスをありがとう、ティム。

T Right. Next, you have to consider your priorities. As I said, turning your hobby into a career can be a rewarding experience. But remember, ₂₆ you will no longer be able to turn to that hobby in order to **relax** like you do now, because it will be your job. You will probably have to find some other way to reduce your stress.

V Yes, I'm aware of that. I am thinking of taking up yoga.

T Also, as I said, your new hobby-based career might mean a decline in your income. But even apart from the finances, and even if you head into your new career with lots of optimism and passion, it might not be as great as it first seemed. You may struggle and work hard for years to get your new operation off the ground.

V I know. Other people have told me I have to prepare for long hours and ₂₇ work all **seven** days of the week.

T All of that work for less reward can definitely be difficult. ₂₈ People commonly find it a **challenge** both physically and emotionally. You might need that yoga to cope with that challenge!

V Tell me about your experience.

T Well, I was lucky. After about a year, I was able to turn my hobby of creating gemstone jewellery into a fairly successful business. Jewellery making is an expensive hobby, but for me, it soon paid for itself.

V Your jewellery work is amazing. I've never seen anything like it.

T Well, it is vital to be authentic and to be different from others. The best way to do that is to ₂₉ go with your own personal **perspective** on things. Your business should reflect you, who you are, and how you see things.

V And I also worry—what if my career switch doesn't work out? It did for you, but what if it doesn't work for me? I'd be afraid to give up and go back to what I did before.

ああ。次に優先順位をよく考えることだね。繰り返しになるけど、趣味を仕事にするのは、やりがいのあることだろう。でも、それを自分の仕事にすると、今みたいに気分転換にその趣味をすることができなくなるということを忘れちゃいけないよ。たぶん君は、ストレスを和らげる別の方法を見つける必要があるだろうね。

ええ、そのことならわかってる。ヨガを始めようと思っているの。

それから、これももう言ったけど、趣味から始めた新しい仕事では、収入が減ることになるかもしれない。でも、お金のことは別にしても、君がどんなに大きな自信と情熱を持って新しい仕事に飛びこんだとしても、それは最初に期待したほどうまくいかないかもしれない。新しい事業を軌道に乗せるまでに、何年も苦労してがんばらなければならないかもしれないよ。

そうね。ほかの人からも、私は長時間の作業を覚悟し、週7日働かなければならないと言われたし。

収入が減ったうえでのそうした仕事は、結局は難しいものになるかもしれない。誰でもそれを、肉体的にも精神的にも試練だと感じるのが普通だろう。君はこの試練に立ち向かうために、そのヨガが必要かもしれないね!

あなたの経験を聞かせてもらえるかしら。

そうだね、僕はついていたんだ。1年くらいで宝石の原石を使って宝飾品を作るという自分の趣味をかなり成功したビジネスにすることができたんだから。宝飾品作りというのはお金のかかる趣味だけど、すぐに元が取れたんだ。

あなたの宝飾品の作品はすてきだね。あのようなものは今まで見たことがないもの。

そう、正統的でありながら、ほかのものとは違っていることが大事なんだ。そうするための最善の方法は、物事に対して自分ならではの見方を持つことさ。君のビジネスは君という人間、君はどんな人物で、物事をどう見ているかを反映しなければならないんだ。

それで、私も心配しているんだけれど、進路を変更してうまくいかなかった場合はどうなるのだろうって。あなたの場合はうまくいったけど、私がだめだったらどうしたらいいのかな。その仕事をあきらめたら、前の仕事に戻る勇気がなくて。

T	Don't be afraid about that. Unfortunately, a lot of people simply don't make a success of their new career, and the best option is to simply **30** go back to your old one. There's no **shame** in admitting your career switch didn't work out.	そのことは心配しなくていいよ。残念ながら、新しい仕事を成功させることができない人は数多くいるし、最善の選択肢は、ただ前の仕事に戻ることなんだ。進路の変更がうまくいかなかったと認めるのは恥ずかしいことじゃないんだ。
V	Thanks very much for sharing all this with me.	私にいろいろと教えてくれてありがとう。
T	No worries. I hope you'll finally have a job you enjoy.	どういたしまして。君がいよいよ楽しめる仕事ができることを願っているよ。

That is the end of Part 3.
You now have 30 seconds to check your answers to Part 3.

これでパート3は終わりです。
ここで、パート3の解答を確認するための時間が30秒あります。

Part 4 本冊P.88 ／ track 15

解答	**31** ▸ Drought(s)	**32** ▸ bats	**33** ▸ inflammation	**34** ▸ 500,000
	35 ▸ expansion	**36** ▸ shaded	**37** ▸ Africa	**38** ▸ wildlife / animals
	39 ▸ areas	**40** ▸ food		

▸ **解説**

メモを完成させる問題

パート4は、切れ目なく一気に音声が流れる点でほかのパートと異なる。その分、難易度が上がるが、最初のプレヴュータイムで問題文を読み込み、音声に備えよう。

ここでは、メモのタイトル（Deforestation is leading to more infectious diseases in humans）と見出し（How Nipah virus initially spread, Malaria, How new diseases emerge）を読むのは必須。その後に、メモの箇条書きにも目を通そう。

31 火災を悪化させた原因を表す名詞を入れる。パラフレーズされにくいキーワードであるIndonesia, 1997を頼りに、解答の根拠となる場所を見つけよう。

32 使役の文型〈make＋目的語＋動詞の原形〉の目的語の部分を入れる問題。migrateから、目的語には生物がくると予想しておく。

33 音声中の265, 105を聞き逃さないように。Within two years（メモ）⇄ By 1999（音声）のように、数字でもパラフレーズされることがある。

34 空欄に死亡者数が入るのは明白なので、数字を聞き逃さないように。every year（メモ）⇄ annually（音声）と、roughly（メモ）⇄ about（音声）のパラフレーズは基本。

35 agricultural expansion（メモ）⇄ expansion of agriculture（音声）は、〈形容詞＋名詞〉⇄〈名詞＋of＋形容詞の名詞化〉の言い換え。 パラフレーズ have increased gradually ⇄ have been steadily rising

36 Peruvian Amazonが重要なキーワードなので、音声中で聞き逃さないようにする。in warm and slightlyが、in warm, partiallyに、少しパラフレーズされている。

37 空欄のある文を読めば「マラリアと森林破壊の直接的な関連は、**37**........ では薄く、サバ州ではかなり強い」と対比構造になっており、空欄には地名が入ると確信が持てる。

38 As well as mosquitoesから、空欄には生物の種類や名前がくると判断できる。

39 メモのTransmissionが音声ではhumans can catch the virusesに、untouchedがhave never been visited by humans beforeに、それぞれ具体的にパラフレーズされている。

40 空欄部分の文型は〈send＋目的語＋for 〜〉（〜を求めて（目的語）を送る）で、この場合の目的語にあたるthemは動物（ネズミ）のこと。

▶ 問題文の訳

Questions 31–40　以下のメモを完成させなさい。それぞれの解答として、1つの単語か1つの数字を記入すること。

森林破壊は人により多くの感染症をもたらす

ニパウイルスは当初、どのようにして広がったのか

- 森林伐採とは、人がその土地をほかの用途で利用できるように樹木を伐採することである。
- **31**　<u>干ばつ</u>　が1997年のインドネシアの森林火災を悪化させた。
- その火災のために**32**　<u>コウモリ</u>　が餌を求めてマレーシアの果樹園に移動した。次に、ブタが果物を食べて病気になった。その後、その致死性の病気が養豚業者にも感染した。
- 2年のうちに、この病気は265人の脳に**33**　<u>炎症</u>　を引き起こし、105人の命を奪った。
- 伐採される森林の面積が大きいほど、感染症の流行が頻繁に発生することになる。

マラリア

- 世界中で、マラリアは蚊によって伝染し、毎年およそ**34**　<u>50万</u>　人が亡くなっている。それはまた、森林破壊に関連があると考えられている。
- 農業の**35**　<u>拡大</u>　により、症例の数が次第に増加している。
- ペルー領のアマゾン川流域でマラリアがどのように広がったのか：森林の端に沿った生息地で蚊が繁殖し、その幼虫が、温かく、少し**36**　<u>日陰になっている</u>　水たまりで見つかった。
- 2003年から2015年の間にかけて森林伐採の面積が10パーセント増加したことにより、マラリアの症例が3パーセント増加した。
- 蚊の生態はその種と生息地域によって異なる。**37**　<u>アフリカ</u>　におけるマラリアと森林破壊の直接的な関連は薄いが、サバ州では関連性がかなり強い。

新たな感染症はどのように発生するか

- 蚊だけでなく、さまざまな森林の**38**　<u>野生生物／動物</u>　もまた、人に致命的な病気を感染させる。
- 人が手つかずの森林**39**　<u>地帯</u>　に進出すると、感染が起こる可能性がある。
- 大規模農園用に森林を伐採したために、動物が**40**　<u>餌</u>　を求めて人間の生息域にやって来て、人々に接触する場合がある。
- 人は、げっ歯類の尿や糞に接触したときに、感染者の36パーセントを死に至らしめるラッソウイルスに感染した。

▶ スクリプトと訳　🇬🇧

Part 4

You will hear a talk about deforestation that is leading to more infectious diseases in humans. First, you have some time to look at Questions 31 to 40. Now listen carefully and answer Questions 31 to 40.

Deforestation is the permanent removal of trees to make room for something besides the forest. This can include clearing the land for agriculture or grazing, or using the timber for fuel, construction or manufacturing. **31** In 1997, clouds of smoke covered the rainforests of Indonesia as an area was burned to make way for agriculture, and the fires were exacerbated by **drought**. This caused a problem that few people predicted. Smothered in haze, the trees couldn't produce fruit, **32** leaving resident **bats** with no other option than to fly elsewhere in search of food, and carrying with them a deadly disease.

パート4

人の間で感染症を増加させる森林破壊についての説明が聞こえてきます。音声を聞く前に、設問31〜40を見る時間があります。では、音声を注意深く聞いて設問31〜40に答えなさい。

森林伐採とは、森林以外の用途のために樹木を恒久的に取り除くことです。その例としては、農業や放牧のための土地の開拓、あるいは燃料や建設、製造業のための木材の利用が含まれます。1997年、もうもうたる煙がインドネシアの熱帯雨林を覆いましたが、その原因は、その一画を農地にするために焼き払ったためで、それによる火災が干ばつによってさらに拡大したのです。これは、ほとんどの人が予期していなかった問題を引き起こしました。煙のせいで呼吸ができなくなった樹木は実を結べなくなり、そこを生息地にしていたコウモリは餌を求めて別の場所に移動せざるをえなくなり、命にかかわる疫病を運ぶことになりました。

32 Not long after the **bats** settled on trees in Malaysian orchards, pigs around them started to fall sick. Researchers presumed that the pigs contracted the virus from eating fallen fruit that bats had nibbled on, and then, pig farmers caught it from the pigs. **33** By 1999, 265 people had developed a severe brain **inflammation**, and 105 had died. It was the first known emergence of Nipah virus in people, which has since seen a string of recurrent outbreaks across Southeast Asia.

As widespread burning continues in tropical forests in the Amazon, and some parts of Africa and Southeast Asia, experts have expressed concern about the health of people living at the frontiers of deforestation. They're also afraid that the next serious pandemic could emerge from our world's forests.

It's also pretty well established that deforestation can be a strong driver of infectious diseases such as malaria. It's a numbers game: The more we degrade and clear forest habitats, the more likely it is that we're going to find ourselves in these situations where epidemics of infectious diseases occur.

34 Malaria kills about **500,000** people annually due to infection by *Plasmodium* parasites transmitted by mosquitoes. It has long been suspected of going hand in hand with deforestation. In Brazil, control efforts have dramatically reduced malaria transmission in the past. It brought 6 million cases a year in the 1940s down to just 50,000 by the 1960s. Since then, however, **35** cases have been steadily rising again in parallel with rapid forest clearing and **expansion** of agriculture. At the turn of the century, there were over 600,000 cases a year in the Amazon basin.

A study in the late 1990s suggested a reason why. Clearing patches of forest appears to create ideal habitat along forest edges for the mosquito *Anopheles darlingi* to breed. This mosquito is the most important transmitter of malaria in the Amazon. Careful surveys **36** in the Peruvian Amazon showed higher numbers of larvae in warm, partially **shaded** pools; the kind that form beside roads cut into forests, and in puddles behind debris where water is no longer taken up by trees.

コウモリがマレーシアの果樹園の樹木に棲みついてから間もなく、周辺にいるブタが病気になり始めました。研究者たちは、コウモリがかじった後に地面に落ちた果物をブタが食べたことでウイルスに感染し、その後、養豚業者がそのブタから感染したと推測しました。1999年までに、265人が重度の脳炎を発症し、105人が亡くなりました。それは、知られている限りニパウイルスが初めて人から見つかった例で、それ以来、東南アジア全域で何度も流行しています。

アマゾン川流域、アフリカや東南アジアの一部の熱帯雨林で広範囲な焼失が続いているので、専門家は森林破壊の最前線に住む人たちの健康について懸念を表明しています。彼らはまた、次の深刻な疫病が世界中の森林から発生するのではないかと心配しています。

森林破壊がマラリアなどの感染症の大きな要因になる可能性があることも、かなり裏づけられています。これは数当て賭博です。森林の生育環境を悪化させたり伐採したりすればするほど、感染症が大流行する状況に陥る可能性が高まるのです。

マラリアは、蚊によって媒介されるマラリア原虫に感染することで、年間約50万人を死に追いやっています。このことは、森林破壊と密接に関係していると以前からずっと疑われてきました。ブラジルでは、過去に封じ込めの努力によってマラリアの感染が劇的に減少したことがあります。1940年代には年間600万件の症例があったものの、1960年代までにはわずか5万件にまで減少しました。しかしその後、急激な森林伐採と農地の拡大に伴って症例は再び次第に増加しつつあります。世紀の変わり目には、アマゾン盆地では年間60万件以上の症例がありました。

1990年代後半に行われた研究が、その原因のヒントを与えてくれました。森林の一部の区域を伐採すると、蚊のハマダラカが繁殖するための理想的な生息環境が森林の端に沿って生まれるようです。この蚊は、アマゾン川流域で最も重要なマラリアの媒介者です。ペルー領のアマゾン川流域での詳しい調査でわかったことは、森林に分け入る道路沿いにできるような、温かく、部分的に日陰になっている水たまりや、水が樹木によって吸い上げられることのなくなった破壊跡の裏にある水たまりなどに幼虫の数がずっと多いということです。

Between 2003 and 2015, they estimated that on average a 10-percent yearly increase in forest loss led to a 3-percent rise in malaria cases. However, it's hard to generalize about mosquito ecology, which varies depending on species and region. **37** In **Africa**, studies have found little association between malaria and deforestation. Perhaps because the mosquito species there like to breed in sunlit bodies of water and favor open farmland over shady forest areas. **37** But in Sabah, a part of Malaysian Borneo, malaria outbreaks also occur in tandem with bursts of forest clearing for palm oil and other plantations.

38 Mosquitoes aren't the only animals that can transmit deadly scourges to people. In fact, 60 percent of new infectious diseases that emerge in people are transmitted by various **animals**; the vast majority of them **wildlife**. These diseases include HIV, Ebola, and Nipah, all of which originated in forest-dwelling animals.

Many viruses exist harmlessly with their host animals in forests because the animals have co-evolved with them. But **39** humans can catch the viruses when they venture into forest **areas** that have never been visited by humans before.

40 Diseases can also occur when disease-carrying species travel out of the forest. For instance, in Liberia, forest clearings for palm oil plantations cause hordes of typically forest-dwelling mice to come into towns close by to find **food**. Humans can contract Lassa virus when they come into contact with food or objects contaminated with faeces or urine of virus-carrying rodents. In humans, the virus causes haemorrhagic fever—the same kind of illness triggered by Ebola virus. And in Liberia, it killed 36 percent of infected people.

Virus-carrying rodents have also been spotted in deforested areas in Panama, Bolivia, and in Brazil. Alfonso Rodriguez-Morales, a medical researcher and tropical disease expert at Colombia's Universidad Tecnológica de Pereira, fears that their range will be wider following the resurgence of forest fires in the Amazon.

研究者は、2003年から2015年の間、平均で森林の喪失面積が毎年10パーセント増加するごとに、マラリアの症例が3パーセント増えたと試算しました。しかし蚊の生態について一般化するのが難しいのは、その種や地域によって異なるからです。アフリカでは、マラリアと森林破壊との間にほとんど関係がないことが研究でわかっています。おそらく、そこの蚊の種は、日当たりのよい水域で繁殖しやすく、日陰の多い森林地帯よりも開けた農地を好むためでしょう。しかし、マレーシア領のボルネオ島にあるサバ州では、パーム油などの大規模農園のために森林をいっせいに伐採したことに伴い、マラリアの流行も同時に発生しています。

命にかかわる疫病を人に感染させる可能性がある動物は、蚊だけではありません。実際、人が発症する新たな感染症の60パーセントはさまざまな動物によって伝染し、その大部分は野生動物です。そうした疾病には、HIV、エボラ、ニパなどが含まれ、そのいずれも森林に生息する動物に起因しています。

多くのウイルスが、森林に生息する宿主の動物に害を与えることなく存在するのは、その動物がそれらと共進化したためです。しかし、人は、それまで人が訪れたことのない森林地帯に足を踏み入れたときに、ウイルスに感染する可能性があります。

病気を運ぶ生物種が森林の外へ移動する場合も、疾病が発生することがあります。例えば、リベリアでは、パーム油の大農場のための森林伐採によって、普通は森林に生息するネズミの大群が、餌を求めて近くの町にやって来ています。人は、ウイルスを運ぶげっ歯類の糞や尿で汚染された食べ物や物に接触するときに、ラッサウイルスに感染する可能性があります。人の場合、このウイルスは出血熱を引き起こしますが、これは、エボラウイルスによって引き起こされるのと同じ種類の病気です。そして、リベリアでは、感染者の36パーセントが亡くなりました。

ウイルスを運ぶげっ歯類は、パナマやボリビア、そしてブラジルの森林伐採地域でも発見されています。コロンビアのペレイラ工科大学の医学研究者で、熱帯病の専門家であるアルフォンソ・ロドリゲス・モラレス氏は、アマゾン川流域での森林火災が再発することによって、その範囲が広がるのではないかと憂慮しています。

That is the end of Part 4.
You now have one minute to check your answers to Part 4. That is the end of the Listening Test. You now have ten minutes to transfer your answers to your answer sheet.

これでパート4は終わりです。
ここで、パート4の解答を確認するための時間が1分あります。これでリスニングテストは終了です。ここで、解答を解答用紙に書き写す時間が10分間あります。

Writing

Writing

実践1 〉 棒グラフの問題　　　　　　　　　　　　　　　　　　　　　本冊P.118

中級者のエッセイ

[Introduction]

パラフレーズ The graph shows the number of men and women in full or part-time education in the UK between 1970 and 1990. 要約 Overall, an increase was seen for all trends except that fewer men were studying part-time by 1990.

[Body 1]

In 1970, the number of men doing full-time study was 80,000. By 1980, it increased to 150,000 and by the end it increased again to 220,000. There were fewer women in full-time studies. In 1970, there were only 60,000 women studying full-time. The figure increased to 220,000 by 1990, which was equal to the male number.

[Body 2]

The number of men and women doing part-time studies was much higher than those in full-time studies. For men, the figure stood at 1 million in 1970. After 10 years, the figure decreased to 850,000 and then slightly increased to 900,000 by the end. On the other hand, initially, there were only 700,000 women involved in part-time studies. It went up to 800,000 and then, in 1990, the figure increased to 1.1 million, which was higher than the figure for males.

(175 words)／※下線＝〈一貫性とまとまり〉のスコアに関わる接続表現

▶ 解説

〈課題の達成度〉

[Introduction]

中級 「男性のパートタイム学習者以外は増加傾向」と、最低限の情報に言及している。

上級 最大の特徴である「パートタイムの学習者がフルタイムの学習者と比較して極めて多いこと」にも触れられている。

[Body]

棒グラフで、横軸の項目が時期（西暦など）の場合、すべての時期と数値にまで言及する必要はない。しかし最初と最後の項目（この場合1970/71と1990/91）と、特徴的な項目には言及するべき。本エッセイでは、両者とも女性のフルタイムの1980/81の数値には触れていないが、ほかは網羅している。

〈語彙力〉

中級 increaseを繰り返し使っているので、少し単調な印象になっている。

上級 increaseだけではなく、climb up to ～（～まで上る）、hit（～に達する）、surge to ～（～に急上昇する）などで増加を表している。double to ～（～に倍増する）などの倍数表現でも語彙力を示せている。

〈文法知識と正確さ〉

中級 There is 構文を繰り返しているので、文法的には正しいが、もう少し構文の種類が欲しいところ。関係代名詞の非制限用法（, which ...）は、付加的に情報を述べる際に効果的に使えている。

上級 There is 構文以外にも関係代名詞などを使っている。特に最終文の分詞構文は、ライティングで好まれる。

[Introduction]
パラフレーズ The chart compares the number of men and women in tertiary education in the UK between 1970 and 1990. 要約 Overall, it can be seen that significantly more men and women were involved in part-time studies than full-time studies. Increases were seen across the board except that fewer men than women were studying part-time by 1990.

[Body 1]
In 1970, the number of men doing full-time studies was 80,000. By 1980, this number had almost doubled to 150,000, and over the next decade, the figure climbed up to 220,000. In relation to full-time studies, there were fewer women. Initially, in 1970, only 60,000 women were studying full-time. This figure increased by slightly more than threefold, which was to 220,000 by 1990 and there ended up being a similar number of both men and women in full-time tertiary level studies.

[Body 2]
On the other hand, initially, the proportion of men in part-time studies was significantly higher than that of women. The figure stood at 1 million in 1970. After 10 years the figure had dropped to 850,000, and then the numbers began to recover, hitting 900,000 by the end of the period. As for women, there were only 700,000 doing part-time studies in 1970. In 1980, this number went up to 800,000, and by the end, it had surged to 1.1 million, outpacing their male counterparts.

(221 words)／※下線＝〈一貫性とまとまり〉のスコアに関わる接続表現

▶ 問題文の訳

下記のチャートは、3つの期間におけるイギリスでの継続教育の男女数と、彼らがフルタイム、パートタイムのどちらで学習していたかを示している。主な特徴を選んで説明することで情報を要約して、関連がある箇所を比較しなさい。

▶ 上級者エッセイの構成

Introduction —— 説明文のパラフレーズ＋要約
Body 1 —— フルタイム（男性：上昇、女性：70年は6万人だけ、90年までに男性と同等に）
Body 2 —— パートタイム（男性：80年に一度下がったが、90年までに上昇、女性：70年は70万人のみ、90年には男性を上回った）

─┤ Vocabulary ├─

中級
□ part-time [形・副] パートタイムの[で]
□ full-time [形・副] フルタイムの[で]
□ on the other hand 他方で
□ involve [動] ～を含む

□ trend [名] 傾向
□ be equal to ～ ～に等しい
□ initially [副] 最初は

上級
□ tertiary education 高等教育
□ in relation to ～ ～に関して
□ outpace [動] ～を追い越す

□ across the board 全面的に
□ threefold [形・副] 3倍の[に]
□ counterpart [名] 同等の人、一方

57

[Introduction]

パラフレーズ The graph shows electricity production from coal, natural gas, hydroelectricity and oil in the world from 1991 to 2009. 要約 During this period, the use of three types of sources increased steadily with only oil declining.

[Body 1]

Firstly, coal was used the most to produce electricity in 1991. The amount was 4,500 TWh. Hydroelectricity was the second most used, producing 2,200 TWh, followed by natural gas and oil, producing 1,900 TWh and 1,400 TWh, respectively.

[Body 2]

Secondly, the use of all forms of energy increased steadily, except for oil which continued to decline during this period. The increase in the use of coal was the greatest from 4,500 TWh in 1991 to 7,600 TWh in 2009.

[Body 3]

Finally, in 2000, natural gas overtook hydroelectricity and became the second most popular source of electricity. Over the 19 years, oil production decreased. By 2009, coal and natural gas were the most used, at 7,600 TWh and 4,200 TWh, respectively.

(153 words)／※下線＝〈一貫性とまとまり〉のスコアに関わる接続表現

▶ 解説

〈課題の達成度〉

[Body]

棒グラフや折れ線グラフの横軸の項目が時期の場合、最低限、最初の数値と最後の数値に言及しよう。本問では、石炭、天燃ガス、水力発電、石油の1991年と2009年に言及している。

中級 水力発電と石油の2009年の数値が漏れている。

Finally ...の文で、2000年に天然ガスが水力発電を抜いたことに言及しているが、数値（2,500TWh）が漏れている。

上級 1991年と2009年はもちろん、特徴的な変化がある2000年の数値にも言及して、増減の程度や数値、各発電源の関係性も描写できている。

〈一貫性とまとまり〉

中級 Firstly, Secondly ...の書き出しは間違いではないが単調なので、高得点を狙うなら上級（It can be seen that, Initiallyなど）を参考にしよう。

上級 各Bodyの1文目で、各段落で述べる内容の概要を端的に表現できている。

〈語彙力〉

中級 increased steadilyを繰り返さず、grew consistentlyなどの類似表現も使うべき。

上級 hydroelectricity（水力発電）を、hydropowerやhydroelectric powerに言い換えている。

数字の増減を描写する語彙が特に上級で豊富（黒い下線部分）。

[Introduction]
パラフレーズ The graph presents the production of four different fuel sources in the world from 1991 to 2009. 要約 Over these 19 years, there was an increase in production for all fuel types except oil, with coal producing significantly more energy throughout the period.

[Body 1]
It can be seen that coal remained the world's largest energy producer over the two decades. In 1991, coal produced by far the most energy with over 4,500 TWh. There was a slow and steady increase in production rising up to about 5,500 TWh in 2000. By 2009, the figure had surged to approximately 7,600 TWh.

[Body 2]
Initially, hydroelectric power was the second highest producer of energy. However, its production was overtaken by natural gas by the end of the period. In 1991, hydroelectric power produced 2,200 TWh of energy, and gas produced slightly less at 1,900 TWh. Hydropower increased to 2,600 TWh by 2000, matching the production of gas. After that, the production of energy by gas skyrocketed, overtaking hydropower, and by 2009, its production had jumped up to 4,200 TWh, while hydropower increased, but at a slower rate. It rose to 3,200 TWh.

[Body 3]
Oil produced the least energy. Its figure stood at 1,400 TWh in 1991, and production remained relatively stable throughout. There was an overall slight decrease in production, dropping to 1,050 TWh by 2009.

(219 words)／※下線＝〈一貫性とまとまり〉のスコアに関わる接続表現

Writing

▶ 問題文の訳

このグラフは、1991年から2009年における、4種類の世界的な発電源を示したものである。主な特徴を選んで説明することで情報を要約して、関連がある箇所を比較しなさい。

▶ 上級者エッセイの構成

Introduction ——	説明文のパラフレーズ＋要約
Body 1 ——	突出して高い石炭（1991年〜2000年に段階的増加、2000年〜2009年に急増）
Body 2 ——	数値が近い水力発電と天然ガス（水力発電が天然ガスに抜かれる）
Body 3 ——	一番低い石油

┤ Vocabulary ├

中級
□ **overtake** ［動］〜に追いつく
□ **A and B, respectively**　AとB、それぞれ

□ **source of 〜**　〜の源

上級
□ **throughout** ［前・副］その間ずっと
□ **surge to 〜**　〜に急上昇する
□ **jump up to 〜**　〜に跳ね上がる

□ **slow and steady increase**　穏やかで安定的な上昇
□ **skyrocket** ［動］急上昇する
□ **remain relatively stable**　比較的安定したままでいる

中級者のエッセイ

［Introduction］

パラフレーズ The table shows the usual method of travel to work for people in four Australian cities in 2016.

要約 Overall, it can be seen that there were some differences among the cities in how people got to work.

［Body 1］

A lot more people drove to work in Adelaide than in the other cities. This percentage was 80%. The figure for Hobart was 76%, and in Sydney, 65.5% drove to work. More people used public transport in Sydney, and the figure stood at 21%, while only 8% and 5.5% of workers used public transport in Adelaide and Hobart, respectively.

［Body 2］

In Hobart, a lot of people walked or used a bicycle to go to work. A total of 8% of workers in Hobart did this. The figure for the other two cities was 4% in Adelaide and 6% in Sydney. More people in Hobart worked from home (10.5%). In Adelaide and Sydney, this figure was at around 8%. People in Hobart work from home more because there aren't many options of other types of jobs.

(153 words)／※下線＝〈一貫性とまとまり〉のスコアに関わる接続表現

▶ 解説

都市別の通勤方法の割合を比較した表なので、グラフ化するなら円グラフが最適。円グラフの問題と同じアプローチで、都市ごとの割合を描写、比較すればよい。

〈課題の達成度〉

［Introduction］

中級 冒頭のパラフレーズすべき文が問題文中の説明文の流用なので、**語数に含まれない**。要約は「都市ごとによって違いがある」だけで情報不足。

上級 要約で、表内のDrive, Walk, Bicycleをまとめてprivate means of transport（個人の交通手段）とまとめ、public transportation（公共交通機関）と大まかに比較できている。

［Body］

中級 Melbourneに言及していない。**重要な項目の漏れは減点になる**ので要注意。また、最終文のPeople in Hobart …は、**主観的な解釈なので不要**。データから読み取れる情報のみを描写しよう。

〈語彙力〉

中級 figureの繰り返しが目立つ。また、表内の語句を流用しがちで語彙力を示せていない。

上級 figureだけではなく、percentageやproportionなどの割合を表す語彙が豊富。

「大半の人々」は2通りで表現（a majority of the people, a large percentage of people）。

〈文法知識と正確さ〉

上級 「円グラフの問題」で使うべき比較構文を正確に使えている（The figures for the other cities were lower, with only 4% in Adelaide, …など）。

受験者によく見られるミス！〜「中級者のエッセイ」の注意点〜
- 「問題文中の説明文」の丸写しはNG。必ずパラフレーズしよう
- 表の重要な項目に触れていない。項目の記述漏れに注意しよう
- データを主観的にとらえている。タスク1では、主観的な意見や解釈は一切不要！

[Introduction]

パラフレーズ The table compares the different ways that people commuted to work in four Australian cities in 2016. 要約 Most notably, a majority of the people drove to work. People tended to use more public transportation in Sydney and Melbourne compared with the other two cities, where they relied more heavily on their own private means of transport.

[Body 1]

The first major point is that more people drove to work in Adelaide than in the other cities. It was a staggering 80%, which was higher than any of the other cities. A large percentage of people also drove in Melbourne. This figure stood at 74.5%. In comparison, the proportion of drivers was 76% in Hobart, and 65.6% in Sydney. Another major feature is that the use of public transport was much more popular in Sydney, where 21% of workers relied on its use, compared to 13.5%, 8% and only 5.5% for Melbourne, Adelaide and Hobart, respectively.

[Body 2]

In Hobart, more people walked or cycled to work; their share was 8% of the total. The figures for the other cities were lower, with only 4% in Adelaide, 4.5% in Melbourne, and 6% in Sydney choosing to walk or cycle to work. In addition, more people in Hobart worked from home (10.5%), which was slightly higher than in the other cities, where the figure stood at around 8%.

(222 words)※下線＝〈一貫性とまとまり〉のスコアに関わる接続表現

Writing

▶ 問題文の訳

下記の表は、2016年のオーストラリアにおける4都市の人々の普段の通勤手段を示している。主な特徴を選んで説明することで情報を要約して、関連がある箇所を比較しなさい。

▶ 上級者エッセイの構成

Introduction ── 説明文のパラフレーズ＋要約
Body 1 ──────── ①車（Adelaideとほかの都市）、②公共交通機関（Sydneyとほかの都市）
Body 2 ──────── ①徒歩と自転車（Hobartとほかの都市）、②在宅勤務（Hobartがわずかに高い）

┤ Vocabulary ├

中級
□ **method of ～**　～の手段
□ **A and B, respectively**　AとB、それぞれ
□ **public transport**　公共交通機関

上級
□ **notably** ［副］特に
□ **compared with ～**　～と比べると
□ **staggering** ［形］驚異的な
□ **in addition**　加えて
□ **majority of ～**　大半の～
□ **means of ～**　～の手段
□ **rely on ～**　～に頼る

中級者のエッセイ

[Introduction]
<u>パラフレーズ</u> The maps show changes to the town of Riverport between 1900 and 2000. <u>要約</u> There were some differences and some similarities.

[Body 1]
In 1900, there was a main road and a bridge connecting the south and north of the area. There was a timber mill and a ship building area in the northern part of the town. There were three wharves and a warehouse for storage. Just to the north of the town centre, there was a railway station.

[Body 2]
By 2000, there was only one wharf instead of three. There was a park on the south riverbank, and the old warehouse had become an art gallery. On the northern side of the river, the timber mill and shipbuilder were gone. Instead, there was a camping area. The railway now continued on to the east, and the old main road had become an interstate highway with a bigger bridge than before.

[Body 3]
The town centre and forest to the northeast of the town remained the same, but the latter was much smaller than before.

(170 words) ／ ※下線＝「地図の問題」で重要となる、位置や方角を表す語句

〈課題の達成度〉
[Introduction]
[中級] 要約が曖昧で情報不足。
[上級] 土地の用途の視点で、主な変化を表現できている。主な変化＝ship building industry（造船産業）がなくなり、recreational facilities（娯楽施設）が増えた。
[Body]
高得点を狙うなら、全要素に触れよう。中級だとFarmland（農地）が漏れている。
〈一貫性とまとまり〉
両者ともに段落構成は「Body 1 ＝1990年の状況」「Body 2 ＝2000年までの変化」「Body 3 ＝変わらない点」で明確。
〈語彙力〉
[中級] 最終文のthe latter（後者）は、forestの繰り返しを避けるよい表現。
〈文法知識と正確さ〉
[中級] There is 構文は地図問題で使える構文だが、使い過ぎで単調な印象になっている。
[上級] There is 構文以外の構文も豊富。**地図の問題では、動作主は重要ではないので受動態を活用しよう**（the main road was extendedやthe old warehouse was also converted into an art galleryなど）。

受験者によく見られるミス！〜「中級者のエッセイ」の注意点〜
・There were some differences and some similarities.（変化している点と変化していない点があった）という、内容がない文を要約に入れている。要約が抽象的にならないように、図の主な特徴に言及しよう

[Introduction]
パラフレーズ The two maps illustrate the changes that occurred in Riverport from 1900 to 2000. 要約 It is evident that the town changed greatly over time. In the year 2000, it no longer had a mill or ship building industry. Instead, it had more recreational facilities such as an art gallery, a camp and a park.

[Body 1]
In 1900, Riverport had three wharves where boats could dock and unload, and beside them stood a warehouse. Across the river, there was a timber mill with a shipbuilder next to it. The town centre had a railway station, as well as a main road with a bridge to the west. To the east of the town lay a forest and some farmland.

[Body 2]
In 2000, many changes could be seen. To the west of the town, the main road was extended and became a large interstate highway with a much wider bridge than before. The south of the riverbank was converted into a recreational park which ran alongside the river. The three wharves were no longer needed and only one was in use at this time, and the old warehouse was also converted into an art gallery. On the opposite side of the river, the timber mill and shipbuilder were no longer in existence, and the area had been redeveloped into a campsite. The railway station remained unchanged, however, the rail line was extended, and it continued past the farmland on to the next station.

[Body 3]
The location and size of the town centre and the farmland did not change over time. The forest to the northeast of town also stayed in the same place, though it was much smaller than before.

(275 words)／※下線＝「地図の問題」で重要となる、位置や方角を表す語句

▶ 問題文の訳

下記の地図は、1900年と2000年のリバーポートの町を示している。主な特徴を選んで説明することで情報を要約して、関連がある箇所を比較しなさい。

▶ 上級者エッセイの構成

Introduction	説明文のパラフレーズ＋要約
Body 1	1900年の状況（すべての要素に言及）
Body 2	2000年までの変化（西：道路→高速道路／南：川岸→公園、波止場は1つに、倉庫→ギャラリー／川の反対側：木材工場と造船場→キャンプ場／線路の拡張）
Body 3	変わらない点（中心街と農地。森は縮小）

┤ Vocabulary ├

中級
☐ **similarity** [名] 類似
☐ **wharf** [名] 波止場 [複] wharves
☐ **the latter** 後者

☐ **connect A and B** AとBをつなぐ
☐ **interstate** [形] 各州間の

上級
☐ **over time** 時間が経つにつれて
☐ **no longer 〜** もはや〜でない

☐ **be converted into 〜** 〜に変換される
☐ **redevelop** [動] 〜を再開発する

中級者のエッセイ

[Introduction]

パラフレーズ The diagram shows the process of how white wine is produced. 要約 There are seven steps in the process of making white wine, but only six if oak barrels are not used. If oak barrels are used, it takes longer to produce the wine. You must put the grape juice in various containers to make the juice into wine. This requires time and adding various ingredients.

[Body 1]

Firstly, the grapes are harvested. Secondly, we use a press for crushing grapes. The juice is put in a settling tank. In this tank, the sediment gets collected at the bottom. The pure grape juice is then put in the fermentation tank. Sugar and yeast are added to this tank. Finally, this fermentation process produces alcohol and CO_2.

[Body 2]

The fermented wine is transferred to oak barrels for a minimum three months. After that it is filtered and bottled and sent to the shops.

(148 words)／※下線＝〈一貫性とまとまり〉のスコアに関わる接続表現

▶ 解説

〈課題の達成度〉

中級 語数が150 wordsを下回っている。

[Introduction]

上級 工程の数を明確に示し、さらに工程の名前を順に挙げており、わかりやすい。

[Body]

この問題タイプでは全工程を網羅すべき。両者の違いは「発酵の段階を1工程と見るか、2工程に見るか」で、どちらもOK。

中級＝全7工程、樽の工程がなければ6（発酵の工程＝2工程）

上級＝主に5工程、樽の工程を含めると6（発酵の工程＝1工程）

中級 Body 2で「樽で3か月貯蔵される工程」は描写できているが、「直接瓶詰めされる工程」が漏れている。1つでも工程が漏れると減点対象になる。

〈一貫性とまとまり〉

工程の順序を明確に説明することが必須。中級までなら、Firstly, Secondlyなどを機械的に使えばいいが、高得点を目指すなら上級の表現を参考にしよう。

〈語彙力〉

中級 図の用語（黒い下線部分）がそのまま使われていることが多い。

上級 言い換えが多く、語彙力を示せている。パラフレーズ crushing grapes ⇄ the grapes being crushed / settling tank ⇄ a tank where the grape juice settles / CO_2 ⇄ carbon dioxide

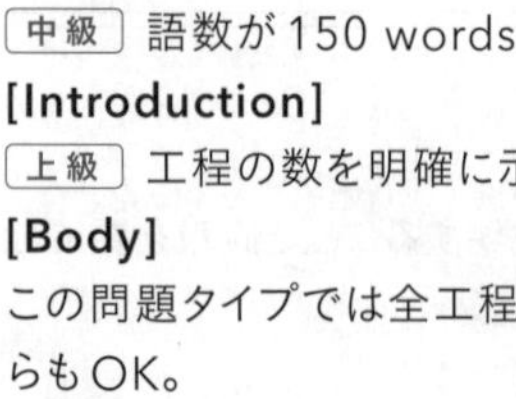

このタイプでは、工程数を明記し、順々に説明します。このとき、工程の数え方に戸惑いがちですが、**数え方に厳密な正解はなく、これはスコアに影響しません。**実際に、本問を読むと、各エッセイの要約で提示している工程数は異なります（中級者は7、上級者は5）。**重要なのは全工程に触れ、順序立てて説明することなのです。**

［Introduction］

パラフレーズ The diagram illustrates the production process of white wine. 要約 Overall, there are five main steps in the production of white wine. The main steps are harvesting and crushing of grapes, separation of sediment from the juice, and then fermentation of alcohol. If oak casks are used, it takes more time and a sixth step is needed. Finally, the wine is filtered and bottled.

［Body 1］

Once the grapes are picked, they are brought to a winery for further processing. The subsequent major step involves the grapes being crushed using a large press to extract the juice. After this, the grapes are transferred to a tank where the grape juice settles for some time and then, sediment from the grapes is separated. In the next step, the grape juice is transferred to a fermentation tank where sugar and yeast are added. After some time, the sugar in the grape juice is converted into alcohol and carbon dioxide.

［Body 2］

Finally, once the fermentation is complete, there are two options for bottling. The first option is that the wine can be bottled immediately. Alternatively, the white wine can be placed in oak casks where it is left for at least three months to age. It is then filtered, bottled, and made ready for distribution.

(208 words)／※下線＝〈一貫性とまとまり〉のスコアに関わる接続表現

▶ 問題文の訳

下記の図は、白ワインがどういう過程で作られるのかを示している。主な特徴を選んで説明することで情報を要約して、関連がある箇所を比較しなさい。

▶ 上級者エッセイの構成

Introduction ── 説明文のパラフレーズ＋要約（全工程に言及）

Body 1 ── 1〜4工程（1：収穫、2：ブドウを潰す、3：タンクに入れて堆積物を分離、4：発酵タンクに砂糖と酵母を入れてアルコールとCO₂ができる）

Body 2 ── 5つ目の工程（「直接瓶詰め」。「しばらく樽で貯蔵」を入れるなら6工程）

┤ Vocabulary ├

中級

□ **barrel** ［名］樽
□ **harvest** ［動］〜を収穫する
□ **fermentation** ［名］発酵

□ **ingredient** ［名］原料
□ **sediment** ［名］堆積物
□ **transfer** ［動］〜を移す

上級

□ **separation** ［名］分離
□ **extract** ［動］〜を抽出する
□ **carbon dioxide** 二酸化炭素
□ **at least** 少なくとも

□ **subsequent** ［形］次の
□ **be converted into 〜** 〜に変換される
□ **alternatively** ［副］代わりに
□ **distribution** ［名］流通

中級者のエッセイ

[Introduction]
パラフレーズ The graph and table show how water was used by different appliances in U.S. households in 2010, and how much water a person used on average over a period of 26 years. 要約 Overall, it is clear that water use in U.S. households during this period increased.

[Body 1]
In 2010, it is clear that toilets used the most water, which was 32 gallons per day. This was followed by showers, which used 28 gallons daily. Faucets used 26 gallons, and washing machines used 23 gallons. Dishwashers and baths used the least. Leaks accounted for the loss of about 17 gallons of water daily, while five gallons were used for other purposes.

[Body 2]
Daily water consumption per person in the U.S. grew over the 26-year period from 1985 to 2010. In 1985, 98 gallons of water per day were used and after this, consumption increased, reaching a peak of 118 gallons in 2005. In 2010, daily consumption declined to only 110 gallons.

(158 words)／※下線＝〈一貫性とまとまり〉のスコアに関わる接続表現

▶ 解説

〈課題の達成度〉

[Introduction]
中級 要約で棒グラフに触れていない。このタイプの問題では、**要約で両方のグラフや表に言及しよう。**

[Body 1]
中級 棒グラフの全8項目を挙げているが、Dishwasher（食洗機）とBath（風呂）の数値がない。

[Body 2]
表をグラフ化するなら、棒グラフか折れ線グラフになる。したがって、これらと同じアプローチで年ごとの増減に言及すればよい。これらのグラフで、横軸の項目が時期の場合、最初の年（1985年）と最後の年（2010年）の数値に言及し、特徴的な年（2005年：使用量が最大）があれば、そこにも触れるべき。

〈一貫性とまとまり〉
両者ともに「Body 1＝棒グラフ」「Body 2＝表」の軸で分けており、明確。

〈語彙力〉
上級 増減を表す語彙がより豊富（黒い下線部分）。

「上級者のエッセイ」では、棒グラフのToilet, Shower, Bathをbathrooms やbathroom useに、Faucet, Dishwasherをkitchensに、Washing machineをlaundry purposesに言い換えています。

[Introduction]

パラフレーズ The graphs show water usage by different appliances in U.S. households in 2010, and daily water consumption per person over a period of 26 years. 要約 It can be clearly seen that water usage per capita increased throughout the period, and that bathrooms accounted for the highest water usage.

[Body 1]

In 2010, of the eight listed household appliances, toilets used the most water with 32 gallons per day, followed by showers (28 gallons), faucets (26 gallons), and washing machines (23 gallons). Dishwashers and baths consumed by far the least amount of water, two and four gallons, respectively. Surprisingly, leaks resulted in about 17 gallons of water being wasted daily, while five gallons were used for other reasons. The water consumption for bathroom use was quite significant, followed by a large percentage of water being used in kitchens and for laundry purposes.

[Body 2]

Daily water consumption per person in the U.S. grew gradually over the 26-year period. In 1985, usage stood at 98 gallons per day, and this figure steadily increased to 118 gallons in 2005. By 2010, however, daily consumption had declined slightly to 110 gallons.

(183 words)／※下線＝〈一貫性とまとまり〉のスコアに関わる接続表現

▶ 問題文の訳

この棒グラフは、アメリカでの電化製品ごとの毎日の水の平均消費量を表している。表は、26年間にわたり、アメリカで1人あたり何ガロンの水を消費したかを示している。主な特徴を選んで説明することで情報を要約して、関連がある箇所を比較しなさい。

▶ 上級者エッセイの構成

Introduction ── 説明文のパラフレーズ＋要約（棒グラフと表に言及）
Body 1 ──── 棒グラフ（消費量が多いトイレ、シャワー、水道、洗濯機。少ない食洗機と風呂。水漏れとそのほか）
Body 2 ──── 表（期間を通じて徐々に増加。1985年は98→2005年は118→2010年は110）

Vocabulary

中級
□ **appliance** [名] 電化製品
□ **It is clear that S＋V.** SVは明らかだ。
□ **account for 〜** 〜を占める
□ **reach a peak of 〜** 〜の最高値に達する
□ **household** [名] 世帯
□ **follow** [動] 〜に続く
□ **consumption** [名] 消費

上級
□ **per capita** [形・副] 1人あたりの [で]
□ **result in 〜** 〜に終わる
□ **steadily** [副] 絶えず
□ **A and B, respectively** AとB、それぞれ
□ **grow gradually** 徐々に増える
□ **decline slightly** わずかに減る

Writing

67

本冊P.140

中級者のエッセイ

[Introduction]

[パラフレーズ] It is expected that there will be shortages of world resources in the future because the population in the world is increasing. Some people think that population control, that is, having fewer children, is the most effective solution for this problem. However, others believe technological development is the key. [意思表明] In my opinion, technology is the best solution.

[Body 1]

[トピック] On the one hand, population control is not always effective. In recent times, China has tried population control with its one-child policy. Families can have only one child. This policy has had some problems. For example, even though the numbers of newborn children were controlled, the population did not decrease. Rapid population increase just stopped. This was because the largest age group was people aged 20 to 40 years old. Some older people passed away every day, but some children were born. As a result, the population was stable. This meant the amount of spending on resources was stable, too.

[Body 2]

[トピック] On the other hand, technological development can change the amount of spending on resources. For example, because of improved efficiency, we can use energy better. Oil is one of the limited resources, but we can use this energy source more efficiently with new technology. Another example is electrical energy. Now we can make this power with natural energy sources such as wind, heat from the ground, waterfalls, and so on. This energy is almost unlimited.

[Conclusion]

To sum up, technological development makes the world's limited resources more efficient. This will possibly create unlimited energy in the future.

(253 words)／※下線＝〈一貫性とまとまり〉のスコアに関わる接続表現

▶ 解説

〈課題への回答〉このエッセイで書くべき [要求ポイント]

①限られた資源を維持するため出生数を減らすのが最善という見解（問題文中の前者の見解）

②技術が答えで、人口管理は不要という見解（後者の見解）

③自分の意見

[中級] Body 1 では、On the one hand, population control is not always effective. から始まり、「前者の見解がいかに効果的ではないか」という議論に終始している。[要求ポイント] ①では、「前者の見解」を紹介すべき。

〈語彙力〉

[上級] 特に上級で、overpopulation（人口過剰）、contraceptives（避妊具）、abductions（拉致）、renewable sources（再生可能資源）など、人口・環境問題の「特定分野の語彙」を広く使えている（黒い下線の部分）。

〈文法知識と正確さ〉

This energy is almost unlimited. など、中級は単文が散見されるが、上級では複文が多い。

[Introduction]
パラフレーズ It is expected that there will be shortages of natural resources in the future due to overpopulation. Some people think that population control is the most effective solution. However, others believe technological development is the key to preserving our non-renewable resources. 意思表明 Personally, I believe that technology will be a far more ethical and effective solution.

[Body 1]
トピック Undoubtedly, as the population increases exponentially, the burden on our limited natural resources accelerates. As cities become overpopulated, trees are being cut down to make way for residential buildings and consequently, the amount of groundwater is being depleted at an alarming rate. It is often stated that if more people have easier access to contraceptives and information about family planning, they tend to have fewer children. As a result, the need for natural resources will be reduced.

[Body 2]
トピック Nevertheless, population control raises the question of whether or not it is an ethical solution. As a prime example, China's draconian one-child policy led to a predominance of male children while girls were aborted. This led to other problems in society, for instance, abductions of women and girls became rampant.

[Body 3]
トピック In my opinion, technological development can significantly change the amount of spending on resources. Due to improved efficiency, we can use energy better. Oil is a limited resource, but with new technology, this power can be used more efficiently. We can also generate electricity with renewable sources like wind, solar, heat from the ground, and so on. The energy produced by these sources is virtually unlimited if properly tapped into.

[Conclusion]
To conclude, technology is a better and more ethical solution than just controlling the size of the world's population. Technological developments make the world's limited resources more efficient. These uses of technology will possibly create unlimited energy in the future and allow much more sustainable population growth.

(299 words)／※下線＝〈一貫性とまとまり〉のスコアに関わる接続表現

Writing

▶ 問題文の訳

世界の限られた資源を維持するため出生数を減らすのが最善という考えがあれば、技術が答えで、人口管理は不要との意見もある。両者の見解を議論し、あなた自身の意見を述べなさい。

▶ 上級者エッセイの構成

Introduction ── 説明文のパラフレーズ＋意思表明（後者の意見を支持）
Body 1 ──── 前者の見解（人口管理が必要：資源枯渇の例と避妊教育という解決策）
Body 2 ──── 前者の見解の問題点（一人っ子政策の問題点と、女性拉致が横行する可能性）
Body 3 ──── 後者の見解（自分の意見、技術発展で解決：再生可能資源による発電）
Conclusion ── Bodyの要約＋意思表明の再掲（人口管理より技術革新）

→Body 1で［要求ポイント］の①を満たしているが、書き手は、この見解に反対の立場なので、Body 2で前者の見解の問題点を書き、その後、自分の意見である後者の見解を紹介するBody 3にロジカルにつなげている。

中級

□ **population control**　人口管理

□ **stable** [形] 安定的な

□ **pass away**　亡くなる

□ **to sum up**　要約すると

上級

□ **preserve** [動] 〜を保護する

□ **undoubtedly** [副] 疑いようもなく

□ **burden** [名] 重荷

□ **deplete** [動] 枯渇する

□ **nevertheless** [副] それにもかかわらず

□ **draconian** [形] 厳格な

□ **rampant** [形] 蔓延した

□ **tap into 〜**　〜を利用する

□ **ethical** [形] 倫理的な

□ **exponentially** [副] 急激に

□ **accelerate** [動] 加速する

□ **alarming rate**　驚くべき速さ

□ **raise the question**　問題を提起する

□ **predominance** [名] 優位

□ **virtually** [副] 事実上

中級者のエッセイ

[Introduction]

パラフレーズ Many young people are motivated and successful at high school. However, many lack motivation and see high school as not related to their interests and needs. 意思表明 In my opinion, this is because the education system is not well organised.

[Body 1]

トピック The reason why each high school student has a different level of motivation is the inflexibility of the high school curriculum. Most high schools in Japan want students to go to university after graduating. If the number of their students who go to higher education is large, the high school's reputation will be better. Thus, the curriculum is designed for this purpose and it may not be related to students' interests or needs at all. This was the case with my high school.

[Body 2]

トピック I believe the best solution is to change the entrance exams to focus more on subjects that a student wants to study at university. In the current system, students have to study many subjects which they are not interested in because of the entrance exams. For example, even if students want to study a language at university, they may need to study math because it is tested in the exam to enter the university. However, this subject is not relevant to their future study. If students can choose only the subjects which are related to their goals, their motivation will be high.

[Conclusion]

In conclusion, it is unfortunately very difficult to keep high school students' motivation high because of the current system. The entrance examination should be changed to keep all students interested.

(254 words)／※下線＝〈一貫性とまとまり〉のスコアに関わる接続表現

▶ 解説

〈課題への回答〉このエッセイで書くべき［要求ポイント］

①原因：多くの若者は士気が高く、高校でうまくやっている一方で、士気に欠け、高校に興味がなく必要性を感じていない者も多い。それはなぜか

②解決策：すべての生徒がうまくやっていくために、何ができるか

→どちらのエッセイも、Body 1で①を、Body 2で②を論じている。

[Introduction]

中級 冒頭2文は問題文中の説明文の流用なので語数に含まれない。結果、合計が250 wordsに届かないので減点になる。

上級 意思表明で［要求ポイント］の①②に言及している。

〈文法知識と正確さ〉

両者ともに、特に解決策を述べるBody 2では「もし〜なら、...になる」と仮定的に提案しているので、If節を活用している。

上級 2文目で、副詞のhoweverを文中に入れて、アカデミックな印象を出せている。また、最終文で、副詞（otherwise）の直前にセミコロン（;）を使い、文同士をつないでいる。高得点を目指すならパンクチュエーションでアピールするのも手。

Writing

[Introduction]

パラフレーズ Some high school students are motivated to study hard in order to pursue their career ambitions. Others, however, struggle because they think that high school is not related to their future goals. 意思表明 In my opinion, this is because the education system is not well organised and pushes students to study subjects which are irrelevant to their interests. I believe changes to the university entrance examination are needed to resolve this issue.

[Body 1]

トピック There are many reasons why high school students have different levels of motivation. One of the main reasons is due to the inflexibility of the high school curriculum. Most of the high schools in Japan want students to go to higher education after graduating because the greater the number of their students who go on to university, the better the school's reputation will be. Thus, the curriculum is designed for the purpose of succeeding in university entrance exams. Some highly-motivated students really want to go on to university, so they are motivated to work hard regardless of the subject. However, other students struggle when they find that the curriculum is hardly related to their real interests or needs at all.

[Body 2]

トピック What is needed to solve this problem is a definite action, namely, changing the entrance exams so that they focus on subjects that are relevant to the degree. In the current system, students have to study many subjects which they are not interested in to get into university. For example, even if students want to pursue a degree in language studies, they need to take mathematics as it is a compulsory subject in the entrance exam. Clearly, such a subject has little relevance to their future study. If they can choose only the subjects which are aligned to their respective goals, their motivation can be kept high.

[Conclusion]

In conclusion, it is unfortunately very difficult to keep high school students' motivation high because of the current system. The university entrance exams should be changed so the high school curriculum can also change to keep all students interested in their studies; otherwise, students' motivation levels will remain low, and fewer students will want to pursue higher level studies.

(357 words)／※下線＝〈一貫性とまとまり〉のスコアに関わる接続表現

▶ **問題文の訳**

多くの若者は士気が高く、高校でうまくやっている。しかし士気に欠け、高校に興味や必要性を見出さない者も多い。これはなぜか。生徒全員の成功を手助けするために何ができるか。

▶ **上級者エッセイの構成**

Introduction ——	説明文のパラフレーズ＋意思表明（日本の教育制度の問題、受験制度（受験科目）を変更すべき）
Body 1 ————	原因（受験カリキュラムについていく生徒と、そうでない生徒）
Body 2 ————	解決策（受験科目が変わればカリキュラムも見直される）
Conclusion ——	Bodyの要約＋意思表明の再掲（受験科目の見直し）

中級

□ **motivation** [名] やる気

□ **reputation** [名] 評判

□ **be relevant to ～**　～に関連している

□ **inflexibility** [名] 融通が利かないこと

□ **be related to ～**　～に関係している

上級

□ **pursue** [動] ～を追い求める

□ **irrelevant** [形] 無関係の

□ **namely** [副] すなわち

□ **respective** [形] それぞれの

□ **career ambition**　経歴上の野心

□ **definite action**　明確な方策

□ **have relevance to ～**　～に関連がある

中級者のエッセイ

[Introduction]
意思表明 I believe there are more disadvantages of social media than advantages to the individual and society.

[Body 1]
トピック The biggest problem with social media is the amount of information available. If the information is correct and right, no problem will arise. However, there are no strict rules to upload correct information, so both individuals and society will be affected easily by the wrong information. For example, if famous people make good comments about a product, the product will be immediately famous even if it is a bad product. Famous people or big companies can control society by information they choose to share and spread. Another example is that a lot of celebrities or influencers use social media to spread misinformation about the coronavirus.

[Body 2]
トピック However, sharing and spreading information easily and quickly is the biggest advantage of social media. For instance, when a big earthquake happened in Japan, warnings about any related disasters that might happen were shared immediately. This helped many people. Also, what victims really need, and which area needs more food were shared. That's why people could help each other more efficiently.

[Body 3]
トピック Another benefit is that the distance between people is reduced. Even if people are in different countries, they can communicate with each other with almost no time lag. Social media has made our society and individuals come closer and the world smaller.

[Conclusion]
To summarise, social media can be used as a tool to influence society and individuals negatively. However, it has also helped people get access to information in the world more easily.

(255 words)／※下線＝〈一貫性とまとまり〉のスコアに関わる接続表現

▶ 解説

〈課題への回答〉このエッセイで書くべき [要求ポイント]
①ソーシャルメディアの長所
②ソーシャルメディアの短所
→outweighがキーワードで、意思表明で「どちらが上回るか」を記述するのが必須。また、中級、上級ともに「短所が上回る」意見なので、長所より短所の数を多く書くべき。

[Introduction]
中級 最初のパラフレーズが抜けており、問題のテーマが提示できていない。

[Body]
中級 短所はBody 1の1点のみで、長所はBody 2、3の2点なので、「長所が上回る」意見に読めてしまう。

[Conclusion]
中級は「短所が上回る」という意見を明確に再提示していないが、上級ではit has more drawbacksと明確に示している。

〈語彙力〉
上級 断定を避ける表現に注目（Body 3：This could be due to the fact that ... ／ ... may lead them to ...）。
ソーシャルメディア関連の「特定分野の語彙」が、特に上級で豊富（黒い下線部分）。

[Introduction]
パラフレーズ Nowadays, social media is the world's most useful communication tool, and undoubtedly, there are both benefits and drawbacks of using this tool for the individual and also for society. 意思表明 I personally feel that the disadvantages are far greater than the advantages.

[Body1]
トピック The possibility of sharing and spreading information easily and quickly is the biggest advantage of social media. For instance, when big earthquakes happen in Japan, warnings about any related disasters are immediately shared. Latest information on what victims really need, and which areas require more assistance is quickly communicated to those who can help.

[Body2]
トピック On the other hand, one of the major problems with social media is the enormous amount of information it conveys. If the information were correct, this would not be an issue. However, since there are no strict rules regarding uploading correct information, people can be easily affected by false and malicious social media content. There are hundreds of examples of fake celebrity-backed investment websites that were set up with the sole purpose of scamming people. The scammers lure people with fake news articles accompanied by celebrity endorsements on social media to attract customers into investing in fake companies.

[Body3]
トピック Another worrying trend is the impact on the mental health of teenagers and young adults, which is at an all-time low. This could be due to the fact that many young people are influenced by social media and feel that their celebrities and peers are living a perfect existence while they are not. These upward social comparisons may lead them to feel inferior and unhappy. Teenage suicides in Japan are becoming much more common now than before the popularity of social media.

[Conclusion]
To summarise, it is true that social media has helped people throughout the world receive information more easily. It can, however, be used in very harmful and negative ways. While there are many advantages to social media, overall, I believe it has more drawbacks for the individual and society.

(324 words)／※下線＝〈一貫性とまとまり〉のスコアに関わる接続表現

Writing

▶問題文の訳
ソーシャルメディアはとても効果的なコミュニケーション手段となっている。同時に個人と社会への影響が懸念されている。ソーシャルメディアの長所は短所を上回るか。

▶上級者エッセイの構成

Introduction ── 説明文のパラフレーズ＋意思表明（短所が上回る）
Body 1 ── 長所（情報の拡散が簡単で速い）
Body 2 ── 短所1（情報が膨大で、規制がない。デマや悪意あるコンテンツ）
Body 3 ── 短所2（若者への心理的影響。他者との比較、自殺の増加）
Conclusion ── Bodyの要約＋意思表明の再掲（長所もあるが、短所が上回る）

→「短所が上回る」という意見なので、長所は1段落にとどめ、短所に2段落を割いている。短所をBody2、3に述べることで、自然にConclusionへつなげている。

中級

☐ **individual** ［名］個人

☐ **celebrity** ［名］有名人

☐ **misinformation** ［名］デマ、誤報

☐ **victim** ［名］被災者、犠牲者

☐ **strict rule**　厳格な規則

☐ **influencer** ［名］インフルエンサー

☐ **disaster** ［名］災害

☐ **influence** ［動］〜に影響を与える

上級

☐ **undoubtedly** ［副］疑いようもなく

☐ **drawback** ［名］欠点、不利

☐ **malicious** ［形］悪意のある

☐ **sole purpose**　唯一の目的

☐ **lure** ［動］〜を誘惑する

☐ **at an all-time low**　史上最低で

☐ **inferior** ［形］劣等の

☐ **benefit** ［名］恩恵

☐ **enormous** ［形］膨大な

☐ **celebrity-backed**　有名人が支援した

☐ **scam** ［動］〜をだます

☐ **endorsement** ［名］（商品などの）推奨

☐ **lead 〜 to ...**　〜を...に誘導する

受験者によく見られるミス！〜「中級者のエッセイ」の注意点〜

• Introductionでは、説明文のパラフレーズをするのを忘れて、意思表明しか書いていない。Introductionでは、必ずトピックの紹介から始めよう

• Introductionに1文しかない。1段落には最低でも2文以上書こう

中級者のエッセイ

[Introduction]
[パラフレーズ] People have an expectation that automation in business will replace humans' jobs in the near future. [意思表明] I think the statement is true and it is a positive development rather than a negative one.

[Body 1]
[トピック] One of the main reasons for automation in business is that it is the only way to deal with the issue of an aging population. Japan is one such example because the number of hardworking young people is going to decrease in a few decades. As a result, there will be a lack of workers, and companies will need to use more robots in business. In this case, automation is essential for the country to help workers and society.

[Body 2]
[トピック] This development is positive for society. If automation happens, businesses will be more efficient and can lower the costs of creating goods and services. Also, human workers can be more expensive than robots. This means companies can make more profit if they automate. Furthermore, another positive point is that it will help keep products clean as there will be no human contact. These days, the dangerous virus, COVID-19, is widespread around the world. Everyone really worries about how clean products are. If there are systems which are automatic and do not need to be touched by people, it will improve the situation.

[Conclusion]
To sum up, the reason why people expect more jobs will shift from people to robots is because of the aging population. This will have more advantages than disadvantages due to the reasons stated above. In addition, there will be no human errors or accidents when using automatic systems.

(263 words)／※下線＝〈一貫性とまとまり〉のスコアに関わる接続表現

Writing

▶ 解説

〈課題への回答〉このエッセイで書くべき［要求ポイント］
①ビジネスにおける自動化が人々の仕事を奪うという見方があるが、なぜ人々はそう思うのか
②この発展は肯定的か否定的か（自分の意見）

中級の構成と改善すべき点

Introduction —— 説明文のパラフレーズ＋意思表明（意思表明で、［要求ポイント］の①に触れていない）
Body 1 ———— 要求ポイント①—高齢化に対する解決策だから（労働力確保）
Body 2 ———— 要求ポイント②—1）コスト減　2）コロナ対策、清潔
Conclusion —— Bodyの要約＋意思表明の再掲（In addition ...の新しい話は入れるべきではない）

中級でも［要求ポイント］の①に触れているが、上級ではBody 1の最終文でTherefore, many people believe ...と、①の問に明確に答えており、読み手にとってわかりやすい。
中級は、Body 2で2つの肯定的な点（コスト削減、コロナ対策）を盛り込んでおり、上級では段落を分けているが、どちらの構成でも問題ない。
両者の最大の違いは、上級はBody 4で否定派の視点にも触れている点。**高得点を狙いたいなら「〜という意見もあるが ...」と、自分とは反対の意見にも触れる**とよい。このように自分の意見に隙を作らないようにすると説得力が出る。

[Introduction]

(パラフレーズ) It is predicted that automation in business will replace many human workers in the near future. (意思表明) I think this is a direct response to the issue of aging workforces in developed countries. Overall, this is a positive development rather than a negative one.

[Body 1]

(トピック) To begin with, this trend of rapid automation is an expected reality in many countries, driven by changes in demographics. Japan is one such example because the proportion of working youth is going to dwindle in a few decades. Consequently, companies will face the challenge of securing their workforce to sustain their businesses. Therefore, many people believe automation is essential for the country to maintain productivity.

[Body 2]

(トピック) In general, automation has many benefits. For instance, as a consequence of increased efficiency and lower labour costs, it can bring down business's cost. The labour costs of hiring workers are substantially higher in the long run, compared to investment in automation. Furthermore, automated factories can run 24 hours, raising the production rate.

[Body 3]

(トピック) An added benefit of replacing people with robots is that it will help keep products clean, due to there being no human contact in their production. These days, the dangerous virus, COVID-19, is widespread around the world. Everyone really worries about how hygienic the products are. If automatic systems are in place and do not require manual handling, it could potentially reduce the chances of spreading contagious illnesses.

[Body 4]

(トピック) In spite of these benefits, a lot of people do express concerns about automation. It is projected that many manual-labour jobs will be replaced by computers or machines, potentially leaving many people unemployed. Many truck drivers in the United States fear job loss due to the technological development of driverless trucks. Either people will have to upskill or become dependent on the state for assistance.

[Conclusion]

To sum up, it's widely believed that automation in business is inevitable as a result of demographic changes. The benefits of efficient and hygienic automation outweigh the drawbacks of society offering fewer jobs to its workers.

(331 words)／※下線＝〈一貫性とまとまり〉のスコアに関わる接続表現

▶ 問題文の訳

今日、ビジネスにおける自動化が急速に人々の仕事を奪うという見方がある。なぜ人々はそう思うのか。これは肯定的もしくは否定的な発展か。

▶ 上級者エッセイの構成

Introduction	説明文のパラフレーズ＋意思表明（[要求ポイント] ①②：肯定的）
Body 1	要求ポイント①高齢化に対する解決策だから（労働力確保）
Body 2	要求ポイント②肯定的な点1：コスト減
Body 3	要求ポイント②肯定的な点2：コロナ対策、清潔
Body 4	否定派の主張（失業者の増加）
Conclusion	Bodyの要約＋意思表明の再掲（[要求ポイント] ①②）

┌─ **Vocabulary** ───┐

中級

☐ **aging population** 高齢化する人口　　　☐ **a few decades** 数十年

☐ **be essential for 〜 to ...** 〜にとって...することは不可欠である

☐ **efficient** [形] 効率的な　　　☐ **widespread** [形] 蔓延した

☐ **shift from 〜 to ...** 〜から...に変わる

上級

☐ **aging workforce** 高齢化する労働力　　　☐ **demographics** [名] 人口統計

☐ **proportion of 〜** 〜の割合　　　☐ **dwindle** [動] 次第に減少する

☐ **consequently** [副] 結果として　　　☐ **as a consequence of 〜** 〜の結果として

☐ **labour cost** 人件費　　　☐ **investment into 〜** 〜への投資

☐ **manual handling** 手作業　　　☐ **contagious illness** 接触伝染性疾患

☐ **driverless truck** 無人トラック　　　☐ **upskill** [動] 技能を向上させる

☐ **become dependent on 〜** 〜に依存的になる　　　☐ **inevitable** [形] 避けられない

└──┘

受験者によく見られるミス！〜「中級者のエッセイ」の注意点〜

• Conclusionで、Bodyに書いていない新情報を盛り込んでいる。
　ConclusionではBodyで触れた情報にのみ言及しよう

Speaking

Speaking

練習問題   本冊P.165 / track 19

▸ Where you live / Being bored

▸ 回答例   E = Examiner 🇬🇧   C = Candidate

E Now, in this first part, I'd like to ask you some questions about yourself. Let's talk about where you live. Is there anything special about the town or city where you live now?

C Yes, the city where I live now is one of the oldest in my country with many historical temples and shrines as it used to be the capital city.

E Do you have many friends who live nearby?

C ₁Unfortunately, I don't. I just moved here three months ago for a new job, so the only people I know currently are my co-workers. I hope some of them will become friends.

E Does your city have many places for people to exercise?

C ₂I think there are not that many places where people can exercise. Although, there is one sports facility which is huge, it was built for the Olympic Games a long time ago.

E Next, let's talk about being bored. What things do you find boring?

C ₃Maybe it's strange to say this, but I feel watching a movie in the theatre is ₄quite boring. I like doing other things while watching movies at home, surfing online stores, for example. However, the only thing I can do at the theatre is watch. So, I feel bored sometimes. Of course, it depends on the movie though.

E When was the last time you felt very bored?

C ₅Around half a year ago at Dubai Airport ₆while I waited for my transit flight. It was early morning, so shops were closed and there was no Wi-Fi access either.

E What do you do to prevent ₇boredom?

C I often read novels when I find the time. I can purchase new books on the internet easily nowadays, and even read them on my tablet or phone.

E Do you think that people are more bored nowadays than in the past?

C ₈I strongly believe so. People these days get bored easily because we are so busy and are not used to having nothing to do. Elderly people know how to enjoy quiet time.

E ₉Why?

C I suppose it's out of necessity! They don't have to work so they are used to finding ways to keep life interesting.

E Thank you.

▶ 解 説

1　1語で感情を表現し、これから話す内容がネガティブな内容であることを相手に伝えられる便利な副詞。

2　「人々が運動できる所はそんなに多くないと思います」。この where は関係副詞で、where people can exercise が先行詞である many places を修飾している。

3　少し変わった回答をする際の前置き。類似表現：Maybe it's just me,

4　boring のように程度に差がある形容詞には、度合いを表す語で修飾するとよい。この場合は quite（かなり）。他に、a bit, a little, a little bit（少し）なども修飾によく使う表現。

5　The last time I felt very bored was ... と試験官の言葉を繰り返しても間違いではないが、この回答のように前置きなしで直接本題に入る答え方も自然でよい。

6　この while は「〜の間」という意味の接続詞。

7　品詞の変化を例文と一緒に整理しておこう。

boredom［名］退屈 → relieve boredom（退屈を紛らす）

boring［形］うんざりさせる、退屈な → It's boring just to sit and watch TV.（座ってテレビを見るだけなんて退屈だ）

bored［形］うんざりした、退屈した → I'm bored with doing homework.（宿題をするのが退屈だ）

8　強い肯定を表す。類似表現：I absolutely think so.

9　話を膨らませられるか試すために Why? と質問を追加することがある。

| Vocabulary |

□ **facility**［名］（図書館・病院などの）施設

□ **transit flight**　乗り継ぎ便　→［類］connecting flight

□ **prevent**［動］〜を妨げる、中止させる　→［名］prevention

□ **be used to -ing**　〜することに慣れている　→［類］be accustomed to -ing

□ **out of necessity**　必要に迫られて

▶ Place

▶ 回答例　　　　　　　　E＝Examiner 🇺🇸　　C＝Candidate

E　Now, I'm going to give you a topic, and I would like you to talk about it for one to two minutes. Before you talk, you will have one minute to think about what you are going to say. You can make some notes if you wish. Do you understand?

C　Yes.

E　Here is some paper and a pencil for making notes, and here is your topic. I'd like you to talk about a place where you would like to spend more time.

－ 1分間の準備時間 －

E　All right? Remember, you have one to two minutes for this, so don't worry if I stop you. I'll tell you when the time is up. Can you start speaking now, please?

C　I would like to tell you about a city that I really love but haven't been to for five years. The city is ①Hanoi, which is the capital of Vietnam. ②I've been to Hanoi five or six times and I lived and I worked there a few years ago. It was great with friendly people, brilliant food, and has a lovely climate. Hanoi has everything, I think.
It's a big city with terrible traffic, but it's also quite beautiful in unexpected ways. ③There are old French buildings built alongside Soviet-style public buildings that were put up to replace the ones that were bombed during the war. There are some lovely parks as well. But the thing that I especially like is the activity and energy in the little streets in the old quarter. I used to wander around there a lot.
You can eat out every day and night, and ④Vietnamese food is delicious, I think. That's something I really miss! Sadly, I haven't had the opportunity to revisit Hanoi for some time, but I hope to go next year. ④I'd like to spend a couple of months reacquainting myself with the people and the places I've been missing for so long.
Of all the cities I've visited, and I've been to quite a few, Hanoi is definitely one that I'd love to spend more time in.

E　Thank you. Do you ever talk to other people about this place?

C　Certainly, and I always recommend to my friends some of the shops and restaurants I like.

▶ 解説

「もっと長い時間、過ごしたいと思う場所」について説明する問題。かつて住み、働いた街として、ハノイを挙げ、魅力として、主に街並みを詳しく紹介しているロングターン。さらにそこまで再訪したい理由として食、人、場所を挙げてトピックの指示を満たしている。

文法面では現在完了形の経験用法と継続用法をうまく使っている。

経験用法

I've been to Hanoi five or six times （ハノイに5、6回行ったことがあります）

Of all the cities I**'ve visited**, and I**'ve been to** quite a few,

（私が訪れたことや何度も行ったことがあるすべての街の中で）

継続用法

a city that I really love but **haven't been** to for five years
（本当に大好きですが5年間ずっと行っていない街）

I **haven't had** the opportunity to revisit Hanoi for some time,
（しばらくの間ハノイを再訪する機会を持っていません）

the people and the places **I've been missing** for so long
（かなり長い間恋しく思っている人々や場所）

最後の例は、恋しい感情が継続していることを強調する現在完了進行形。

街を描写する文では、主格の関係代名詞が2つ入っているので、整理しておこう。

There are old French buildings built alongside <u>Soviet-style public buildings</u> **that** were put up to replace <u>the ones that</u> were bombed during the war.
（戦争中に爆撃された建物の代わりに建てられたソ連風の公共施設と並んで古いフランスの建物があります）

この文の主節はThere are old French buildings。

built ... the warが過去分詞句としてold French buildingsを修飾している。

文の後半に2つの関係代名詞（that）がある

①先行詞：Soviet-style public buildings　修飾する部分：that were put up ... the war

②先行詞：the ones　修飾する部分：that were bombed during the war（onesはbuildingsのこと）

[You should say ポイント]

ロングターンの下線部分（①〜④）で、以下の①〜④に言及している。

①where this place is（場所はどこか）

②how you know about this place（どのようにその場所を知っているか）

③what this place looks like（その場所はどんな様子か）

④why you wish you could spend more time there（なぜ、そこでもっと過ごすことを望むのか）

メモの例

where	how I know	what ... looks like	why more time
Hanoi	lived	French bldg	food
Vietnam	worked	Soviet-style public bldg	miss
	5-6 times	parks	people and place
		little streets	reacquaint

┤ **Vocabulary** ├

□ **alongside** [前・副] 〜と並んで

□ **put up** 建設する

□ **quarter** [名]（都市の特定の）地区、街

□ **public building** 公共施設

□ **replace** [動] 〜を取り替える

□ **reacquaint oneself with 〜** 〜との旧交を温める

▸ Places to visit / City living

▸ 回答例　　　　　　　　　　E = Examiner 🇬🇧　　C = Candidate ⬤

E We've been talking about a place where you would like to spend more time and I'd like to discuss with you one or two more general questions related to this. Let's consider first of all, places where people like to relax in cities. In cities, where do people like to go to relax?

C Hmm, let me think ... I guess in large cities people like to go to sport parks. They generally have a lot of different sports facilities for various kinds of sports, for example swimming pools, gyms, tennis courts, and so on. Some of them also have big gardens with a lot of trees. Many children and older people like to walk around and play, and sometimes families go there to have picnics.

E Why do you think natural places like forests or the seaside are pleasant to be in?

C ₁That's interesting to think about. ₂I guess the answer is because humans are also animals. We cannot live among only man-made buildings. That's why there are parks or rivers even in big cities such as New York, London, or Tokyo. If the parks were not important or pleasant for us, we would have already demolished them and built more buildings or railways to make our lives more convenient. Many people say walking in parks a few times a week can significantly reduce anxiety and levels of depression, so I think in order to maintain good mental health we should spend some time in nature.

E Some people prefer to stay in their homes rather than go out and visit beautiful places. Why is that?

C ₃I guess some people can find going to new places stressful, even if it is a pretty place. They may feel under stress being in an unfamiliar setting and cannot really relax. ₃Personally, I think people like to stay at home as it is more comfortable and everything that we need or want is there.

E Now, let's talk about different ways to improve cities. What are some of the things that governments can do to make cities better places to live?

C ₁That's a difficult question ... I've never thought about it but in my opinion, the government should better manage roads in and around cities because I hear from my father that the traffic during rush hour is terrible. Many people spend a lot of time in their cars. If the traffic is well managed, people can spend more time with their families.

E How can local people improve their neighbourhoods?

C I think making a safe environment for children is the best way to improve the area. Local people can take turns standing along the streets to check children are OK while they are coming back from school. This will protect children and also prevent traffic accidents.

E In modern cities, do you think it's difficult for people to find time to be alone?

C I think spending time alone is not easy ₄if people are living in cities, especially big cities like Tokyo. Maybe at home is the only place where people can be truly alone, but this is also possible only if they are living alone.

E How important is it to find time alone?

C ₅It's very important because we need a moment to collect our thoughts and de-stress.

E ₅Why?

C When we are continually surrounded by people and chaos, it can severely affect our mental health. So when we spend time alone, we can have time to recuperate from the stress we get from the outdoor environment.

E Thank you. That's the end of the Speaking Test.

▶ **解 説**

パート2の練習問題がDescribe a place where you wish you could spend more time.だったので、パート3ではそれに関連して「場所」と「都市生活」という抽象的なトピックになっている。

1 すぐに答えるのは難しい場合は、こういったフレーズで間をつなごう。

2 Whyで聞かれているので、まずはbecauseで答えて、それから詳細を述べている。詳細を先に述べると伝わりづらいので注意する。

3 「美しい場所に行くよりも家にいるのを好む人がいるのはなぜですか」と聞かれて、まずはI guess, some people can ...を使い一般論で答え、後半で、Personally, I think ...と個人的な意見も追加している。**パート3で個人的な意見も述べていいが、このように付加的に述べる程度にした方がいい**だろう。また、Personally, と挿入し、個人的な話を始めるサインを示すとわかりやすい。

4 「都会に住んでいるなら」と、条件をつけるためにIf節を使っている。これは現実には起こりえないことを仮定する仮定法ではないので、If節の時制は現在形にするのが正しい。

5 試験官の質問を繰り返しながら1文で答えただけなので、試験官はWhy?で深掘りしようとしている。**Why?と聞かれる前に理由を述べられるのがベスト。**

┤ Vocabulary ├

□ **man-made** [形] 人工の → [類]artificial

□ **take turns -ing** 交替で〜する

□ **collect** [動]（考えを）まとめる

□ **recuperate from 〜** 〜から回復する、元気になる

□ **find＋O＋C** OがCであると気づく

□ **only if S＋V** SVの場合に限り

□ **de-stress** [動] くつろぐ

Part 1

▶ Hometown / Neighbours / The weather

▶ 回答例 E = Examiner 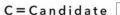 C = Candidate ●

E Now, in this first part, I'd like to ask you some questions about yourself. Let's talk about your hometown. What kinds of jobs do people in your hometown do?

C Many people work in factories. There are three big factories in my hometown. I don't know what the factories make but a lot of people work there, doing various jobs.

E In which part of your hometown do most people live?

C Mainly around the stations. There are two stations, so many apartments are located between them. However, since there are no houses in that area, families with children live a bit further away from the stations.

E ₁Where did you play in your hometown when you were a child?

C When I was a kid, I used to play at parks around my home. Unfortunately, some of them are no longer there.

E Why not?

C That's because ₂new apartments have been built where the parks used to be. My hometown has gone through rapid development over the last ten years.

E Let's move on now and talk about your neighbours. How often do you see your neighbours?

C ₃I've rarely seen my neighbours because I'm living in an apartment, and I think most of the people living there are single, so everyone keeps their distance.

E Do you invite your neighbours to your home?

C No, I've never invited my neighbours to my place.

E Why not?

C Because I don't know them well enough to do so. I don't feel comfortable asking them to come to my place. Usually, people keep to themselves in big cities like Tokyo.

E Do you think you are a good neighbour?

C I guess so. I haven't had any problems with other residents. I try to be quiet and follow the rules of the apartment. I think these are the two most important things to consider when living close to others.

E Has a neighbour ever helped you?

C No, never. But I think ₄if I needed help and asked them, they would help me. However, I haven't had any instances when I needed their help. Also, I haven't helped any of my neighbours. Of course, ₄I would help them if they needed it though.

E Let's talk about the weather now. What kind of weather did you like best when you were a child?

C I definitely liked the hot summer weather when I was a kid because I always wanted to play outside, especially in the mountains or rivers.

E Does the weather affect your mood?

C Yes, definitely, it affects me in both good ways and bad. Rainy weather puts me in a bit of a bad mood, but snow makes me happy because it doesn't often snow where I live. So, I feel it's lucky when it snows.

E What is the best weather for studying or working?

C I think the weather doesn't affect studying or working. But if I think about going to school or work, sunny weather is the best, definitely not rainy weather ₅as I feel it makes people a bit depressed.

E Would you like to live in a country that has very hot or very cold weather?

C ₆It's very hard to decide because I like both types of weather and the activities I can do in both climates. If I need to choose one, I would say very hot weather, but not if it's humid.

E Thank you.

▶ 解説

1 最初の2問は現在のことだが、ここでいきなり過去の質問に切り替わるので答え方に注意する。

2 「かつて公園があった場所に新しいマンションが建設されてきています」。現在完了形の受け身形。

3 How often do you see ...と現在形で聞かれているが、「マンションに住んでから現在まで近所の人とめったに会っていない」という、過去から現在までの継続を表現したいので現在完了形で答えている。

4 仮定法過去を2回使っており、文法力のアピールになる。仮定法過去は「現在における、実現しそうにない仮定」を表す。訳はそれぞれ「もし私が助けを求めたら、彼らは私を助けるでしょう」「彼らが必要としているなら、私は彼らを助けるでしょう」。

5 「雨は人々を少し憂鬱にさせるように感じるので」。このasは、理由を表す接続詞。

6 ときに断言できない質問がきたときは、このように素直に答えたうえで、理由を述べて話を広げよう。

┤ **Vocabulary** ├

☐ **further away from ～** ～からより離れて

☐ **used to ～** 以前は～したものだった、（used to be は「～だった」）

☐ **put ～ in a bad mood** ～の気分を損ねる

☐ **no longer** もはや～でない

☐ **keep to oneself** 人と付き合わない

☐ **a bit of ～** 少しの～

Part 2 本冊P.187 ／ track 25

▶ Something you were given

▶ 回答例 E = Examiner 🇦🇺 C = Candidate

E Now, I'm going to give you a topic and I would like you to talk about it for one to two minutes. Before you talk, you will have one minute to think about what you are going to say. You can make some notes if you wish. Do you understand?

C Yes.

E Here is some paper and a pencil for making notes, and here is your topic. I'd like you to describe something you were given that was very useful.

― 1分間の準備時間 ―

E All right? Remember, you have one to two minutes for this, so don't worry if I stop you. I'll tell you when the time is up. Can you start speaking now, please?

C The thing I'm going to describe is ①my bicycle. It's not an expensive bike or anything, but I've found it very useful ever since I got it.
②My husband gave it to me a couple of years ago because we had been talking about how I was getting a bit fat, but I'd never got around to buying one myself! Well, not long after he gave it to me, ③I had to take my car to the garage for major repairs, and I thought I might take the opportunity to ride to work. It was a nice 20-minute ride each way, and pretty flat, so not too demanding. The first day I did the ride, ④I felt quite good about myself, so the next day and the day after that, I rode again.
By the time I got my car back, I'd decided that ③bike riding would be part of my daily exercise routine. It's quite easy once you're into the routine, I think. As I said, that's a couple of years ago, and I haven't looked back.
④Now, I feel much healthier than I was before. And I also feel younger and virtuous, as well. And, by the way, I bought my husband a bike last year too, and we sometimes go bike riding at the weekends—a happy and healthy family!

E Thank you. Do people often give you things that you find are useful?

C To be honest, no. I think I must be a difficult person to buy for, so I end up being given books which I seldom read!

▶ 解 説

「とても役立った頂き物」を説明する問題。妻からもらった自転車の話で、この時点で［you should say ポイント］の①②をクリアできている。③の「役立った点」は、大きく分けて2つあり、1つ目は車を使えないときに自転車通勤ができた点、2つ目は運動習慣となった点である。④は、シンプルに動詞のfeelを使って表現すればよい。
トピックの指示はすべて過去形になっているので、受験者は基本的には過去形を使っているが、伝えたいニュアンスに合わせて完了形をうまく取り入れている。詳細を見ていこう。

過去完了進行形
My wife gave it to me a couple of years ago because we **had been talking** about how I was getting a bit fat, but I'd never got around to buying one myself!
（私が太ってきているのに一向に自分で買わないことを夫婦で話していたので、妻が2、3年前に私にくれました）
主節は、My wife gave it to me a couple of years agoの部分。because節で過去完了進行形を使っている。夫婦で話をしていたのは過去のある時点まで継続していたことなので、この時制が適切。

過去完了形
By the time I got my car back, I**'d decided** that bike riding would be part of my daily exercise routine.（車が戻ったときには、自転車に乗ることは日常の運動習慣の一部になっていたんです）
主節は、I**'d decided** that bike riding would be part of my daily exercise routine。
I'd decidedは、I had decidedの省略形。
過去の一時点（車が戻ったとき）に、結論づけて（I'd decided）完了したことを表現したいので過去完了形がふさわしい。このdecideは「決定する」ではなく「結論づける」「判断する」というニュアンス。

現在完了形
As I said, that's a couple of years ago, and I haven't looked back.
（さっきも言ったように、これは数年前の話で、それ以来ずっと続いているんです）
look backは否定形と一緒に使い、「後退していない」という意味になる。「自転車が習慣になったときから現在まで継続していること」を表すので現在完了形を使っている。

[You should sayポイント]
ロングターンの下線部分（①〜④）で、以下の①〜④に言及している。
① what this thing was （物は何か）　③ why it was useful （なぜ役立ったか）
② who gave it to you （誰がくれたか）　④ how you felt when you used it （使ったときどう感じたか）

メモの例

what	who	why	how I felt
bicycle	wife	car = major repairs	healthy
not expensive		ride to work	younger
		daily routine	virtuous

┤ **Vocabulary** ├

□ **get around to -ing** やっと～に取り掛かる   □ **not long after S＋V** SVから間もなく

□ **demanding** ［形］過酷な、きつい   □ **by the time S＋V** SVするときまでには

□ **into** ［前］～の中へ →be into the routineで「習慣化する」。intoは場所だけではなく状況も表す。

□ **look back** 後退する、後悔する、ふりかえる（否定文で使う）   □ **virtuous** ［形］立派な、高潔な

□ **end up -ing** 結局～することになる

Part 3 本冊P.188 ／ track 26

▸ Giving / International aid

▸ 回答例   **E＝Examiner**   **C＝Candidate**

E   We've been talking about an item that was given to you, which is very useful and I'd like to discuss with you one or two more general questions related to this. Let's consider first of all popular gifts in your country. What are some examples of popular birthday gifts that people give to each other in your country?

C   ₁Hmm, I am not sure which birthday gifts are popular in Japan. ₁For children, maybe animation merchandise is one of them, but the popular products keep on changing every year because new animations become popular each year. ₁For adults, I think gift cards are popular as people can choose ₂what they want to buy with them.

E   When giving something, how important is it that the gift is wrapped up beautifully?

C   ₃I don't think wrapping is important at all because anyway, the wrapping will be opened quickly after you get the gift. ₄Even if the wrapping is beautiful, it will be thrown away at the end of the day. I've never heard of someone valuing wrapping paper in the same way as they value the gifts.

E   Some say that giving a person your time, that is, listening to them or helping them, is the best gift. What do you think about that?

C   ₅Possibly it's true. Spending time with the person can be the best present. However, in my opinion, presents should be given on special occasions.

E   Why is that?

C   Well, listening to or helping your friends or family should be a normal thing, so it can be the best present for someone, but not for me.

E   Let's move on now to talk about countries giving international aid at times of crisis. When there are natural disasters such as earthquakes, floods, or tsunamis, what sort of help will the victims need from their own country or from other countries?

C   I'm pretty sure what the victims need, ₆from my experience of seeing the news and being one of them, is food, of course.

E Can you think of other things that are needed?

C Let me think, I guess the next most important thing is tissue paper for hygiene. You need this for the toilet, cleaning up dishes, tables and such. Towels can be useful, but you can't wash them after serious natural disasters because usually the water supply is stopped.

E Some people say that it is better to build local infrastructure, for example, bridges and dams, than to just give money to poor countries. What do you think about that?

C I agree. ₇Those projects are far more important than donating money. People might have enough money by donation to buy food for a few months, but this is not a long-term solution. Building projects can create employment opportunities ₈, which means people can earn money and gain skills. Also, this will help in giving them a safer and more comfortable life.

E ₉Some say that rich countries give aid to poor countries as a way of spreading their influence in the region rather than actually helping people. What do you think?

C I am sure that most countries give aid in order to help the poorer countries because ₁₀if they wanted to increase their influence, they could give expensive loans instead. However, often the aid doesn't reach the poor people and the money is not enough to help everyone. I think ₁₁developed countries should help people who live in ₁₁developing countries by teaching and sharing their knowledge and technological skills rather than just providing money.

E Thank you. That's the end of the Speaking Test.

▶ 解説

1 受験者にとっては答えにくい質問だったので、filler wordsでうまく間を埋めている。国民全体では規模が大き過ぎて語りにくいため、For children, For adultsと年齢で細分化して話を広げている。

2 「大人に関しては、買いたいものが選べるためギフトカードが人気だと思います」。what 以下が関係代名詞の節で、chooseの目的語になっている。

3 not ... at allは、強い否定表現。類義語：no ... whatsoever

4 接続詞的な働きをする〈Even if S＋V〉で複文を作っている。意味は「たとえSVでも」。

5 Possibly it's true. で「そうかもしれません」。It's true. よりも肯定の度合いは下がる。

6 このように挿入句を入れることで複雑な文を作り、文法力をアピールするのも効果的。

7 質問が、betterやthanを含む比較級なので、受験者がどれだけ比較級を使いこなせるかを判断する問題。〈more＋形容詞＋than ～〉の基本的な比較級で答えている。farはmoreを強調する副詞で、ここでは「お金を寄付するよりもはるかに重要です」となる。

8 employment opportunitiesだけだと抽象的なので、関係代名詞の非制限用法で情報を補足している。

9 質問が長いので注意して聞こう。「豊かな国々は実際に人々を助けるというより、その地域で影響力を広める手段として貧しい国々を援助しているという意見があります。どう思いますか」
aidはhelpより堅い語で、力のある者が弱い者を助ける意味合いが強い。

10 because節の中に仮定法（If節）が組み込まれている。「もし影響力を強めたいなら、代わりに高額な貸付を行うはずだから、大半の国々は貧しい国々を助ける目的で援助しているに違いないです」

11 rich countries→developed countries / poor countries→developing countriesに言い換えている。

┤ Vocabulary ├

□ **merchandise** [名] 商品

□ **special occasions** 特別な機会

□ **long-term solution** 長期的な解決

□ **keep on -ing** ～し続ける

□ **hygiene** [名] 衛生

□ **aid** [名]（食料、医薬品、武器などの）援助

Practice Test 1

WRITING

WRITING TASK 1

> 上級者のエッセイ

[Introduction]
パラフレーズ The maps of Hamford show how the downtown area of the town changed over 50 years from 1930 to 1980. 要約 These changes were quite significant. In short, compared to 1930, downtown Hamford in 1980 had lost some of its green areas but had gained a railway, an art museum and residential buildings.

[Body 1]
In 1930, there was a garden and sculpture park in the northeast of the town. By 1980, however, the garden and sculpture park had been removed to make way for a railway line. This railway line ran along the northern edge of the downtown area. A new art museum was built next to the railway in the east of the town. By 1980, new apartment complexes had been built in the southwest section of downtown Hamford.

[Body 2]
Apart from these major construction projects, Hudson Street and Ellison Road stayed much the same. The location of shops, galleries, the Madrigal Theatre, public library, and city hall remained the same as they were in 1930.　　　　　(164 words)／※下線＝「地図の問題」で重要となる、位置や方角を示す語句

▶ 問題文の訳

下記の地図は、50年の期間における、ハムフォードという町の中心地の変遷を示している。主な特徴を選んで説明することで情報を要約し、関連のある箇所を比較しなさい。

▶ エッセイの構成

Introduction ── 説明文のパラフレーズ＋要約
Body 1 ──── 大きな変化（ガーデンと公園の代わりに鉄道。美術館と集合住宅の出現）
Body 2 ──── 変わらない点（通りや店、ギャラリー、映画館、図書館、市役所）

▶ 解説

〈課題の達成度〉
[Introduction]
要約が明確で、地図上の全要素（変化している点、変化していない点）に言及している。
〈一貫性とまとまり〉
in short（要するに）、compared to ～（～と比較して）、apart from ～（～を除いて）など、接続表現が明確。
〈文法知識と正確さ〉
過去に完了したことを伝える文脈で、過去完了形を適切に使っている。ほか、受動態や比較の文（the same as ...）も使い、文法の運用範囲が広い。

| Vocabulary |

□ **residential**［形］住居の　　□ **sculpture**［名］彫刻　　□ **apartment complex**　集合住宅
□ **construction project**　建設事業　　□ **stay much the same**　ほぼ変わらない

[Introduction]

パラフレーズ There has been a significant increase in the number of violent crimes around the world in recent years. Some suggest we should have longer prison sentences. Others are opposed to this approach, arguing that harsher penalties do not deal with the root causes of crime. 意思表明 I agree with the latter point of view, and believe that it is not a lack of suitable punishment, but rather, a lack of education that leads to crime.

[Body 1]

トピック Those who advocate for increased prison terms think that severe penalties will stop criminals committing a crime. They think, furthermore, that some criminals cannot be rehabilitated, and that prison is the only place for them. Psychopaths are one example of such criminals. Research has shown that psychopaths lack the psychological resources to rehabilitate themselves. Such people may never be able to return to society as law-abiding citizens. Nevertheless, these are a very small minority of prisoners.

[Body 2]

トピック While keeping some violent criminals under strict surveillance is a necessity, simply imposing heavier punishments on prisoners indiscriminately generally does very little to prevent crime, and it is not a sustainable option. Often it is said that prisoners simply learn how to become more effective criminals while in prison. Therefore, the focus of prisons should be on teaching prisoners the skills that will help them to make an honest living after they have left prison. Hence, if the government wants to implement measures that effectively prevent a crime, re-education in prisons is the most logical solution. In fact, studies show that individuals who participated in some kind of educational program while in prison were less likely to re-offend.

[Conclusion]

In conclusion, while prisons play a role in rehabilitating criminals before they return to society, increasing the length of imprisonment does not deal with the fundamental causes of crime. Therefore, if prisoners are a threat to society, I believe the solution is education rather than brutal punishment, and this approach will ultimately reduce violent crime.

(322 words)／※下線＝〈一貫性とまとまり〉のスコアに関わる接続表現

▶ 問題文の訳

多くの人が、凶悪な暴力犯罪に対する最善の対応は、実刑の期間を延ばすことだと考えている一方で、長期にわたる実刑は犯罪抑止にならないと考える人もいる。双方の見解を論じ、あなた自身の意見を述べなさい。

▶ エッセイの構成

Introduction ── 説明文のパラフレーズ＋意思表明（後者の意見に賛成、教育の欠落が問題）

Body 1 ──── 実刑長期化に賛成する人の見解と彼らが支持する理由

Body 2 ──── 厳罰化に抑止効果はなく、教育制度の充実が必要（自分の意見を深掘り）

Conclusion ── Bodyの要約＋意思表明の再掲

▶ 解説

〈課題への回答〉このエッセイで書くべき [要求ポイント]

①凶悪な暴力的犯罪に対する最善策は長期実刑だという見解

②長期にわたる実刑は犯罪抑止にならないという見解

③自分の意見

→本問は、「対立する2つの見解を論じ、自分の意見を述べる問題」。[要求ポイント]の3つについて具体的な理由も含めて詳細に書かれている。自分が支持する反対派の意見については2つの具体例（①受刑者は刑務所でもっと効果的な犯罪者になる方法を学ぼうとする。②刑務所で教育された者は再犯しにくい）を挙げ、一貫して明確に議論が展開できている。

〈一貫性とまとまり〉
Bodyでのトピックセンテンスが明確。その後にサポーティングセンテンスを書き、具体的な理由や詳細で主旨を支えている。

〈語彙力〉
rehabilitate（犯罪者を社会復帰、訓練させる）、law-abiding citizens（順法精神のある市民）、re-offend（再犯する）など、犯罪関連の「特定分野の語彙」が豊富。

〈文法知識と正確さ〉
複文が多く、各文で多くの情報を伝えられている。特に、Body 2のトピックセンテンスでは、厳罰化に賛成派の意見の肯定的な点を認め、譲歩するためにwhile（〜の一方で）を使い、その後の主節で、反対派である自分の意見につなげている。

┤ Vocabulary ├

- □ **harsh penalty**　厳罰
- □ **advocate**［動］〜を擁護する、主張する
- □ **impose**［動］〜を課する
- □ **implement measures**　措置を実行する
- □ **fundamental cause**　根本原因

- □ **point of view**　観点、視点
- □ **surveillance**［名］監督
- □ **hence**［副］それゆえに
- □ **imprisonment**［名］投獄
- □ **brutal**［形］無情な、情け容赦ない

READING

READING PASSAGE 1　　　　　　　　　本冊P.193

1 ▸ feeding　　**2** ▸ pathogens　　**3** ▸ cereal fermentation
4 ▸ antimicrobial　　**5** ▸ kept　　**6** ▸ commercial products
7 ▸ probiotics / good bacteria / beneficial bacteria
8 ▸ immune system

▶ 解説

「要約を完成させる問題」では、多くの場合はパッセージの一部をまとめた要約が出題されるが、本問は全体の内容を要約したもので、難易度が高め。

1　段落1の中盤にある文、While there can be ... から解く。

2　食品汚染の原因を表す名詞を入れる。空欄2のある文は、段落2の1、2文目を言い換えたもの。

3　段落3、中盤のOne important answer ...の文に注目する。パラフレーズ One important answer ⇄ One traditional solution。importantとtraditionalは直接的な言い換えではないが、当段落の1文目にtraditional food preparation methodsとあり、手がかりになる。

4　空欄4のある文は、段落5の2文目と中盤の文（It is also hypothesized ...）の言い換え。パラフレーズ the germs ⇄ pathogens / during fermentation ⇄ in the fermentation process

5　段落5の後半 The fermented foods ..., be kept for a longer timeから解く。

6　要約の are less in demand から段落7の2文目へ（当段落1文目のis going out of fashionもヒントになる）。節（where commercial products are more available）と句（the availability of <u>commercial products</u>）のパラフレーズにも慣れておこう。

7,8　要約の最終文は、発酵食品の利点を列挙しており、これは段落8の1文目にあるa wide range of other benefitsにリンクする。7は、当段落の2、3文目、8は、終盤にあるYour immune system is made more robust.を根拠に解答する。

▶ 問題文の訳

Questions 1–8　次の要約文を完成させなさい。それぞれの答えとして、文章1から2つ以下の単語を選ぶこと。解答用紙の空欄1～8に解答を記入すること。

乳児のための発酵食品

栄養不良は、不十分な **1** 　食事　 と食品の汚染によって引き起こされる。この食品汚染は **2** 　病原体　 と不適切な保存方法によって引き起こされる。古くからある解決策の1つは **3** 　穀物の発酵　 である。

発酵によって食物の酸性度が高まり、発酵過程における **4** 　抗菌　 作用のために、病原体が死滅する。汚染の度合いが低いため、発酵食品はより長く **5** 　保存する　 こともできる。

現在、発酵食品は以前ほど需要がないが、これは、**6** 　市販の製品　 が手に入るからである。これが残念なのは、発酵食品は **7** 　善玉菌　 を多く含み、消化しやすく、体がビタミンやミネラルを吸収するのを助け、**8** 　免疫システム　 を高め、食欲を増してくれるからである。

9 ▸ C　　**10** ▸ C

▶ 解説

複数の選択肢から選ぶ問題

9　パッセージの中で全体的に発酵食品の利点（汚染を止める、保存性がある）が述べられているので、Cが正解。パッセージの特定の箇所をスキャニングする力ではなく、全体の主旨を理解しているかを問う問題。

10　「要約を完成させる問題」の要約文（空欄4の文）を読めば、酸化は発酵によるよい作用だとわかり、パッセージに戻らなくても解答できる。パッセージを参照する場合は段落2へ。汚染の原因が列挙されている。

Questions 9-10　正解となるA, B, CまたはDの文字を選びなさい。解答用紙の空欄9〜10に正解となる文字を記入すること。

9　食物の発酵が研究されている主な理由は何か。
- **A**　食物の栄養価を高めることができる。
- **B**　人気が低下しつつある伝統的な食品の調理方法である。
- **C**　食物の汚染をくい止めるとともに保存性を高めてくれる。
- **D**　世界中で人気がある。

10　食物の汚染の原因ではないものは、
- **A**　料理に使う水である。
- **B**　高温で食品を長期間保管することである。
- **C**　食物の中の酸が多過ぎることである。
- **D**　台所の衛生状態の悪さである。

解答	11 ▸ NO	12 ▸ YES	13 ▸ YES

▶ 解 説

特定する問題

11　段落3の最終文にあるreduce the risk of contaminationを参考にする。

12　問題文のless popular in citiesから、段落7の中盤、their use is becoming less popular, particularly in urban areasへ。

13　段落8の最終文から解答を導こう。

▶ 問題文の訳

Questions 11-13　次の記述は、文章1の筆者の主張と一致するか。解答用紙の空欄11〜13に、次のように記入すること。

　　　記述が筆者の主張と一致する場合はYES
　　　記述が筆者の主張と相反する場合はNO
　　　それについての筆者の考えが不明な場合はNOT GIVEN

11　発酵食品は汚染とは無縁である。

12　伝統的な発酵食品は、都会ではどちらかというとあまり人気がない。

13　発酵食品の方が風味のよいことが多い。

▶ パッセージの訳

次の文章1に基づく設問1〜13には、約20分を費やす必要があります。

乳児のための発酵食品

離乳期――母乳だけでは（乳児の）成長に不十分になったときに半固形の食品に置き換え始める時期――における栄養失調は、世界に数多く存在する貧しい地域の家庭の子どもに蔓延している。栄養失調につながるさまざまな要因が考えられるが、直接的な原因は、子どもの成長と発達にとって不十分な食事、および主に汚染された食物の摂取を原因とする下痢などの再発性感染症であることがわかっている。その結果、多くの幼い子どもたち、特に6か月から2歳までの乳児は、体重の減少や成長と発達の阻害に悩まされている。

食品は、たいてい食物、調理器具、水、そして調理者の手についている病原体によって汚染される。冷蔵装置がないために食品を高い外気温で保管しなければならないと、問題はさらに深刻になる。離乳食の場合、母親が仕事で忙しく、食物、水、燃料が日常的に不足していると、その日の毎回の食事に新鮮な食品を用意できない可能性がある。

さまざまな国々の昔ながらの調理方法を対象にした研究は、そうした問題に対して安価で実用的な解決策を教えてくれる。それ

は、誰にもなじみがあり、それぞれの土地に固有で、文化的にも受け入れやすい家庭での食品加工法に基づいている。浮かび上がった重要な解決策の1つは、穀物の発酵である。それは、多くの家庭において、食物の調理と保管には適さない現在の条件下でも、汚染のリスクを下げてくれることが証明されている。

この方法は、世界の多くの地域における伝統的な食品の保存法だったもので、古代から利用されてきた。発酵食品が持つ抗菌性と比較的高い安全性は、1900年代初頭から記録されており、数多くの研究でも示されてきた。よく知られた発酵食品の例としては、醤油、テンペ（インドネシア）、ある種のチーズ、キムチ（韓国）、みそ（日本）、ザワークラウト（ドイツ）、そして酢などがある。アフリカのガーナなどでは、トウモロコシの生地を粥として調理する前に発酵させるのが普通である。ケニアでは、主に穀物からなる粥とミルクが昔から発酵されてきた。ミルクをヨーグルトの形で保存することは、暑い気候の中で暮らす多くの家庭に知られている。

発酵の作用が食物の汚染の防止や低減につながる基本的な仕組みは何だろうか。考えられる答えは、発酵中に食品の酸性度が高まることのようである。これは、下痢の原因となる細菌が、発酵食品の中では未発酵食品の中ほど急速に増殖できない理由を説明している。また、発酵中に生成される抗菌物質の作用により、食品に存在する細菌の一部が死滅するか、増殖がくい止められるという仮説も立てられている。したがって、発酵食品は生鮮食品に比べて長期間保存することができる。調理済みの未発酵食品の汚染レベルは保存期間が延びるとともに増加するが、発酵食品は汚染が少ないままであることが示されている。

基本的な仕組みがどうであれ、確かなことは、発酵作用が時間と金銭の両方の点で家庭の負担を増やすことなく食品の汚染を減らしてくれるということである。その調理方法は簡単である。穀物の粉を水と混ぜて生地を作り、あとは発酵させればよい。場合によっては、酵母を加えたり、以前に発酵させた生地のごく一部を混ぜたりすることが必要となる。その後で、生地を粥に調理して子どもに与えればよい。

有益ではあるものの、残念ながらこの方法は時代遅れになりつつある。ケニアの乳児に与えられる発酵食品に関する研究では、食物は今でも子どもに食べさせるために家庭で発酵されることが多いものの、市販の製品がより入手しやすい都市部では特に、それがあまり行われなくなっていることが示された。もちろん、市販製品は大量の宣伝が行われているが、そうした製品が結果的に子どもの成長にとって優れていることを示す証拠は一般的にほとんど存在せず、本当に不十分な衛生状態では、その危険性は明らかである。

そして、食品の安全性の向上とは別に、今では発酵食品には、ほかにも幅広い利点があることがわかっている。砂糖とデンプンの変換は、食品中の自然で有益なバクテリアを増加させる。プロバイオティクスまたは「善玉菌」として知られるそうしたバクテリアは、さまざまな健康問題、特に消化器系の健康を改善すると考えられている。発酵食品はまた、消化しやすい。例えば、発酵はミルクに含まれる乳糖をより単純な糖（ブドウ糖とガラクトース）に分解する。これは、あなたが乳糖不耐症であれば、ヨーグルトやチーズなどの製品を消化しやすくしてくれる可能性がある。発酵はまた、私たちの体が吸収できるビタミンとミネラルの量を増やしてくれるだけでなく、腸内の善玉菌がビタミンB群を生成し、ビタミンKを合成するのを助けてくれる。あなたの免疫システムは、より強固なものになる。最後に、発酵食品は、元のままでは不快な風味をしばしば取り除いてくれるので、食欲を増進させると報告されている。

明らかに、発酵食品は今こそ貧しい国々で普及させる必要があり、先進国でもより望ましい栄養を提供してくれる可能性がある。

解答

14 ▸ centuries   15 ▸ longest period   16 ▸ Malaysia
17 ▸ technological advancements / technological revolution
    / new inventions
18 ▸ public spaces   19 ▸ radical change

▸ 解説

文を完成させる問題

14 問題文のsixやchurches or cathedralsから段落1へ。数字はパラフレーズされにくいので重要なキーワードとなる。

15 問題文のEmpire State Buildingと20th centuryから段落3へ。当段落の2文目が問題文と一致。

16 空欄前を読み、国名を入れる問題だと事前にリサーチしておこう。段落3の中盤のMalaysia was the first country to break the United States' recordを解答の根拠にする。

17 答えの根拠となる箇所がパッセージ中に複数箇所ある珍しい問題。段落4の中盤にある、exploit the technological advancements which made tall buildings possibleか、段落6の1文目にある The American technological revolution of ... a wave of new inventions that helped architects to build higher than ever beforeから解く。

18 Early office towersの特徴を述べているのは段落8。当段落の最初にEarly office towers ... didn't provide any public spacesとある。

19 zigguratから段落9へ。終盤のThis was a radical change in the shape of tall buildings, and the second generation of skyscrapers. と問題文が一致する。

▸ 問題文の訳

Questions 14-19   次の文を完成させなさい。それぞれの答えとして、文章2から1つまたは2つの単語を選ぶこと。解答用紙の空欄14〜19に解答を記入すること。

14 およそ6 __世紀__ の間、最も高い建物は教会か大聖堂だった。

15 エンパイア・ステート・ビルディングは、20世紀に __最も長期間__ 、世界一高い建物という記録を保っていた。

16 現代において、アメリカ以外で最も高い建築物を最初に建てた国は __マレーシア__ だった。

17 企業は、 __技術の進歩__ によって中心街に大きなオフィスを建設し始めることができた。

18 初期の高層オフィスビルには __共用スペース__ がなかった。

19 ジッグラトのスタイルは、以前のデザインからの __根本的な変化__ だった。

解答

20 ▸ FALSE   21 ▸ TRUE   22 ▸ TRUE   23 ▸ NOT GIVEN
24 ▸ FALSE   25 ▸ NOT GIVEN   26 ▸ FALSE

▸ 解説

特定する問題

20〜26の文の中に、年代や都市名などパラフレーズされにくい語が多く、これらはキーワードとして重要である。キーワードを探してパッセージをスキャニングしよう。

20 「特定する問題」にall, none, alwaysなど断定形の語がある場合は、本当に断定できるのか注意するべき。1880s, insurance companiesを手掛かりに段落4の中盤のThe booming insurance businesses of the mid-19th century were among the first enterprisesへ。firstとallは明確に違うのでFALSEを選ぶ。

21 1884や12から段落4の最終文へ。the first tall buildingは「それ以前にその高さのビルはなかったこと」を意味し、問題文のThe tallest buildingとのパラフレーズになっている。

22 1896から段落5の1文目にすぐ行き着くはず。2、3文目は1文目をサポートする詳細を述べており、解答の根拠は、最終文のThis specification still largely applies today.まで出てこないので注意しよう。

23 段落 6 に技術革命が 3 つ列挙されているが、エレベーターが「主な理由」とは言及されていない。

24 housing に触れているのは段落 7 の後半。前半では、初期の高層ビルはオフィス利用されていたことが述べられているが、On the other hand 以降は、対比的な内容（住宅街は低層のまま）がきている。

25 Hong Kong から段落 7 の最終文へ。住居の例として挙げられているだけで、最も高いオフィスビルの建設でニューヨークと競争したという記述はないので NOT GIVEN が正解。

26 1915 から段落 9 の最初の文へ。高さを制限したのではなく階段状の間口を設定したので、問題文とパッセージの内容が相反する。よって FALSE が正解。

▶ 問題文の訳

Questions 20-26 次の記述は、文章 2 で述べられている情報と一致するか。解答用紙の空欄 20〜26 に、次のように記入すること。

　　　記述が情報と一致する場合は TRUE
　　　記述が情報と相反する場合は FALSE
　　　記述に関する情報がない場合は NOT GIVEN

20 1880 年代、最も高い建物は、みな保険会社によって建てられた。

21 1884 年に最も高かった建物は、12 階建てだった。

22 高層ビルの基本的な考え方は、1896 年から変わっていない。

23 より高い建物を建て始めることができた主な理由は、エレベーターの発明だった。

24 住宅用の高層ビルには早い時期から大きな需要があった。

25 香港は、最も高いオフィスビルの建設でニューヨークと競争した。

26 ニューヨークは、通りが暗くなるという理由で 1915 年に建物の高さを制限した。

▶ パッセージの訳

次の文章 2 に基づく設問 14〜26 には、約 20 分を費やす必要があります。

高層ビル小史：現代における高層ビルの誕生

伝説上のバベルの塔から有名なブルジュ・ハリファまで、人間は常により高い建物を建設することに情熱を注いできた。歴史を振り返ると、高い建物はしばしば、宗教によって信仰心を高めるために建てられており、14 世紀初頭からおよそ 6 世紀にわたって世界で最も高い建物は常に教会か大聖堂だった。高さ 160 メートルのリンカーン大聖堂は 1311 年に完成したが、その尖塔は 1549 年に崩落した。その後、1890 年に完成したウルム大聖堂まで、ヨーロッパのさまざまな教会や大聖堂がずっと記録を保持していた。

しかし、そうした壮大な歴史的偉業は、20 世紀と 21 世紀の高層ビルによって影が薄くなっている。今日の最も高い建物の最上階から外を眺めると、都市は街路や高層ビルが密集した塊として、おもちゃの模型のように眼下に広がっている。

20 世紀のほぼ全期間、世界で最も高い建物は常にアメリカにあった。ニューヨークの有名なエンパイア・ステート・ビルディングは 380 メートルの高さで、1931 年からおよそ 40 年間、最も長くその記録を保ったが、昨今の変化の速さを考慮すると、今後それほど長期間にわたり記録を保持する建物は現れないだろう。1998 年、その名誉は東半球に移り、ペトロナス・ツインタワー（452 メートル）が完成すると、世界で最も高い建物を建設したというアメリカの記録をマレーシアが初めて破ることになった。次に台湾の台北 101（509 メートル）が 2004 年からその記録を持った建物となり、その後ブルジュ・ハリファ（828 メートル）が 2010 年にその地位を引き継いだ。

では、どのようにして、この飛躍的な高層化が実現したのだろうか。その答えは、1880 年代、シカゴとニューヨークに第一世代の高層ビルが出現した時にさかのぼることができる。19 世紀半ばに急成長した保険業界は、高層ビルの建設を可能にした技術の進歩を利用した最初の企業群だった。1871 年の大火の直後に建設されたシカゴのホーム・インシュアランス・ビルは、1884 年末にウィリアム・ル・バロン・ジェニーによって竣工したが、12 階建てで、工業化時代における最初の高層ビルだと一般に見なされている。

建築家のルイス・サリバンとダンクマー・アドラーは、1896 年に初めて「高層オフィスビル」という用語を作り出した。彼らの定義によると、最初の 2 つの階が入り口と店舗に割り当てられ、その下には供給施設用の地階、その上に数階のフロア、最上

部には屋根裏の階があることになっていた。いくつかの垂直ダクトによって、建物全体に電力と熱、空気の循環がもたらされる。このような仕様は今日でも広く採用されている。

1880年から1890年にかけてのアメリカの技術革命は、建築家にかつてないほど高い建物を建築することを可能にする新たな工夫を相次いでもたらした。例えば、新型の圧延装置でＩ字型の断面に形成されたベッセマー鋼は、従来の鋳鉄よりも背が高く、より柔軟なフレーム設計を可能にした。また、新たに特許を取得したスプリンクラーヘッドのおかげで、建物は、火災時のリスクを軽減するために課されていた厳格な23メートルの高さ制限を回避することができた。さらに、交流電源の特許取得により、エレベーターを電力で動かして10階以上に引き上げることができるようになった。

初期の高層ビルにはオフィスが入っていた。タイプライター、電話、全米一律の郵便制度もこの10年間に登場し、この新しいテクノロジーは事務作業に革命をもたらし、管理機能を市内のビジネス街にある単独の高層ビルに集中させることができるようになった。その一方、パリ、ロンドン、マンハッタンなど、自動車が登場する前の時代からある密集した都市の住宅街は大半が低層の長屋式住宅のままで、よく知られた例外といえばニューヨークのセントラルパーク周辺のいくつかの高層マンションや超過密な香港の9階建ての建物などだけだった。

初期の高層オフィスビルは街区全体を占有し、建物は大きな窓と通気口を持ち、角ばったＵやＯ、またはＨの形をしていた。このことによって、建物内部に自然光と外気が取り入れられたが、共用スペースは用意されていなかった。また、外観はあまり変化を持たせられなかった。シカゴは1893年に40メートルの高さ制限を設けたが、ニューヨークは大きな高層ビルで先行した。

その結果、1915年にブロードウェイに40階建てのエクイタブルビルが完成すると、街路が暗くなることを恐れたニューヨーク市は「ゾーニング法」を導入した。これは、街路への日照を確保するために、新築のビルに階段状の間口を設けることを義務づけるものだった。この「ジッグラト（古代メソポタミアの神殿のようなピラミッド型の建築）」のデザインでは、基礎部分は街区を占めるものの、ビルが上へ伸びていくにつれて数階ごとに間口を後退させることを意味した。これは高層ビルの形状の根本的な変化で、高層ビルの第二世代となった。ジッグラトのスタイルは、当時流行したアールデコ運動の建築における最もはっきりとした象徴となった。

しかしながら、1920年代後半になると、利益優先の高層ビル開発ブームは歯止めがかからなくなり、クライスラー・ビルディングとエンパイア・ステート・ビルディングの完成で1931年に最高潮に達した。オフィスビルの供給過剰、1930年代の不況、そして第二次世界大戦は、アールデコのブームに終止符を打った。次に高層ビルが登場するのは1950年代になってからのことで、戦後の時代は（高層ビルの）第三世代をもたらした。それは「インターナショナル・スタイル」と呼ばれるもので、現在、世界各地の数多くの都市で見られるような、暗いガラスと鉄骨の枠で囲まれた箱型の建物で、空調設備があり、建物の前面を後退させたところに広場が設けられている。そうしたビルの外観は、1970年代に入っても、しばらくはほとんど長方形のままだった。

READING PASSAGE 3　　　　　　　本冊P.200

解答			
27 ▸ 38[thirty(-)eight]	**28** ▸ environmental changes	**29** ▸ Robusta
30 ▸ geographic ranges	**31** ▸ store	**32** ▸ conservation
33 ▸ communities		

▸ **解説**

メモを完成させる問題
27 段落Bの2文目と一致。[パラフレーズ] have fertile pollen transfer ⇄ interbreed
28 段落Bの最終文と一致。長い文だが、asの節は挿入であり、ここを精読しなくても答えは導ける。
29 問題文の中のキーワードであるcoffee leaf rustから段落C, Dへ。段落Dの1文目から答えを導く。
　　　[パラフレーズ] are resistant ⇄ is not very affected
30 Threats to coffee speciesのタイトルを読み、One threat ...から始まる段落C以降を追う。段落C, Dは、メモで言うとClimate change + diseasesに該当し、30の解答根拠は、段落Eの2文目までいかないと出てこない。

31 段落Gの2文目 don't store well と、メモの are difficult to store がパラフレーズになっている。メモの Threats to coffee species の箇条書きのうち、最初の4行は段落C～Eの内容で、本問だけ離れているので注意しよう。

32 メモの3つ目のタイトル（The future）と、メモ内の botanical gardens から段落Hへ。当段落の最終文にある species where they grow が完全にメモと一致するので探しやすい。

33 段落Hの最終文。work with がパラフレーズされておらず、解きやすい問題。

▶ 問題文の訳

Questions 27-33 次のメモを完成させなさい。それぞれの答えとして、文章3から2つ以下の単語か1つの数字を選ぶこと。解答用紙の空欄27～33に解答を記入すること。

コーヒー

コーヒー種
- 4つの主要品種と、ほかの **27** _____ 38 _____ は、自然に交配することが多い
- 多様性は、コーヒーを **28** 環境の変化 から守るために重要である
- **29** ロブスタ種 は「コーヒー葉さび病」の影響をあまり受けない

コーヒー種への脅威
- 気候変動＋病気
- 多くの種は、特定の狭い **30** 地理的範囲 にのみ自生する
- 土地活用をめぐる争い
- 木材や薪のための過剰伐採
- コーヒー豆は **31** 保管する のが難しい

未来
- 植物園ではコーヒーの品種を簡単に保存することはできない
- コーヒーがどこで成長するにしても品種の **32** 保護区域 がなければならない
- 現地の **33** 地域社会 と協力する必要がある
- 遺伝的多様性は、持続可能なコーヒー生産の尺度の1つであるべきだ

---

 34 ▶ C　35 ▶ H　36 ▶ A　37 ▶ F

▶ 解説

情報を組み合わせる問題

34 段落Cのトピックセンテンス（1文目）で判断できる。文中の climate change, affect（effectの動詞形）に注目。

35 Kew Royal Botanic Gardens を読んで反射的にEを選ばないように。recommendation, Kew Royal Botanic Gardens の2つをキーに、ガーデンが主張、示唆している段落Hを選ぶ。当段落の the Kew Gardens study argues の argue（主張する）が決め手になる。

36 段落Aで、コーヒー種が列挙・比較されている。

37 問題文の species, re-surfaced がキーワード。段落Fの最初の文だけではなく2文目も読まないと答えに確信が持てないが、このように細部の情報をマッチングさせることもある。

▶ 問題文の訳

Questions 34-37 文章3には、A～Iの9つの段落がある。次の情報が含まれている段落はどれか。解答用紙の空欄34～37に、正解となる文字A～Iを記入すること。

34 気候変動の影響の一例

35 キュー王立植物園からの提言

36 比較的よく知られているコーヒー種の比較

37 再び姿を現したコーヒー種

Test-1

解答	38 ▸ B	39 ▸ D	40 ▸ D

▶ 解説

複数の選択肢から選ぶ問題

38 Bが、段落Aの中盤にあるRobusta is sometimes openly mixed with Arabica ... to reduce costs. と一致する。

39 問題文のCrossing different varieties of coffeeが段落Bの3文目にあるinterbreedにつながる。選択肢Dのadaptable to changeが、段落B最後のadaptable to environmental changesにパラフレーズされている。

40 段落Cのスキャニングで解こう。選択肢のA〜Cは、当段落内で言及されている。

    A = becoming entrenched globally

    B = the early 20th century ... by the turn of the millennium

    C = over 1.7m lost jobs and US$3.2 billion in damage and lost income

    Dは、段落Dの1文目にあるRobusta varieties, which are resistant to leaf rustと矛盾する。

▶ 問題文の訳

Questions 38-40　　正解となるA, B, CまたはDの文字を選びなさい。解答用紙の空欄38〜40に正解となる文字を記入すること。

38 ロブスタ種がアラビカ種と混合されるのは

  A　アラビカ種の品質を高めるため。

  B　コストを節約するため。

  C　新しいコーヒー製品を生産するため。

  D　異なる風味を生み出すため。

39 コーヒーのさまざまな品種の交配は

  A　病気になりやすい新しい品種を生み出す。

  B　コーヒー葉さび病の発生につながった。

  C　気温と降雨量に依存する。

  D　変化に適応できる、より優れた種を生み出す。

40 コーヒー葉さび病について、正しくないものはどれか。

  A　コーヒーが栽培されているすべての主要地域に影響を及ぼした。

  B　約1世紀の間、存在している。

  C　栽培者の収入に影響を与えた。

  D　すべてのコーヒー種に同程度の影響を及ぼした。

▶ パッセージの訳

次の文章3に基づく設問27〜40には、約20分を費やす必要があります。

コーヒー：野生種の60パーセントが気候変動により絶滅の危機に瀕している

A　あなたはどのようなコーヒーを飲んでいるだろうか。それが高品質のものならば、ほぼ間違いなく、風味のよさで知られるアラビカ種（アラビアコーヒーノキ）の豆から作られている。その例としては、ジャワコーヒー、エチオピアのシダモ、高価なジャマイカのブルーマウンテンなどがある。インスタントブレンドが好みならば、それはおそらく別の種、味はより苦いが価格が安いことで知られているロブスタ種（ロブスタコーヒーノキ）の豆だろう。ロブスタ種は、市販の商品ではアラビカ種と混合されていると明記されることもあるが、コストを抑えるために「100パーセントアラビカ種」と謳った商品にこっそりと混ぜられることもよくある。3番目の種であるリベリカコーヒーノキは、西アフリカと中央アフリカの原産で、熱帯にある国々で地元での消費用として広く栽培されているが、味が比較的苦いため、世界的に取引されてはいない。4番目の種であるユーゲニオイデスコーヒーノキは、当初はロブスタ種と交配され、その結果として交配種であるアラビカ種が生まれた。

B　野生には、実に100種類以上のコーヒーノキがある。上に述べた4種類とは別に、38の類縁種が商用の品種と授粉により

交配することが知られ、もしくは推測されている。さらに、商用の品種と遠縁に当たるものが82種あるが、科学者は実験室でそれらを商用のコーヒー種と交配することができる。さまざまなコーヒーの種の存在が重要なのは、それらがコーヒーを守ることに役立ってくれる可能性があるからである。というのも、そうしたすべての品種が商用のコーヒー種の遺伝的多様性を広げるのに役立ち、環境の変化に対する適応力を高めてくれるからである。

C　1つの脅威は気候変動から生じているが、それは気温と降雨パターンの変化が植物の成長に影響を与え、コーヒーの収穫量を危機に陥れるからである。気候の変動はまた、植物を病気によりかかりやすくしている可能性がある。すべての主要な商用コーヒー生産国は「コーヒー葉さび病」の影響を大きく受けたことがあり、それは20世紀初頭にアフリカ全土からアジアへ、そして南アメリカに広がり、千年紀の変わり目には全世界に定着するようになった。中央アメリカで2011年から2012年の収穫期にかけて始まったコーヒー葉さび病の大流行は、この地域の農場の70パーセントに影響を及ぼし、170万人以上の雇用の喪失と32億米ドル相当の被害と収入の減少をもたらした。

D　異種交配がどのように役立つかの一例として、葉さび病に耐性のあるロブスタ種は、アラビカ種の耐性を強める上での鍵となってきた。しかし、気候変動と病気のリスクが高まるとともに、ほかの脅威や課題にも直面する中で、野生のコーヒー種が世界のコーヒー供給を維持する上で重要な資源となっている。アラビカ種は、生育に適した土地の範囲が著しく限られており、ロブスタ種は葉さび病以外の病気に対して脆弱だからである。

E　イギリスのキュー王立植物園が主導した最近の研究は、コーヒー種の60パーセント以上が絶滅の危機に瀕しているという文脈の中で、この品種の価値を評価した。コーヒー種は、エチオピア高原の特定の標高に自生する野生のアラビカ種の個体群などのように、特定の地理的範囲で少量だけ生育するため、特に絶滅の危機にさらされやすい。野生のコーヒー種、そして商用種の野生種は、土地の活用をめぐる争いと、木材や薪のためにコーヒーノキが過剰に伐採されることにより、ほとんどすべてが減少している。野生のコーヒーの類縁種の多くは数十年もの間にわたって発見されておらず、絶滅している可能性がある。

F　インド洋に浮かぶ離島、ロドリゲス島のカフェ・マロンは、1877年に一度だけ確認されてその存在が知られていた。1世紀後、ある男子学生が野外観察中に「珍しい」木をスケッチし、それを教師に見せたところ、それは生き残っていたカフェ・マロンであることが確認された。唯一生き残ったこの野生のコーヒー種の実例は、ロドリゲス島の森林をより広範囲に保護しようという機運を生んだ。この種は、キュー植物園の研究室でも培養されている。

G　残念なことに、ほかの種についてはあまり希望が持てないかもしれない。コーヒーの種子は、小麦やトウモロコシなどのほかの作物の野生種とは異なり、あまり保存がきかないのである。そのため、コーヒーの多様性と回復力を維持しようとしても種子バンクでの保管に頼ることはできない。実験室で植物を凍結したり、試験管でサンプルを育てたりすることも1つの選択肢かもしれないが、既存の商用品種以外では研究されてこなかった。

H　植物園でさまざまなコーヒー種を保存することも、遺伝的多様性を守る上であまり現実的な解決策ではない。コーヒー種は互いに容易に授粉し合い、保存しようとしている資源を「汚染」してしまうからである。一部の専門家は、コーヒーの多様性を集団ごとに維持することを提案しているが、キュー植物園の研究では、コーヒー種の持続可能性は、これらの種を自生地に保護区域を設けて保存することと、それらが分布するアフリカとアジアの地域社会との協力にかかっていると主張している。

I　遺伝的多様性の保全は、「フェアトレード」や「レインフォレスト・アライアンス認証」など、持続可能なコーヒー生産に向けた既存の取り組みの中に含める必要がある。コーヒー取引の継続性を確保することは、コーヒーが生み出される生態系と、コーヒー豆からコーヒーカップの生産に至るまで、関係者の生計を守ることを意味する。（そうすることで）私たちはまた、新しい風味や、最初からカフェインが少ない、あるいはまったく含まないコーヒーも期待できる。

LISTENING

PART 1

本冊P.204 / track 27

解答	
1 ▸ Finley **2** ▸ 53[fifty(-)three] **3** ▸ RICH113978MW	
4 ▸ 10:30[ten thirty] (am / a.m.)	
5 ▸ 7(th) November / November 7(th) / 7th of November	
6 ▸ airport	

▸ **解説**

フォームを完成させる問題

4 9 am, 10と、ディストラクターが2つもあるので注意しよう。

5 Friday ... which is the 8th I believeがディストラクター。NovemberはNov / Nov. と書いてもよい。

▸ **問題文の訳**

Questions 1-6 それぞれの答えとして、3つ以下の単語か1つの数字、もしくはその両方を使って以下の予約用紙を完成させなさい。

グレン・レンタカー：ドライバー情報

姓：**1**　　フィンリー　　　　　　　名前：リチャード

年齢：**2**　　　53

国籍：イギリス

免許番号：**3** RICH113978MW

引き取り

日付：11月3日

時間：**4**　（午前）10時30分

場所：市内の営業所

返却

日付：**5**　　11月7日

時間：午後5時

場所：**6**　　空港

解答	
7 ▸ hatchback **8** ▸ automatic **9** ▸ Freedom (Plan)	
10 ▸ 5.5%[percent]	

▸ **解説**

メモを完成させる問題

7 まずは店員の発言、We have four types of car available to rent. We have small hatchbacks, four-door sedans, station wagons, and four-wheel drives. を落とさずに聞き、その中で客が何を選ぶか、解答を絞っていこう。

10 先に6.5%が出てくるが、飛びつかないように。

▸ **問題文の訳**

Questions 7-10 以下のメモを完成させなさい。それぞれの答えとして、2つ以下の単語か1つの数字、もしくはその両方を記入すること。

		オプション	
車の種類：	**7**	ハッチバック	
変速装置：	**8**	オートマチック	
追加装備：	−		
料金プラン：	**9**	フリーダム（・プラン）	
税金：	**10**	5.5 パーセント	

▶ スクリプトと訳

Part 1

You will hear a telephone conversation involving a man renting a car. First, you have some time to look at Questions 1 to 6.

Now listen carefully and answer Questions 1 to 6.

A = Alana 🇦🇺   R = Richard 🇬🇧

A Good morning, Glen Rent-a-Car. How can I help you?

R Good morning, I'd like to rent a car for next week, please.

A Certainly, Sir. I'll need to ask you a few questions first. Can I have your name?

R It's Richard **Finley**. That's **F-I-N-L-E-Y**.

A OK, Mr Richard **Finley**. And your age?

R Oh, yes. I'm ₂**53**.

A You're not Australian, are you?

R No, I'm British.

A Do you have an international driver's license? You'll need one if you want to drive in Australia.

R Yes, I do.

A Can you tell me the license number, please?

R Yes, just a moment … Umm … let me see. Ah yes, here it is. The number is ₃**RICH113978MW**.

A ₃**RICH113978MW**. Thank you. Now, you said you want the car for next week. When did you want to pick it up exactly?

R Umm … well, I want to pick it up on Monday …

A OK, next Monday, that's the 3rd of November. Would you like to pick it up first thing in the morning at 9 am?

R Umm … can we make it later? I have an appointment at that time. Better make it 10. No … let's say ₄**10:30**. Just to be safe.

A OK, would you like to pick up the car from our airport office or our city office?

パート1

レンタカーを借りようとしている男性が電話で会話をしているのが聞こえてきます。最初に、設問1～6を見る時間があります。では、音声を注意深く聞いて、設問1～6に答えなさい。

A＝アラナ　R＝リチャード

おはようございます、グレン・レンタカーです。ご用件をお伺いいたします。

おはようございます。来週レンタカーを借りたいのですが。

かしこまりました、お客様。まず、いくつか質問をさせていただく必要があります。お客様のお名前をお教えいただけますか。

リチャード・フィンリーです。つづりはF-I-N-L-E-Yです。

はい、リチャード・フィンリー様。ご年齢は？

ああ、はい。53歳です。

お客様はオーストラリア人ではないのですね。

ええ、私はイギリス人です。

国際運転免許証はお持ちですか。オーストラリアで運転されたいのなら、それが必要です。

はい、持っています。

その免許番号を教えていただけますか。

はい、ちょっと待ってください…ええと…どれどれ。ああ、これだ。番号はRICH113978MWです。

RICH113978MWですね。ありがとうございました。では、お客様は来週、車が必要とおっしゃいました。具体的には、いつ車を取りに来られたいですか。

ええと…そうですね、月曜日に取りに行きたいのですが…。

はい、来週の月曜日というと11月3日ですね。朝一番で午前9時に取りに来られたいですか。

ええと…もう少し遅い時間にしてもらえますか。その時間に約束があるので。10時にした方がいいです。いや…10時30分にしましょう。念のために。

わかりました。その車は、空港にある当社の営業所、それとも市内の営業所で受け取りたいですか。

R	Well, I'll be in the city then, so I'll collect it from your city office.	ええと、私はその時間は市内にいるので、そちらの市内の営業所で引き取ります。
A	How long would you want to rent the car for?	車を借りたい期間はどれくらいですか。
R	I'd like to return it on the following Friday … which is the 8th I believe.	次の金曜日にお返ししたいと思います…それは8日のはずですが。
A	Actually, that Friday is the **5 7th of November**. Please drop it off before 5 pm as our office closes at that time.	実際には、その金曜日ですと11月7日ですね。車は午後5時までにお返しください。営業所はその時間に閉まりますので。
R	I'd prefer to return it to the **6 airport** if possible as we will be heading straight back to Britain that night.	その夜はイギリスにまっすぐ帰国する予定なので、車はできれば空港でお返ししたいと思います。
A	That's fine, Sir.	問題ありません、お客様。

Before you hear the rest of the conversation, you have some time to look at Questions 7 to 10. Now listen and answer Questions 7 to 10.

残りの会話を聞く前に、設問7〜10を見る時間があります。では音声を聞いて、設問7〜10に答えなさい。

A	Now, what kind of car would you prefer?	では、どのような種類の車をご希望ですか。
R	What are my choices?	どのようなものから選べますか。
A	We have four types of cars available to rent. We have small hatchbacks, four-door sedans, station wagons, and four-wheel drives.	レンタルできる車には4つの種類があります。小型のハッチバック、4ドアセダン、ステーションワゴン、そして四輪駆動車です。
R	Hmmm, it's only me and my wife … so maybe just the smallest car you have …	うーん、私と妻の2人だけなので…そちらにある一番小型の車で…。
A	So, how about a **7 hatchback**?	では、ハッチバックでよろしいですか。
R	Yes, that would be fine. Thank you.	はい、それで結構です。ありがとうございます。
A	Would you prefer automatic or manual transmission?	オートマチック車とマニュアル車のどちらがよろしいですか。
R	Well, my wife will also be driving so better make it an **8 automatic**.	ええと、私の妻も運転するので、オートマチックにした方がいいです。
A	OK, that's an automatic hatchback … Now would you like any extras, such as roof racks, a GPS navigator, or maybe a child seat?	はい、ではオートマチックのハッチバックですね…では、ルーフラック、GPSナビゲーター、チャイルドシートなどの追加装備は必要ですか。
R	Hmm … I don't think so.	ええと…いらないと思います。
A	And will you be travelling over a long distance? I'm asking because we have two pricing plans. One is the Freedom Plan which includes unlimited kilometres and the other is our Budget Plan which is limited to 500kms or less per week.	それから、長距離を移動しますか。というのは、2種類の料金プランがあるからです。1つは走行キロ数に制限のないフリーダム（無制限）・プランで、もう1つは1週間に500キロメートル以下に制限されているバジェット（低予算）・プランです。
R	Well, we will be travelling interstate, so we should take the **9 Freedom Plan**.	ええと、州間高速道路を走るつもりなので、フリーダム・プランにするべきでしょうね。
A	So, now I have to mention there are some additional costs. Firstly, there's a 6.5% tax.	では、ここで私はいくつかの追加費用があることをお伝えしなければなりません。まず、6.5パーセントの税金がかかります。
R	6.5%? Wow, that's a lot.	6.5パーセント？ わあ、それは高いですね。
A	Sorry, that's the old rate. It has gone down. Now you pay **10 5.5%** road tax.	失礼、それは以前の税率です。今は下がっています。現在は5.5パーセントの道路税を払うことになります。

R	Umm ... OK. I didn't know that. Let me talk to my wife before I make the final decision. I'll get back to you in 10 minutes.	うーん…わかりました。私はそれを知りませんでした。最終決定をする前に、妻と相談させてください。10分後にまたご連絡します。

That is the end of Part 1. You now have one minute to check your answers to Part 1.

これでパート1は終わりです。今から1分間パート1の解答を確認する時間があります。

PART 2
本冊P.206 ／ track 28

解答	11 ▶ tasting(s)	12 ▶ ethnic	13 ▶ accompanied	14 ▶ dogs
	15 ▶ rail	16 ▶ areas	17 ▶ Industry	

▶ 解説

表を完成させる問題

11 表に記述されている順序と音声の流れが一致しているので、The Festival will feature over 250 artisan coffee and gourmet food stalls. が聞こえたら、次に答えが流れると予想できる。

12 表の meet your favourite barista が、音声では visit your favourite barista になっていることに気づき、その後の音声を聞き逃さないようにしよう。

13 空欄前の be から、解答は形容詞、過去分詞、現在分詞あたりがくると判断できる。16がキーワード。

14 Unfortunately はネガティブな情報が続くサインなのでヒントになる。 パラフレーズ are ... allowed ⇄ permit

15 事前に空欄前後を見て、乗り物を表す名詞が入ると予想しておく。And how do you get there? を聞き取り、その後に集中しよう。

16 問題文の表現が、音声では Some of them are named after areas of London which are well-known ... に言い換えられている。famous と well-known の言い換えは基本で頻出。

17 the festival consists of two events を聞き逃さずに、その後に出てくるイベント名を聞き取ろう。

▶ 問題文の訳

Questions 11-17 以下の表を完成させなさい。それぞれの答えとして1つの単語か1つの数字、もしくはその両方を記入すること。

ロンドン・コーヒーフェスティバルの呼び物には何があるか。	ロンドンのコーヒー業界の祝典 コーヒーやグルメ料理の屋台 コーヒーの **11** ＿＿試飲＿＿ と国際的なバリスタによる実演 テーマごとのライブのショーや音楽
チケットには何の料金が含まれているか。	コーヒーの淹れ方の講習会 お気に入りのバリスタとの対面 市場での **12** ＿エスニック＿ 料理や屋台料理の食べ歩き
来場者への追加情報	16歳未満の子どもは **13** ＿付き添い＿ が必要 車椅子の利用が可能 **14** ＿＿犬＿＿ は中に入れない
開催日	4月2日から5日
アクセス方法	徒歩もしくは **15** ＿＿鉄道＿＿ かバスを利用

Test-1

109

場所	ロンドン、ブリックレーン15番地 フェスティバルの会場の中には、ロンドンの有名な **16** ＿＿＿**地区**＿＿＿ と同じ名前がついているものがある。
2種類の重要な催しは何か。	- **17** ＿＿**インダストリー**＿＿ ・デイズ：木曜日から金曜日（4月2日から3日）に開催。各種ワークショップ、セミナー、商品の試飲などを含む - 一般来場者向けの催し：金曜日の午後から日曜日に開催。無料の試飲会、屋台の食べ物、コーヒーを使ったカクテルなどを提供

解答 **18** ▶ 50[fifty] %[percent]　　**19** ▶ Kenya　　**20** ▶ fundraising

▶ 解説

制限内の語数で答える問題

18 fifty と fifteen を聞き分けられるか試している問題。-ty と -teen の聞き分けは頻出。

19 Project Waterfall は固有名詞なので、音声でもそのまま登場している。

　　 パラフレーズ was set up ⇄ was established

20 2017 がキーワードなので、その後を聞き逃さないように。

▶ 問題文の訳

Questions 18-20 以下の設問に答えなさい。それぞれの答えとして、2つ以下の単語か1つの数字、もしくはその両方を記入すること。

18 チケットの総売り上げのうち、どれくらいの金額が慈善団体に渡るか。

19 「プロジェクト・ウォーターフォール」は、どの国で設立されたか。

20 2017年に、ロンドン・コーヒーフェスティバルはチケット販売に加え、どのようにして資金を集めたか。

▶ スクリプトと訳 🇬🇧

Part 2
You will hear a talk about the London Coffee Festival. First, you have some time to look at Questions 11 to 17.
Now listen carefully and answer Questions 11 to 17.

パート2
ロンドン・コーヒーフェスティバルについての説明が聞こえてきます。最初に、設問11～17を見る時間があります。では音声を注意深く聞いて、設問11～17に答えなさい。

Good evening everyone. The London Coffee Festival returns for its 10th anniversary next month, and promises to be an unmissable event for discerning coffee lovers and those working with coffee.
So, the London Coffee Festival celebrates the bustling and vibrant coffee scene in that city. With over 30,000 coffee lovers and foodies, professional baristas, coffee shop owners and top decision-makers expected to attend, the London Coffee Festival promises to be an unmissable event for all coffee lovers and industry folk alike. The festival will feature over 250 artisan coffee and gourmet food stalls. There will also be **11** some coffee **tastings** as well as demonstrations by world-class baristas, with

皆さん、こんばんは。ロンドン・コーヒーフェスティバルは、来月の開催で10周年を迎え、舌の肥えたコーヒー愛好家やコーヒー業界で働く人たちにとって必見のイベントになることでしょう。
というわけで、ロンドン・コーヒーフェスティバルは、この街の賑やかで活気のあるコーヒー業界の成功を祝います。3万人を超えるコーヒー愛好家やコーヒー専門家、プロのバリスタ、コーヒーショップの経営者、トップリーダーたちの参加が見込まれるロンドン・コーヒーフェスティバルは、すべてのコーヒー愛好家と業界人のどちらにとっても、必見のイベントになることでしょう。このフェスティバルでは、250を超える職人のコーヒーとグルメ料理の屋台を大きな呼び物にしています。また、コーヒーの試飲会や世界トップクラスのバリスタによる実演が行われるほか、

live entertainment and music in the uniquely themed zones.

Purchase a ticket and you can also expect to learn about the various ways to make and brew coffee at home, to visit your favourite barista at the True Artisan Café, and to graze your way through ₁₂ the **ethnic** food and street food markets. You won't go home hungry, thirsty, or caffeine-free!

The London Coffee Festival is child-friendly, although ₁₃ we ask that any child under the age of 16 is **accompanied** by an adult. Arrangements will be made to ensure that all guests can access every section of the festival space. All staff and security will be briefed and ready to assist in any way we can. All event spaces are wheelchair accessible with a combination of ramps and lifts within the Old Truman Brewery. Unfortunately ₁₄ the venue does not permit **dogs** other than service dogs.

Now I'm sure you are all excited. Make sure you include this in your event reminder. The London Coffee Festival will be held from the 2nd to the 5th of April at the Old Truman Brewery, which is at 15 Brick Lane. And how do you get there? ₁₅ The Brewery is easily reached by **rail**, bus or on foot.

Let's talk about the 'festival zones'. ₁₆ Some of them are named after **areas** of London which are well-known, like Soho, Hyde Park and Shoreditch. However, all the fun will be taking place under one roof—so don't get lost!

Right, the festival consists of two events: ₁₇ **Industry Days**, from Thursday to Friday, 2nd to 3rd of April and general public celebrations from Friday afternoon to Sunday.

What does 'Industry Days' mean? Well, it is an exclusive programme which includes a series of workshops, seminars, product tastings and other industry specific experiences. The Lab area of the festival will also host numerous free, relevant seminars and workshops that will provide attendees with the latest market insight, innovative ideas and ready-to-implement training and vocational skills.

The second event consists of general public celebrations, from Friday afternoon to Sunday, with free tastings, street food, coffee-based cocktails, live music, DJs, art exhibitions and much more.

特別なテーマごとの会場でライブのショーや音楽も楽しめます。

チケットを購入すれば、ご家庭でコーヒーを淹れるさまざまな方法を学んだり、トゥルー・アーチザン・カフェ（本格職人のカフェ）でお気に入りのバリスタを訪れたり、エスニック料理や屋台料理の集まる市場で食べ歩きすることができます。帰る頃には、たっぷり食べ、たっぷり飲み、あるいはカフェインを十分に取っていることでしょう。

ロンドン・コーヒーフェスティバルは、お子様も入場できますが、16歳未満のお子様には大人の同伴が必要です。すべての来場者がフェスティバル内のどの部分でも利用できるように配慮されています。運営スタッフと保安員はみな、できる限りのサポートに当たるよう指示を受けています。すべてのイベント会場は車椅子で利用でき、オールド・トルーマン醸造所内にはスロープとエレベーターが備えられています。申し訳ありませんが、会場内には介助犬以外の犬は入ることが認められていません。

今、皆さんはきっと、わくわくしていることでしょう。あなたのスケジュール表にこれを入れておいてください。ロンドン・コーヒーフェスティバルは、4月2日から5日まで、ブリックレーン15番地にあるオールド・トルーマン醸造所で開催されます。では、どのようにしてそこまで行くのかですって？　この醸造所へは、鉄道、バス、徒歩で簡単にお越しいただけます。

「フェスティバル・ゾーン」についてご説明いたしましょう。そのいくつかは、ソーホー、ハイドパーク、ショーディッチといった、ロンドンの有名な地区にちなんで名づけられています。ただし、楽しいイベントはすべて1つの建物の中で行われるので、迷子にならないでください！

そう、このフェスティバルは2つの催しで構成されています。木曜日から金曜日、すなわち4月2日から3日までの「インダストリー・デイズ」と、金曜日の午後から日曜日までの一般来場者向けの催しです。

「インダストリー・デイズ」の意味ですか。ええ、これは、一連のワークショップ、セミナー、商品の試飲、そのほかこの業界特有のことがらを含む参加者限定のプログラムです。このフェスティバルの「ラボ」エリアでも、関連する多数の無料セミナーやワークショップが開催され、参加者に最新の市場分析、革新的なアイデア、そしてすぐに実践できるトレーニングや専門知識を提供します。

2つ目の期間は、金曜日の午後から日曜日までの一般来場者向けのいくつかの催しで構成され、それには無料の試飲会、屋台の食べ物、コーヒーを使ったカクテル、ライブ音楽、ディスクジョッキー、美術展などが含まれます。

Test-1

Before you hear the rest of the talk, you have some time to look at Questions 18 to 20.
Now listen and answer Questions 18 to 20.

There is one thing you need to know about where the money goes. **18** **Fifty percent** of all ticket sales for the London Coffee Festival will go towards Project Waterfall, the charitable component of the festival. The London Coffee Festival provides a unique opportunity for branded coffee chains, independent coffee shops and industry suppliers to collaborate and celebrate the success of the industry while giving back to an extremely worthy cause. **19** Project Waterfall was established in 2005 in **Kenya**, to provide clean water to coffee growing communities, and it has since spread to neighbouring countries like Uganda and Ethiopia.
The aim of Project Waterfall is to raise more than £1 million to deliver safe drinking water and sanitation projects for up to 100,000 people, specifically in coffee-producing countries in Africa. The latest project is currently providing clean water to communities in the Mbulu District of Tanzania in partnership with the service delivery provider, WaterAid. In 2017 **20** the London Coffee Festival raised as much as £280,000 towards this worthy cause through ticket sales, and through **fundraising** on site.
Right, for more information, visit: www.londoncoffeefest.com

That is the end of Part 2. You now have 30 seconds to check your answers to Part 2.

残りの説明を聞く前に、設問18〜20を見る時間があります。では音声を聞いて、設問18〜20に答えなさい。

収益金の用途について、お知らせしなければならないことが1つあります。ロンドン・コーヒーフェスティバルのチケット売り上げの50パーセントは、このフェスティバルの慈善部門である「プロジェクト・ウォーターフォール」に渡ります。ロンドン・コーヒーフェスティバルは、有名コーヒーチェーン、個人経営のコーヒーショップ、コーヒー関連業者がお互いに協力し、この業界の発展を祝う貴重な機会を提供するとともに、1つの非常に大きな価値を持つ理念に奉仕します。プロジェクト・ウォーターフォールは、コーヒーの栽培地に清潔な水を提供するために2005年にケニアで設立され、それ以来、ウガンダやエチオピアなどの近隣諸国に活動を広げています。

プロジェクト・ウォーターフォールの目標は、100万ポンド以上を集め、特にアフリカのコーヒー生産国において最大10万人の人たちに安全な飲料水と衛生事業を提供することです。最新の事業においては、現在、給水サービスの提供者である「ウォーターエイド」と協力してタンザニアのムブル地区の住民に清潔な水を供給しています。2017年には、ロンドン・コーヒーフェスティバルは、チケットの販売と会場での募金活動を通じて、この有意義な理念に向けて28万ポンドもの資金を集めました。

では、より詳しい情報は、www.londoncoffeefest.comをご覧ください。

これでパート2は終わりです。今から30秒間パート2の解答を確認する時間があります。

PART 3

本冊P.207 / track 29

解答	21 ▶ B	22 ▶ A	23 ▶ B	24 ▶ C

▶ 解説

複数の選択肢から選ぶ問題

21 選択肢Bのequipmentが、音声ではstuffに言い換えられている。
22 選択肢Aのlandscapeが、音声ではthe terrain, or how rough the physical features of the land areになっている。terrainをor以下で言い換えているように、難しい単語の後は易しい語句で説明が続くことも

ある。

23 パラフレーズ diversify your workouts ⇄ do a variety of exercises

24 選択肢Aのwater、選択肢Bのpillsも音声に登場して典型的なディストラクターとなっているので注意しよう。

▶ 問題文の訳

Questions 21-24 正解となるA, BまたはCのうち正解となる文字を選びなさい。

21 キリマンジャロに登るには、初心者は
  A ガイドが必要だ。
  B いまだに彼らの装備を運ぶ必要がある。
  C 6つの公式なルートのうち、どれを歩いてもいい。

22 ルートの難易度は、主に _____ によって決まる。
  A 地形
  B 天気
  C ルートの距離

23 特別なフィットネストレーニングについて、どのようなアドバイスがされたか。
  A 毎日運動する必要がある。
  B トレーニングの種類を増やすべきである。
  C 1か月以上運動をすべきである。

24 キリマンジャロに登るとき
  A 余分の水を運ぶ必要がある。
  B さまざまな薬を携行する必要がある。
  C 高山病にかかるかもしれない。

| 解答 | 25 ▸ rainforest | 26 ▸ valley | 27 ▸ sunset | 28 ▸ 7[seven] |
| | 29 ▸ desert | 30 ▸ darkness | | |

▶ 解説

メモを完成させる問題

25 空欄の前にaがあるので、単数名詞を入れればいい。メモのmost of the dayが、音声ではpretty much continuallyに言い換えられており、厳密に言えば意味は違うが、こういったパラフレーズもある。

26 空欄の前を見れば、空欄には名詞が入ると判断できる。メモでは、形容詞のsteepが解答のvalleyを前から修飾しているが、音声では、関係代名詞節のthat is really quite steepが後ろからa valleyを修飾している。

29 パラフレーズ resembles ⇄ looks like

30 inの後に地名がくるだろうと限定的に考えてしまわないように。in darkness（暗闇の中を）のほかに、in the rain（雨の中を）などの言い方もある。

▶ 問題文の訳

Questions 25-30 以下の旅程表を完成させなさい。それぞれの答えとして、1つの単語か1つの数字、またはその両方を記入すること。

```
┌─────────────────────────────────────────────┐
│           マチャメ・ルートの旅程表              │
│  第1日                                        │
│   ・キリマンジャロ国立公園の管理事務所からスタート。 │
│   ・1日のほとんどは 25  熱帯雨林  の中を登る。    │
└─────────────────────────────────────────────┘
```

第2日
- 川沿いを歩く。
- 傾斜の急な **26　谷** を登る。
- キャンプ・シラーで1泊する。

第3日
- 高度に慣れる必要がある。
- ラバタワーで昼食をとる。
- 大きな岩のある台地で1泊する。
- すばらしい **27　夕日** を見ることができる。

第4日
- 厳しい地形を乗り越えなければならない。
- **28　7** キロメートル歩く。

第5日
- この標高では、風景は **29　砂漠** に似ている。
- この地点からは、ほかの山々の頂がはっきり見える。

第6日
- **30　暗闇** の中を登る。
- 日の出を見るのに間に合うように頂上に到着。
- キャンプ・ムウェカで1泊する。

▶ スクリプトと訳

Part 3
You will hear a conversation about a student climbing trip to Mount Kilimanjaro. First, you have some time to look at Questions 21 to 24.
Now listen carefully and answer Questions 21 to 24.
J = Joe 　T=Tiffany

パート3
キリマンジャロ山に登山旅行をしようとしている学生の会話が聞こえてきます。最初に、設問21〜24を見る時間があります。では音声を注意深く聞いて、設問21〜24に答えなさい。
J＝ジョー　T＝ティファニー

J　Hi Tiffany, sorry I missed that meeting with Professor Albin about the Mount Kilimanjaro climbing trip. Can you please fill me in?

T　Sure, let me just get my notes out …

J　It's quite a big trip, so it's going to require a lot of planning and preparation, right?

T　Certainly. Well, there will be 10 students going, and we'll be accompanied by three experienced climbers …

J　That's reassuring.

T　Mount Kilimanjaro is the world's highest free-standing mountain, but it's not the most gruelling or dangerous mountain to climb. So

やあ、ティファニー。アルビン教授とのキリマンジャロの登山旅行についてのミーティングに出られなくてごめん。詳しく聞かせてくれる？
もちろん、ちょっとノートを出すね…。
かなり大掛かりな旅行だから、たくさんの計画と準備を必要とするよね。
その通り、10人の学生に、3人の経験豊富な登山家が付き添う予定だよ…。

面白そうだね。
キリマンジャロ山は世界で最も高い独立峰だけど、登るのが最も過酷で危険な山というわけではないの。だから、どうやら私たちは大半が初心者だけど、チームの経験豊

apparently, even though we are mostly beginners, the experienced climbers in the team can show us the way and we don't need to get a local guide.

J It's a bit surprising that beginners like me can climb Kilimanjaro.

T Yes, but ₂₁ the professor said you will still need to carry all of your own stuff, so you'll need to be physically fit. It also depends on the route you take. It seems there are six official routes, but the Lemosho Route is really the only one suitable for inexperienced climbers.

J Did he say what makes the route easier or more difficult?

T He said the weather could be an issue, but ₂₂ the most important factor is the terrain, or how rough the physical features of the land are. If you're climbing over rocks, then that's going to be more difficult than just walking up a slope. But Professor Albin did strongly recommend that you need to complete some special fitness training before going on a climb.

J I already exercise every day. Is one month training going to be enough do you think?

T Yes, the professor specifically said that one month should be enough, provided you're already quite fit. You'll only need to make a few adjustments to your regular routine.

J What are the adjustments?

T Let me just check my notes ... Well, the most important thing is ₂₃ to do a variety of exercises as there isn't just one exercise that will successfully prepare you for mountain climbing. Climbing takes a lot of overall strength and uses a wide range of muscle groups. The professor recommended we use the full range of equipment in a gym.

J OK, I'll definitely do that.

T There were a couple of other things ... Have you ever hiked at such a height above sea level before? ₂₄ Some people get sick the first time they try climbing at that height.

J Oh? Is that right? I'll take note of that. I've heard you can take some pills to help with that. And I was wondering about water. Will I have to take a supply of drinking water with me?

T Well, there are lots of natural springs on Kilimanjaro, so I doubt if that will be a problem.

富な登山家が教えてくれるから、地元のガイドを雇う必要はないね。

僕のような初心者がキリマンジャロに登れるなんてちょっと驚きだよ。

もちろん。だけど、教授はあなた自身で荷物を運ぶ必要があるって言ってたから、鍛える必要がありそうだね。登るルートにもよるけど。どうやら公式で6つのルートがあるみたいだけど、レモショー・ルートが経験の浅い登山者に唯一適しているんだね。

教授は、何がルートを簡単にするか難しくするか話してた?

教授は、天気が問題になりうるけど、一番重要な要因は、地形、つまり土地がいかにでこぼこしているかだと言っていたよ。もし岩を登るなら、ただ斜面を歩いて行くよりも難しいでしょ。でもアルビン教授は、登山前に、特別なフィットネストレーニングを終えておく必要があることを強く勧めていたよ。

僕はすでに毎日運動しているよ。1か月のトレーニングで十分だと思う?

うん、教授は、すでにかなり調子がいいなら1か月で十分だろうと言っていたよ。普段やっていることに、いくつか変更を加えるだけでいいよ。

変更というと?

ちょっとノートを確認させてね…。まず、一番重要なのは、さまざまな運動をすること。登山のよい準備となる運動は1つだけじゃないよ。山登りには総合的な体力が必要で、多くの筋肉群を使うの。教授は、ジムにあるすべての設備を使うべきだって勧めていたよ。

わかった、絶対にそうするよ。

いくつかほかにもあって… 今までにそんなに海抜の高いところでハイキングをしたことはある? 初めてそれくらいの高さで登山をしようとすると、病気になる人も出てくるよ。

へえ? そうなの? メモしとこうっと。それに効く薬があるって聞いたけど。それから、水についてなんだけど、飲み水を持参する必要はある?

そうね、キリマンジャロには天然の泉がたくさんあるから、それは問題にはならないと思う。

Before you listen to the rest of the conversation, you have some time to look at Questions 25 to 30.
Now listen and answer Questions 25 to 30.

残りの会話を聞く前に、設問25～30を見る時間があります。では音声を聞いて、設問25～30に答えなさい。

J Did the professor talk about the actual route we will take?

T Yes, he gave us a lot of information about that. Here, I've got a printout of the map and the itinerary that he gave us. The route is apparently called the Machame Route and it takes six days to get to the top. The map shows the daily itinerary. On Day 1, you start here, at the Kilimanjaro National Park office. You walk along a road, and then you start climbing. **25** You are in a **rainforest** pretty much continually until you arrive at Camp Machame.

J Sounds nice. I expect that the first part of the walk is fairly level and not very demanding.

T On Day 2, you leave the trees and pass alongside a river for quite a while, and then **26** you go through a **valley** that is really quite steep. After that, you cross over this terrific gorge just before you reach Camp Shira.

J I see it on the map. It seems already quite high at that point. It says 3,850 metres above sea level.

T Yes, and apparently you can feel it. On Day 3, you could start to feel the symptoms of high altitude sickness. The professor said it is vital to take it easy in order to acclimatize properly. On this day you climb slowly and have lunch at Lava Tower, and in the late afternoon you end up on a small plateau among some large rocks. **27** The **sunset** at this place is supposed to be really good.

J I can imagine. Let me see. Day 4 looks quite tough. The map shows rough terrain, so that must be tiring. But it looks like **28** you walk only about **seven** kilometres on Day 4, which doesn't seem far.

T Yes, the professor said it's not that far, but because it's hard going and it feels like twice the distance.

J And then, the next day, that's Day 5, it says here you ascend to 4,600 metres. The map says the environment up there is dry and sandy, so **29** it looks like a **desert**, although of course deserts are normally flat, whereas we will be on

教授は、僕たちが歩く実際のルートについて話してた？

うん、それについてはたくさんの情報をくれたよ。彼が私たちにくれた地図と旅程表のプリントアウトだよ。このルートはマチャメ・ルートと呼ばれるもので、頂上まで6日かかるの。この地図を見れば、日ごとの旅程がわかるよ。1日目はここ、キリマンジャロ国立公園の管理事務所からスタートするの。道なりに歩き、それから登りが始まるよ。キャンプ・マチャメに到着するまで、ほとんどずっと熱帯雨林の中だよ。

いいね。徒歩の最初の方はまずまず平坦で、さほどきつくないといいな。
2日目は、森林地帯を出て川沿いをかなり長い間歩くと、とても険しい谷を通るの。その後、キャンプ・シラーに到着する直前にこのすばらしい峡谷を渡るのよ。

地図にも書いてあるね。すると、もうここでかなり高い地点にいることになるね。海抜3850メートルとあるよ。

うん、それを感じられるよ。3日目には、高山病の症状を感じ始めるかもしれない。教授は、うまく順応するためには、無理をしないことが大切だと言っていたよ。この日はゆっくりと登り、ラバタワーで昼食をとって、午後遅くには大きな岩に囲まれた小さな台地に行き着くよ。この場所の夕日は、とてもすばらしいよ。

目に浮かぶようだ。えっと、4日目はかなり大変そうだね。地図によると、起伏の多い地形だから、疲れるだろうな。でも、4日目は7キロメートルくらいしか歩かないようだから、あまり遠くまで行かないようだね。

うん、教授は、そんなに遠くまで離れていないけど、進むのが大変だから、距離は2倍あるようにも感じると言ってたよ。
それから、次の日の5日目だけど、ここに4600メートル地点まで登ると書いてある。地図によると、そこの環境は乾燥していて砂地だから砂漠みたいだね。もちろん、砂漠は普通平地で、そこは急斜面だろうけど。

116

a steep incline.

T	I think that's right. There is a note here that says because it's above the tree line you get wonderful views of neighbouring peaks.	そうだね。ここのメモによると、森林限界線より上だから、すぐ近くの山々の頂のすばらしい景色を眺められるよ。
J	Here on the itinerary it mentions that, on Day 6, you wake up just after midnight. What is the meaning of that?	旅程のここには、6日目は真夜中過ぎに起きると書かれているね。これはどういうこと？
T	That's so you can get to the top by dawn as I understand it.	それは、私の知っているところでは、夜明けまでに頂上に着けるようにするためだよ。
J	₃₀ So you have to hike through **darkness**? Isn't that really dangerous?	ということは、暗闇の中を歩かなければならないの？とても危険じゃないの？
T	Well, you have to be careful, of course. This part is probably the most challenging part of the hike. But when you reach the summit, at nearly 6,000 metres, and see the sunrise, I'm sure it is more than worth it. After that you climb down to Camp Mweka and spend the night there.	ええ、もちろん注意する必要があるよ。この部分はたぶん、このハイキングの中で最も難所の部分じゃないかな。でも、6000メートル近い高さの頂上に着いて日の出を見たら、その苦労以上の価値があるよ。その後でキャンプ・ムウェカまで降りて、そこで1泊するの。

That is the end of Part 3. You now have 30 seconds to check your answers to Part 3.

これでパート3は終わりです。今から30秒間パート3の解答を確認する時間があります。

PART 4 本冊P.209／track 30

| 解答 | **31 ▸ crime**　　**32 ▸ equality**　　**33 ▸ half**　　**34 ▸ common good**
35 ▸ 2[two] years　　**36 ▸ public servants**　　**37 ▸ alone**
38 ▸ daily rush　　**39 ▸ indoors**　　**40 ▸ gardens** |

▸ 解 説

メモを完成させる問題

パート4では、途中にプレヴュータイムがないので難易度が上がる。最初にあるプレヴュータイムで問題文に目を通しておこう。

31 空欄から〈of + 名詞〉の形になると判断できる。メモの What makes Danish people happy? が音声では But what makes the Danish people so happy? に言い換えられているので、その後に集中する。

32 メモの The country has a high level of **32** equality と、音声の Denmark has a high level of equality が単純なパラフレーズになっている。

33 空欄の前後から量を表す語が入ると予想をつけておく。as much as ～ は「～もの」と、値や数字の大きさを強調する表現。 パラフレーズ as much as ⇄ up to

34 パラフレーズ support ⇄ contribute to

35 for almost の for は期間を表す前置詞なので、空欄には年月を表す数字が入ると判断する。 パラフレーズ jobless people ⇄ people who lose their jobs / almost ⇄ up to

36 Trust is an essential value ... が聞こえてきたら、Danes are happy to pay taxes から Trust and safety に話題が移ったと判断して集中しよう。メモの Honesty や government はパラフレーズされずに音声で流れるので、解答を特定するヒントになる。 パラフレーズ low levels of ⇄ is very rare

37 メモの Young children が、音声中では children as young as age 8 or 9 と、具体的な年齢にパラフレーズされている。このように問題文の抽象的な内容が、音声では具体的に言い換えられることも多い。

38 'Hygge' は一般的な言葉ではないので、メモでは 'Hygge' means ... と定義している。音声でも 'Hygge' を定

義づけしている箇所を聞き取ろう。

39, 40 メモの39, 40の空欄前後を読めば、winter, summerの対比になっているので、それぞれの季節における 'Hygge' の過ごし方を集中して聞き取ろう。

> パラフレーズ practised ⇄ experienced
>
> tendには「（動物・人・植物など）を世話する」という意味があり、それがメモのtake care ofにつながる。

▶ 問題文の訳

Questions 31-40 以下のメモを完成させなさい。それぞれの答えとして、2つ以下の単語か1つの数字、もしくはその両方を記入すること。

デンマーク：幸せの国

なぜデンマーク人は幸せだと感じているのか

- 教育と公的医療が無料であること。
- **31** <u>犯罪</u> の発生率が低いこと。
- 同国には高い水準の **32** <u>平等</u> と共同体意識があること。

デンマーク人は喜んで税金を払う

- 収入の **33** <u>半分</u> もが、税金として支払われる。
- 彼らは高い税金によって、子どもや高齢者、病人のための社会的セーフティーネットを確保する **34** <u>公共の利益</u> が支えられると思っている。
- 彼らは失業者を **35** <u>2年</u> 近く支援するために税金を払っている。ただし、その人たちは仕事を見つける努力をしなければならない。

信頼と治安

- 誠実さは重要である。彼らには安定した政府があり、**36** <u>公務員</u> や企業による不正は少ない。
- 治安がよい。小さな子どもも公共交通機関を利用して **37** <u>1人で</u> 移動することができる。

「ヒュッゲ」

- 「ヒュッゲ」とは、**38** <u>日々の慌ただしさ</u> から離れて生活を楽しむことを意味する。
- 「*Hygge*」の語は2017年にオックスフォード辞典に追加された。
- 冬の間、それは人々がボードゲームをしたりする **39** <u>屋内で</u> 行われる。
- 夏の「ヒュッゲ」は、小さな別荘で **40** <u>庭</u> の手入れをしたり、パーティーを開いたりして時間を過ごすことを意味する。

自己実現が幸せへの鍵

- 幸福と自己実現の間には深い関係がある。
- 人々は人生で望むことをする自由を与えられている。

▶ スクリプトと訳 🇬🇧

Part 4

You will hear a talk about one of the world's happiest countries. First, you have some time to look at Questions 31 to 40.

Now listen carefully and answer Questions 31 to 40.

パート4

世界で最も幸せな国の1つについての話が聞こえてきます。最初に、設問31〜40を見る時間があります。では音声を注意深く聞いて、設問31〜40に答えなさい。

Today we're going to look at what makes Danish people so happy. According to international

今日は、デンマーク人がとても幸せだと感じている理由を調べてみます。いくつかの国際的な調査では、その結果

surveys, the results usually rank Denmark among the world's happiest countries.

When international surveys ask citizens around the world how happy they are with their daily lives and personal circumstances, Denmark often comes in among the top three happiest countries in the world. But what makes the Danish people so happy? Is it the tuition-free access to high-quality education, or the free public health care? Or is it 31 the relative lack of **crime**?

According to the World Happiness Report, happiness is closely linked to equality and people's willingness to participate in activities that promote a community. Denmark scores highly on both. 32 Denmark has a high level of **equality** and a strong sense of common responsibility for social welfare. Even though there are nine major political parties in Denmark, none of them seriously supports dismantling the Danish welfare state.

33 People living in Denmark pay some of the world's highest taxes—up to **half** of their income. On top of this, they pay a 25% value-added tax on most items, and a tax of up to 150% on new cars.

But most Danish people will tell you that they are happy to pay taxes because they can see what they get in return. Most healthcare in Denmark is provided with no fee to the patient. University students pay no tuition and receive a grant to help cover expenses while studying. Childcare is subsidised. And the elderly receive pensions and are provided with carers who visit them at home.

34 Most of them also believe that it is everyone's responsibility to work if they can, and pay taxes to contribute to the **common good**. If everyone pays their fair share, a social safety net can remain in place to support the very young, the very old, and the sick. 35 The social safety net also supports people who lose their jobs for up to **two years** while they look for new jobs, although a system is in place to make sure they are actively looking for work.

Trust is an essential value in Danish culture and society, and a significant factor in Danish happiness. In Denmark, the default is to trust one another when it comes to business or personal relationships. Honesty is expected. 36 The government is stable and corruption in business or among **public servants** is very rare.

はたいていデンマークを世界で最も幸せな国の1つに位置付けています。

いくつかの国際的な調査で、世界中の人たちに対して日々の生活や個人的な境遇にどれくらい満足しているのかを尋ねると、デンマークはしばしば世界で最も幸せな国の上位3カ国に入っています。では、どうしてデンマーク人はそんなに幸せだと感じているのでしょうか。質の高い教育を無料で受けられることでしょうか、それとも無料の公的医療でしょうか。あるいは、犯罪がほかの国と比べて少ないことでしょうか。

「世界幸福度報告」によると、幸福は平等と、コミュニティーを育むための活動に参加しようという人々の意欲と密接に関連しています。デンマークはどちらでも高いスコアを獲得しています。デンマークには高い水準の平等があり、社会福祉に対して強い責任感を共有しています。デンマークには9つの主要な政党がありますが、デンマーク流の福祉制度を解体することを本気で表明している政党はありません。

デンマークに住む人たちは、世界で最も高いレベルの税金を払っており、それは最大で収入の半分にもなります。これに加え、彼らはほとんどの商品に25パーセントの付加価値税を払い、新車には最大で150パーセントの税金を払います。

ところが、ほとんどのデンマーク人は、自分たちが見返りに得られるものがわかっているので、喜んで税金を払っていると言うでしょう。デンマークのほとんどの医療は、患者に無料で提供されています。大学生は授業料を支払うことがなく、就学中の費用をまかなう助けとなる奨学金を受け取ります。育児にも補助金が出ます。そして高齢者は年金を受け取り、自宅を訪問してくれる介護人が用意されます。

彼らのほとんどはまた、働けるうちは働き、公共の利益に貢献するために税金を支払うことはすべての人の責任だと考えています。誰もが公平な分担をすれば、社会的なセーフティーネットを維持できて、若年層や高齢者、病気の人を支えることができます。この社会的なセーフティーネットはまた、仕事を失った人たちが新しい仕事を探している間、最長で2年間の支援をします。もちろん、失業者が積極的に仕事を探していることを確認するためのシステムも備わっています。

信頼ということがデンマークの文化と社会では必須の価値であり、デンマーク人の幸福度の重要な要素となっています。デンマークでは、ビジネスや人と人との間の関係については、お互いを信頼することが当たり前のことです。誠実さは当然のことなのです。政府は安定しており、企業や公務員による不正は非常にまれです。

The relatively high level of safety in Denmark compared to many other countries means that Danish children enjoy much more freedom and independence than their counterparts elsewhere in the world. It is common to see ₃₇ children as young as age 8 or 9 travelling **alone** on public transport— the other passengers keep an eye on them. It is also common practice for parents to take their babies outside in their baby carriages to nap, even during the chilly Danish winter. And it is usually safe to walk or bicycle in Denmark at any time of the day or night.

Perhaps most importantly, however, they value a cultural construct called 'hygge'. The Danish concept of hygge is hard to translate, but in general ₃₈ it means taking time away from the **daily rush** to enjoy the good things in life. The word was added to the Oxford Dictionary in June 2017, and it is defined as the quality of warmth and comfort that produces a feeling of happiness.

₃₉ During the long Danish winters, hygge is mostly experienced **indoors**—playing board games or chatting with friends over a hot beverage. But it can also be hyggeligt (adjective) to take a winter walk in nature and observe how plants and animals cope with the cold weather.

During Denmark's short and often unreliable ₄₀ summers, hygge is centred around Danish summer houses— small, basic homes-away-from-home, where Danes tend **gardens** and throw big lunch or dinner parties that feature delicious locally-grown strawberries.

I can also see a strong relationship between happiness and empowerment. Danish people feel empowered to change things in their lives. What is special about Danish society is that it allows people to choose the kind of life they want to live. They rarely get caught in a trap. This means they're more satisfied with their lives.

That is the end of Part 4. You now have one minute to check your answers to Part 4. This is the end of the Listening Test. You now have 10 minutes to transfer your answers to the answer sheet.

ほかの多くの国々と比べてデンマークの治安が比較的よいということは、デンマークの子どもたちが世界のほかの地域の子どもたちよりもはるかに多くの自由と自立性を享受していることを意味します。8歳か9歳の子どもが1人で公共交通機関を利用しているのはよく見かける光景です。そして、ほかの乗客は彼らを見守っています。寒いデンマークの冬の間でさえ、親がベビーカーで赤ちゃんを外に連れ出して昼寝させることも一般的な習慣です。そして、デンマークでは、昼夜を問わず出歩いたり自転車に乗ったりするのは、いつでも安全です。

一方で、おそらく最も重要なことは、彼らが「ヒュッゲ」と呼ばれる文化的枠組みを大切にしていることです。デンマークのヒュッゲの概念を翻訳するのは難しいことですが、概して言えば、日々の慌ただしさから離れる時間をとり、人生に幸せをもたらすものを楽しむことを意味します。この単語は2017年6月にオックスフォード辞典に追加され、「幸福感を生み出す思いやりと快適さの質」と定義されています。

デンマークの長い冬の間、ヒュッゲは主に屋内で発揮されます。ボードゲームをしたり、温かい飲み物を飲みながら友だちとおしゃべりしたりします。しかし、自然の中で冬の道を散歩し、植物や動物が寒さの中でどのように生きているのか観察することも、ヒュッゲ的なことと言えるでしょう。

デンマークの短くてしばしば不安定な夏の間、ヒュッゲの舞台はデンマーク風のサマーハウス —— 小さくて質素な別荘 —— が中心となります。そこでデンマーク人は庭の手入れをしたり、地元産のおいしいイチゴを目玉とする盛大な昼食会やディナーパーティーを開いたりします。

私は、幸福と自己実現の間には深い関係があることにも気づいています。デンマーク人は、自分の人生に変化を起こすことに意欲を持っています。デンマーク社会の特徴は、人々が自分の生きたいと思う人生を選択できることです。彼らはめったに落とし穴に陥ることはありません。つまり、彼らは何よりも自分の人生に満足しているのです。

これでパート4は終わりです。今から1分間パート4の解答を確認する時間があります。リスニングテストはこれで終了です。答えを解答用紙に転記する時間が10分あります。

— SPEAKING —

▶ Study / Running / Insects

▶ 回答例   E = Examiner   C = Candidate

E   Good afternoon. Can you tell me your full name, please?

C   My name is Mika Suzuki.

E   Can I see your identification, please?

C   Here you are.

E   Thank you. Now in this first part, I'm going to ask you some questions about yourself. Let's talk about what you do. Do you work or are you a student?

C   I'm a university student.

E   What are some of the everyday tasks you do when you study?

C   I study Biology, so I need to write a lot of reports.

E   Why?

C   Because at university, most subjects require you to write two to three reports. So as I study multiple subjects each semester, report writing takes up a lot of my time.

E   How did you choose your college?

C   Actually, I chose to study English in high school, but I decided to change to Nutrition. The main reason that I chose Nutrition is because I really like eating.

E   Tell me about one of the things that surprised you when you first started at your college.

C   I was surprised to learn that nutrition has an impressive effect on preventing disease. For example, I learned that heart disease is caused by consuming too much salty food.

E   Next, let's talk about running. How often do you run?

C   I don't run very often. I sometimes have to run to catch trains because I don't want to be late for school.

E   ₁Do you run more or less now than when you were a child?

C   ₁Definitely, I run less now. When I was a child, I played with my friends outside and even when I was around 15 years old, I used to run during PE class.

E   Do you think everybody should run at least once a week?

C   I don't think so.

E   Why not?

C   I know it depends on the person, but in my opinion, walking is enough to keep our body healthy. Also, some of us cannot run due to our physical health.

E   Is using a running machine in a gym as good as running outdoors?

C   Yes, I think so. Our bodies don't know where we are running, inside or outside, so we can still lose weight and stay healthy if we use a running machine.

Test-1

E Now, let's talk about insects. ₂What are the most common insects where you live?

C ₂I've never thought about it because I'm not interested in insects. But I would say mosquitos are the most common insects in Japan.

E Do you find anything about insects interesting?

C No, I don't really find insects interesting, ₃but some people really focus on them as they believe insects have unknown benefits for medical science.

E Do you have a favourite insect?

C ₄If I have to choose one, I would say butterflies.

E Why?

C As I mentioned earlier, I don't like insects, but I like butterflies because they have beautiful wings.

E Do you think that we should protect insects in the same way as we protect bigger animals?

C Yes, I think not only bigger animals but also insects are affected by global warming. Some kinds of insects have already disappeared from Earth. For this reason, we should definitely protect them.

E Thank you.

▶ 解説

1 more or less ... than 〜で聞いており、受験者が比較級を使えるか試している問い。

2 時に、このように突拍子もない質問をされるのは、IELTSスピーキングテストの特徴の1つ。知識の深さは採点されないので、まずは落ち着いて。**試験官はあなたの「瞬発力」や「対応力」を採点している。**

3 パート1は身近な話、個人的な話で対応することが多いが、この受験者は昆虫のトピックでは深掘りできなかったため、some people ...と話題を一般的な方向に広げている。「瞬発力」「対応力」の好例。

4 「好きな昆虫を選ぶなら...」と単純に仮定しているだけで、「起こりえないことの仮定を表す仮定法過去」ではない。よって、If節の動詞はhadではなくhaveにする。

┤ **Vocabulary** ├

☐ **Biology** [名] 生物学
☐ **prevent disease** 病気を防ぐ
☐ **in one's opinion** 〜の意見では
☐ **medical science** 医学
☐ **not only 〜 but also ...** 〜だけではなく...も

☐ **Nutrition** [名] 栄養学
☐ **depend on 〜** 〜による
☐ **due to 〜** 〜のため
☐ **in the same way** 同じように

PART 2

本冊P.210 / track 32

▶ Feeling tired

▶ 回答例   E = Examiner   C = Candidate

E Now, I'm going to give you a topic and I would like you to talk about it for one to two minutes. Before you talk, you will have one minute to think about what you are going to say, and you can make some notes if you wish. Do you understand?

C Yes.

E Here is some paper and a pencil for making notes, and here is your topic. I'd like you to talk about a time when you felt very tired.

－１分間の準備時間－

E   All right? Remember, you have one to two minutes for this, so don't worry if I stop you. I'll tell you when the time is up. Can you start speaking now, please?

C   I'm going to talk about a time when I felt very tired. ① It was on the first day of my first ever job. I was still a student, but wanted to move out of the family house, so I found a part-time job in a ② warehouse. The factory started early, at about 7:30 in the morning as I recall, and it was in the winter. The warehouse was cold, I didn't know anyone, and as I said, it was my first job. ③ The staff showed me what to do—it was simple. I just had to pack some car parts in boxes.
The first box took me about 15 minutes to pack, and there were about a hundred boxes to do that day. Eventually, one of the guys there, ③ Satoshi, took pity on me and offered to give me a hand. He was very efficient and after watching him work, I got the hang of it quickly. I finished up about 5:30 that evening.
So, this was a big step for someone like me, who had been living an easy life until then—just studying, sitting around, never doing much physical work. ④ So being exhausted from the tough day at work, I felt a sense of accomplishment. I learnt a lot while I was working at that place. I think the main thing I learnt was that if you just keep working at something, no matter how big the task is, you can get it done. Well, another thing that I can remember is, how much I enjoyed taking a bath after that long tiring day at work. I think a hot bath is the best way to recover from physical exhaustion. I still enjoy taking baths after work as it helps to get rid of any muscle pains, and it's so relaxing.

E   Thank you. Do you ever tell people about this time?
C   Yes, occasionally. I'm still in touch with Satoshi.

▶ 解 説
とても疲れたときのことを説明する問題。車の部品をパッキングする倉庫での仕事について、つらかった環境や仕事内容だけではなく、同僚が手助けしてくれて仕事を達成するプロセスまで具体的に述べられている。最後に仕事を通じて学んだことを話している。そこまで話し終わった段階で時間がまだ余っていたので、Well, another thing that I can remember is ... と続けて、仕事の後、風呂に入って疲れをいやすことについて話を広げ、2分間フルに話し続ける努力をしている。

[You should say ポイント]
ロングターンの下線部分（①〜④）で、以下の①〜④に言及している。
①what made you tired　（疲れさせたこと）
②where it was　（それはどこで起こったか）
③who was there　（そこに誰がいたか）
④how you felt about being tired　（疲れたことについてどう感じたか）

┤ Vocabulary ├

□ **recall** [動] 〜を思い出す　　　　　　　□ **eventually** [副] 結局
□ **take pity on 〜**　〜を憐れむ　　　　　□ **get the hang of 〜**　〜のコツをつかむ
□ **physical work**　肉体労働　　　　　　　□ **no matter how 〜**　どんなに〜でも
□ **be in touch with 〜**　〜と連絡を取っている

▶ Being tired / Work and leisure

▶ 回答例　　　　　　　　　　E = Examiner 　　C = Candidate ●

E We've been talking about a time when you felt very tired and I'd like to discuss with you one or two more general questions related to this. Let's consider first of all being tired. On what occasions do people commonly feel tired?

C ₁Can you please rephrase that question?

E When do people feel tired most often in daily life?

C OK, if we are talking about mental tiredness, I think taking exams is ₂exhausting. Especially, when you don't like the subject, I think this will make you feel more stressed. Also, meeting new people, for example, when starting at a new school is tiring. I think people feel tired when they are in stressful situations.

E What are some of the different ways that people deal with tiredness?

C People feel tired for different reasons and depending on their situation, they also have different ways of dealing with it. ₃For example, if I have stress at work and I feel very tired afterwards, I like to go home, take a long bath and eat a nice dinner, to relieve stress. However, my brother likes going to a bar with his friends after work to stop thinking about work. It depends on the person, I think.

E Do you think most people get enough sleep nowadays?

C I don't think so. People are basically very busy and have too much to do. ₄A lot of students are in a similar situation as me. Mostly I can see that students hardly get five or six hours sleep due to the fact that they have clubs, cram schools and homework. When we look at ₄the older generation, people who have jobs often leave for work in the morning, very early and return late at night. It seems people get very little sleep these days.

E ₅Why are people so busy?

C I am not sure if this is always true, but I believe there is too much competition nowadays and people need to work very hard: first, to get good jobs, and then, to get promotions at work.

E Now let's talk about working hard. What makes some people work hard, while others don't work hard?

C I honestly think the biggest reason is what kind of financial situation you are in. It doesn't mean how much money you have, more like what kind of lifestyle you want. If someone wants to have a simple lifestyle, they don't need to work too hard.

E Why is that?

C Well, if you are living in the countryside, there are very few expensive restaurants and shops, so you don't need to spend much money. However, if someone wants to have a fancy lifestyle in the big city, they really need to work a lot.

E So, country people work less hard compared to city people?

C ₆No, that's not exactly what I meant. I was trying to say that since cities are more expensive to live in than small towns or villages, people living in the country can enjoy a good lifestyle even if they don't make a lot of money. Also, life in the countryside is slower and people have more time for hobbies.

E Why do you think that some people like to do physically exhausting activities such as long-distance running as a form of leisure activity?

C I don't think someone who does extreme activities thinks the activities make them tired. ₇Generally people feel that doing such kinds of exercise is actually in effect increasing the amount of energy you have. It is also proven to be very beneficial for your mental health. ₈That sense of accomplishment that someone gets after running long-distance gives people a confidence boost to deal with the constraints of everyday life.

E Do men and women have different ways of relaxing?

C ₉To some extent it could be true. There are certain activities that men are more likely to do compared with women. For example, it seems as though fishing or online gaming is more popular with men, whereas shopping as a free-time activity either online or instore is possibly liked more by women. Another example could be surfing—I would say it is more common for men to do this sport. But, it's not to say that women can't do it, they do.

E Thank you very much. That's the end of the Speaking Test.

▶ 解説

1 質問自体を変えてくれることはないが、こう聞けば、より簡単な言葉で言い換えてくれる。

2 exhausting は形容詞で「ヘトヘトにさせる、疲労困憊させる」といった意味で、tiring よりも疲れの度合いが上がる。

3 For example 以降で「疲れにどう向き合うかが、いかに人それぞれか」を示すために、自分と兄弟の行動が違うことを伝えている。個人的な例から一般論につなげられている。

4 下線 4 から、代わりに For instance, I usually sleep around five hours only every night. I wish I could sleep more, but it's not easy. I need to go to school, sports club, cram school and do homework and self-study to get good grades. I can sleep a lot only on Sundays. などと語っても文法的には正しいが、**個人的な話に終始しているので、パート 3 としてベストな回答とは言えない**。回答例では students, older generation と、世代別に一般的な傾向を語っている。

5 パート 3 ではこのように Why? と聞き返されることがよくある。

6 「それは私が言おうとしていたことと少し違います。私の言おうとしたことは…」は、自分の伝えたい意図と違う解釈をされた場合に使えるフレーズ。

7 〈Generally people feel that S＋V.〉で「一般的に、人々は SV と感じている」。一般論で語るパート 3 では重宝するフレーズ。

8 That から long-distance までが主語。that someone gets after running long-distance の that は目的格の関係代名詞。

9 「ある程度はそうでしょう」。白黒はっきりつけられないときに使えるフレーズ。

Vocabulary

□ **deal with ～**　～に対処する

□ **hardly**［副］ほとんど～でない

□ **in effect**　事実上、要するに

□ **whereas**［接］～であるのに

□ **afterwards**［副］その後で

□ **cram school**　学習塾

□ **constraint**［名］制約

□ **instore**［副］店内で

Practice Test 2

WRITING

WRITING TASK 1

上級者のエッセイ

[Introduction]

パラフレーズ The graph shows the average size of the audience for each performance at four Canadian theatres over a 15-year period. 要約 Of these four theatres, Harpe's Theatre consistently had the biggest audiences and Little Black Box had the smallest. As for audiences for the other two theatres, New Stages became more popular over the years, while The Dragonfly's attendance fluctuated throughout.

[Body 1]

In 2000, the average size of the audience at Harpe's Theatre was about 220. In contrast, it was slightly less than 50 for Little Black Box. Over the next 14 years, the audience size for Harpe's Theatre was fairly consistent, peaking at around 240 in 2008, and then gradually decreasing back to its initial figure of 220 by 2014. For Little Black Box, the audience size steadily increased from about 40 in 2000 to around 75 in 2014. Nevertheless, it remained the least popular theatre of the four.

[Body 2]

New Stages' audience size increased significantly from about 90 in 2000 to 160 in 2006. The average audience size for The Dragonfly fell from approximately 125 in 2000 to a low of about 80 in 2002 before reaching its highest average in 2006, which was 170. From 2007 onwards, the average audience size for a performance at New Stages stayed at around 160, whereas for The Dragonfly, it fell to around 130 in 2014.

(222 words) ／※下線＝〈一貫性とまとまり〉のスコアに関わる「接続表現」

▶ 問題文の訳

下記のグラフは、2000年から2014年のカナダの4つの劇場における平均的観客規模を示している。主な特徴を選んで説明することで情報を要約し、関連のある箇所を比較しなさい。

▶ エッセイの構成

Introduction —— 説明文のパラフレーズ＋要約
Body 1 ———— Harpe's Theatre と Little Black Box の観客規模の推移
Body 2 ———— New Stages と The Dragonfly の観客規模の推移

▶ 解説

〈課題の達成度〉

[Introduction]

要約で4つの劇場に触れ、比較しながら全体的な傾向を表現できている。

[Body]

横軸の一番左（2000年）の数値と、一番右（2014年）の数値を用いて説明できている。

ほか、特徴的な数値（Harpe's Theatre の2008年や The Dragonfly の2002年と2006年など）にも言及できている。

段落分けが的確。各Bodyでは述べる軸を決めてから書き出そう。

Body 1の軸：最も人気のある劇場と最も人気のない劇場

Body 2の軸：似た傾向の2つの劇場

〈文法知識と正確さ〉

Introductionの最終文で、前置詞ではなく副詞のthroughout（その間ずっと）を用いて、当段落1文目にある名詞句

15-year period を繰り返さずに済んでいる。

The Dragonfly's attendance fluctuated throughout.

throughout = throughout the 15-year period

また、分詞（peaking at）を用いた複雑な文が書けている。

Over the next 14 years, the audience size for Harpe's Theatre was fairly consistent, peaking at around 240 in 2008, and then gradually decreased back to its initial figure of 220 by 2014.

ほかにも副詞の nevertheless を活用するなど、幅広い文法を用いている。

⊢ Vocabulary ⊢

- [ ] **consistently** [副] 一貫して
- [ ] **fairly** [副] かなり
- [ ] **steadily** [副] 着実に
- [ ] **fall from ~ to ...** ～から...に下がる

- [ ] **fluctuate** [動] 変動する
- [ ] **peak at ~** ～で最高値に達する
- [ ] **significantly** [副] かなり、大幅に
- [ ] **fall to ~** ～に下がる

WRITING TASK 2

[Introduction]

パラフレーズ The rapid innovation within the auto industry indicates that in the near future, there will be automobiles that can be driven without a human behind the wheel. Some predict that when driverless vehicles are fully operable, there will no longer be a need for traditional cars with human drivers. 意思表明 In my opinion, this is a positive development, which will remove business costs related to drivers' wages and accidents, making businesses more profitable.

[Body 1]

トピック One of the most significant advantages of driverless vehicles is that businesses will not have to pay salaries to their human drivers. Obviously, labour costs make up a significant portion of a business's operating expenses. For example, in Japan, an average taxi driver's wage can range from 2,800 to 3,500 dollars a month. Another positive point to consider is the cost of accidents related to human-driven cars. Even experienced drivers are not perfect and can end up causing accidents. The cost to a business of damages related to cars can range from repairing a vehicle to, in the worst-case scenario, the death of their employee.

[Body 2]

トピック Although I strongly believe that driverless vehicles are desirable, there may be consequences in the short-term that can be negative. Switching to driverless vehicles will mean that transport workers will no longer have jobs. Other related services, such as crash repairs, car insurance, and driving schools will also go out of business. Finding new occupations for all of these workers will be a major challenge for companies, governments, and the workers themselves.

[Conclusion]

To conclude, the emergence of driverless vehicles should be welcomed, as the advantages it brings in terms of lower costs related to labour and a reduction in traffic accidents are very obvious. Nevertheless, the short-term problems this might cause will require a lot of imagination from all sections of government and society to make sure the change is achieved with as little pain as possible.

(317 words) ／※下線＝〈一貫性とまとまり〉のスコアに関わる「接続表現」

▶ 問題文の訳

テクノロジーの発展で、人間の運転手を必要としない自動運転車が開発されている。自動運転車の技術が完成したら、人間が操作する車から自動運転車に取って代わるだろう。これは肯定的もしくは否定的な発展か。

▶ エッセイの構成

Introduction ―― 説明文のパラフレーズ＋意思表明（肯定的）
Body 1 ―― 一番の利点（運転手にかかっていたコストの削減）とほかの利点（事故が減り、損失が減る）
Body 2 ―― 短期的には否定的側面もある（輸送関係者の失業、関連産業への影響）
Conclusion ―― Bodyの要約＋意思表明の再掲（自動運転車は歓迎すべきものだが、否定的側面には政府や社会の働きかけが必要）

▶ 解説

〈課題への回答〉このエッセイで書くべき［要求ポイント］

①人間が操作する車から自動運転車に代わることは肯定的もしくは否定的な発展か。

→本問は、「肯定的か否定的かを答える問題」。［要求ポイント］は1つだけで、肯定的な意見を支持して書いているが、高得点を狙うなら否定的側面にも触れるとよい。

〈語彙力〉
自動車関連の「特定分野の語彙」が豊富。例：auto industry（自動車業界）、behind the wheel（運転して）、driverless vehicles（自動運転車）、repairs（修理）など。

〈文法知識と正確さ〉
although, asなどの適切な接続詞で複文を構成し、表現に厚みを出せている。

Vocabulary

□ **predict**［動］〜を予期する	□ **operable**［形］操作可能な
□ **profitable**［形］有益な	□ **portion of 〜** 〜の一部
□ **operating expense** 営業経費	□ **consequence**［名］結果
□ **emergence of 〜** 〜の出現	□ **reduction in 〜** 〜における減少

READING

本冊P.214

READING PASSAGE 1

解答

1 ▸ psychological	**2** ▸ behave	**3** ▸ pixels (randomly)	
4 ▸ positivity bias	**5** ▸ memories	**6** ▸ male participants	
7 ▸ first encounters			

▸ 解説

メモを完成させる問題

長いメモだが、パッセージ中の各見出しとメモ中の見出し（Physically Attractive と Attractiveness is important など）が大体対応しているので答えの根拠を探しやすい。

1　段落 2 の最後の These positive illusions, ... psychological well-being by creating a positive self-image. と一致。 パラフレーズ well-being ⇄ health

2　段落 4 の中盤に ... but also on how we behave towards them とある。メモ中の **2** behave ... positively の具体的な内容は、Indeed 以下に書かれている。 パラフレーズ them ⇄ attractive people

3　The study の 1 行目は 1 回目の実験、空欄のある 2 行目は 2 回目の実験について。段落 6 の最終文 ... groups of pixels, accounting for a third of the total image, were randomly removed から解く。

4　段落 7 の最後に結果が書かれている。段落 7 中盤の ... one-third of faces led to the largest positivity bias ... と一致。

5　Discussion の最初が Overall, these findings ... から始まるので、段落 8 でも研究結果や考察が続くと判断する。段落 8 中盤の participants resort to what they know about faces ... and their representation of a prototypical face in their memories ... に注目する。

6　Interestingly, it was seen that the bias is more pronounced in male participants. と一致。

7　段落 9 中盤の ... the impact of this bias might only apply to impressions and interactions in first encounters の言い換えになっている。

▸ 問題文の訳

Questions 1-7　以下のメモを完成させなさい。それぞれの答えとして、文章 1 から 1 つまたは 2 つの単語を選ぶこと。解答用紙の空欄 1～7 に答えを記入すること。

魅力的な顔に関する研究

魅力に対する正のバイアス
・私たちは自分を実際よりも魅力的だと考える傾向がある
・好意的な自己印象を持つことは、**1**　精神的な　健康につながる

魅力の重要性
・私たちは、魅力的な人には、ほかにも多くの望ましい性質があると考える
・私たちは魅力的な人に対してより肯定的に **2**　振る舞う

研究
・完全な写真と、それより小さいもの、3 分の 1 だけのもの、ぼやけたものを比較した
・さらに一部の **3**　画素　を削除した写真を使用した

結果
・3 分の 1 だけの写真が最も大きい **4** 正バイアス を生んだ
・人は不完全な顔写真を自分の **5**　記憶　にある顔と一致させる
・より大きな正のバイアスが **6** 男性の被験者 によって発揮された

解答				
8 ▶ FALSE	**9** ▶ TRUE	**10** ▶ TRUE	**11** ▶ FALSE	
12 ▶ NOT GIVEN	**13** ▶ TRUE			

▶ 解説

特定する問題

8 問題文のmany people, opinionsを頼りに段落2の... they might think that the opinions they have are held by many more people than is the caseへ。「実際よりもはるかに多くの人」とあるので、accuratelyと矛盾する。**fairlyのように強く言い切る副詞があるときは注意して検証しよう。**

9 段落2の... positive biases, help to promote psychological well-being ...と一致。

10 Physically Attractiveの最初の段落の2文目と一致する。

11 justice systemをキーワードに、法律や裁判に関する語をスキャニングで探そう。段落4最終文は問題文と反対の内容。

12 顔の3分の1だけを表示したものに正のバイアスがかかると言及されているが、出会い系アプリで採用するべきとは書かれていない。出会い系アプリは、パッセージ中、Physically Attractiveの最後に出てくるが、問題文に無関係の内容。

13 evolutionaryがキーワード。Discussionの真ん中の段落、最初の文と一致する。

▶ 問題文の訳

Questions 8-13 次の記述は、文章1で述べられている情報と一致するか。解答用紙の空欄8〜13に、次のように記入すること。

記述が情報と一致する場合はTRUE
記述が情報と相反する場合はFALSE
記述に関する情報がない場合はNOT GIVEN

8 私たちは、自分の意見に賛成してくれる人の数をかなり正確に予測することができる。

9 自分自身に対する正のバイアスは、私たちの気分をよくしてくれる。

10 私たちは、魅力的な人はまた、そうでない人よりも親切だと思う。

11 魅力的な人は、司法制度において優遇されることはない。

12 出会い系アプリでは、自分の顔の3分の1だけを表示するべきである。

13 この正のバイアスには、進化論的な根拠があるのかもしれない。

▶ パッセージの訳

次の文章1に基づく設問1〜13には、約20分を費やす必要があります。

私たちは不完全な顔の方を、より魅力的だと判断する

最近の調査によると、人は不完全な顔写真（例えば、顔の一部がはっきりしない、など）を見ると、その人物を完全な写真を見た場合よりも容姿が魅力的だと認識する。言い換えれば、人は不足している情報を自分で埋めて、その顔を実際よりも魅力的なものとして思い描く。

正のバイアス

正のバイアスは、人間の認知ではよく見受けられる。例えば、人が自分のことを考えるとき、非現実的なほど肯定的であることが多い。自分が実際よりも周囲の環境をうまくコントロールできていると思い込んでいたり、自分の意見が実際よりもはるかに多くの人から支持されていると思ったりすることがある。人が自分を他人と比較するとき、いわば「自分は平均より優れている」と思うことによって、自分を平均的な人よりも魅力的で、親切で、誠実であると感じることになる。そうした前向きの錯覚、あるいは正のバイアスは、肯定的な自己イメージを生み出すことによって精神的な充足をもたらすのに役立ってくれる。

Test-2

人が他人を認識するときにも、非現実的な期待を抱くことがあると考えるのには十分な根拠がある。研究文献が示しているのは、人が他人について限られた情報しか持っていないとき、その人の性格について肯定的な印象を持つ傾向があるということである。しかし、そのような錯覚は、人の容姿にも当てはまるのだろうか。私たちが他人の顔について不完全な情報しか与えられないとき、その人を魅力的だと思うのだろうか。

容姿が魅力的

この問いが重要なのは、正バイアスが私たちの人間関係に重大な影響を与える可能性があるからである。私たちがより魅力的だと認識するような人はまた、より社交的で、幸せで、健康で、裕福で、学校の成績がよく、専門知識が豊富で、優秀な人材だと思われている。魅力的な人々に対するこのような「後光効果」は、私たちが他人をどう認識するかだけでなく、その人に対してどう振る舞うかにも重要な役割を果たす。実際、私たちは、より魅力的であると感じる人により多くの注意を払い、より多くの手助けや配慮をする傾向がある。魅力的だと思われている人は、裁判官からより軽い判決を下される可能性さえある。

これが重要なもう1つの理由は、最近では不完全な情報を使って他人の容姿を判断することが多いからである。それは、知らない人を遠くから、または暗い場所で見かけるような場合である。それと同様に、ネット上での人との出会いでは、小さい、不完全な、あるいは部分的にぼやけている自己紹介写真に基づいて美的な判断を下すことがある。こうしたネット上の分身は重要である。例えば、組織は就職希望者についての情報を集めるためにソーシャルメディアを利用する傾向が増しているので、ネット上の画像にどこか不完全なところが少しでもあると、雇用する可能性のある人材に対する雇用主の第一印象に影響を与えるかもしれない。また、最近の出会い系アプリの人気にも注意が必要だ。そこでは、人が自分のさまざまな写真を投稿しているからだ。

本研究

本研究では、1回目の実験の被験者が、96人の顔の魅力を4種類の写真から判断するように求められた。その4種類とは、顔全体が写った写真、サイズの小さな写真、顔の3分の1しか見えない写真、ぼやけた写真である。2回目の実験では、新たに1つの変更を加えてその効果が再検証された。変更した1枚は、画像全体の3分の1に相当する量の画素を写真からランダムに削除することで顔の66パーセントだけが表示されていた。なお、欠けている部分は顔全体に分散していた。

この4種類の条件で96人の顔の魅力度の評価を比べてみると、被験者は、小さい顔、3分の1だけの顔、ぼやけた顔のほうが、完全な写真よりも魅力的だと判断したことがわかった。顔の3分の1だけを表示したものは、最大の正バイアスをもたらし、小さいサイズのものは、最も少ない（しかし依然として有意な）バイアスをもたらした。同様の結果が2回目の実験でも観察され、完全な画像と比べると不完全な画像には明らかな正バイアスがあった。

議論

全体的に見ると、一連の調査結果は、人が不完全な顔を知覚するとき、不足している情報を肯定的な要素で埋めるという仮説を裏づけている。不完全な顔写真を示され、その魅力度を判定するよう指示された被験者は、自分が顔（構造や特徴）について知っていることと、記憶にある理想的な顔の描写を頼りにして、新たに全体的な表象を作り出しているようである。興味深いことに、この錯覚は男性の被験者のほうがより顕著であることがわかった。また、この錯覚は美的な判断に限定したものだが、その錯覚が十分に強力な場合には、ほかの側面（人の性格など）にも一般化できる。

初対面の人の魅力について肯定的な錯覚をすることは、人類の進化において重要な仕組みだったのかもしれない。というのも、それが人間同士の交流を促進した可能性があるからだ。ただし、この錯覚の影響が及ぶのは、初対面のときの印象と対応に限られるのかもしれない。相手について知り、より多くの情報を得るにつれ、第一印象が薄れていくことはよく知られている。したがって、今後の研究にとって興味深い課題は、その相手に対するその後の対応に及ぼす正バイアスの影響である。

なお、この研究の制約の1つとして、すべての実験がネット上で行われたということを念頭に置く必要がある。ネット上の実験で集めたデータは、研究室の実験で集めたデータと遜色がないことを示す研究もあるが、上に述べたいくつかの結論は、研究室で、そしてこの研究に直接関連するような状況（例えば、ソーシャルメディア、人材募集、ファッション業界、芸能界、広告、マーケティングなど）で追試される必要がある。

解答	14 ▸ ix	15 ▸ x	16 ▸ i	17 ▸ iii	18 ▸ v	19 ▸ xi	20 ▸ vi

▶ 解説

「段落に合う見出しを選ぶ問題」 では、各段落のトピックセンテンスで主旨を把握し、見出しを選んでいこう。ダミーの見出し（ii Sugar in the Mediterranean, xii The addictiveness of sugarなど）はパッセージ中に記述はあるが、主旨ではなく細部や例なので選ばないように。

14 段落Cの1文目がトピックセンテンスで主旨を表す。パラフレーズ refined ⇄ processed
歴史的記述もあるが、significance（重要性）を表すものではないのでviiiは合わない。

15 段落Dも1文目が主旨を表す。xの内容が、large-scale refinement and tradeと一致する。

16 段落Eも1文目がトピックセンテンスだが抽象的なので読み進める必要がある。transatlantic slave trade, the expansion of industrial productionなどから奴隷貿易の経済的な役割を述べていると判断できる。

17 段落Fの1文目が明確な主旨を表す。もしemancipate（解放する）の意味を知らなくても、2文目以降は奴隷解放後のことしか書かれておらず、iiiとマッチする。

18 段落Gの1文目に注目する。パラフレーズ closely aligned ⇄ closely related

19 1文目のin the 21st centuryでxiにつながる。似ているviiは、指示文を読んだ時点で選択肢から排除しておくこと。

20 段落Iの1文目が主旨を表し、後半のwhat we can do to mitigate its malign influenceが解答の根拠に。もしmitigate, malignの意味がわからなくても、sugar tax, displayed health warningsなど解決策が列挙されているのでviを選ぼう。

▶ 問題文の訳

Questions 14-20　文章2には、A～Iの9つの段落がある。次の見出しリストから、各段落にふさわしい見出しを選びなさい。なお、段落Aと段落Bの見出しはすでに記入されている。解答用紙の空欄14～20に正解となる番号i～xiiを記入すること。

見出しリスト

　i　奴隷貿易の役割

　ii　地中海産の砂糖

　iii　奴隷制の終了後

　iv　起源となった場所

　v　よく似た製品

　vi　いくつかの解決策

　vii　砂糖が今日重要な理由

　viii　砂糖の歴史の重要性

　ix　初期の加工糖

　x　より大規模な製糖業

　xi　現在への影響

　xii　砂糖の中毒性

解答	21 ▸ NOT GIVEN	22 ▸ FALSE	23 ▸ TRUE	24 ▸ FALSE
	25 ▸ TRUE			

▶ 解説

特定する問題

21 段落Aの中盤に「糖分の多い炭水化物が食料経済を支配するようになっているすべての国で肥満症が蔓延して

いる」との記載はあるが、それ以外の国については触れていないので、Obesity is only a problem in countries where sugar-based carbohydrates dominate the food economyと、肥満症がこのような国に限定した問題だとは判断できない。

22 pigsから段落Bの3文目へ。**and then** humans **later** beganとあり、同時に食べているように記述している問題文と相反する。

23 refined sugarから段落Cへ。expensiveを探してスキャニングすると、最終文に行き着く。

24 固有名詞Portugal, Brazilをもとに簡単に段落Dへ行けるはず。Dの1文目にThe first place ... the Atlantic island of Madeiraとあり、問題文に相反する。

25 addictiveを頼りに段落Gの最終文へ。... tobacco is widely acknowledged to be addictive, sugar can also ... that are indistinguishable from addictionからTRUEが正解と判断できる。

▶ 問題文の訳

Questions 21-25　　次の記述は、文章2で述べられている情報と一致するか。解答用紙の空欄21〜25に、次のように記入すること。

　　　　記述が情報と一致する場合はTRUE
　　　　記述が情報と相反する場合はFALSE
　　　　記述に関する情報がない場合はNOT GIVEN

21　肥満症は糖分の多い炭水化物が食料経済を支配している国々でのみ問題である。

22　当初、人間はサトウキビをブタに与え、自分でも食べた。

23　精製された砂糖はかつて高価だった。

24　大規模な製糖産業はポルトガルとブラジルで始まった。

25　砂糖は中毒性があることが知られている。

解答　**26 ▶ A**

▶ 解説

複数の選択肢から選ぶ問題

26　Madeiraは段落Dの1文目にあり、奴隷貿易と無関係。選択肢B, Cは奴隷貿易を説明している段落Eに、Dは段落F（奴隷解放後の文脈）に登場する。

▶ 問題文の訳

Question 26　　正解を、A, B, C, またはDから選びなさい。次のうち、奴隷貿易に関係しているとされなかったものはどれか。

A　マデイラ島での大規模生産

B　銅の生産

C　銀行業

D　ビクトリア朝の社会基盤

▶ パッセージの訳

p.219〜220の文章2に基づく設問14〜26には、約20分を費やす必要があります。

砂糖の歴史──誰にも必要ではないが、誰もが欲しがる食品

A　砂糖ほど、人間への恩恵がほとんどないにもかかわらず、世界中で多くの土地を占有している物質はないように思われる。最新のデータによると、サトウキビは穀物と米に次いで世界で3番目に金銭的価値のある作物で、世界中で2694万2686ヘクタールの耕作地を占有している。それが主に生み出してきたものは、商業的な利益は別として、何世紀にもわたって続いている世界的な公衆衛生上の危機である。肥満症の蔓延は、がん、認知症、心臓病、糖尿病などの関連する疾患とともに、糖分の多い炭水化物が食糧経済を支配するようになっているすべての国に広がっている。したがって、今こそ一歩下がって砂糖の古い起源について考え、それがどのようにして、私たちの日常、社会、そして健康に差し迫った脅威をもたらすようになったのかを理解することが有益だろう。

B　人類の生理機能は、砂糖をほとんど含まず、精製された炭水化物を実質的にまったく含まない食事によって進化した。実のところ、砂糖はおそらく偶然に私たちの食生活に入り込んだと思われる。サトウキビは、もともとブタを肥やすために使う「飼料」作物であり、後になって人間がその茎を噛むようになったと考えられる。古い植物の断片やDNAから得られた証拠は、サトウキビが東南アジアで進化したことを示している。研究者たちは現在、パプアニューギニアのクック湿地でサトウキビ栽培の初期の痕跡を探している。そこでは、タロイモやバナナなどの近縁種の作物が栽培されたのは紀元前8000年頃にまでさかのぼる。サトウキビは、オーストロネシア語族とポリネシア語族の航海者によって運ばれて、およそ3500年前に東太平洋やインド洋の周辺に広がった。

C　初めて化学的に精製された砂糖が登場したのは、約2500年前のインドだった。その技術は、そこから東は中国、西はペルシャと初期のイスラム世界へと広がり、とうとう13世紀に地中海に達した。キプロスとシチリアは砂糖生産の重要な拠点となった。中世（西暦500年から1500年）の時代、それは日常的な調味料というよりも、貴重で高価なスパイスと見なされていた。

D　大規模な精製と売買のためにサトウキビが栽培されたことが明らかな最初の場所は、15世紀後半の大西洋上のマデイラ島だった。その後、新たにサトウキビ農場に好ましい条件がブラジルにあることに気づいたのはポルトガル人で、そこでは奴隷制に基づくプランテーション経済が確立された。1647年の少し前に、ブラジルのサトウキビがカリブ海諸島に持ち込まれると、それは西ヨーロッパの砂糖ブームを満たすための産業へと成長していった。

E　この食品は、誰も必要としていなかったが、誰もが切望するようになり、現代世界を形作る原動力ともなった。ブラジルやカリブ海諸島の大規模サトウキビ農園で働く労働力に対する大きな需要が生まれた。その需要は大西洋間の奴隷貿易によって満たされ、その結果として1501年から1867年の間にアフリカから南北アメリカに、およそ1257万人の人間が運ばれた。そして当然ながら、アフリカの支配層から奴隷を購入するためには、銅や真ちゅう、ラム、布、タバコ、銃などの商品が必要だった。そうした商品は、特にイギリスの中部地方や南西地域における工業生産の拡大を通じて確保された。現在あるような銀行業や保険業も、その起源は18世紀の大西洋の奴隷経済に行き着く。

F　1834年になって大英帝国で奴隷がようやく解放されたとき、補償を十分に受けたのは奴隷ではなく、奴隷の元所有者だった。その資金の多くは鉄道や工場など、ビクトリア朝の社会基盤を整備するために使われた。その一方で、多くの元奴隷は「徒弟」制度という名目の下で、以前の所有者のために働き続けることを余儀なくされた。

G　多くの点で、砂糖とタバコの物語はとてもよく似ている。どちらの製品も当初は奴隷の労働力によって生産され、最初のうちは健康に有益だと考えられていた。さらに、砂糖とタバコはどちらも古代に起源を持っているが、17世紀半ば以降の突然の大量消費こそが、現在私たちがそれらから連想する健康上のリスクを生み出したのである。非伝染性疾患の「産業による拡大」という状況は、大企業の営利上の動機によって生み出されており、両者に当てはまる。また、タバコは中毒性があると広く認められているが、砂糖もまた中毒と見分けがつかないような行動反応を引き起こすことがある。

H　しかし、21世紀になり、砂糖の支配力は、タバコはもとよりアルコールなどの同種の害悪よりも強力になっている。砂糖はあらゆるところ——現代の食生活で摂取するカロリーのおよそ20パーセントを占めている可能性がある——に存在するだけでなく、世界の経済と文化的な伝統の重要な部分ともなっている。おそらく、よりわかりやすい比較は、私たちの化石燃料への依存だろう。化石燃料は、単に悪癖または悪い習慣であるだけでなく、私たちの生活様式、そしてそれが採掘される地域の地理や政治にとって重要なものである。同様に、砂糖の台頭は、世界貿易や社会経済的な発展、奴隷制、アフリカ系民族の離散、現代の文化規範などの重要な要因となっている。

I　サトウキビの進化論的および歴史的起源から、砂糖が現代文化を支配している理由と、その悪影響を軽減する方法についての洞察が得られるかもしれない。気候変動など、21世紀の多くの重要課題と同様に、この問題を特定する科学的方法は明らかであるように思われる。足りないのは、それに対処しようという一般市民および政治の側の決心である。その例としては、砂糖税案や健康上の警告を目立つように表示する方法などがある。砂糖は今もなお私たちの食料生産に深く根づいており、2013年には糖料作物が世界の農業収穫量の6.2パーセント、総金銭的価値の9.4パーセントを占めたので、必要な変化を起こすには、そのような大胆な社会経済的措置が必要である。

| 解答 | 27 ▸ F | 28 ▸ E | 29 ▸ F | 30 ▸ B | 31 ▸ D |

▶ 解説

情報を組み合わせる問題

27　問題文のateをキーワードにエッツィの歯に言及している段落Fを参照すると、中盤にa diet of milled grain productsがある。

28　問題文のmedicinesを頼りにエッツィの健康状態に触れている段落Eへ。最終文にmedical kitとある。birch fungusとnaturalの言い換えを見抜こう。

29　問題文のstill puzzling scientistsのpuzzling（困らせる）が特に重要なキーワード。段落Fの後半which no one has been able to explainを探し出せるかがポイント。各段落の主旨を理解しただけでは解けず、細部のスキャニングが必要なので難しい問題。また、問題文のscientistsだけでスキャニングをしようとすると、段落Bに行ってしまうので注意。

30　問題文のbodyだけを頼りにすると段落Aに飛びついてしまうが、how well ... preservedもあわせて考えると、段落Bの中盤His condition was remarkable ... all completely intact.がマッチする。

31　問題文のwhere, ancestors, came fromをヒントに、祖先はどこから来たか、具体的な場所を明記している段落Dへ。最終文のwhich is rooted, like farming, in the Middle Eastが根拠に。

▶ 問題文の訳

Questions 27-31　文章3には、A〜Jの10の段落がある。次の情報について述べている段落はどれか。解答用紙の空欄27〜31に、正解となる文字A〜Jを記入すること。

　　　　　　　　注意：いずれの文字も何度でも使ってもよい。

27　エッツィが食べたもの

28　エッツィが、どのように天然の薬品を使ったと思われるか

29　エッツィに関して科学者が今でも解明できないこと

30　エッツィの遺体が、どれだけよく保存されていたか

31　エッツィの先祖は、どこからやって来たのか

| 解答 | 32 ▸ rare mutation | 33 ▸ arsenic | 34 ▸ plant fibre / threads |
| | 35 ▸ grass net | 36 ▸ ballistic principles | |

▶ 解説

文を完成させる問題

32　relativesから段落Cへ行けるが、細部まで読み込まないと解けない問題。パラフレーズ Sharing a rare mutation ⇄ they had the same rare mutation

33　Working with metalから、段落Eのworking with copper extractionへ。alarming amounts ofとhigh levels ofの言い換えに気づけたら解答に確信が持てるはず。

34　clothes, animal skinsをヒントに段落Hを特定する（パラフレーズ garment, robe ⇄ clothes ）。段落内でスキャニングする際のキーワードはsewn。3文目のcleverly stitched together with threads of plant fibreから解く。

35　carried, belongingsから段落Iの1文目に。パラフレーズ the things he took with him ⇄ his belongings

36　arrowsから段落Iへ行けるが、段落全体でarrowsの詳細を述べているので注意深く読もう。パッセージのwere known and appliedが、問題文ではunderstandingにまとめられている。

Questions 32-36 以下の文を完成させなさい。それぞれの答えとして、文章3から1つまたは2つの単語を選ぶこと。解答用紙の空欄32〜36に解答を記入すること。

32 彼の現代の「親類」は、 珍しい突然変異株 が同じだったことから特定された。

33 金属を扱う作業は、高いレベルの ヒ素 をもたらした。

34 彼の衣服は主に、動物の皮を 植物の繊維 で縫い合わせて作られていた。

35 彼はおそらく自分の携行品を 草で編んだ籠 で持ち運んでいた。

36 彼の矢のデザインは、ある程度 弾道の原理 の知識があることを示した。

解答				
37 ▶ FALSE	**38** ▶ TRUE	**39** ▶ NOT GIVEN	**40** ▶ FALSE	

▶ 解説

特定する問題

37 段落Gの3文目以降で、were unlikely to have been used for purposes of identification by other tribes ... It is likely that the designs marked the passage from youth to manhoodとあり、問題文と相反するのでFALSEが正解。

38 段落Hの3文目the robe had been cleverly stitchedのcleverlyがskillfullyと同義。

39 arrowに言及しているのは段落Iだけ。どういう作りなのかが述べられており、「誰が」作ったのかには言及していない。

40 段落Jの1文目yew, which is the best wood in Central Europe for bow-making and the wood the famous English longbows were made ofから、イチイは弓の素材として一般的だとわかる。

▶ 問題文の訳

Questions 37-40 次の記述は、文章3で述べられている情報と一致するか。解答用紙の空欄37〜40に、次のように記入すること。

記述が情報と一致する場合はTRUE

記述が情報と相反する場合はFALSE

記述に関する情報がない場合はNOT GIVEN

37 入れ墨は、おそらくエッツィがどの部族に属するのか示すために使われた。

38 エッツィの衣服は巧みに作られていた。

39 エッツィは自分で矢を作った。

40 エッツィの弓に使われた木材は、実際には、めったに弓に使われないものだった。

▶ パッセージの訳

次の文章3に基づく設問27〜40には、約20分を費やす必要があります。

アイスマン「エッツィ」
学者たちは、アルプス山中で凍ったまま発見された古代人に驚かされ続けている。

A 1991年、オーストリアとイタリアの国境にあるエッツタール・アルプスを調査していたハイカーのグループが、氷に半分埋まった人間のミイラ化した死体を偶然に見つけた。発見したのは標高1万530フィートの高地であったため、このグループは当初、その遺体は遭難した登山者のものではないかと思っていた。現場をさらに検証するために派遣された地元警察は、それがいずれかの世界大戦中に亡くなったイタリア兵士の遺体である可能性をほのめかした。

B 彼が生きていた時代について驚くべき真実が明らかになったのは、考古学者たちが、その発見された山地にちなんでエッツィと名づけられた彼を調べる機会を得た後のことだった。科学者たちは放射性炭素年代測定法を用い、彼がなんと5300年前にアルプスで亡くなっていたと特定した。彼の保存状態は驚くほど良好で、その脳、内臓、そして片方の眼球までも含め、どれも損傷がまったく見られなかった。彼が発見されてから、エッツィは科学界の紛れもない有名人となった。というのも、それが古代世界についての洞察を提供し、従来のいくつかの仮説を一掃したからである。以下に述べるのは、研究者がアイスマンと

彼の持ち物、彼の不自然な死の状況から解明した謎の一部である。

C　アイスマンと現在とのつながりは、今や最新のDNA研究によって明らかになっている。アイスマンの男性性染色体上の異常なマーカーを調べた遺伝学者は、オーストリアのチロル地方でエッツィの遺伝子上の近縁者が少なくとも19人いることを発見したと報告している。この照合作業は、インスブルック医科大学のウォルター・パーソンが率いる調査の中で、3700人の匿名の血液提供者からのサンプルを使って行われた。両者は珍しい突然変異株を共有しており、「アイスマンとこの19人は共通の先祖を持ち、それはおそらく1万年から1万2000年前に生きていた人たちではないかと思われる」とパーソンは語った。

D　この調査結果は、エッツィと彼の先祖が農耕民であったことを示す以前の研究を裏づけている。今回の研究では、父から息子に渡されるY染色体マーカーを手がかりに、アルプスを経由してヨーロッパに農業をもたらした新石器時代の人の移動を追跡した。エッツィは、ハプログループGと呼ばれるY染色体グループに属しており、これは農耕と同様に中東に起源がある。

E　詳しく調査されたもう1つの分野は、エッツィの健康状態である。その結果は、あまり好ましいものではなかった。というのは、彼は関節の摩耗、動脈硬化、胆石など、40以上の症状を抱えていたからだ。彼は、おそらくライム病（シカダニに咬まれて引き起こされる）にかかっており、体内に危険な量のヒ素があり（おそらく銅の精錬作業のため）、彼の腸には寄生虫の卵があった。興味深いことに、彼は腸内の寄生虫を殺すことが知られているカンバタケを、一種の寄生虫用の医薬品として携行していた。

F　エッツィには歯医者も必要だった。歯の詳しい検査で、進行した歯周病と虫歯の痕跡が発見された。彼の歯は、おそらく製粉された穀物で作られた食事のせいでかなりすり減っており、彼の歯には青みがかっていたが、これは誰も説明できないでいる。彼には親知らずがなく、前歯2本の間には「歯隙」として知られる隙間があった。

G　彼には50以上にも及ぶ、さまざまな入れ墨があった。これは針を使って彫られたものではなく、皮膚に細い傷をつけ、そこに炭をこすりつけて作ったものである。そのどれも衣服で隠されていたので、ほかの部族と識別する目的で使われた可能性は低く、何らかの精神的な意味を持っていたに違いない。その装飾は、世界中の古代文化で行われていたように、若者から成人男性になった印を表していたのかもしれない。

H　エッツィは高山の寒さへの備えは万全だった。彼の基本的な衣服はシカ、シャモア、アイベックスなどの皮を継ぎ合わせた裏地のない、ゆったりとした上着だった。この上着は何か所も修繕されていたが、植物繊維の糸で巧みに縫い合わされており、見た目はモザイク状のパターンになっていて、生皮をまとった原始人というかつてのイメージとはまったく異なっている。彼は、さらなる保温のために、20世紀初頭までチロル地方の羊飼いが着ていたものに似た、縄を編んで作ったケープを服の上に着ていた。彼の使い古された靴は革でできており、防寒のために干し草が詰められていた。

I　彼は草で編んだ籠を持っていたが、それはおそらく携行品を運ぶためと思われ、彼の道具の中にはガマズミ材やミズキの枝を削って造られた羽根付きの矢が数本と、それを入れる毛皮製の矢筒（弓矢を入れる筒）があった。12本の矢は未完成だったが、2本は矢じりと羽根がつけられており、いつでも放てる状態だった。羽根は、空中で矢を回転させ、正しい方向を保てるような角度で樹脂のような接着剤で取り付けられていたので、弾道の原理は当時から知られていて、実際に用いられていたと断定することができる。

J　まだ弦を取りつける刻み目がなかった弓は、中央ヨーロッパで弓を作るのに最適とされ、有名な英国の長弓にも使われたイチイ材で作られている。イチイはアルプス地方では比較的珍しいので、このような最高級の材料を見つけるために、かなりの努力が払われたのは確かである。

LISTENING

解答	
1 ▸ Merlina **2** ▸ one(-)way **3** ▸ 23(rd) **4** ▸ economy **5** ▸ stopover **6** ▸ 8:20[eight twenty](am / a.m.) **7** ▸ booking fee **8** ▸ 1,642 / 1642 **9** ▸ October 2025 **10** ▸ vegetarian	

▸ 解 説

メモを完成させる問題

1 ジョーが間違えて聞き取り、それをマーリーナが訂正している流れをつかもう。

2 下線2の直前のジョーの発言、And can I confirm the type of ticket—is it the usual return ticket? が、次に解答が流れるサインになっている。

4 マーリーナがエコノミーを指定した後、金額に難色を示しているが、結局はlet's just go with thatと了承している。

5 ジョーの発言、And the cheaper fares often involve some more inconvenient travel schedules. の the cheaper faresはエコノミー料金のこと。

6 いろいろな都市の出発／到着時刻が出てくるので注意。メモのArrival, Christchurchから、ターゲットを絞ろう。

9 OctoberはOct/Oct.と書いてもよい。

10 終盤のDo you have any special travel requirements?を聞き逃さないように。ホテルの予約のやり取りでも最後に特別な要望があるか聞くケースがある。典型的な流れとして頭に入れておこう。

▸ 問題文の訳

Questions 1-10 以下のメモを完成させなさい。それぞれの答えとして、2つ以下の単語か1つの数字、もしくはその両方を記入すること。

航空便予約

個人情報
- 氏名：**1** マーリーナ・アダムス
- 国籍：カナダ人

予約内容
チケット種別：**2** 片道
出発日：8月**3** 23日
等級：**4** エコノミー
スケジュール面での不便さ：長い **5** 乗り継ぎ時間
クライストチャーチへの到着時間：**6** （午前）8時20分

支払い
クレジットカード決済の利点：**7** 予約手数料 が不要
合計料金：**8** 1642 ドル
クレジットカードの有効期限：**9** 2025年10月
特別な要望：**10** ベジタリアン 用の食事

Part 1

You will hear a woman making a flight reservation at a travel agent. First, you have some time to look at Questions 1 to 6.

Now listen carefully and answer Questions 1 to 6.

J = Joe 🍁   M = Merlina 🍁

J	Good morning.
M	Morning.
J	Can I help you, Madam?
M	Yes, I'd like to make a flight reservation please.
J	Of course. Is that just for yourself, Madam, or will you be travelling with someone else?
M	I'll be travelling alone.
J	Fine. Can I have your name, please?
M	₁**Merlina** Adams.
J	M-E-R-I-N-A ... Merina?
M	No, with an L, ₁**Merlina, M-E-R-L-I-N-A**.
J	Oh, OK. Sorry. And your nationality is Canadian?
M	Yes, that's right.
J	And can I confirm the type of ticket—is it the usual return ticket?
M	No, I'm planning to stay there for quite a while, so just ₂**one way** please.
J	OK. What's your destination, Madam?
M	Well, I'm flying to Christchurch, New Zealand. I'm going to stay with my daughter who lives there.
J	That's quite a long trip. When do you plan to leave?
M	I'd like to leave on ₃the **23rd of August**, but I do understand I might not arrive until the following day.
J	₃**23rd** of August. All right. And would you prefer economy class or business class?
M	₄**Economy,** thanks—the cheapest possible fares you can get.
J	OK. Let me see. Um, hmm ... It looks like the best we can do is about $1,650.
M	Whoo. That's expensive. Is that the cheapest flight you have?
J	I am afraid it is. It's high season, Madam, and even that price may be available only for a limited time. And the cheaper fares often involve some more inconvenient travel schedules. With this booking you'll have a very

---

パート1

女性が旅行代理店で航空便の予約をしているのが聞こえてきます。最初に、設問1〜6を見る時間があります。では音声を注意深く聞いて、設問1〜6に答えなさい。

J＝ジョー　M＝マーリーナ

おはようございます。

おはよう。

どのようなご用件でしょうか、お客様。

はい、航空便の予約をしたいんです。

承知いたしました。それはお客様お1人の分だけ、それともどなたかとご一緒に旅行されるのでしょうか。

1人で旅行することになっています。

わかりました。お客様のお名前を教えていただけますか。

マーリーナ・アダムスです。

M-E-R-I-N-A...メリーナですか？

いいえ、Lがついて、マーリーナ、M-E-R-L-I-N-Aです。

ああ、わかりました。すみません。それで国籍はカナダでいらっしゃいますね。

ええ、そうです。

次に、チケットの種別を確認させてください。通常の往復航空券でよろしいですか。

いいえ、しばらくあちらに滞在するつもりなので、片道だけお願いします。

わかりました。お客様の目的地はどちらですか。

ええと、ニュージーランドのクライストチャーチに行くんです。そこに住んでいる娘のところで過ごす予定で。

それはずいぶん長距離の旅ですね。いつ出発されるご予定ですか。

8月23日に出発したいのだけど、到着するのは翌日になるということはよくわかっています。

8月23日ですね。わかりました。それから、エコノミークラスとビジネスクラスのどちらにされますか。

エコノミークラスでお願いします。手に入る中で一番安い料金で。

わかりました。そうですね。ええと...ご用意できる最安のものは1650ドルくらいのようです。

うーん。それは高いですね。それが今ある一番安いものですか。

ええ、あいにく。今は旅行シーズンですから、お客様。それに、この価格でさえ、手に入る期間は限られるかもしれません。それから、安い料金であるほど、運航スケジュールがあまり便利でないことが多いのです。この予約の場合、香港での乗り継ぎ時間がとても長くなります。

long ₅stopover in Hong Kong.

M I really am on a strict budget, so let's just go with that. And what are the departure and arrival times?

J It leaves here, Toronto, just after midnight, arriving in Hong Kong at 7:55.

M Leaving Toronto at midnight? Not a convenient time! But it's good to arrive in Hong Kong early in the morning. And what about the second flight?

J The flight for Christchurch leaves Hong Kong at 11:05 pm and arrives at ₆8:20 the following morning.

M Umm ... ₆8:20 am is not that bad. It's all fine then ...

Before you listen to the rest of the conversation, you have some time to look at Questions 7 to 10. Now listen and answer Questions 7 to 10.

J OK. That's an Air Canada flight from Toronto, Canada, to Hong Kong, then transferring to an Air New Zealand flight to Christchurch, New Zealand.

M So, I'll have to transfer to a different carrier for the second flight? Why?

J Because Air New Zealand is a lot cheaper for that leg. Would you like to pay by credit card or make an online payment?

M Ummm ... by credit card please.

J That's good because for credit card payments ₇there is no **booking fee**, although a small credit card surcharge still applies. If you pay any other way there is a fee of $30 per passenger.

M OK, that's good, like I said, I really am on a strict budget. So, the fare again was ...?

J Let me check ... The total fare would be ₈$ 1,642.

M OK, ₈**one six four two** ... Here's my credit card and my Canadian passport.

J OK, I'll just write down your credit card number, and the expiry date ... hmm let me see, ah yes ... ₉**October 2025** ... Thank you ... Here's your card.

M Thank you. Is there anything else?

私の予算はとても厳しいから、それにしましょう。それで、出発時刻と到着時刻はどうなっているのですか。

この便は深夜の0時ちょっと過ぎに、ここトロントを出発し、香港には7時55分に到着します。
トロントを真夜中に出発するんですか。あまりいい時間じゃないですね！でも、朝早く香港に着くのはいいですね。それで、乗り継ぎ便は？

クライストチャーチ行きの便は、香港を午後11時5分に出発し、翌朝の8時20分に到着します。

うーん…午前8時20分なら、そんなに悪くないですね。だったら、何も問題ないでしょう…。

残りの会話を聞く前に、設問7〜10を見る時間があります。では音声を聞いて、設問7〜10に答えなさい。

わかりました。それは、カナダ航空のカナダ・トロント発、香港行きの便で、ニュージーランド航空のニュージーランド・クライストチャーチ行きの便に連絡しています。

ということは、私は二度目の飛行では別の航空会社の便に乗り換える必要があるのね。それはどうしてですか。
この航路では、ニュージーランド航空の方がずっと格安だからです。お客様のお支払いは、クレジットカードかオンライン決済のどちらになさいますか。
そうね…クレジットカードにします。
それがいいと思います。クレジットカード決済ですと、予約手数料がかかりませんから。もっとも、少額のクレジットカードの追加料金は変わらずに適用されますが。それ以外の方法でお支払いの場合、乗客1人につき30ドルかかります。
ええ、それでいいです。さっき言ったように、私の予算はとても厳しいですから。ということは、料金はいくらですか。
確認させてください…。合計金額は1642ドルとなります。

ええ、1,642…こちらが私のクレジットカードとカナダのパスポートです。
結構です。ちょっとお客様のクレジットカード番号と有効期限を書き留めさせていただきます…ええと、はい…2025年10月…ありがとうございました…カードをお返しします。
ありがとう。ほかに何かすることがありますか。

J	Do you have any special travel requirements? Special meals for example?	ご旅行中で何か特別なご要望はございますか。例えば、特別な機内食とか。
M	Yes, I was going to say ... I'm a 10 **vegetarian** so definitely no meat meals on the planes.	ええ、そのことを言おうと思っていたところです … 私はベジタリアンなので、機内食で肉類はまったくだめなんです。
J	OK, I will make a note. Finally, can you please sign this booking form, Madam?	わかりました。そう書き留めておきます。最後に、この予約用紙にサインをしていただけますか、お客様。
M	Sure.	ええ。

That is the end of Part 1. You now have one minute to check your answers to Part 1.

これでパート 1 は終わりです。今から 1 分間パート 1 の解答を確認する時間があります。

PART 2

本冊P.226 ╱ track 35

解答 **11-14 ▸ B, E, G, H（順不同）**

▶ **解 説**

「**複数の選択肢から選ぶ問題**」では、複数の正答を選ぶパターンもある。それぞれスクリプト中の下線と選択肢の文が一致する。

Bのwalkingは、音声ではstrollingにパラフレーズされている。

EのMost attractionsは、音声ではnearly all tourist sitesにパラフレーズされている。

Hのoutside the cityは、音声ではBeyond the cityに、plenty ofはteeming withにパラフレーズされている。

▶ **問題文の訳**

Questions 11-14 この話し手は、ブダペストを訪れるとよい 4 つの理由を述べている。その理由を A～H の中から 4 つ選びなさい。

A この街は、特産のビールが好きな人にはうってつけだ。
B ここは散歩するのに適している。
C 川岸はこの街で最高の場所だ。
D 有名な近代建築が数多くある。
E ほとんどの観光名所には公共交通機関で行くことができる。
F 買い物はとても安くつく。
G この街はとても異なる 2 つの地域に分かれている。
H 街の外にはたくさんの野生生物が見られる。

解答
15 ▸ (still) quiet 16 ▸ stone sculpture(s)
17 ▸ Parliament[parliament] 18 ▸ cake(s) 19 ▸ chambers
20 ▸ (red) wine

▶ **解 説**

表を完成させる問題

15 roadsが、音声ではcobbled streetsにパラフレーズされている。

16 前置詞includingの後なので名詞相当語句を入れる。問題文ではfrom the Middle Agesが後ろからstone sculpture(s)を修飾する形だが、音声では、medieval stone sculpturesとmedieval1語で前からかかっている。

17 パラフレーズ views ⇄ sights / such as ⇄ like。どちらも基本的で頻出。

18 問題文のcoffee and 18............ から、空欄には飲食物がくると予想する。問題文のfamous forが、音声ではa strong tradition ofになっており、このパラフレーズは見抜きにくいが、coffeeが音声でも登場するので大きなヒントになる。

19 UNESCO-listedは固有名詞が入っている語なので、音声でも流れる可能性が高い。空欄にはUNESCO-listed sitesの一例が入るというところまで事前に予想しておこう。

20 問題文中のfamous forが、音声ではhas a stellar reputation for 〜（〜に輝かしい評判を持つ）にパラフレーズされている。strongには「飲食物の香りが強い」という意味があり、それが音声中では full-bodiedになっている。

▶ 問題文の訳

Questions 15-20 以下の旅程を完成させなさい。それぞれの答えを2語以内で記入すること。

日程	行き先	詳細
1日～3日	ブダ城地区	- ケーブルカーで到着。 - 街路が **15**（まだ）**静か**な 早朝に出発する。
	ハンガリー国立美術館	- 中世の **16 石像** や見事な現代絵画を含む芸術作品を収蔵するハンガリー国立美術館を見学する。
	マーチャーシュ聖堂と漁夫の砦	- 1000年以上前にハンガリーに定住した遊牧民の部族を表す7つの塔を見学する。
	ドナウ川	- 遊覧船に乗り、**17 国会議事堂** の建物など、川からのすばらしい眺めを楽しむ。 - より刺激的な旅をしたければ、スタンドアップパドルでのサンセットツアーに参加する。
	ペスト繁華街	- ヴァーツィ通りは何でも買える数々のショップが立ち並ぶ目抜き通り。 - おなかが空いていれば、コーヒーと **18 ケーキ** で有名な由緒ある美しいカフェに立ち寄る。
4日～5日	ペーチ	- 特別な歴史的遺産のある大学都市で、古代の埋葬 **19 室** などのユネスコ世界遺産もその1つ。
	ヴィラーニー	- 風味の強い **20**（赤）**ワイン** で有名な村

▶ スクリプトと訳 🇬🇧

Part 2
You will hear a talk about a four-day trip to Budapest. First, you have some time to look at Questions 11 to 14.
Now listen carefully and answer Questions 11 to 14.

Budapest, the capital city of Hungary, is a city to rank alongside the very best in Europe. The site was first settled in prehistoric times, and now it's home to about one-fifth of the country's population. It is famous for its broad boulevards, its buzzing bars, and the elegant sweep of the River Danube. ₈ Most visitors to Budapest enjoy spending their days

パート2
ブダペストへの4日間の旅行についての説明が聞こえてきます。最初に、設問11〜14を見る時間があります。では音声を注意深く聞いて、設問11〜14に答えなさい。

ハンガリーの首都ブダペストは、ヨーロッパで最も美しい街の1つに数えられる都市です。この土地は先史時代に初めて人が定住しましたが、今ではこの国の人口のおよそ5分の1が暮らしています。この街は広い並木通り、にぎやかなバー、優雅に流れるドナウ川で有名です。ブダペストへの観光客はたいてい、いくつもの市場や旧市街を散歩したり、世界有数のギャラリーや美術館を訪れたり、

strolling through the markets and the old town, enjoying world-class galleries and museums, and indulging in some fabulous food and drinks. ₈ Many of these places lie within walking distance of each other.

If a visitor is tired of walking, ₑ nearly all tourist sites can be easily reached by superb buses, trams and a metro system that was the first of its kind in continental Europe. The shopping districts are also within easy reach of the centre by using the various transport systems, so no lengthy journeys required. The River Danube defines Budapest, cutting it in two. On one side of the river lies Buda, and on the other, Pest. ₉ These halves could not be more different in character, and the contrast between the two sides of the river is one of the fascinations of the city. Buda is home to the old town, the Castle District, on a hill overlooking the riverbank, and ancient monuments like Matthias Church. Facing Buda, across the water, is Pest, with grand, 19th-century and modern architecture. You can appreciate the contrast best by crossing the Danube over one of its magnificent bridges.

ₕ Beyond the city, there's so much more besides. Many visitors go on wine-tasting trips to sample wines in rustic cellars. ₕ Others follow hiking trails through extraordinary landscapes, teeming with wildlife, and still others cruise down the Danube through the Hungarian heartland.

Before you hear the rest of the talk, you have some time to look at Questions 15 to 20. Now listen and answer Questions 15 to 20.

Spend the first two days with a ride up to the Castle District aboard its funicular railway. ₁₅ Go early in the morning, when the cobbled streets are **still quiet**. The old town has witnessed many sieges over its history, including a struggle between Russian and German forces during World War II that caused huge damage. It's all been beautifully pieced back together. The green-domed Buda Castle Palace holds ₁₆ the Hungarian National Gallery, offering a fascinating spread of exhibits, from medieval **stone sculptures**, to vast 20th-century canvases. At the heart of the district is the vibrant Matthias Church, and beside it, the Fishermen's Bastion, its seven turrets representing the nomadic tribes that first settled in

すばらしい食べ物や飲み物を味わったりして過ごします。そうした場所の多くは、お互いに歩いて行ける距離にあります。

観光客が歩くのに疲れたら、ほとんどすべての観光スポットは、快適なバス、路面電車、そしてヨーロッパ大陸で最初に完成した地下鉄網を利用して簡単に行くことができます。ショッピング街も、さまざまな交通機関を利用して市内から簡単に行けるので、長い移動時間は不要です。

ドナウ川はブダペストを特徴づけるもので、この街を二分しています。川の片側にはブダ地区があり、その反対側にはペスト地区があります。それぞれには非常に異なる特徴があり、川の両側の際立った違いがこの街の魅力の1つとなっています。ブダ地区には、川岸を見下ろす丘の上に広がる旧市街の「ブダ城地区」やマーチャーシュ聖堂などの史跡があります。川の反対側でブダ地区に面しているのは、壮大な19世紀から現代までの建築物が立ち並ぶペスト地区です。この違いを最もよく鑑賞する方法は、いくつかある大きな橋の1つでドナウ川を渡ることです。

この街の外にも、いろいろな楽しみがあります。多くの観光客は、ワイン試飲旅行に出かけ、素朴な貯蔵庫でワインの味見をします。別の観光客は、野生生物が豊富な美しい風景の中のハイキングコースをたどったり、ドナウ川を船で下ってハンガリーの中心部をめぐったりします。

残りの説明を聞く前に、設問15～20を見る時間があります。では音声を聞いて、設問15～20に答えなさい。

最初の2日間は、ケーブルカーに乗って「ブダ城地区」に出かけましょう。石畳の街路がまだ静かな早朝に出発です。旧市街は、その歴史を通じて数多くの包囲戦を経験しており、それには甚大な被害をもたらした第二次世界大戦中のロシア軍とドイツ軍の戦闘も含まれます。その破壊の跡は、美しく修復されています。緑色のドーム型をしたブダ城の宮殿内にはハンガリー国立美術館があり、中世の石像から莫大な数の20世紀の油絵まで、魅力的な美術品が展示されています。この地区の中心部には豪華絢爛なマーチャーシュ聖堂があり、その隣にある「漁夫の砦」の7つの塔は、1000年以上前にハンガリーに最初に定住した遊牧民の部族を表しています。その回廊からのドナウ川の眺めは、この街のどこから見た場合にも劣らず美しいものです。

Hungary over 1,000 years ago. The views of the river from its arcades are as good as any in the city.

The views from the river itself are excellent, too. **17** Regular sightseeing cruises depart from the pier at Vigadó Square, drifting past waterside sights like the **Parliament** building. The more adventurous can even take a sunset tour on a stand-up-paddle or SUP.

Pest's downtown is a lively spot. Váci Street is its main artery, lined with boutiques and souvenir shops that open on to squares surrounded by 19th-century Art Nouveau mansions. Opposite the southern end is the Great Market Hall, a striking building topped with multi-coloured majolica roof tiles, where it's possible to buy everything from dried paprika to handmade lace.

There are plenty of places to rest while exploring. **18** Budapest has a strong tradition of coffee and **cake**, and there are superb historic cafés. Pest in particular is packed with top-quality places to eat and drink, with six Michelin-starred restaurants, including Onyx——which became the first Budapest restaurant with two Michelin stars in 2018.

Southern Hungary is the base for the final two days of this itinerary. Pécs has both yesteryear charm and the contemporary energy of a university city. Its historical heritage is special. **19** Here you'll find UNESCO-listed early Christian burial **chambers** dating to the 4th century, with biblical scenes painted on the walls.

Before leaving, take a short hop south to Villány. It might be small, little more than a single street in fact, but **20** this village has a stellar reputation for full-bodied **red wine**. Wander through the white-washed cellars that line the main street, enjoy a glass or two, and buy a bottle as a souvenir of your visit.

That is the end of Part 2. You have 30 seconds to check your answers to Part 2.

ドナウ川自体から見える風景もまた、すばらしいものです。定期的に運航する遊覧船は、ヴィガドー広場の桟橋から出発して国会議事堂などの水辺の観光スポットを通過します。もう少し冒険心のある人なら、スタンドアップパドル（SUP）でサンセットツアーに参加することもできます。

ペストの繁華街は活気に満ちた場所です。ヴァーツィ通りはその目抜き通りで、ブティックや土産物店が立ち並び、19世紀のアールヌーボー様式の邸宅に囲まれたいくつかの広場とつながっています。この通りの南端の向かい側にはグレートマーケットホール（中央市場）があります。これは、屋根が色とりどりのマジョリカ瓦で覆われた見事な建物で、乾燥パプリカから手編みレースまであらゆるものが手に入ります。

観光中に休憩できる場所はたくさんあります。ブダペストは昔からコーヒーとケーキが有名で、すばらしい老舗のカフェが何軒もあります。特にペストには、ミシュランの星を獲得した6軒のレストランを含む最高級の飲食店が数多くあり、2018年にブダペストで初めてミシュラン2つ星を獲得したオニキスもその1つです。

ハンガリー南部は、この旅程の後半2日間の拠点です。ペーチは、古き時代の魅力と大学都市としての現代的なエネルギーの両方を併せ持っています。その歴史的遺産は特別なものです。ここには4世紀にまでさかのぼる初期キリスト教の埋葬室があり、それはユネスコ世界遺産にも登録されていて、壁には聖書からのいくつかの場面が描かれています。

帰る前には、少し南に足を延ばしてヴィラーニー村に向かいましょう。この村はこぢんまりとして、実際に道は1本しかありませんが、濃厚な風味の赤ワインでとても有名です。メインストリートに立ち並ぶ白いしっくい塗りのワイン貯蔵庫を散策し、1、2杯飲んだ後で、この地からのお土産としてワインを1本買うのもよいでしょう。

これでパート2は終わりです。今から30秒間パート2の解答を確認する時間があります。

<table>
<tr><td>解答</td><td>21 ▸ B</td><td>22 ▸ A</td><td>23 ▸ A</td><td>24 ▸ C</td></tr>
</table>

▸ 解 説

複数の選択肢から選ぶ問題

21 下線21の3つ前のフォード博士の発言、Not many of the other members of class appear to be that interested in the Great Migration. がCと矛盾する。Aは記述がない。

22 B, Cは、下線22より前にあるシンディの発言で肯定されている。

23 what it boiled down to was 〜は「要するに〜だった」。

24 I was just really surprisedから下線24につながる。

▸ 問 題 文 の 訳

Questions 21-24　正解をA, BまたはCから選びなさい。

「大移動」に関する論文

21 なぜシンディは「大移動」をトピックに選んだのか。
　A　彼女は、もともとシカゴ市の出身だから。
　B　彼女は、このテーマについて書かれた本が特に気に入ったから。
　C　彼女のクラスメートの多くが大移動に興味を持っていたから。

22 シンディは、イザベル・ウィルカーソンがどの点で間違っていたと考えているのか。
　A　移民の統計。
　B　2回の移動があったという事実。
　C　移動が起こった時期。

23 シンディによれば、なぜ移民の数が急増したのか。
　A　アメリカが第二次世界大戦後に好景気を迎えた。
　B　人々が兵役につくことを避けたがった。
　C　ニューヨークは、もはや移民の唯一の目的地ではなかった。

24 シンディがロサンゼルスへの移民に驚いたのはなぜか。
　A　ロサンゼルスへのアフリカ系アメリカ人の移民はあまり多くなかった。
　B　ハリウッドが多くのアフリカ系アメリカ人労働者を引きつけた。
　C　ロサンゼルスの文化に関する彼女の以前の考えが間違っていた。

<table>
<tr><td>解答</td><td>25 ▸ A</td><td>26 ▸ B</td><td>27 ▸ C</td><td>28 ▸ C</td><td>29 ▸ A</td><td>30 ▸ B</td></tr>
</table>

▸ 解 説

特徴を組み合わせる問題

25 下線25が問題文のパラフレーズだが、問題文は主語が「アフリカ系アメリカ人の移民」なのに対して、下線では主語が都市で、「移民」は目的語となっている。

26 パラフレーズ a large African-American community ⇄ a vibrant black community

27 州の名前は簡単にパラフレーズされないので貴重なキーワードになる。

28 問題文のtransformed its cultureがThe cultural impact was huge.につながる。

29 問題文のsuccessをそのまま音声に探そうとしても出てこず、具体的にfound prosperityとパラフレーズされ

ているので注意しよう。

30 Carolinas は、ノースカロライナ州とサウスカロライナ州の地域を指す語。

▶ 問題文の訳

Questions 25-30 それぞれの記述はどの都市に関するものか。正解を A, B または C から選びなさい。

街		
A ロサンゼルス	**B** ニューヨーク	**C** シカゴ

大移動

25 ほとんどのアフリカ系アメリカ人の移民は、第二次世界大戦の開戦時に到着し始めた。

26 大移動の前から、アフリカ系アメリカ人の大規模なコミュニティーがあった。

27 アフリカ系アメリカ人の移民のほとんどは、ミシシッピ州とルイジアナ州からやって来た。

28 アフリカ系アメリカ人の移民が、その都市の文化を変えた。

29 アフリカ系アメリカ人が、ここで早い段階で成功を収めた。

30 ノースカロライナ州とサウスカロライナ州から多くのアフリカ系アメリカ人の移民を引き寄せた。

▶ スクリプトと訳

Part 3
You will hear a student, Cindy, and her tutor, Dr. Ford, discussing a paper Cindy has written on the Great Migration. First, you have some time to look at Questions 21 to 24.
Now listen carefully and answer Questions 21 to 24.
D = Dr. Ford   C = Cindy

D Well, Cindy, thank you for coming along to talk about your paper on the Great Migration.

C Thank you, Dr. Ford. I'm looking forward to hearing what you think about it.

D Well, just to be clear, when we say Great Migration, we are talking about the migration of African-Americans from the south of the USA to the northern and western states. I was wondering, what made you choose this topic in the first place? Not many of the other members of class appear to be that interested in the Great Migration.

C Actually, I didn't know much about the topic at first. I'd grown up with the idea that the big cities of the United States like Chicago had always had major African-American populations. I hadn't realized that it was only in the early 20th century that African-Americans arrived there in large numbers. And then, I read this book by Isabel Wilkerson.

D Ah, yes. *The Warmth of Other Suns*. It really is a fantastic book.

パート 3
学生のシンディと彼女の指導教授であるフォード博士が、シンディーが「アフリカ系アメリカ人の大移動」をテーマにして書いた論文について話しているのが聞こえてきます。最初に、設問 21～24 を見る時間があります。では音声を注意深く聞いて、設問 21～24 に答えなさい。
D ＝フォード博士　C ＝シンディ

さて、シンディ、あなたの「アフリカ系アメリカ人の大移動」の論文について話をしに来てくれてありがとう。

こちらこそ、フォード博士。博士がそれについてどう思われるのかをお聞きするのが楽しみです。

ちょっとはっきりさせておきたいのですが、私たちが「大移動」と言うとき、それはアフリカ系アメリカ人がアメリカ南部から北部や西部の州へ移り住んだことを指します。私は不思議に思っていたんですが、そもそも、あなたはなぜこのテーマを選んだのですか。クラスのほかの学生で、この大移動に興味を持っている人は多くないようですが。

実は、私は最初、このトピックについてあまり知識がありませんでした。私は、シカゴのようなアメリカの大都市のどこでも、かなりの数のアフリカ系アメリカ人がずっと暮らしてきたと思っていたんです。大勢のアフリカ系アメリカ人が大都市にやって来たのは 20 世紀初頭のことだったなんて、思いもよりませんでした。そして、その後で私はイザベル・ウィルカーソンのこの本を読んだのです。

ああ、そうですね。『ほかの太陽の暖かさ』。それは、とてもすばらしい本です。

C **21** I loved it. That's when I made up my mind.

D Do you agree with Wilkerson that actually there were *two* Great Migrations?

C Yes, and I think Wilkerson is right about the timing of the migrations. The first migration happened in the first three decades of the century. Then, in the 1930s it seemed to stop, probably because of the lack of jobs in the northern cities. Then the second Great Migration started during World War II, when industry needed African-Americans from the south to work in the cities of the north and west. But **22** I think she may be wrong about the figures.

D Yes, I saw that in your paper. You feel that the second migration was much greater than the first?

C I do. All the latest statistics I found show much higher levels of migration after 1940.

D And why do you think those numbers shot up like that?

C It's certainly true that World War II had a big effect. During those years, there was a massive demand for cheap labour to work in the armament factories. But when the war was over, the numbers increased more. **23** What it boiled down to really was the postwar boom, which was driven mostly by consumer spending. Detroit, Chicago, Los Angeles all grew exponentially in the postwar years.

D You mention Los Angeles. You wrote in your paper that migration to that city was very different.

C Yes, it was. But at first, I was just really surprised that there was so much African-American migration to Los Angeles. It wasn't so much the total numbers, as the fact that **24** I'd always associated that city with Hollywood and maybe Hispanic culture, not Black culture.

私はとても引きつけられました。そのときに、私は決めたんです。

あなたは、実際には大移動が2回起こったというウィルカーソンの主張に同意しますか。

はい、ウィルカーソンの主張する移動の時期は正しいと思います。最初の移動は、20世紀の最初の30年間に起こりました。やがて、1930年代になると、おそらく北部の都市での仕事口が減ったために、それは止まったように思えました。その後、第二次世界大戦中に2回目の大移動が始まりましたが、このとき、産業界は南部からのアフリカ系アメリカ人に北部と西部の都市で働いてもらう必要があったのです。ただし、彼女は、その人数については間違っているかもしれないと思います。

ええ、あなたの論文にもありましたね。あなたは、2回目の移動は最初のものよりも、規模がはるかに大きかったと思うのですね。

そうです。私が見つけた最新統計のどれもみな、1940年以降にはるかに大きい規模の移動があったことを示しています。

それで、なぜその数字がそんなにも急上昇したのだと思いますか。

第二次世界大戦が大きな影響を及ぼしたのは確かです。その時期、兵器工場で働く安い労働力への大きな需要がありました。でも、戦争が終わったとき、その数はさらに増えました。結局、実際に何が原因だったかというと、それは戦後の好景気で、それは主に個人消費によって引き起こされたものでした。デトロイト、シカゴ、ロサンゼルスはすべて、戦後になって飛躍的に拡大しました。

ロサンゼルスと言いましたね。あなたは論文の中で、その都市への移動がほかとは非常に異なっていたと書いています。

はい、そのとおりです。まず、アフリカ系アメリカ人のロサンゼルスへの移動が非常に多かったことにとても驚きました。というのも、その総数というよりもむしろ、それまでの私がいつも、この都市からハリウッドやヒスパニック文化を連想していたからです。黒人文化ではなく。

Before you hear the rest of the discussion, you have some time to look at Questions 25 to 30. Now listen and answer Questions 25 to 30.

残りの話し合いを聞く前に、設問25〜30を見る時間があります。では音声を聞いて、設問25〜30に答えなさい。

D The most interesting part of this paper, to my mind, is the differences between destination cities. We were talking about Los Angeles just now ...

C Yes, ₂₅ Los Angeles and other Californian cities, like Oakland and San Diego, only really began to receive African-American migrants when World War II broke out. New York, of course, had had a large black population for many decades by that stage.

D That's very true. ₂₆ Even before the first Great Migration, New York had a vibrant black community in Harlem. Other cities lagged behind in that regard.

C That's true. But if there is one city that was totally changed by the Great Migration, it wasn't New York but Chicago. I'm talking mainly about the culture. You see, ₂₇ the majority of the migrants came from states like Mississippi and Louisiana, which were famous for their music, the blues and jazz, and ₂₈ when they arrived in Chicago, they brought their music with them. The cultural impact was huge.

D According to Wilkerson, a lot of the Louisiana blacks migrated to California.

C Some did, but not that many. Anyway, ₂₉ migrants to Los Angeles came from all over, even from Texas. They generally found prosperity much quicker than the people who went to Chicago or New York, mostly because of the availability of better jobs.

D I think I'm right in saying that the greatest number of migrants ended up in New York. You didn't mention that in your essay.

C No, I didn't. I kind of took that for granted. It was by far the biggest city, you see, and the proportion of African-Americans was not as high as in Chicago. ₃₀ But one interesting thing was that it got most of its migrants from states like Virginia and the Carolinas. That was something I learned.

D It's fascinating.

C Totally.

That is the end of Part 3. You now have 30 seconds to check your answers to Part 3.

この論文で最も興味深い部分は、私の考えでは、目的地となった都市の間にある違いです。ついさっき、私たちはロサンゼルスについて話していましたが…。

はい、ロサンゼルスと、オークランドやサンディエゴのような、ほかのカリフォルニアの都市がアフリカ系アメリカ人の移民を実際に受け入れ始めたのは、第二次世界大戦が勃発したときのことでした。もちろん、ニューヨークはその時点までに何十年にもわたって多くの黒人人口を抱えていました。

まったくそのとおりです。最初の大移動の前でさえ、ニューヨークにはハーレム地区に活気に満ちた黒人コミュニティーがありました。ほかの都市は、その点では遅れをとっていましたね。

確かにそうです。でも、大移動によって一変した都市が1つあるとすれば、それはニューヨークではなくシカゴでした。私は特に文化のことを話しているのですが。というのも、移民の大部分はミシシッピやルイジアナなど、音楽、例えばブルースやジャズで有名な州からやって来て、シカゴに彼らの音楽を持ち込んだのです。その文化的な影響はとても大きいものでした。

ウィルカーソンによれば、ルイジアナの黒人の多くがカリフォルニアに移住しました。

そのような人たちもいましたが、数はそれほど多くはありませんでした。いずれにせよ、ロサンゼルスへの移民は全国から、テキサスからさえやって来ました。彼らはたいてい、シカゴやニューヨークに行った人たちよりもはるかに早い時期に裕福になりました。その主な理由は、よりよい仕事に恵まれたからです。

私が、最も多くの移民がニューヨークにたどり着いたと言ったのは間違っていないと思います。あなたはその点を論文の中で言及していませんでしたね。

ええ、しませんでした。それは言うまでもないことだと思ったので。なぜって、それは群を抜いて最大の都市でしたし、アフリカ系アメリカ人の割合はシカゴほど高くありませんでしたから。ただ、興味深いことの1つは、ニューヨークは、ほとんどの移民をバージニアやノースカロライナ・サウスカロライナなどの州から受け入れたということです。私はそれを初めて知りました。

それはとても興味深いですね。

まったくです。

これでパート3は終わりです。今から30秒間パート3の解答を確認する時間があります。

<table>
<tr><td rowspan="4">解答</td><td>31 ▸ supplies</td><td>32 ▸ nationality</td><td colspan="2">33 ▸ 13 [thirteen]</td></tr>
<tr><td>34 ▸ eardrums</td><td>35 ▸ mammals</td><td colspan="2">36 ▸ reserve</td></tr>
<tr><td colspan="2">37 ▸ neighbouring [neighboring]</td><td>38 ▸ scans</td><td>39 ▸ doubts</td></tr>
<tr><td>40 ▸ progress</td><td></td><td></td><td></td></tr>
</table>

▶ 解説

メモを完成させる問題

34 メモのbreakが音声ではruptureになっており難易度が高くなっている。パラフレーズ deliberately ⇄ on purpose / so that diving is easier ⇄ to make diving easier

35 空欄前のOtherに修飾され、かつthat spend a long time underwaterに後ろから修飾される複数名詞の先行詞が入ると予想できる。

36 spleenの意味がわからなくても慌てずに「spleenの働きを聞き取ること」に集中しよう。スクリプト中の下線36の少し前で、The spleen is an organ in the body that regulates red blood cells. とspleenを定義づけている。専門性の高い語句は、このように端的に説明してくれることが多い。

39 抽象的な語であるOther researchersが、音声ではsome geneticistsと具体化されており、注意が必要。パラフレーズ relating to ⇄ about

40 in progressは「進行中の」。パラフレーズ We are not yet sure whether ⇄ It is perhaps too early to tell whether

▶ 問題文の訳

Questions 31-40　以下のメモを完成させなさい。1つの単語か1つの数字、もしくはその両方を使って記入すること。

バジャウ族：海の遊牧民

・東南アジアのバジャウ族は「海の遊牧民」として知られている。

バジャウ族の生活様式

・バジャウ族は、人生のほとんどを海で過ごす。

・彼らが陸地に上がるのは、嵐から避難したり**31**　生活必需品　を購入したりする場合だけである。

・彼らは海上で、数か国の間を移動する。

・彼らのほとんどは、**32**　国籍　を持っていない。

並外れた潜水技術

・バジャウ族は並外れた水中ダイバーである。

・彼らは最長で**33**　13　分間、水中に潜っていられる。

・若いバジャウ族は、潜水を楽にするために、意図的に**34**　鼓膜　を破ることがある。

バジャウ族の脾臓

・水中で長時間過ごすほかの**35**　哺乳類　は大きな脾臓を持っている。

・そのような脾臓は、血液のいわば**36**　貯蔵庫　として機能するため、血液の供給が少ないときに役立つかもしれない。

・大きな脾臓を持っていることは、ダイバーにとって好都合かもしれない。

ほかの集団との比較

・科学者たちは、バジャウ族を**37**　近隣の　部族であるサルアン族と比較した。

・バジャウ族の脾臓は、はるかに大きかった。

・科学者はまた、バジャウ族とほかの民族のゲノムの**38**　スキャン　を行った。

それは本当に自然淘汰なのか
・一部の研究者は、進化がバジャウ族の体の特徴に影響を与えたと考えている。
・別の研究者は、自然淘汰の影響に関して**39** <u>疑問</u> を持っている。
・私たちはまだ、バジャウ族が**40** <u>進行中</u> の進化の証拠であるかどうかは確信が持てない。

▶ スクリプトと訳 🇬🇧

Part 4
You will hear a talk about the Bajau people. First, you have some time to look at Questions 31 to 40. Now listen carefully and answer Questions 31 to 40.

パート4
バジャウ族の人々についての説明が聞こえてきます。最初に、設問31〜40を見る時間があります。では音声を注意深く聞いて、設問31〜40に答えなさい。

Good morning everyone. This morning I'm talking about the Bajau people of Southeast Asia. Sometimes called 'sea nomads', the Bajau have lived at sea for at least a thousand years, probably many more, living on small houseboats that float in the open waters of the Southeast Asian archipelago. Let's start, first of all, with their way of life. Their lives are spent almost exclusively on water. They make their homes in houseboats called 'lepas', which are their primary residences, although some Bajau also occupy houses built on stilts, in shallow water near land. Generally, **31** they come ashore only to trade for **supplies** and to shelter from storms. The majority are born at sea, live their entire lives there, and eventually die at sea. However, since they are predominantly Muslim by faith, they bury their dead on land. Those Bajau who maintain a nomadic existence sail the seas off Indonesia, Malaysia and the Philippines, but because they travel constantly to and fro across national borders, **32** the majority of Bajau have no **nationality** and would find it hard to settle even if they so desired. Their main source of income is fishing, and it is the way they catch fish that has drawn the attention of anthropologists and other scientists.

The Bajau are celebrated for their extraordinary skill in diving. It has long been noted that they can hold their breath far longer than the average human being, sometimes **33** staying under the surface for **13** minutes or more at a time. It has been calculated that each day, in total, they may spend up to five hours underwater, catching as much as ten kilograms of fish and octopi per diver.

皆さん、おはようございます。今朝、私は東南アジアのバジャウ族の人々についてお話しいたします。「海の遊牧民」とも呼ばれることがあるバジャウ族は、少なくとも1000年、おそらくはそれ以上の年月にわたって海に住み、東南アジアの多島海に浮かべた小型の船の上で暮らしてきました。
まず、彼らの生活の様子を見てみましょう。彼らは毎日を、ほぼ水の上で過ごします。彼らは、「レパ」と呼ばれる船に家を作り、それを主な住居としています。ただし、バジャウ族の中には、陸地に近い浅瀬に建てた高床式の家に住む者もいます。だいたい、彼らが陸地に上がるのは、生活必需品を手に入れたり、嵐から避難したりするときだけです。彼らの大多数は海で生まれ、そこで一生を過ごし、最後には海で死ぬことになります。しかし、彼らのほとんどは信仰の上ではイスラム教徒なので、死者は陸地に埋葬します。遊牧民の生き方を続けているバジャウ族は、インドネシア、マレーシア、フィリピンの沖合を航海しますが、いくつもの国境をひんぱんに横断するので、バジャウ族の大多数は国籍を持たず、たとえ希望しても定住することは難しいでしょう。彼らの主な収入源は漁業で、人類学者や科学者たちの注目を集めているのは彼らの漁の方法です。

バジャウ族は、並外れた潜水の技術を持つことで広く知られています。彼らは以前から、普通の人間よりもはるかに長く息を止めることができ、時には一度に13分以上も水中に潜っていることができるとして注目されていました。彼らは毎日、合計すると最長5時間を水中で過ごし、漁師1人あたり10キログラムもの魚やタコを捕まえることがあると考えられています。その際には、彼らは獲物の種類に応じて、簡単な水中銃あるいは素手を使います。

To do this they use simple spear-guns or their bare hands, depending on the type of prey. They can dive to incredible depths of more than 230 feet wearing neither wet suits nor flippers. **34** Incredibly, they sometimes rupture their own **eardrums** on purpose at an early age to make diving easier.

Now, we turn our attention to the Bajau spleen. Because of their remarkable lifestyle and their ability to push the boundaries of human endurance, the Bajau have attracted the attention of researchers. Biologists have long known that **35** other **mammals** that spend a long time underwater possess unusually large spleens. The spleen is an organ in the body that regulates red blood cells. Researchers believe it might be relevant to underwater survival because **36** it holds a sort of **reserve** of blood, which can be vital at times of physical crisis such as shock. A large spleen might, therefore, be a natural advantage to a human being unable to take a breath for several minutes.

Scientists were anxious to discover whether there was any difference in size between the Bajau spleen and the spleen of other ethnic groups that did not share their underwater lifestyle. When **37** the researchers compared the spleens of the Bajau with those of a **neighbouring** tribe called the Saluan, they made a remarkable discovery. A Bajau spleen is on average 50% larger than a Saluan spleen. **38** They went on to further compare the Bajau with the Saluan and the Han Chinese, by carrying out genetic **scans** of several members of each ethnicity. The results revealed at least 25 sites in the human genome that differentiated the Bajau from the other groups, and one of these points related directly to spleen size.

Perhaps the most important claim from this research is that natural selection may be able to work on human populations in a relatively short time. Natural selection works by making certain individuals, with certain characteristics, more likely to reproduce than others who do not have those characteristics. In the case of the Bajau, this would mean that individuals with large spleens would have a reproductive advantage. However, **39** some geneticists have **doubts** about the process. The Bajau have been living the sea life for just a few thousand years, which is not long at all in evolutionary terms. Scientists admit that it's often difficult to show that a gene has undergone recent evolutionary adaptation in living people. **40** It is

彼らはウェットスーツもフィンも着けずに、230フィート以上という驚くべき深さにまで潜ることができます。信じられないことですが、彼らはダイビングが楽にできるように、幼い頃に意図的に鼓膜を破ることがあります。

ここで、バジャウ族の脾臓に注目します。彼らの特異な生活様式と、人間の忍耐力の限界を押し上げる能力のために、バジャウ族は研究者の注目を集めてきました。生物学者は、水中に長時間いられるほかの哺乳類が並外れて大きな脾臓を持っていることに以前から気づいていました。脾臓は、赤血球の量を調節する内臓です。研究者たちは、そのことが水中での生存に適していると考えています。なぜなら、それがいわば予備の血液を蓄えることで、血液循環の悪化のような肉体的な危機に陥った際にきわめて重要になるからです。したがって、大きな脾臓は、数分間息を吸うことができない人間にとって当然有利に働く可能性があるわけです。

科学者たちは、バジャウ族の脾臓と、彼らのような水中での生活とは縁のないほかの民族グループの脾臓との間に、サイズの違いがあるかどうかを突きとめようとしました。研究者たちがバジャウ族の脾臓を、近隣の部族であるサルアン族のものと比較したとき、彼らは驚くべき発見をしました。バジャウ族の脾臓は、サルアン族の脾臓よりも平均して50パーセントも大きいのです。彼らはさらに、バジャウ族をサルアン族および漢民族と比較するために、それぞれの民族から数人分の遺伝子スキャンを行いました。その結果、バジャウ族をほかのグループと区別するヒトゲノムの少なくとも25の部位が判明し、そのうちの1つは脾臓のサイズに直接関係するものでした。

おそらく、この研究の最も重要な主張は、自然淘汰は比較的短期間で人間の集団に作用するかもしれないということです。自然淘汰は、特定の性質を持った特定の個体が、そうした性質を持たないほかの個体よりも子孫を残しやすくするように作用します。バジャウ族の場合、これは大きな脾臓を持つ個体が子孫を残す点で有利であることを意味します。しかし、遺伝学者の中には、その過程に疑問を持っている人たちもいます。バジャウ族が海で暮らすようになってから、わずか数千年しか経っておらず、それは進化論の観点からは決して長い期間ではありません。科学者たちは、現存する民族の中で遺伝子が最近になって進化的適応をしたことを証明するのは、なかなか難しいと認めています。東南アジアのバジャウ族が進行中の進化の生きた証拠であるかどうかを判断するのは、おそらく時期尚早でしょう。しかし、先駆けとなるこれらの分析か

perhaps too early to tell whether the Bajau of Southeast Asia are really living examples of evolution in **progress**. However, the evidence of these initial tests certainly indicates that there is a need for further research.

That is the end of Part 4. You now have one minute to check your answers to Part 4. This is the end of the Listening Test. You now have 10 minutes to transfer your answers to the answer sheet.

らの証拠は、さらなる研究の必要性があることを明らかに示しています。

これでパート4は終わりです。今から1分間パート4の解答を確認する時間があります。リスニングテストはこれで終了です。今から解答を解答用紙に転記する時間が10分あります。

SPEAKING

▶ **Where you live / Colours / Keeping animals in zoos**

▶ 回答例　　　　　E = Examiner 🇬🇧　　C = Candidate

E　Good afternoon. Can you tell me your full name, please?

C　My name is Mika Suzuki.

E　Can I see your identification, please?

C　Here you are.

E　Thank you, that's fine. Now in this first part, I'm going to ask you some questions about yourself. Let's talk about where you live. Which room in your home would you most like to improve?

C　My kitchen. ₁I wish it was bigger.

E　Why?

C　It's because there is almost no space to dry dishes or cut vegetables. It's not so bad but a little inconvenient.

E　Would you say where you live is noisy or quiet?

C　Definitely noisy. I live in central Tokyo, and I can't sleep well during the weekend because there are many bars around my house.

E　Would you say your neighbourhood is a good place for young people to live?

C　₂I think the area I'm living in is good for young people. There are many cafés and malls nearby. Also, it's safe to walk home alone at night.

E　Next, let's talk about colours. Are there any colours you really don't like?

C　I don't like the colour red. I don't know the reason why but maybe it's because I like the opposite colour on the wheel, green. I don't have anything in red. I have stuff in many other colours but nothing in red.

E　Why not?

C　₃Hmm, I don't know why, perhaps because red is such a strong colour. I also think it's difficult to match other colours with red especially when it comes to clothes.

E　₄Has your choice in the colour of your clothes changed very much since you were younger?

C　Hmm, I think so. ₄I liked black, white, or gray colours only when I was younger. However, ₄I like more colourful clothes now, like green and blue, because they look good on me.

E　Is the colour of personal goods, like mobile phones, for example, important to you?

C　At times, yes. Especially, for items like my mobile phone or bags which I use frequently, I will choose the colours I like. But if it's something like stationery, I'm easy as long as it's not red.

E　Do you think the colours that people wear tell us anything about their personality?

C　Sometimes, yes. No one wears colourful clothes if they don't want to be seen by many people, for example. However, I think simple colours such as black and white are common and don't show any personality.

E Let's talk about keeping animals in zoos. Do you think that every city should have a zoo?

C I honestly don't think so. If it's a national park, yes, but not a zoo. I kind of feel animals in the zoos are sad, so I'm not interested in the idea.

E Why do you think zoo animals are sad?

C Well, for one thing, the animals in zoos are living within concrete walls, and they have such limited space to live in. They are kept in cages overnight too. So, I think zoos violate the rights of animals.

E When did you last visit a zoo?

C I don't remember exactly when, but maybe it was when I was 7 or 8 years old. I went to a zoo near my hometown on a school trip.

E Who likes zoos the most, young people or older people?

C I think children below 10 years old are fascinated to see their favourite animals from books and TV in real life. Few adults except children's parents visit zoos because older people are not that curious about animals usually.

E ₅Do you think that zoos will become more or less popular in the future?

C ₅I think they will be less popular because now we can see animals in videos on the internet easily. However, in the past, people couldn't see animals up close in action unless they went to the zoo.

E Thank you.

▶ 解説

1 「台所がもっと広かったらいいのですが」。〈I wish S＋過去形…〉は、If 節を伴わない仮定法で、現実では起こりえない願望を表す。

2 「私が住んでいる地域は若者にとってよいと思います」。I'm living in が the area を修飾する関係代名詞節で、本来 the area の後ろに入る関係代名詞の which が省略されている。

3 理由を聞かれて答えがわからない場合は正直に I don't know と言ってよいが、そこから想像力を働かせて話し続けよう。

4 質問は「若かったときから服装の色は大きく変わりましたか」で、現在完了形で聞かれている。回答は、昔と今に分けて答えているので、それぞれ過去形と現在形を使っている。試験官が質問で使った時制と異なるが、問題ない。

5 質問は「今後、動物園はもっと人気が出るでしょうか、もしくは人気がなくなるでしょうか」。この more or less は「多かれ少なかれ」という意味ではないので注意。受験者が比較級を使えるか試している質問。

┤ Vocabulary ├

□ **nearby** [副] 近くに
□ **look good on 〜** 〜に似合う
□ **fascinate** [動] 〜を魅了する
□ **be curious about 〜** 〜に興味がある
□ **unless S ＋ V** SVしない限り

□ **the opposite colour on the wheel** 補色
□ **kind of 〜** （動詞を修飾して）少し〜
□ **except** [前] 〜を除いて
□ **in action** 活動中で、動いて

▶ Person with a special skill

▶ 回答例　　　　　　　　　　　　　E＝Examiner 🇬🇧　　C＝Candidate ⬤

E　Now, I'm going to give you a topic, and I would like you to talk about it for one to two minutes. Before you talk, you will have one minute to think about what you are going to say. You can make some notes if you wish. Do you understand?

C　Yes.

E　Here is some paper and a pencil for making notes, and here is your topic. I'd like you to describe a person you know who has special skills.

——1分間の準備時間——

E　All right? Remember, you have one to two minutes for this so don't worry if I stop you. I'll tell you when the time is up. Can you start speaking now, please?

C　The person I'd like to talk about is ① Maya, my cousin, who is the lead singer and songwriter in a local band. ① Maya wasn't great at schoolwork, but she always had a love of music, and this was her real passion from when she was quite young. I remember how she used to love singing songs at family gatherings.

② She mainly plays the guitar, but she loves to try out lots of other instruments. Not only can she play multiple instruments, she also has a talent for writing melodies, which isn't easy. And she likes a wide range of musical styles too. She's gone through different styles as a songwriter. Her earlier songs reminded me of pop music by Hikaru Utada, the famous J-pop star. Lately, there's been a Latin influence … you know, bossa nova, salsa, etc.

③ Maya is someone who has taught herself. She never had formal musical training other than music classes at school. She soaks up musical influences like a sponge. I suppose it's obvious that ④ I admire her very much, but not just for her skill as a songwriter.

④ She's a charming girl as well … very humble and affectionate. It's fair to say that she has a natural talent that brings pleasure to a lot of people, and which makes her happy and fulfilled. She's certainly inspired me to practice my music more and even to try my hand at song writing. Although I'm not up to her standard yet, music is a big part of my life as well. One of my dreams is to perform at a local live spot with Maya someday.

E　Thank you. Do you know other people who have this particular skill?

C　Yes. I know a few musicians because, as I said, I play music a bit, too.

▶ 解説

「特別なスキルを持つ人」について説明する問題。音楽のスキルがあるいとこについて、彼女がどのように音楽に取り組んできたかからどのようにスキルを身につけたかまで、詳しく伝えられている。④のポイントに関しては、admire（～を尊敬する）のほか、She's a charming girl...など、彼女に対する率直な印象を述べている。

[you should say ポイント]
ロングターンの下線部分（①～④）で、以下の①～④に言及している。
① how you know this person（その人をどうやって知ったか）
② what their skill is（彼／彼女のスキルは何か）
③ how they learnt this skill（彼／彼女はそのスキルをどう身につけたか）

④ how you feel about this person（その人についてどう感じるか）

┤ Vocabulary ├

□ **schoolwork** [名] 学業

□ **a wide range of ~** 幅広い~

□ **soak up** 吸収する

□ **affectionate** [形] 優しい

□ **try out** 試してみる

□ **remind ~ of ...** ~に...を思い出させる

□ **humble** [形] 謙遜した

□ **fulfilled** [形] 充実した

PART 3 本冊P.232 ／ track 40

▶ Learning a skill / Rewarding skills

▶ 回答例　　　　　　　　　E＝Examiner 🇬🇧　　C＝Candidate

E We've been talking about a person you know who has special skills, and I'd like to discuss with you one or two more general questions related to this. Let's consider first of all, learning a new skill. What do you think is the best way to learn a new skill?

C I think on the job is the best way to learn a new skill. Even if ₁you don't want to do some tasks because ₁you don't know how, ₁you have to do them somehow at work. Also, ₁you need to research how to do them, so ₁you will get some knowledge as well.

E Do you think anyone can learn anything, or do you need some natural talent to begin with?

C I think people can learn anything even if they don't have any natural talent. However, it takes time. If you keep doing the same thing, you will be able to become good at it. Unfortunately, I don't think people can be professional athletes or artists without talent though.

E Why not?

C I'm not sure if this is the right way to put it, but to be able to reach the level of a professional in sports or arts, hard work alone won't be enough. You also have to be born with that special gift.

E Do young people learn new skills more easily than older people?

C Definitely, young people learn new skills faster because they have more adaptable brains. Also, they are both mentally and physically energetic.

E ₂Why is this important?

C It means they can spend more time and energy to learn new skills. Of course, older people can learn new skills as well, but I don't think they can learn as fast and easily as young people.

E Now, let's talk about rewarding skills. Society rewards some skills, like sporting talent, for example, much more than other skills. Why is that?

C ₃I think some skills, which make people's lives better or make people excited, are more valued. For example, sports make people excited whether it's a famous sport or not. Also, IT skills or scientific knowledge improve people's lives. So, I think skills that have a good influence on people are more important.

E How does being good at something influence a person's life?

C Hmmm, it's quite a difficult question to answer. Being good at something has a lot of positive effects on one's life, especially when it comes to employment. The amount of job opportunities people get really depends on what kind of skills they have.

E ₄Can you give me an example?

C For example, if you are good at a language, you can become a teacher, translator, or even a tour guide.

E As technology advances, what sorts of new skills will young people have to learn in the future?

C ₅I would definitely say IT skills, especially system engineering skills. I believe we cannot live without computer technology anymore, at least for the next few centuries. There ₆will be more and more job opportunities in this field. I think this skill ₆will be the same as writing skills in the near future. Possibly, people ₆will communicate with each other using computer languages soon.

E Thank you. That's the end of the Speaking Test.

▶ 解説

1 このyouは、試験官ではなく世間一般の人を表す。peopleを主語にする場合より、カジュアルな響きになる。

2 パート3はディスカッションなので、このように試験官が掘り下げる質問をすることもある。このthisは「精神的にも肉体的にも活気に満ちていること」を指す。

3 「人々の生活をよりよくし、ワクワクさせるスキルがより評価に値するのだと思います」。I think some skills are more valued.に、関係代名詞節のwhich make ... excitedが挿入されている。

4 この前の回答が抽象的なので、試験官が具体例を求めている。試験官から促される前に例を挙げられるのがベストだが、焦らず答えよう。

5 I would say ...は、元々は控えめな意思表明だが、この場合definitelyが入っているので断言している。

6 未来に関する質問なので、シンプルに助動詞のwill（～でしょう）を多く使って答えている。

┤ Vocabulary ├

☐ **adaptable** ［形］適応できる   ☐ **reward** ［動］～に報いる

☐ **whether it's ～ or not**   ～であろうがなかろうが

☐ **have a good influence on ～**   ～によい影響を与える

☐ **when it comes to ～**   ～の話になると   ☐ **more and more**   ますます多くの

☐ **possibly** ［副］ひょっとして

桐原書店